ROSEWOOD

LIKE JUDGMENT DAY

An Essay on *Rosewood* by John Singleton
as Told to Akosua Busia

Sheriff Ellis Walker (Michael Rooker), James Taylor (Loren Dean), Deputy Earl (Jaimz Woolvett), and Duke (Bruce McGill) lead the mob to the Carrier home in Rosewood.

The first time I became aware of Rosewood and the incidents that took place there was in the summer of 1994. I was walking through an airport on my way to a speaking engagement at a university in Birmingham, Alabama, when I stopped at a newsstand and picked up a copy of *Esquire* magazine. As I thumbed through the pages, this article caught my eye:

THE ROSEWOOD MASSACRE
Seventy-one years after a rampaging white mob
lynched a small black town in the Florida
swamp, the survivors have finally told their
story. A Gothic drama of race wars, justice
delayed, and the ultimate TV tie-in.

I quickly scanned the article, which featured excerpts from interviews with the survivors, and chronicled the fact that the Florida legislature had granted those survivors, as well as those whose ancestors could be verified as victims of the massacre, reparations. I was especially intrigued by the story of Sylvester Carrier, whom the article described as "the Rosewood black resented the most…a proud, somewhat imposing man [who] did not defer to whites." I was struck by the descriptive details surrounding the murder of Sylvester's mother, Sarah Carrier, and the killing of his uncle, James Carrier, who had been forced by the mob to dig his own grave. I remember standing there reading the magazine,

Sarah Carrier (Esther Rolle) and her grandson Arnett (James Coleman) at the Rosewood depot with one of the Bryce brothers.

Folks came from near and far searching the swamps for Fannie Taylor's assailant.

and then putting it back on the rack and walking away with an attitude of *Well, there you have it. That's America.*

Born and raised on the West Coast, I've always had an instinctive and strong aversion to the South in connection to people of African descent. There has been so much black blood spilt in America as a whole—and especially in the South—that when I think of the South it evokes only negative images: slavery, whippings, bodies hanging from trees. I never thought I would approach any subject in film that dealt with the South, especially if it took place in an era when lynchings routinely occurred. Walking away from the airport newsstand that day in 1994, I tried to put what I had read out of my mind and focus on the task ahead, which I hoped was to inspire the students I was about to address, many of whom wanted to follow in my footsteps and become filmmakers.

A few months after skimming the Rosewood article, I was approached by Peters Entertainment, which I already had a relationship with because we'd worked together on my directorial debut, *Boyz N the Hood*. Jon Peters and Tracy Barone, President of Peters Entertainment, asked me to meet them for lunch at the Bel Air Hotel. There, Jon told me that he had acquired the rights to the Rosewood survivors' stories. I replied that I was familiar with the ordeal.

James Carrier (Paul Benjamin) and Emma Carrier (Isabell Monk) attempt to rest with the children as they hide in the woods from the mob.

Sitting over lunch in palatial surroundings, breaking bread with a white man and woman, not even a lifetime after the racial destruction of Rosewood, I began to think about how the events of Rosewood might be turned into a movie. As I considered how it might be done, the idea became increasingly interesting to me.

Typically in American cinema, moviemakers have been afraid to approach the hard-core issues of race and social order. Rosewood seemed like a ripe historical subject to make into a provocative film, one that might paint a portrait of an America people rarely want to discuss. Ours is a morbid history. Most of us try to avoid it. Black people don't want to remember having been the victims of lynchings and rapes. We don't want to linger on the separation of our families, living under Jim Crow, and all the horrors that kind of life entailed. And white folk don't want to remember perpetrating that kind of persecution.

As I said, I did not want to deal with anything having to do with the South— I didn't even want to *go* to the South. But I have lived enough to learn that wounds don't heal by being ignored, and wrongs are not righted by denying the truth. I thought about the Rosewood victims whose voices had been silenced

Sheriff Walker
(Michael Rooker)
and Deputy Earl
(Jaimz Woolvett)
waiting before
they hang the
drifter Mann
(Ving Rhames).

for so long, and about the fact that life was affording me an opportunity to add to their newfound breath. Prompted by my haunting memory of the "Gothic drama" the article I had read that summer described, I agreed to sign on to direct the movie for Peters Entertainment.

The first thing I set out to do was talk to the survivors. In January 1995, executive producer Tracy Barone, screenwriter Greg Poirier, and I took a trip to Orlando to meet some of the Rosewood survivors and put them on videotape. We met with Minnie Lee Langley, Wilson Hall, Arnett Goins, and Willie Evans.

Talking to them—especially Minnie Lee Langley—was an experience I will never forget. As the frail but wise-looking old lady sat down at the head of the table, I moved in next to her and asked her how she was feeling. She replied in a soft uncomplaining voice that her legs were hurting. "My name is John Singleton," I said with a smile as I extended my hand, hoping to put her—and myself—at ease. She shook my hand and spoke so softly I couldn't make out the words. "Pardon me?" I asked.

"Minnie Langley," she repeated with a slight hint of a smile, full of wisdom and the permission an older person gives to let a young one know that they can relax…just a little bit.

"It's very nice to meet you," I responded, meaning it sincerely. Making the arrangements to travel to Florida, it had occurred to me that given the ages of the survivors, time was of the essence. One hoped, but could not assume, that they would all live to see the film come to fruition, and it was important to get as many firsthand accounts as possible.

SKETCH OF CARTER'S BARN-"ROSEWOOD"
BY P. ALBERT

First I asked Minnie when she was born. "July 4th, 1915," she replied.

"You were born the fourth of July," I enthused. She returned my enthusiasm with an expressionless gaze. "Independence Day!"

"Mmmhmm," she said, nodding wanly and turning away from me.

"So every day on your birthday you had fireworks, huh?" I laughed and she didn't respond. It occurred to me that it meant nothing to her, being born on the great American holiday. The great nation of America hadn't given her celebrations, but instead had uprooted her and overturned her childhood. As my laughter trailed away, she turned back toward me with a slight hint of a smile, and nodded.

"Yes," she said quietly.

"What do you remember about Rosewood?"

"Lived there all my life until they ran us away," Minnie replied, her voice gathering strength. She paused and gazed into space. "What I remember about Rosewood?" she said finally, breaking the silence. "Well, I'll tell you: One evening my grandmother and I was on the porch, and those crackers came from down that railroad—just as far as I could see down that railroad they was coming on horseback…"

From then on Minnie Langley began to tell me a moving personal account of the events of the Rosewood massacre, as witnessed by her nine-year-old

eyes. She was related to all the key people in the incident: Aaron Carrier was her uncle; Sarah Carrier was her grandma. Sarah's son, Sylvester Carrier, was the uncle who scooped Minnie up in his arms and sat her between his legs, then hid her in a box while the mob fired through the windows of their family home, which they proceeded to burn to the ground.

As Minnie Lee Langley told her story of how she fled, how she hid in the marshes with the other children as the white posse hunted them like animals, I could sense the fear she had experienced and feel the horror of the incident. The more details she revealed, the more I ached for her and wondered at what cost she kept such a calm demeanor. One of her relatives had told me that whenever she talked about Rosewood, she had a tendency to almost pass out. I felt terrible that telling me the story was causing her anguish, but I was riveted—I had to hear it.

Toward the end of the interview Minnie Lee Langley said, "They destroyed us. Can't go no place to call home no more," and it struck me that seventy-two years later, she still considered Rosewood her home.

"So where do you live now?"

She leaned over and rested her head against her palm, her affect suddenly that of a lost child. "Jacksonville…" she said, her voice barely a whisper. "I live in Jacksonville." The rest of us found it hard to break the silence. It was as if the horrors of Rosewood had taken place much more recently than they had. I sat and watched her and felt as though I were seeing the nine-year-old

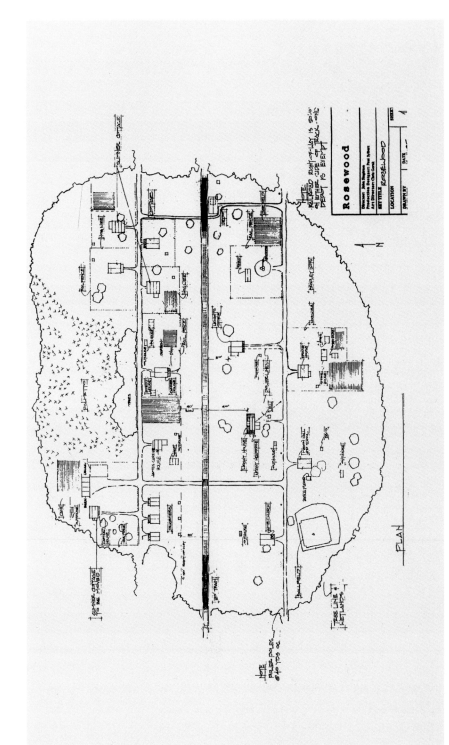

Director John Singleton speaks with Don Cheadle (Sylvester Carrier) and Ving Rhames (Mann).

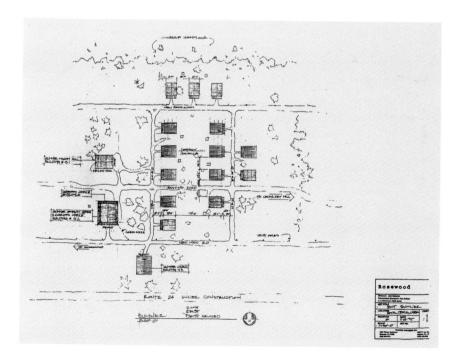

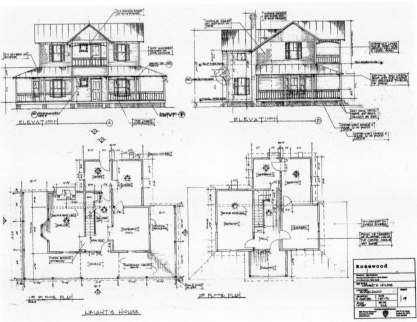

Mann (Ving Rhames) and
Arnett (James Coleman)
lead the children out of
the woods.

girl that Minnie had been when she emerged from her hiding place in the woods early one January morning in 1923, shivering with cold, deprived of food and water for days, having fearfully watched through palmetto fronds as white men hunted and killed black human beings.

"So what do you think about us doing a movie about this?" I asked eventually. She looked up slowly. "It's all right with me."

I could tell she was getting tired, but I needed to know one more thing. "Sylvester got away?"

"So I heard…I ain't seen him since."

I saw sorrow and weariness wash through her body, and I knew I should not push her any further. "We're gonna let you rest now."

The instant the words left my mouth, Minnie Lee Langley collapsed her head onto the table. Did she need food? Did she need water? She stayed collapsed with her head in her arms, until finally, without looking up, she shook her head to our varying offers of sustenance. Lost for words, but eager to

comfort her, I reached out and touched the sleeve of her yellow coat, and sliding my hand down her arm, I held her slender wrist. She looked up at me and said, "We ready to go home now?"

Did she mean to Jacksonville? To her hotel room? To Rosewood? I wasn't sure. But what I had suddenly become sure of was that I had to make this movie. Prior to conducting the interviews, I had been indecisive, but the more I talked to the people who endured the incident, the more I felt compelled to tell their stories to others, so that those who heard the stories could in turn pass them along to someone else. Making a movie is one of the best ways to get a story out to as many people as possible. I got an eerie feeling that the voices of their ancestors were pushing through these survivors, letting me know that as a black man with opportunity it was my duty to tell what had happened to them. "You *have* to make this movie," one of the survivor's daughters said to me during a break from interviewing. "God brought you here to make this movie. This is your destiny. You *have* to make this movie." My ears got hot, and I felt so humbled.

The night I returned to Los Angeles I determined in my heart and mind to put everything aside, including a film I had been prepping, and focus on the making of the Rosewood movie. I had read various screenplays in order to find

John Wright (Jon Voight) stands in disbelief as they burn his neighbors' homes.

exactly the writer who could bring history to life. I had chosen Greg Poirier because I was attracted to his style of writing action sequences. I knew I wanted action in the picture. I wanted the entire film to focus on those four days from New Year's Eve to the torching of the town, chronicling the ferocity and hysteria that took place.

Next I traveled to Rosewood itself. I went there with Arnett Doctor, an extraordinary man who took it upon himself to investigate his heritage and who spearheaded the families' pursuit of a legal claim against the state of Florida. His mother, Philomena Doctor, was a Rosewood survivor who died in 1991. When alive, she spoke of the Rosewood incident only on Christmas day, and had ordered him to tell no one outside the family until after she passed away.

There is nothing left of the original town of Rosewood except John Wright's large, white, two-story frame house, built ninety years ago, with its outside well, and the old depot where the train used to stop. Paper-shell pecan trees grow in the area, amidst soft cypresses hanging with moss. Even though the sky was blue, we shivered against the cold. Near Wright's old house, a few white families now live in trailer parks dotted with packs of howling hounds.

We walked into the woods, and Arnett Doctor showed me a cemetery deep in the forest, where the headstones of his relatives dating back to 1903 had

Sheriff Walker (Michael Rooker) attempts to obtain the truth from Fannie Taylor (Catherine Kellner).

Sheriff Walker (Michael Rooker) holds Aaron Carrier (Phil Moore), attempting to discover who assaulted Fannie Taylor.

Sarah Carrier (Esther Rolle) and director John Singleton talk between scenes.

been overgrown with shrubbery. Three acres of land was all graves, representing hundreds of former Rosewood residents. Doctor's great-grandfather Ed Goins is buried there. Goins owned three-quarters of the land in Rosewood and was the largest land-owner—black or white—in the entire county; many believe that envy of this kind of black wealth was the root cause of the Rosewood massacre.

Some of the white people who now live on the land came out of their trailers when we arrived. They were slightly upset that we were around because they thought we were from the press, and they feared that since the black families of Rosewood had been granted reparations, they would come back to reclaim their land. It became clear that we would not be able to shoot the film on the actual site of Rosewood; we needed to find a place where we could re-create the town.

In the late summer of 1995, we began hunting locations. We tried to find a free area, bordered by trees, where we could carve a small town right out of the wilderness. It had to be a place that resembled the terrain around Rosewood and was big enough for us to transplant or construct thirty or more houses. The ideal location was not easy to find. One property we came across that fit our ideal was a place in the Seminole woods. We were going to rent the property,

but two murders that had been committed there the year before gave us pause. One of the caretakers, an old backwoods man who had been living on the land for forty-five years, was opposed to a young couple who had inherited the property, so he murdered them and put them out in the woods. The other, more deciding, drawback was the fact that a hunting club used the land, and we were scheduled to shoot the movie during hunting season. Nobody wants to make a film while they risk being shot at.

   We found a suitable site to build on at the Royal Trails Ranch in Lake County, approximately three hours from the original Rosewood. It took the next three-and-a-half months to assemble the sets of Rosewood and Sumner.

In order to make the towns look authentic, Academy Award–winner Paul Sylbert, the production designer, talked to Minnie and other survivors about what they remembered, and he gathered as many records and photographs as he could find. As Sylbert observed, "Sumner was geometric and regimented. Rosewood was organic and free-flowing." Half a dozen turn-of-the-century frame houses and one nineteenth-century church were trucked in from the

region and fifteen additional houses were built. Dirt was transported; gardens were planted. It really was something to see, since not many films build an entire environment from scratch anymore.

During pre-production I had sat up in my apartment in Lake Mary, Florida, listening to the Blues—Bessie Smith and Ma Rainey—immersing myself in the era and its music, and at times I became depressed. It's hard to really put yourself back there and not feel a certain sense of sadness. I finally replaced those sad songs with music by Wynton Marsalis, who came on board to compose the music for the film.

I've always admired Wynton's work. I met him when I was doing the final mixing on *Boyz N the Hood*, and was in awe. When *Rosewood* came up, I felt it would be the right project for us to work on together, so I sent him the script and

GINA FLANAGAN

Duke (Bruce McGill) teaches his son Emmett (Tristan Hook) to tie a noose as Rosewood burns in the background.

was thrilled when he said he wanted to do it. Music plays a large part in the picture, helping set the socio-economic culture of the southern United States. Wynton and I decided not to go with the usual Eurocentric, Wagneresque music that is usually put on dramatic pictures to heighten the tension. We wanted American folk music—black and white—to be played, so that viewers could enter the whole texture of the period with as many of their senses as possible.

That November the reconstruction of Rosewood was still under way. I was working on pre-production for the movie with Tracy Barone and co-producer Penelope L. Foster when Arnett Doctor called to inform us that Minnie Lee Langley had passed away and that her funeral would be that week in Jacksonville. I was shocked. Even though I had figured that some of the survivors wouldn't live to see the film, the news still came as a blow. It was a very intense time for me, because we were a month away from production, and we were still discussing the film's budget with the studio. I wanted the scope of the picture to be much broader than what the financiers intended, and the discrepancy created tension. I had lived the film for a whole year, and like all of my movies, it had ceased to become a job. I wanted in my heart and soul to see the film come to fruition, but I knew it was going to take a lot of money.

In the midst of this effort to get *Rosewood* made, I left production on a Friday to attend Minnie Lee Langley's funeral. I drove the three hours to Jacksonville

Scrappie (Elise Neal),
Philomena (Benea Ousley),
and Gertrude (Bridgid Coulter).

with Liba Daniels, my assistant. After we got there, friends and family got up one by one to talk about Minnie. When they finished, there was a moment when they asked if anyone wanted to step forward and say a few words, and I almost felt compelled to say something, but it wasn't my place. I just hoped to make a movie about an incident that this woman had actually endured.

The words Minnie Langley had spoken on camera for a *60 Minutes* interview ran through my mind. When asked what advice she would give to her grandchildren today, she said, "Don't ever stay in a place where white folks can surround you, because if anything happens somewhere else, they'll run you from your home just like they did us."

As I sat in the pew at Minnie's funeral, listening to excerpts being read from her testimony before the Florida legislature, my resolve to make the movie was invigorated. Here was a woman who grew up under Jim Crow, when black people were not supposed to speak even one word out of line, and she had stood before the Florida legislature, fighting through an era of silence, with the courage to tell the truth about what happened to her and her family. I knew that I had to persevere.

Assembling talented actors for the movie was harder than I had expected. I found that a lot of actors were hesitant to participate in a picture like this because of the subject matter. Many Hollywood names are a lot less apt to take challenging roles when the subject deviates from the norm. The goal of a

Hollywood actor is mostly to stay in the factory as long as possible, and not to take too many risks. That automatically weeded out the cautious from involvement with the picture, so all the actors that did sign on ended up being the strongest ones that we could ever have hoped to get. Case in point is Jon Voight, who portrays John Wright, Rosewood's only white resident. Jon Voight is known for taking roles in films that have tough themes, like *Deliverance, Midnight Cowboy,* and *Coming Home,* so I was pleased he chose our project.

I will never forget my initial meeting with Jon Voight on the Warner Bros. lot. He had read the script and wanted to meet me to get my take on it and find out exactly what I wanted to do with the picture and the role of Wright. We sat on different ends of the same couch, checking each other out—two bulldogs, each of us asking ourselves, "Should I go down the road with this guy?" It's a funny image, and months later, just a few days before the end of shooting, we had a conversation about that first meeting. We smiled at each other, and laughed about the way we had eyed each other, the camaraderie we now had, and what we had accomplished together.

Ving Rhames, who plays the character of Mann, was originally my choice to play Sylvester Carrier. I thought I would find one of the few really well-known black actors to play the role of Mann, the drifter that rides into Rosewood, who starts the movie as the stranger in town but later becomes the hero. I thought that any actor would jump at the chance, but it turned out they all either had higher-paying acting roles on tap or that *Rosewood* just didn't offer the kind of role they wanted. So I started to look at Ving and thought, "Why not make this guy the lead?" That thought solidified when I sought out my mother's advice; my mother said that Ving would be perfect because Ving is not a man cut in a mold but is a real "rounded" man, like those men were in the South in the twenties. So in the end she made me see that Ving fit the role better than any other star could have.

I had decided on Ving for the character of Mann, but that left the role of Sylvester still wide open. I had no problem filling that position. I had seen Don Cheadle's portrayal of Mouse in *Devil in a Blue Dress* and was so impressed with his performance that I had called him up afterward and told him that we had to work together. I didn't know what the project would be when I noted that performance, but now I suddenly realized he would make a great Sylvester.

I cast many of the white actors who played the posse from seeing them on screen. I found Michael Rooker, who played Levy County sheriff Ellis Walker, this way. Rooker is a really animated actor, full of energy and quick-witted comments, which we termed "Rookerisms." He is like a human tornado when he comes on the set.

We were lucky enough to have several great finds in this picture, like Catherine Kellner, who plays Fannie Taylor. She simply embodied the character of Fannie—she just had that trouble-maker look—and it's always great as a director to find a perfect instrument of your vision of a character. I could advise Catherine with a key word and her performance would shift on the drop of a dime, and she would perform exactly as I had envisioned. She was wonderful to watch.

Bruce McGill, cast as Duke, went into the depths of his psyche to play a despicable racist with some glimmer of complexity. Duke was very vicious, ornery and ugly, but Bruce's performance brings the audience to understand why Duke makes the decisions he does. Duke was a man who taught his son how to hunt, how to fish...and how to make a noose to lynch a black man.

I had watched Badja Djola in several movies, but had finally seen him in person at actress Rosalind Cash's funeral—as he walked out of the church, I knew he would be perfect to play John Bradley, so I called him at once and

TWO SHOT - MANN + SCRAPPIE KISS DEEPLY...

ANOTHER ANGLE - MANN + SCRAPPIE KISS - SYLVESTER RIDES
UP IN B.G. - S: "I AIN'T GOT ALL NIGHT!"

MANN MOVES AWAY FROM SCRAPPIE ...

offered him the role. I had also seen Esther Rolle outside the same church, and later, when the actress hired to portray Sarah Carrier pulled out at the last moment, I cast Ms. Rolle as Aunt Sarah. Another actress I met at Rosalind's funeral was Akosua Busia, whom I later called out of writing hibernation in Ghana to play Jewel.

In January 1996 we finally had the first read-through of the screenplay before embarking on a week of rehearsals. It was a very exciting day for me.

Many of the cast members had flown in from various parts of the country, and along with the local actors, we all met at Sanford High School. The crew and I introduced ourselves to the assembled cast. Most met Johnny Jensen, director of photography, Jerry Ballew, the assistant director, and Penelope L. Foster, the co-producer, for the first time, though many actors had already met and been fitted by Ruth Carter, *Rosewood*'s costume designer.

I asked the more than forty people in the room to hold hands, and I said a prayer for the journey that we were about to embark on. I prayed to God that our talents would be well used, that we would remember those who had gone before us and endured in their lives some of the arduous situations we were about to reenact, and that in honor of them, we would keep our grace and our humor and our willingness to cooperate with one another through the difficult times of filming.

Having prayed, we slowly began to read the script aloud and shared a real sense of enthusiasm. I think everyone felt as though we might be on the road to something very important. We ate lunch together in that schoolroom, then I asked various actors who were going to have to work with one another for weeks of filming to mingle and get to know each other.

After that, we had improvisations for about a week. Everyone sat in a large mobile hut outside the production offices, and I set up the actors in situations that had nothing to do with the script but everything to do with the people they were playing. I loved watching the different groups coalesce with each other and seeing actors really discover their characters as they created and researched backstories for their roles. The more we worked, the more I understood the characters in the picture, as well as the actors portraying the characters.

On the last two rehearsal days, we had "Character Therapy." I made each actor sit in the middle of the room in turns, and we assembled all the other actors in a circle around him or her. Everyone had to stay in character as they peppered the actor in the center with questions. What came out of this session was phenomenal. Don Cheadle as Sylvester interacting with the crackers of Sumner within a discussion situation was fascinating and informative. Or Jon Voight as John Wright, talking about why he, as a white man, is living amongst the blacks in Rosewood, and why, married to his new wife, Mary Wright, played by Kathryn Meisle, he is having an affair with Jewel, his black mistress.

Some of the white actors like Bruce McGill (Duke) had the courage to be disliked, and spouted forth racist comments with ease and conviction, perfectly capturing the mind-set of the era. At one point Duke reduced his 12-year-old son, Emmett (Tristan Hook), to floods of tears. But rather than backing down, Tristan, as Emmett, resisted playing the stereotypes of white racism and stood up and defended himself against his bigoted father in favor of his black friend, Arnett (James Coleman). I realized then that it would be best to take advantage of Tristan's diffidence and fire and keep the character of Emmett very naive, so that he would be malleable enough to be molded by his father but individual enough that he would ultimately decide to follow his own path. At the end of the rehearsal period, I had garnered many ideas about how to guide my actors.

On the first day of shooting we hit the ground running. I came onto the set on horseback and said, "Okay, let's go." We started off shooting in Sumner at the sheriff's office, with the scene where the sheriff learns from Emmett that Fannie Taylor has been beaten up. Seeing that first day of dailies on the big wide screen after all the months and months of preparation was exhilarating.

The whole movie was poignant to shoot, but certain moments I remember vividly. Thirteen-year-old Benea Ousley, who played Philomena, had never been in a movie before: we found her because she had participated in many oratory competitions where she recited a poem based on the Rosewood incident.

Her great-aunt was the real Philomena, Arnett Doctor's mother, who had been one of the Rosewood survivors. Every time that Benea acted, I felt that she was being guided by some force outside herself. Despite her inexperience, she brought a very simple and soulful essence to the piece. Her decisions and the way that she carried herself on film were mature beyond her years. In one scene that was set in the woods, Benea worked herself to such an emotional pitch that the other children reacted off her. Pretty soon all the children were so far into their characters and their desperate situation that many of them began to cry with her, to the point that it almost moved *me* to tears.

Another interesting scene—one of the most difficult scenes to shoot—took place in the church. The people of Rosewood held a meeting about the lynching of Sam Carter in the hunt for Fannie Taylor's supposedly black attacker, and Mr. Wright walked in. As the script was written, Aunt Sarah revealed to everyone, including Wright, that she had witnessed a white man beating up Fannie. Jon Voight pointed out that his character shouldn't receive that information: he felt that if he knew about the white man, his character would help them by immediately taking Aunt Sarah to the sheriff and putting a stop to the mob. My attitude, shared with some of the other black cast members in the scene, was that in 1923, John Wright probably wouldn't have reacted that way, and even if he *did,* it wouldn't have made any difference; it wouldn't have stopped anything.

Sometimes I felt that Jon Voight was uncomfortable playing an early-twentieth-century white southern man with a superior attitude, and also felt that the unease was testimony to how strong of character he is. I learned a lot about subtlety watching him go through the paces of playing the character, who is not at all unlikable but who is edgy and a fraternizer with rednecks.

We all went back and forth on the issue, with everyone's emotions riding high, and finally rehearsed the scene differently than it was written. Aunt Sarah gave out the information that the attacker was white, and John Wright walked up from the back of the church, approached Aunt Sarah, and tried to take her to the sheriff. Then Sylvester jumped up in front of Wright and said: "No, you're not taking my momma anywhere."

Suddenly I saw Badja Djola, as John Bradley, pick up his shotgun—again, not in the script but not hashed out by the group that day either! As the director, I had to take fast control of the situation. In the finished movie, Aunt Sarah refuses to speak in front of the white man, so the congregation stares Wright

Arnett (James Coleman)
leads the children to safety.

down, and the preacher asks him to leave before Aunt Sarah will tell what she knows. It was a compromise we could all live with.

Jon Voight is one of the least selfish actors I've ever met. He makes everyone around him better, because he is really working toward the success of the whole movie. He'll come on the set for an extra day just to work with other actors in scenes that don't even concern his character. I really admire him for that, and feel that he became a unifying force on the picture. As director, I'm at the core of the whole process, but it indicates that the production takes on a life of its own when other participants feel strongly and passionately about the entire movie and not just their piece of it.

Despite the many wonderful people involved in the filming—cast, crew, and production—getting *Rosewood* made was very challenging for me. To do what we set out to do within the financial constraints was a monumental task. Even given those constraints, there was more money involved in this than in any of my previous pictures, which in itself was a huge responsibility. It was also tough for me because *Rosewood* is the first picture that I've made out of my element—it's my first truly location picture. I'm from Los Angeles; I've never made a movie outside of L.A.; I've never even *lived* outside of L.A. To make *Rosewood,* I lived in Florida for eight months.

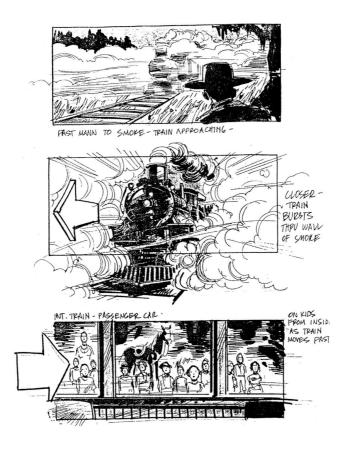

FAST MANN TO SMOKE - TRAIN APPROACHING -

CLOSER - TRAIN BURSTS THRU WALL OF SMOKE

INT. TRAIN - PASSENGER CAR

ON KIDS FROM INSID: AS TRAIN MOVES PAST

More than a third of the picture was shot during the night, wrapping at six or seven o'clock in the morning. And we had several locations with environmental conditions that were hard to contend with. Because we were shooting in sets that mimicked actual places, we shot in swamps and forests, with snakes, ticks, and mosquitoes. Add large groups of very young children acting to the mix as well as endless torrents of rain, and the logistics were endless. Just one rain would set us off schedule for days, because when it rains in the swamps, the whole look of the area changes. We had done exhaustive research, so where in most films I might be able to adapt to a changed situation, here I would get bent out of shape if circumstances forced us to make changes. Toward the latter part of the shoot we worked with the hazards of fire in the surrounding forest, as we depicted the town being burnt to the ground. For the film's final sequences, the production employed eight technicians and over thirty Lake County Fire Rescue members.

When I finally got back to L.A., my whole body and mind seemed to sigh with relief, although I must admit that being out of the city had started to feel good to me. Watching all the footage through as I edited the film, one of my favorite scenes has turned out to be the one where Ving Rhames, as Mann, has left Rosewood and is riding in the countryside on a big black stallion when some rednecks in a truck spot him and start shooting at him, and he takes off into the woods, where the trees are only six feet apart. Through gunshots, Mann, still firmly riding that horse, weaves in and out of the trees. We wanted close-ups of his face, so Ving asked to replace the stunt double and performed the scene himself. Mann finally jumps off the horse and runs from the posse, but at a certain point he turns around and faces them down. It's one of the most heroic scenes I've ever shot because it's intellectually as well as physically exciting to see a character in that day and age—after you expect him to run—turn around and fight back.

I believe *Rosewood* is a very important addition to the history of American film. No black man has had the opportunity before to direct a film like this in this context, and on so wide a canvas. I feel very proud and grateful to have had this experience. So much in *Rosewood* is relevant. You can deconstruct the Susan Smith case, where a woman who killed her two children in 1994 blamed it on a black male carjacker, and say that Susan Smith is a direct descendant of Fannie Taylor. Or you can look at the lynching scenes in *Rosewood* and recognize them in the news seventy years to the day after Rosewood, when three white laborers kidnapped and burnt a black tourist named Christopher Wilson. *Rosewood* families say this is the massacre's legacy. Look at the fact that just as in Rosewood, so many black Masonic halls and churches are being burned in contemporary America. The center for Democratic Renewal has recorded thirty-six cases of arson or serious vandalism at black churches in the South in the past eighteen months. So far, most of those arrested have been white men.

There is so much relevance not just in Rosewood but also in places like Greenwood, North Carolina, where forty black-owned city blocks were leveled and then looted in 1921, and in all the other "Rosewoods" in America: black people were, and still are, the scapegoats for America's problems. Even after the original Rosewood investigation in the 1980s, WFLA-TV reported that many white people nine miles west of Rosewood, around Cedar Key, still "sneer at the massacre." The broadcast captures Quitman Hodges, a longtime Cedar Key councilman, saying on-camera that "them people didn't own

nothing out there to begin with," and that the Rosewood incident is all "poppycock." Yet later in the interview he says, "I know what happened, but I ain't gonna tell you and let you broadcast it." Why not? Especially if it is all "poppycock?" What does Hodges not want the world to know? Thankfully, others who had been silent decided at last to speak. Frightened survivors who had changed their addresses—some even their names—took courage and spoke out. Bringing their story to the screen is one of the most worthwhile ventures I have ever embarked on.

—Hollywood
Summer 1996

[continued on next page]

"Scrupulous reporting that reads like a vivid novel. The Rosewood tragedy speaks to every American, and its survivors' patient struggle for redress forms the heart of this book."

—Morris Dees

"POWERFUL...absorbing...no-holds-barred."   —*Charlotte Observer*

"Even the casual history buff repeatedly encounters similar stories from post-slavery America: grotesque murders, massacres and lynchings through the mid-1960s, committed with the grinning encouragement of white neighbors and the tacit approval of law enforcement. And yet the story of this rural community carries the power to shock anew. It was a crime against not just flesh and bone but a *community*, a crime that tore up a people's history by the roots. D'Orso's beautifully drawn *Like Judgment Day* resurrects that community while it documents its destruction, showing us the faces and lives of those who survived and helping us to fit Rosewood into the quilt of our history....[D'Orso] does a brilliant job of telling the story simply, movingly....He lets us get to know his characters without canonizing or demonizing any of them."

—*St. Petersburg Times*

"ASTONISHINGLY COMPLETE...a gripping drama."

—*Houston Chronicle*

"D'Orso's considerable storytelling talents provide a gripping account of Rosewood and the shameful history of lynching in the South. Extensive interviews illustrate both the tragic aftermath for the victims of Rosewood and the sense of release that they felt when their sufferings were finally honored."

—*Library Journal*

"SUPERB....This book moves, fueled by a poignant story, thorough research and very crisp writing."

—*Fort Lauderdale Sun-Sentinel*

"D'Orso has tackled what is probably America's thorniest problem—race relations—and shown us a path from ruin to reconciliation."

—*Arizona Republic*

"AN HONORABLE TRIBUTE to the survivors of a racist nightmare and a call to higher standards of humanity."

—*Mobile Register*

BOULEVARD BOOKS, NEW YORK

LIKE JUDGMENT DAY

THE RUIN AND REDEMPTION
OF A TOWN CALLED
Rosewood

Michael D'Orso

AN ESSAY ON *ROSEWOOD*
Published by arrangement with Warner Bros., a Time Warner
Entertainment Company
Text and photos © 1996 Warner Bros.

LIKE JUDGMENT DAY

A Boulevard Book / published by arrangement with Michael D'Orso

PRINTING HISTORY
Boulevard edition / December 1996

Lyrics from "If That Ain't Country" by Deborah Lynne Coe and Fred Spears,
© 1977 by Showfor Music (administered by Bluewater Music Corp.),
reprinted by permission. All rights reserved.

Book design by Deborah Kerner.

The Putnam Berkley World Wide Web site address is
http://www.berkley.com/berkley

ISBN: 1-57297-256-4

BOULEVARD
Boulevard Books are published by The Berkley Publishing Group,
200 Madison Avenue, New York, New York 10016.
BOULEVARD and its logo are trademarks
belonging to Berkley Publishing Corporation.

PRINTED IN THE UNITED STATES OF AMERICA

10   9   8   7

TO *Liliane*,

FOR THE GOOD THINGS

Florida,
at the beginning of the century

SCALE OF STATUTE MILES.
0 10 20 30 40 50 60 70 80 90 100
75 MILES TO THE INCH

CONTENTS

Prologue   1

PROLOGUE

This much is known.

Dawn broke keen and crisp that day, the first dawn of the new year, the coldest anyone in Rosewood could remember. A half century later they would remember how cold it was, how frost glistened on the palms and palmettos, how sheets of ice sparkled in the swamp and crystals of rime coated the moss sagging from the branches of the oaks that shaded the village's narrow dirt lanes. A soft breeze blew in from the west that morning, from the Gulf, riffling the moss and rustling the leaves. Years later they would remember that, too, the ones who were still alive.

It was a morning to stay inside, to stoke the flames in the wood-burning stoves and climb back beneath the quilts. Some of the women and children had that choice, those who weren't already up and gone to warm the kitchens of the white people's homes over in Sumner. As for Rosewood's men, most of them had risen hours before, stepping out into the moonlight and walking in groups of three and four to the mill. No matter that this was New Year's Day. The saws were still turning at the mill, the stacks of cedar and cypress waiting to be sliced. It was the cedar, the russet-toned timber that had risen from this

Florida swamp since the time of Christ, that gave Rosewood its reason for being, as well as its name.

It was a three-mile hike down the sandy road to the sawmill in Sumner, the sand white as sugar, and most of the men in Rosewood had made the trek that morning. Others had stayed to stoke the flames at the turpentine still just east of the village in a little place called Wylly, and some were even deeper in those dark, wet woods, loggers with hand saws, felling the trees that fed the mill. Then there were the trappers, running their lines for mink and otter and coon, for furs they could peddle up in Gainesville, or down at Cedar Key, or right there by the tracks that cut through the swamp on the way to the coast. Railcars would stop at the small depot in Rosewood just to pick up those fresh pelts, to ship them on to furriers and catalog houses up north. There was something special about Florida fur, people said, especially people up north.

They were sleeping in Sumner as well that morning, the white women and children whose own husbands and fathers had left before daylight to restart the mill after its holiday shutdown. Among them was James Taylor, thirty years old, soft-spoken, a friendly enough man, with a young wife named Fannie and two small children still asleep in their four-room company-owned home just up the lane from the Cummer and Sons mill. James Taylor's job was to coax the stiff saw blades awake each morning, loosening the steel discs with splashes of oil. That done, he would stroll back home for breakfast, then return to put in the rest of his day's work.

Oiling the mill machinery, that's where James Taylor was that morning when the front door to his home burst open and out onto the porch stumbled his wife, sobbing, shrieking, her face battered, her mouth bleeding. Neighbors, mostly women, clambered out onto their own porches, some rushing to her side, others sending word up the sawdust-sprinkled drive in the direction of the mill, word that picked up speed as it spread. Something about an attack. By a nigger. Over at James Taylor's house.

By the time they laid Fannie Taylor on a friend's bed, weeping, hysterical, moaning for her babies, a crowd had gathered at her front gate. Her children were safe, carried to a neighbor's home, and a posse was already forming, a dozen men, two dozen, the mob swelling by the minute.

By the time James Taylor got there, Rob Walker, the county sheriff, had arrived. He brought word that a black convict had escaped the day before from a county road gang. The man's name was Jesse Hunter, and bloodhounds were already on the way.

It was Jesse Hunter's scent the throng believed—had no doubt—was on Fannie Taylor's clothing when pieces of it were brought out and rubbed on the hounds' noses, and the dogs shot away, bolting through the back yard, baying and snorting, out an open gate, up onto the gravel bed of the railroad tracks, then to the left, to the east, toward Rosewood.

The sun was getting high now, the January light slanting off the whitewashed and weathered homes of the small black village—nearly thirty homes, some hardly more than shanties, others the size of the finest two-story houses in Sumner, all arranged among a network of dirt lanes winding through thickets of cedars and oaks. A few of the homes had lawns, several had fruit trees, some kept arbors of grapes. There were three churches, a general store, a Masonic lodge, a school, a baseball diamond—everything a town of a hundred and fifty could need. A prosperous town. A town that took care of itself. A black town in a white place in a white time. Western Florida, 1923.

They heard the hounds first, far off in the distance, the howls echoing through the brooding swamp. Then the voices of men, angry voices, hungry voices.

"Kill him!" the voices rumbled. "*Kill* the nigger!"

Children who had just stepped out to play were pulled inside. Doors were locked. Curtains drawn. Those bold enough to peek outside saw a parade of white men surging past, some wearing Stetsons, others bareheaded, most brandishing longarms—rifles and shotguns, battered and beaten from years of use. But some of the weapons were new, gleaming, grabbed off store shelves and torn fresh from their wrappers just that morning.

The dogs stopped at a small house in a grove of trees at the far edge of town, whining until the door was pushed open, then rushing in to paw at a gun, a water bucket, a bed. Then out the back, where fresh wagon tracks cut the sand and the scent stopped.

The house belonged to a man named Aaron Carrier, a soldier during World War I, now a civilian again, come back home to the place he'd been born. But Aaron Carrier was not in his house. And there was no sign of the wagon. The whites, furious, frustrated, fanned out through town until they arrived at the home of Aaron's mother, Emma, who answered the pounding on her door to confront a mob of white men.

"Where is he?" one shouted. "Where's your boy? We want him. Now!"

Emma blocked the doorway.

"He's sick," she said. "Sick in bed. He's *been* sick. He didn't do nothin'. What you want him for? He didn't do *nothin'*."

The mob pushed her aside, stormed into the house and found Aaron, up in his mother's bedroom. They dragged him out, ordered him to talk, but he said nothing. So someone called for a rope, and as Emma screamed from the porch, they tied one end around Aaron's wrists and the other to the bumper of a car, a black Model T. The driver hit the gas and Aaron Carrier's body was dragged up the hard dirt road, his shirt torn by the gravel, his skin seared by the sand. A quarter mile they dragged him, and then they stopped, the driver saying he was tired of wasting his gasoline on this nigger. "Kill him!" someone shouted, and that's when Aaron Carrier spoke.

"I didn't do nothin' wrong," he said, his voice cracking from pain and fear. "It was Sam Carter took him."

Some of the group stayed with Carrier in case his story was untrue, and the rest fanned out to find Carter. Throughout the afternoon they swarmed the village, more than four dozen white men, warning women and children foolish enough to step outside to get back into their houses. Rosewood men were stopped, startled as they arrived home near sundown. Some were told to get inside and stay there. Others were warned to get out of town and don't come back. All did as they were told. No one fought back, not yet.

Finally, at dusk, a wagon rolled up to a small, empty house off by itself beneath a cluster of trees at the southwest edge of town. The lone driver stepped down, a forty-seven-year-old man named Sam Carter. That was his wagon; this was his house. The mob sprang from behind some bushes, grabbed him, demanded to know who he'd hidden that day. When he didn't answer, they pulled him toward one of his oaks, its thick lower limbs worn smooth by the ropes he'd used for years to hoist broken parts from crippled wagons. Sam Carter was a blacksmith.

One of those ropes was now looped around Carter's neck, tightened, then pulled taut by the crowd, some jeering, some cheering as the body rose off the ground. They were hanging Sam Carter not to kill him but to choke him, to squeeze the truth out of him.

He squirmed, kicked, finally was able to force out the words. "I'll *tell* you!" he gasped. *"I'll tell you!"*

They let him down, but they weren't done. They were far from done. They dragged him to a stump, tied him down and took knives to his ears, to his fingers and thumbs, slicing off body parts for keepsakes. There were some in the mob bent on finding the black man brazen enough to lay hands on a white woman, but there were just as many, maybe more, fueled by moonshine, high on hate, who were simply thirsty for blood. Nigger blood. They, like the hounds, now had the scent, and they wanted more.

By the time they loosened the ropes, Sam Carter was half dead, weak from pain and fear, the sand he lay on wet with his blood. Yes, he muttered, he would take them to the fugitive. It was dark now, as they hoisted Carter into his wagon and turned it where he pointed, south toward the swampy expanse of forest they called Gulf Hammock.

"Here," Carter said, when they reached a spot at the edge of the jungle. The glow from their lanterns was swallowed by the surrounding blackness. "Here's where I put him out."

But the dogs could smell nothing. A man stepped from the crowd, cane liquor on his breath, a shotgun in his hands. He leveled the rifle at Sam Carter's head.

Carter stared blankly at the white man, then said something anyone raised in those woods would understand, a phrase used by people who hunted for their livelihood, who knew the uselessness of slaughtering an animal for anything other than food or clothing. It was a phrase used by country folk for any pointless act.

"You can kill me," Sam Carter muttered, "but you can't eat me."

"You black son of a bitch," said the white man, spitting in the sand. "You didn't do it, neither."

Then he pulled the trigger, and Sam Carter's face was gone. More of his body parts were taken, to be stored in jars, pulled out and chuckled over for years to come. Someone grabbed his pocketwatch. It too would show up from time to time, in a bar, in a barbershop, around Sumner or Cedar Key, Chiefland or Bronson. "Let's see what time it is by old Sam Carter," someone would laugh, and the watch would come out.

The crowd had a corpse now, but still they weren't finished. They hanged the body back up from a tree and riddled it with bullets. Then, finally, they cut down what remained of Sam Carter, dumped it on the road and headed back to town.

No one knew what to do next. Sam Carter was dead, and Aaron Carrier was gone, taken from the mob by a man named Pillsbury, superintendent of the sawmill, who had spirited the beaten black man away. No one would see Aaron Carrier in Rosewood again, not that week, not ever.

Fannie Taylor's attacker was still at large, and the mood back in Sumner was dark. Work went on at the mill the next day, and the next, some of the men from Rosewood returning to their jobs while others stayed away. The air was tense, and there was talk among whites of returning to Rosewood, of taking back up their guns and going for more than a mere fugitive this time. There was talk of emptying that town, for good and forever.

Some of that talk reached Rosewood, and some of the men sent their families away, hoping it would soon be safe to bring them back. Most, though, did nothing, believing the worst was over.

There was reason to believe that. There had never been much trouble to speak of between the people of Rosewood and Sumner. Blacks from Rosewood would routinely pass through Sumner by wagon or on foot, on their way to Cedar Key for some fishing or just a day at the beach. Black and white children from both towns would often play in the woods together, chasing rabbits, stalking snakes, picking wildflowers. Both towns had ball teams, and though it was forbidden on the face of it, the fact was that the Sumner club would often slip over to Rosewood on a Saturday afternoon to take the field against the blacks. More often than not, they went home with a whipping.

But that was fine. It was fun, and truth be told, fun was hard to come by in those parts, in those times. The high point of the day in both towns was sunset, when the train would stop through with the mail. Men, women and children, they would all gather at their depot, the whites in Sumner and the blacks in Rosewood, the men lighting pipes in the gathering dusk, the women sitting with babies on their laps, all catching up on the day's news, gossiping, anxious to see if there might be something for them in that night's mail bag, but just as content to simply sit together, to socialize. Then the train would pull up, and pull out, and they'd all head home.

So there was reason to believe this outbreak, this killing, was just a passing thing. But Sylvester Carrier knew better than that. "Man," the townspeople called him, simply "Man." He was thirty years old, dark, tall. There was no hunter in the county to match him, black or white, no shot so sure. He made his living from the woods, and each time he went into that forest, they said, he emerged sagging under the weight of wild turkey and deer, possum and quail.

When he was home among his own, on Sundays, at weddings, at funerals, he would dress in black—black suit, black tie, stiff black Stetson hat. No man in town looked so fine, they said, but only one woman shared his favors—his wife Gertrude. They'd been married ten years, the two of them living with Sylvester's mother Sarah and his sisters in a trim two-story house, with a mail-order piano in the parlor, a piano on which Sylvester sometimes taught lessons. His sisters, Annie and Lelland and Bernadina, were called "Sweetie" and "Beauty" and "Honey" by all who knew them, and each Sunday they would walk together, the whole Carrier family, to the Rosewood Methodist Church, where Man would sit at the organ and sing with the choir, sing solo with a voice so rich it brought tears to the eye.

But the whites never saw that side of Sylvester Carrier. What they saw looked dangerous. There were more than a few whites around Sumner who saw the blacks of Rosewood as nothing but thieves—cattle rustlers and hog killers. Sylvester Carrier and his father, Hayward, had done time for cattle rustling, worked nearly a year on one of those road gangs, everyone knew that. They swore they were set up, father and son, framed, and they hated the white men for that.

Which was another thing that made Sylvester Carrier dangerous. This man was angry, and he was proud, too proud. He had no fear of white men. He kept to himself, never looked for a fight—no black man could survive a fight with whites in that time and that place—but he stepped forward and stood his ground when there was ground to be stood. People still talked about the afternoon Sweetie and Beauty came home from Sumner upset, told Sylvester some white boys over there had made indecent statements to them. Sylvester asked where it happened, went straight to the house, walked into the yard and called the men out, warned them that if this happened again, someone would die.

A man like that had a keen nose for trouble, and Sylvester Carrier could smell it now. He gathered his kin from around town, more than a dozen of them, mostly children—cousins and nieces and nephews—and brought them all together under his parents' roof. Sarah Carrier was there, but not her husband Hayward; he had left on a hunting trip at the start of the week and wouldn't be back for another.

Aaron Carrier's parents, Emma and James, were there, James limping as he walked, his left side paralyzed from a recent stroke. With them came a group of their children and grandchildren, ten of them, including a nine-year-old girl named Minnie Lee Mitchell and her big brother Ruben. In all, there were nearly twenty people squeezed into the Carrier house—two men, one old and crippled, the rest women and children, the little ones squeezed into an upstairs bedroom while the grownups slept in the remaining rooms in the house.

While Sylvester Carrier was collecting his family, word spread among the whites that some sort of buildup was going on over at Sarah Carrier's place, that the niggers were stockpiling arms and planning an attack. That was what Henry Andrews heard up in Otter Creek, and that's why he fired up a railroad motorcar full of armed men on the night of January fourth, a Thursday night, and headed toward Rosewood.

Andrews was the chief sawmill superintendent at Cummer's small Otter Creek operation. Short and stocky, he was known for his quick temper, his habit of kicking workers when they moved too slowly for his taste. "Boots," they called him. He had never cared for Sylvester Carrier, and now, with the light of a full moon showing the way, he was bound to do something about it.

By the time Andrews's crew reached Rosewood, about nine P.M., they had been joined by a Sumner shopkeeper and sometimes quarters boss named Poly Wilkerson. In country as remote as this, formal law enforcement was spread thin—one county deputy was responsible for covering the area from Otter Creek to the coast, a distance of twenty miles, with Rosewood and Sumner midway between. So mills like Cummer and Sons created their own sheriffs of sorts, hiring men they called quarters bosses to patrol the workers' communities, keeping the peace and acting as an arm of the law when needed.

Poly Wilkerson had held that job in Sumner for a while, carrying out his duties with relish—too much relish, his superiors soon decided. Weary of hearing complaints from workers about Wilkerson's heavy hand, the mill management had recently let him go. Wilkerson had not taken the dismissal well, challenging his replacement at gunpoint one evening out front of the small Sumner hotel, and backing down when the man beat him to the draw. Poly Wilkerson cared for few people, white or black, and few cared for him, but one thing he did have a taste for was trouble, and that Thursday night he was hungry.

Hearing that Henry Andrews was headed down from Otter Creek, that something was stirring in Rosewood, Wilkerson filled his Model T with a few friends and drove up. The two groups collected in front of the Carrier house, the moon flooding the yard with white light. The house was dark and still. The air was frigid, so cold that the small posse, no more than a dozen all told, built a fire over by the tracks.

Sylvester Carrier had heard them coming and doused all the lights. Now he sat with two loaded rifles by a darkened front window, watching as the white men built their fire. He could see their faces clearly in the bright moonlight.

Sarah could see them, too. She knew most of these men. She'd helped raise some of them from babies, knew their names, had even wet-nursed a couple.

As the men approached the porch, a dog suddenly charged around the side of the house, a puppy the children called Shant Tail. Poly Wilkerson raised his pistol and shot it dead. Wilkerson then shouted for Sarah to come out, her and the children. He said he didn't want to hurt any women or children. He said he had come for Sylvester.

Sarah had seen enough.

"Y'all go on home," she hollered out a window, scolding the throng as if they were still children. "Just get yourselves on home."

Then a gunshot cracked, the window burst, and Sarah Carrier fell back, a bullet through her head.

Then the night exploded with the roar of buckshot as the posse emptied its weapons at the home's windows and wooden walls. Splinters and shards of glass filled the air, falling to the ground like snowflakes.

Inside the house it was chaos and darkness, adults shouting from downstairs, the children huddled above, terrified and confused, but unharmed. All but one, a boy whose face was soaked with blood. It was Ruben, Minnie Lee's brother. He had peeked out a window the instant a bullet came bursting through. The glass had shattered in his face, and now Ruben's left eye was gone.

At the foot of the stairs crouched Sylvester, waiting with a pump-handled shotgun and Winchester rifle. His sisters and cousins were scattered around him, hugging the floor, looking for a chance to get up the stairs to the children.

One, Sarah's twenty-year-old daughter, the one they called "Honey," made her move, rushing up the steps to see to the children. Her nightgown was splashed with her mother's blood. Mama Sarah was dead, she told the children, and some of the small ones pushed past her, rushing downstairs in a panic. One, Minnie Lee, was grabbed by Sylvester, pulled between his legs just as the front door burst open.

Sylvester squeezed one of his triggers, and with a deafening blast, Poly Wilkerson fell back on the porch, shot through the face. A voice shouted, Sylvester fired again, and Henry Andrews dropped dead as well.

One of the mob moved toward the bodies on the porch but was driven back by a fusillade from inside the house. Another tried climbing toward an upstairs window but was knocked back with a bullet wound to the head.

Word swept to Sumner like the wind. A gun battle in Rosewood. White men shot dead by blacks. White wounded lying in the street. Someone called Cedar Key, where a news reporter, a stringer, was roused and put out a dispatch on the wires. By one A.M., carloads of armed men from as far as Gainesville, forty miles to the northeast, had grabbed their guns and were rushing toward Rosewood. There had been a Ku Klux Klan rally and parade in Gainesville New Year's Eve, a hundred hooded men marching past a courthouse square packed with cheering onlookers. The hoods were now gone, tucked back in drawers and closets, but among the cars now rolling toward Rosewood were many carrying Klansmen.

Meanwhile the siege continued. Two more whites were wounded as attacks on the darkened house continued. The moonlight made for easy targets. By four A.M. the posse pulled back to wait for sunup.

By then some of the women in the house had made it upstairs, pulling the children together, waiting for a chance to get out. When they saw the mob retreat, felt the comfort of silence for the first time in hours, they made their escape out the back, all of them, children and grownups, all who were left alive.

At dawn, bolstered by reinforcements, the whites approached again, a throng now two hundred and fifty strong. No gunfire this time. Inside they stepped, into a scene of carnage—splintered glass, shattered wood, walls pocked with bullet holes, sofa pillows and mattresses strewn on the floor. And two dead bodies. One was Sarah Carrier's, shot through the head. The other was a man's, her son Sylvester.

Out the rear door dripped trails of blood, down the steps, across the sandy back yard and on into the woods. They had escaped, all but these two, crawled away during the siege through cover of trees and the night, and now they were out there, out in the swamp.

Now there was no holding back. Axes were taken to everything still intact in the house. Lamps, dishes, chairs, tables. Finally, the piano. All smashed to shards in a burst of fury. Cans of kerosene appeared. Matches. And now the morning sky was darkened with billowing black smoke.

Cars continued to arrive, from as far now as Jacksonville, the streets filling with white rage. Another house went up in flames. Then another. The Methodist church, Man's church, was set ablaze. Then the other two churches as well, their bells tolling languidly, rocked by the wind and rising heat as flames licked the pews below.

The mob surged like a wave, first one way, then another, shooting not just in the air but at anything that moved. Lexie Gordon, fifty-five, a light-skinned widow with a milk cow in her yard, had sent her grown daughters into the swamp at the first sounds of gunshots. She was sick with typhoid fever, too weak to follow. Now, at the sound of voices on her porch, she pulled herself out of bed. When smoke began curling through her front windows, she tried to flee out the back. Silhouetted by the flames, she was an easy target. A quick burst of bullets, and Lexie Gordon lay dead.

And the cars kept coming, now rolling in from across the state line, from Georgia. Some didn't wait to reach town to begin shooting. One carload came upon a lone figure at the edge of the forest, twenty miles east of Rosewood. His name was Mingo Williams, but he was known throughout the county as "Lord God," the name his mother called him when he was a baby. He was fifty now, living alone, not in Rosewood, but in a small cabin out in the piney woods. He was drawing turpentine sap from some of those pines when a car filled with white men pulled up beside him.

"What's your name, boy?" they asked.

"Lord God," he answered.

A rifle was raised, a blast from its barrel, and Mingo Williams lay dead in the dirt, shot through the jaw.

Rosewood was a ghost town now, its streets crowded with outsiders, its residents scattered into the surrounding swamp, some wearing nothing more than nightshirts, shivering and huddling as they heard the crackle of gunfire and saw smoke climbing toward the clouds.

Saturday morning, with most of the village reduced to ashes, an elderly black man emerged from the swamp and approached Pillsbury, the mill super-intendent. The old man was James Carrier. He had limped into the woods with the rest of his family during the gun battle. He had hidden with them for a day and a night, and now he was limping back to plead for their safety. He asked Pillsbury for protection, and the white man obliged, locking the old man in one of the village's few unburned homes.

But that afternoon a crowd collected outside the house, calling for the man who might give them the names of the criminals they now sought, black killers as well as a rapist. The mob pulled James Carrier from the house and carried him to the fresh graves of his sister-in-law Sarah and her son Sylvester. The mob wanted names. They especially wanted Jesse Hunter's name. James Carrier had nothing to give them, and so, after forcing him to hollow out his own grave with his one good arm, they shot him dead.

Now there was nothing left to kill. Most of the refugees in the swamp had made their way to safety in nearby hamlets. Some were hiding in the homes of Sumner whites for whom they worked. Others had been rescued by railcars brought from Cedar Key under cover of night by a pair of white conductors, two brothers, John and William Bryce, men who had never understood the hatred so many of their neighbors felt toward the blacks. Under a dark, blessedly cloudy sky, the Bryces' train rolled slowly, quietly, through the dense mossy woods, its crew calling into the darkness for women and children to climb aboard. Only women and children. The mob's targets were men and older boys. Taking on a male might mean death for them all.

John Wright too could risk taking no one but women and children under his roof. He was one of a handful of whites who called the woods around Rosewood home, the only white man who lived in the village proper. The town's largest store was run by John Wright and his wife. His house, two stories high, its porches trimmed with filigree and flowers, was the village's finest. Children from Sumner would often hike the three miles to John Wright's yard just to sample the sweet grapes he grew on his arbors.

As the mob torched building after building, hour after hour, it passed the Wright home by, knowing it belonged to a white man. They did not know Wright had filled some of those rooms with black women and children, hiding them until the train pulled up Saturday night at the rail platform in his back yard, where quickly, quietly, a line of shivering survivors was loaded into darkened cars and spirited away to Gainesville, never to return to Rosewood again.

There was nothing to return to. Sunday afternoon, the last twelve homes still standing among the smoke and ashes were set aflame. The marauders were weary now, their fury spent, their prey long gone. Sheriffs and deputies had arrived from Bronson and from neighboring Alachua County, but by the time they got there, there was no one left to save. The town was empty. As for the burning, they just watched.

A week had passed since the bells of Rosewood rang in the new year. Now those bells lay smoldering among the twisted steel and blackened ruins, the charred carcasses of cats and dogs, the smoking soot of a place that would never exist again.

By sundown, the white men were gone, back down the sandy Florida roadways to their own towns, to their own homes and families.

And the black men, women and children of Rosewood, they were gone, too. Simply gone.

$\mathscr{A}$WAKENING

Old News

It was a Friday afternoon, payday, and a steady stream of men and women was shoving its way through the front doors of Lundy's Liquor Store, looking to cash their checks and maybe pick up a pint or two, something for the weekend. Each time the glass doors swung open, the springtime sounds of the city rushed in, sharp hoots and shouts from the pedestrians pushing past on the sidewalk outside, the blare of horns and the blast of radios from the sedans surging up Tangerine Avenue toward the east, toward the purple twilight above downtown St. Pete.

The liquor store's safe was stuffed with cash, and Arnett Doctor was working the counter, manning the register, bagging bottles, making small talk with the customers. He was a tall man, with piercing eyes and a strong body, solid save for a belly gone soft with middle age. On his hip, tucked beneath his light cotton shirt, was a pistol, a snub-nosed .357 Magnum, what the people on the street called a "spoiler." Wearing a pistol was part of the job in a place like Lundy's. Doctor knew as well as anyone how liquor and cash made for a deadly

Sarah Carrier, with son Sylvester and daughter Willie

combination. He knew too how poverty could make it even worse, and plenty of the people passing through the doors of Lundy's were poor.

Doctor had grown up with half of them. The rest he knew at least by face. Most lived within a mile or so of the store, many in the public housing project just down the street. Jordan Park, it was called, a tangle of beige two-story buildings sprawled across twenty-six acres of bare dirt and broken glass. When the first tenants had moved there in the spring of 1940, Jordan Park was hailed as a place of hope, like so many such projects across America. There were fresh lawns to water, bright beds of gardenias and hibiscus to weed. Now, forty-two years later, the grass and the flowers, along with the hope, were gone, and Jordan Park had become one of the bleakest, most violent neighborhoods in the state of Florida.

Doctor counted himself lucky never to have lived there. His mother had spent her life working two jobs, sometimes three, just to keep herself and her children out of a place like that, out of the projects. Cleaning white families' homes, cooking and caring for white women's children, that's what Philomena Doctor had done for longer than Arnett could remember, since long before he was born. Most of what he had, he owed to his mother, but even more, most of what he *was,* he owed to her. She loved more fiercely than anyone he had ever known, but she could hate just as hard, and Arnett was the same way, with the same hair trigger, the same volcanic temper, the same river of hurt that ran so deep inside it was hard to understand where it came from.

Much of it came from the simple fact that he was black, born in the '40s, come of age in the '50s and '60s, all in the Deep South, enough right there to fuel a lifetime of fury. For his mother, born before World War I, black and a woman besides, it was unimaginably worse. She had given up a lot in her life— to be married, to have children, then to be divorced and have to raise a son and daughter by herself. But it wasn't the things she lost that hurt Phil Doctor half as much as the things she never had, the things she always swore should have been hers had circumstances been different. And for that she blamed only white people. She cursed the white man. Warned Arnett from the time he was a baby that he could never trust a white man or woman. He might share his days with them, she said, he might work for them or beside them, but he must never allow them to come close enough to hurt him. And that is what they would do, she assured him time and again. They would hurt him, use him, take his life if he let them. She had seen it before.

He had seen it, too, early on, back in Lacoochee, the small sawmill town where he was born, an hour into the central Florida forests and open cattleland north of Tampa. Arnett was just a boy then, but he would never forget the lynching. And that's what it had been, though the authorities never called it that. The body was found by the railroad tracks out toward the river, not far from the sawmill where half the town worked. It was a black man, middle-aged, dead, hit by a passing train, probably drunk. At least that was the way it was officially reported, the way the white world put it to rest.

But the blacks knew better. Arnett's mother and father, their kinfolk and friends, every black person in the town of Lacoochee knew better. Arnett was only ten at the time, still too young to know many things, but even he knew better than to believe this was anything but murder.

The man was a friend, a neighbor. His name was Wallace Jordan. He lived with his wife and a house full of sons three doors down from the Doctors. Some of his boys were Arnett's playmates. Jordan drove deliveries for a grocery store in town, a white man's store, and word was he had glanced the wrong way at the storekeeper's wife one afternoon, not something a black man in a place like Lacoochee could dare to do, not in the 1950s. By that evening Wallace Jordan's beaten, mutilated body had been driven to the edge of town, already a corpse by the time it was dumped on the Seaboard tracks.

Arnett never understood how someone could get away with something like that, how the grownups, his own mama and daddy, could talk about it behind closed doors, then go on as if nothing had happened. Things like that weren't supposed to happen in America. People weren't supposed to die like that with nothing done about it, no questions asked, no questions answered.

But black people had been dying like that in this country for a long time. Arnett learned this as he grew older. Even in a city as serene as St. Pete—a town known among Florida's blacks as a better place than most to make a life, the town to which Arnett's mother chose to take him and his sister Yvonne after deciding to leave her husband, a resort town, a lovely town—even there black people had died the way Wallace Jordan went down. More than once, for sure, but the death most remembered, though there were those who would rather forget, was the hanging of John Evans.

He was a common laborer, hunted down by a mob of whites in the winter of 1914, captured and hanged without trial for a murder no one bothered to prove he committed, strung up from a light pole in the center of the city while a taunting crowd of fifteen hundred men and women emptied their weapons into his swaying corpse. The police were nowhere to be seen until the next morning, when they arrived to cut down and dispose of John Evans's bullet-shredded body.

That was a dark stain on St. Petersburg's past, but it was old news by the time Phil Doctor arrived with her two kids in the summer of 1957. There was a lot of old news in this town. The local chapter of the Ku Klux Klan was no longer as bold as it had been in the '20s, when the hooded throngs, including many of the city's most prominent citizens, routinely staged proud parades up the sands of Pass-a-Grille Beach, the glow of their torches glimmering off the waters of Tampa Bay.

By the '50s, the KKK hoods had faded away, replaced by coats and ties and respectable titles like the White Citizens Council. But like almost every city throughout the South, St. Petersburg remained a divided place. Its nicest neighborhoods, its best beaches, the front rows on its buses and trolley cars, the box seats in its baseball field, Al Lang Stadium, where the New York Yankees and St. Louis Cardinals—Mickey Mantle and Stan Musial—sharpened their skills each spring, even the bright green downtown benches built for the retirees who spilled out of the city's apartments each morning to roam its sun-bleached sidewalks, they were all understood, if not clearly marked, to be for whites only.

Arnett wove his way through that world each day, shining shoes in the afternoons with his mother's brother, his Uncle A. T., their pockets filling with nickels and quarters. Evenings Arnett would fetch tubs of drinks and barrels of ice for the black acts that played the Manhattan Casino, a cavernous club above a warehouse down at the heart of 22nd Street, the main artery through the black section of the city, St. Petersburg's Harlem, so to speak. In its heyday, in the late '50s, the Manhattan was jammed each evening with five hundred, six hundred, seven hundred sweat-soaked couples jitterbugging and lindy-hopping to the likes of Billy Eckstine and Buddy Johnson, Brook Benton and Floyd Rawlings, Louis Armstrong, big stars with big wallets, most of them happy to lay a five-dollar tip on a kid clever enough to find them something cool to drink on those sweltering subtropical nights.

Mornings Arnett would head downtown, wending his way through the whites-only sections to get to the beach, the black beach, a stretch of sand they called South Mole. It had no buoys, no lifeguards, not even a way to get to the water other than a dirt path through thorny sand spurs and bushes. But when you did get there, you could look out across the harbor at the Million-Dollar Pier, the diamond of St. Petersburg's bayfront, with its massive Mediterranean Revival–style casino perched out on those pilings, surrounded by sailboats and yachts bobbing like jewels in the water of Tampa Bay.

Some days Arnett would start swimming toward that pier and not stop till he was half a mile from shore, so far out that there wasn't another soul in sight, just sleek mullet sharks darting beneath him and shimmering man-of-wars floating past, their tentacles sparkling in the tropical sun. And then he would dive, down into the darkness, deep down where the sunlight stopped and the temperature plunged and everything was still and silent and black. And he would stay there, floating in the blackness till his lungs caught fire and he had to surface.

He loved going down like that, staying down. It was the quietest, most peaceful place he had ever known. For a while, he dreamed he would do that when he grew up, make a living as a deep-sea diver. But that was only for a while. Time went past, and he soon saw there were some things there was no use dreaming about. Black boys didn't grow up to be deep-sea divers, not in any world he knew. And the more he got to know about this world, the more he grew angry, just like his mother.

But where Philomena Doctor made it her business to avoid whites wherever she could, Arnett made it his business to confront them, to face them down, to make them answer for what was tearing him apart. He had friends who were calmer, more accommodating, maybe wiser than he was. But he had his mother's temper, her fiery spirit, and there was no getting away from it. More than once in his life that temper would come close to getting him killed. The first time was in the spring of 1960.

Martin Luther King, Jr., was gathering the forces down South, John F. Kennedy was eyeing the White House up north, and civil rights was all the old-timers were talking about down at Buddy's barbershop, where Arnett and his uncle shined shoes. The movement was cresting from Montgomery to Miami, and Arnett was eager to be in the midst of it, right there in St. Pete, which is why he had stood and recited a pledge the year before at an NAACP meeting, raising his right hand and becoming a member of the city's newly formed Youth Council.

Soon he was its president. And not much later, on a warm spring afternoon close to Easter, he gathered a group of his friends, about two dozen of them, the girls dressed in skirts and blouses, the boys in starched shirts and slacks, some wearing sportcoats, and led them downtown to St. Pete's Center Theater, a whites-only movie house, where they paraded in a small circle, demanding that the doors be opened to blacks. The marquee above their heads flashed the feature film showing that night. "King of Kings," the story of Christ.

They were just kids, but that didn't matter to the man who burst from inside the building, white-haired, pink-skinned, in his sixties, half-dressed, wearing a T-shirt and brandishing a .45-caliber pistol as the crowd of onlookers pulled back.

"Nigger," the old man hissed, pressing the barrel of the gun against the side of Arnett's head, "if you don't get your ass out of here, your brains are gonna be splattered all over this sidewalk."

Arnett could see the blue uniform of a policeman at the back of the crowd. The officer was just standing there, looking on like the rest of them, making no move to stop what was about to happen. The cop couldn't know, nor could the old man squeezing that pistol, nor could any of the kids who had come with Arnett—none of them knew that he had a gun of his own shoved in the rear pocket of his trousers, a tiny .22-caliber revolver, a gift from the local president of the Congress of Racial Equality.

Non-violence was the way of the NAACP, Arnett knew that, and he knew as well that it was illegal for him to carry that weapon. But there was no way he was going to take an insult, much less an open threat, lying down. He just didn't have it in him. He had never used that gun before, never had to, but he was ready to use it now. He was scared half out of his wits, but he was ready to use it now.

"You do what you have to do," he said, his eyes locking on the white man's. "And I'm damn well gonna do what I have to do."

Arnett felt nothing but the moment. No past, no future. Only now. Right now. He had been there before, frozen and beyond fear in an instant that stretched like eternity. He would be there again. And right now, in this instant, he was ready to blow a hole through this white man's heart.

Slightly, almost imperceptibly, Arnett moved his hand toward his back pocket. Maybe the man saw that movement, or maybe he simply saw all he needed to see in in this black boy's eyes. Either way, the man backed down. Pulled his pistol away, cursed and charged back into the building.

Arnett and the other boys were taken to jail. The girls, including one to whom Arnett quietly passed his revolver before the police moved in, were allowed to go home. That was the last Arnett ever saw of that gun.

The first his mother learned of his whereabouts was watching that evening's six o'clock news. The broadcast began with footage of the arrest. It showed a line of black teens being led into a paddy wagon. At the front of the line was Arnett, and Philomena just about had a seizure when she saw him. She didn't even know her boy was *in* the goddamned NAACP.

When Arnett finally got home late that night, after officers of the organization's adult chapter had gone downtown and negotiated for the boys' release, Philomena attacked him, whipping him with a belt, beating his back, his chest, his legs, sobbing and shaking, cursing, swearing that he was going to die, just the way Wallace Jordan had died, just the way so many had died.

Arnett didn't flinch. He had seen his mother like this before, and he would see it again. He would see it when he went into the Army in '63, shipped off to the Pacific, then to places he couldn't tell her about, couldn't tell anyone about, because the U.S. wasn't supposed to be in those places, not yet. But Arnett was there, and his mother knew it, knew he was risking his life for the sake of the white man, because this war—if it was a war—would be like all the others, a white man's cause with black men doing more than their share of the dying.

Arnett didn't die. He killed, though he couldn't talk about it, but he didn't die. Twelve years after he enlisted he came home, world-traveled, trained in intelligence, versed in foreign languages, and more comfortable with whites than he had ever dreamed possible. The Army had done that, but his mother didn't give a damn. All she cared about was the fact that he was alive and back beside her, her only son.

He had a wife now, too, but it was not going well. Thelma was her name, and they were at each other all the time. Arnett had married her after she'd told him she was pregnant. It was the right thing to do, he figured, and so he did it right, a military wedding, raised sabers and all. A baby daughter was born five months later, but she was too small to survive. They hardly had time to name her—Patrice—before she died, six hours after she was delivered.

The marriage was a mess. Arnett and Thelma fought constantly. It was better when he had been wearing a uniform. At least that had kept him away from the house. Now he was home all the time, having to face her, and worse, having to face her parents. Arnett still had his temper, and it was getting the best of him again. More than once he threatened Thelma's mother and father, warned them to stay out of his business, that his troubles with his wife were between him and her. Finally, one night, he told them he'd kill them if they didn't keep away. Them and Thelma too. In a fit of rage, he pulled a gun. Waved it. Soon after that he told Thelma he wanted out, that he was filing for divorce. "Do it," she said, "and I'll see you in hell or in prison."

She saw him in prison. The day after the divorce was granted, Thelma's family filed assault charges with the state's attorney's office—aggravated assault—and Arnett wound up doing time. It wasn't hard time, he would say years later. When you do hard time, he would explain, you do it on their terms. Real time is done on *your* terms, and that's how Arnett insists he did his. Three years, all told. He saw the insides of jails in St. Pete and Clearwater, was sent to prisons in Avon Park, Lake Butler, Zephyrhills, Largo. He was all over the state during those three years, serving cafeteria food to inmates in one place, putting on a coat and tie in another and going outside the gates to help run a Special Olympics. He took college classes, too—a couple of business law courses and one in logic. They were behind bars, but they counted.

When he finally came out, in the summer of 1981, came home to St. Pete, Arnett Doctor fit no profile. He was an ex-con who spoke with the polish of a professor, a veteran who had carried a carbine in the jungles of Asia and now packed a sidearm on the streets of St. Pete. He had put his life in the hands of the white man, both in the Army and in prison, and he had survived without scars, without bitterness, though trust remained an issue. His mother made sure of that. The worst hurt he had to show for his life up till then, besides the loss of sheer time, was the feet he tore up during boot camp back in '63. The pain still jerked him awake most nights, the tangle of tendons and tissue stabbing like needles beneath his skin. Sometimes it got so bad he could hardly stand, which was why he had taken to carrying a cane.

The cane was there that Friday afternoon, propped in a corner behind the counter as he made change for his customers. He had been at Lundy's a year now, had worked his way up to manager and was looking to leave soon, to start his own business, maybe something janitorial. He was thirty-nine and in a hurry, a man with connections and some catching up to do. He didn't need any more trouble in his life, which is why he recoiled when he saw a white man appear in the door.

White people didn't come to Lundy's. They didn't come to this *neighbor-*

hood unless they had business, and the business they had was normally something to do with drugs. But this man was not looking for drugs. He was looking, he said, for a man named Arnett Doctor.

"Who wants to know?" asked Arnett. The man looked harmless enough, with a thick brownish beard and unruly hair that hung almost to his shoulders. He wore a checked flannel shirt, wrinkled khaki trousers and sneakers. He reminded Arnett of some of the holdover hippies he had seen when he came out of the service. But this man was no hippie. His deep voice was thick with a southern twang, the voice of a cracker. Educated, but still a cracker. And that set Arnett on edge. His mother had warned him about all white folks, but crackers, she said, they were the worst.

The man introduced himself, said his name was Gary Moore, said he was a reporter for the *St. Petersburg Times*. He extended his hand. Arnett hesitated. He shook the hand, but he didn't speak.

"I was told you might be able to help me out," said the reporter.

"And how's that?" asked Arnett.

"Well, I've been investigating an incident that happened up in Levy County."

Arnett felt his chest suddenly swell. He could hear his heartbeat thudding inside his head, the pounding of his pulse.

"Actually," the man continued, "it's something that happened back in 1923 . . ."

Arnett's hands were clenched now, his knuckles straining against the skin.

". . . at a place called Rosewood."

A Wall of Darkness

Arnett had been to Rosewood before. Once.

It was the summer of 1962, a year before he left to join the Army, and he was with his buddies, Bobo and George. They used to run together, the three of them, cruising the streets of St. Pete nearly every night in Bobo's '57 Buick Roadmaster. The car was a dream, silver and gray and snow white on the outside, black crushed velvet inside, with an engine that got cooler the faster and farther it was driven. Weekends they would take it out of town, hit the highway and open it up, toward Lakeland, Orlando, Ocala, any place that offered bright lights, cold drinks and warm women.

They were always looking for women, and they always came armed, because the kinds of clubs they walked into, a man would be a fool to enter without a weapon. Clubs like the One Stop Inn over at Plant City. Arnett would never forget the night the three of them stopped in there, met some young ladies, danced a while, had a few drinks, finally got up to leave and found themselves facing a crowd of locals, eight or nine of them, blocking the door, making

Philomena and Walter Doctor

it clear they objected to some city boys walking in off the street and hitting on their women.

Arnett didn't blink. He pulled out his piece, a .38, and just the sight of that pistol was enough to part the crowd. The locals backed away, let Arnett and his buddies leave the same way they'd come in, with their new lady friends in tow, and so the night was counted a success, although Arnett and Bobo and George never did go back to the One Stop Inn.

They were headed for Tallahassee that June afternoon in '62, when, about two hours north of Tampa, Bobo suddenly yanked the wheel and turned the car toward the coast.

"What the hell are you doing?" Arnett asked as the Roadmaster lurched left onto a narrow two-lane highway, just past a small sign that read Otter Creek.

"This place you been telling us about for so long," said Bobo, "I want to see it for myself. Rosewood. That's where we're going."

Arnett hadn't told his friends much about Rosewood, nowhere near all that he knew, and he knew nowhere near as much as he wanted to. Still, what he had told them was more than they could believe, and who could blame them? Who could believe there had once been a town up here in this godforsaken swamp country, a busy town filled with black people, three hundred of them at its peak, at the turn of the century, land-owning people with their own homes and businesses. Hard to believe there could have been anything at all out here in the middle of nowhere. Harder still to believe it could have been here one day and be gone the next, swept away overnight, the houses burned to the ground, the land seized, the people driven into the bogs, never to return, and nothing done about it, not after forty years, no mention of it in any history book, as if none of this had ever happened, as if the place had never existed.

Crazy, that's how it sounded to Arnett's buddies. As far as they figured, the place never *had* existed. This was just another one of Arnett's stories, and Arnett could *tell* a story. Sometimes it sounded crazy even to himself, even now, even after a lifetime of hearing the whispers, of hiding as a child around doorways and under windows, listening through walls to the words of the grownups, hearing them talk in hushed tones, late at night, after they thought the children were asleep and it was safe to speak, to speak about Rosewood.

Arnett was six when he first heard of it. It was Christmas day, 1949, and it was cold, bitter cold. They were living in Lacoochee then, he and his sister and his mama and daddy, living in the only house he had ever known, a company house back in what they called the quarters, across the Seaboard tracks, hard against the piney woods, in the crowded corner of town where the black sawmill workers lived. Dirt lanes and two-room huts, no electricity, no plumbing, outhouses out back, wood-burning stoves in the kitchens—that was the quarters.

Arnett's father was what they called a stacker up at the mill, pulling the fresh-cut planks of cedar and cypress as they were sliced off the logs, piling them to the side for the wagons to pick up and haul across the yard to the trains. He worked six days a week, every week of the year but Christmas, because Christmas they shut down the saws. And so Arnett's father was home that wind-whipped afternoon when Philomena came out on the porch and called the kids inside, hollered to Arnett to go find his sister and come on in the house.

They had a tree up, and there was a fire going in the fireplace. As he came in the door, Arnett could see his father was agitated, but then his daddy was always on edge around Christmas, because Philomena always got so sad that day. She'd sink into a tailspin and wind up back in her bedroom, stretched out on the mattress, crying and calling out her grandmother's name. *Mama, Mama,* she'd wail, and Arnett never knew why. All he knew was his father would follow her in there, close the door, and that's where the two of them would stay, for hours sometimes, until it was close to dark and finally his daddy would come out, drained and deathly quiet, and they would sit down to dinner, the three of them. Sometimes Arnett's mother would join them and sometimes not.

But this day it was different. Arnett's father was not so much sad as he was angry. He was facing Philomena as Arnett and his sister walked in.

"Why do you want to *do* this, Phil?" he said. "Why you want to tell them about this now? Just leave it alone. Why don't you leave it *alone?*"

She wouldn't even look at him. He grabbed his jacket, stormed out the door and slammed it behind him. Arnett's mother motioned the children to take a seat on the floor. He could feel the cold coming up through the bare wood. Arnett could see small slivers of light in the cracks between the planks, daylight shining up from beneath the house. He wished he was back outside with his friends, playing cowboys, showing off the new Hopalong Cassidy holster and cap guns he'd unwrapped that morning. But his mother wanted him here, told him and his sister to take off their coats, that she had something important to talk to them about. Arnett fixed his eyes on the tree, staring at the shiny tinsel as his mother began to speak.

"I want to tell you about something," she said, "and I want you to listen carefully. This is very important."

The fire spit and crackled behind her as she wiped her eyes with a handkerchief. His mother was still slim then, and strong. She could carry a washtub under one arm and a load of firewood under the other. She could carry Arnett if she had to, and his sister, too.

"I want you to know who you *are*," she said, narrowing her eyes. "You are *not* like everyone else. You are special. Your ancestors were special people, people of importance. Your granddaddy owned land, a lot of land, just like Mr. Cummer."

Arnett never doubted anything his mama told him, but this was hard to believe. The Cummers owned all of Lacoochee. That sawmill was theirs, along with untold thousands of acres of woodland around it. The houses where most of the men who worked at the mill lived, those belonged to the Cummers. The commissary where the mill hands and their families shopped, that belonged to the Cummers, too. The Cummers themselves lived in a mansion up at the other end of town, across the tracks, a huge three-story home like something out of the movies, set back behind moss-hung oaks, surrounded by hundreds of acres of private woods loaded with fish and game, patrolled by armed guards who arrested anyone caught trespassing. Before they took you to jail, these guards would give you a good beating just to make sure this wouldn't happen again.

Arnett had been up on that Cummer property. He'd been inside the Cummer house as well. His Aunt Becky did laundry and cleaning for the Cummers, and sometimes she would bring him along with her. His father did yard work there, too, and occasionally he would bring Arnett with him. But Arnett's mother never set foot in that house or on that land. She wanted no part of the Cummers.

That world always seemed so far away, even when Arnett was right there, inside that big house. He never met the Cummers, just watched them come and go like white shadows. He never dared to even dream about such a life, but now his mother was telling him his own people had once had something like that—their own land, their own businesses, their own big houses with living rooms and lamps and sofas. Not just two rooms and a kitchen, like the shotgun shacks they lived in now. They owned pianos, his mother said. And organs. They had horses and buggies, and on Sundays they rode to church like royalty.

Royalty. That's what Arnett's mother said her people had been. The Goinses and the Carriers, the two families her father and mother came from, they were the most important people in the town of Rosewood, she said. Her great-uncle, Martine Goins, he was the best businessman in those parts, the way she described him, a man respected by blacks and whites alike. He ran a turpentine operation so big it had housing for some of the men who worked there, quarters just like the Cummers', quarters right there in Rosewood.

That's where she was from, Arnett's mother said. Not Tampa or Gainesville, cities Arnett knew his mother had lived in back before he was born, places he had heard of. No, she was from Rosewood. And so, she was now telling him, were many of his aunts and uncles, and more than a few of his neighbors right there in Lacoochee. They were all from this place called Rosewood. But they could never go back, none of them, his mother said, because there was nothing left to go back to.

And then she began crying, her pride giving way to pain as she told Arnett and his sister, in scattered, sketchy detail, how the town had vanished, in shouts and gunshots and flames.

She was there, she said, at the white woman's house that winter morning in 1923, one village away from Rosewood, in a place called Sumner. Her parents were gone that month, working at a lumber camp near a little spot known as Otter Creek, and so Philomena and her younger brothers, A. T. and George, were staying with their Grandma Sarah, Sarah Carrier. "Mama," that's what Philomena called her. Every morning Sarah walked to Sumner to do house-work and laundry for white folks, and that New Year's morning she brought Philomena with her.

Not long after they arrived, as they were hanging clothes on the line outside this white woman's house, Sarah and Philomena saw a man slip through the back door. It was a white man, but it was not the woman's husband.

They had seen this man before. He was an engineer with the railroad, and he was known to be the woman's boyfriend. Her lover. Most of Rosewood knew it. Most blacks in Sumner knew it. Grandma Sarah knew it. She had seen the man come and go from this house more than once. She never said a word, never even looked up as he passed. She knew better than that.

Normally the man came and left in silence, but this day there was a commotion, some banging and yelling from inside the house. Then the man burst out the back door, hurried across the yard, stepped over the fence without opening the gate, and rushed up the railroad tracks, on foot, toward Rosewood.

Some time passed, a half an hour or so. Philomena and Grandma Sarah were just finishing up their work when the white woman burst out her door, screaming that she'd been attacked, that a black man had beaten her. It wasn't to protect her lover that she lied, said Arnett's mother. The man had just beaten her bloody. It was to protect herself from the beating or even worse she might get from her husband if he knew.

Men came, his mother said. Dogs too. A mob formed. Grandma Sarah tried to step in, to tell them this was wrong, to tell these people what had really happened. But they pushed her away, told her to shut up, her and her little pickaninny, shut up and get on home.

And so the whites would never know, would never *hear* of the notion that it had been one of their own who had done this. It had to be a black man. And so it was.

After a week, Arnett's mother said, it was over. The town was gone. No one ever came back, she said. Not then, not ever. And that, she explained, was why she cried every Christmas, because for her the holidays meant nothing but memories of that week, of Rosewood, of what she had lost and what they, Arnett and Yvonne, had lost, too. She was eleven years old when it happened, she told them. Just a girl, she said. But she would never feel like a child again.

It was dark by the time Arnett's mother was done. Time to take a bath and go to bed. Christmas Day was done.

Arnett hardly slept that night, his mind was swirling with so many questions, his six-year-old chest heaving with so many feelings. He heard his father stumble in late, drunk, but the next morning it was as if nothing had happened. His daddy was up and joking like always, his mother was in the kitchen, breakfast on the table, and Arnett's friends were outside, hollering for him to come and play.

Arnett never heard much more from his mother about Rosewood than what she told him and his sister that Christmas. It became their annual ritual, Philomena sitting the children down on Christmas Day and telling them the Rosewood story. It was always the same, nothing new added, and no questions allowed. None. Arnett's mother spoke, and the children listened.

Every other day of the year, the subject was taboo. Arnett got more than one whipping for mentioning it to a playmate or comparing notes with a cousin. Over the years he was able to squeeze a few tidbits out of some of his relatives, the older ones, like his Aunt Beauty and Aunt Sweetie, who were willing to answer a question or two with a promise not to tell his mother.

But Arnett was never able to learn as much as he wanted. His aunts were eager to talk about what the town had been like before it was destroyed, about their deep family lines, both the Goinses' and the Carriers', about their roots up in the Carolinas and the Indian stock they had come from, about what they had made of themselves by the turn of the century in this hamlet in the woods. But when it came to details of the attack itself, Arnett knew only bits and pieces, and the things he knew raised more questions than they answered. He didn't even know where Rosewood *was,* not until Bobo took that turn that Saturday afternoon.

"It's on the map, man," Bobo said, pointing at a tiny dot over near the coastline. Arnett had never searched a map, never dreamed the place might still exist. But sure enough, there it was, in tiny letters along State Route 24, halfway up the coast. He moved his finger down the map, inland, southeast to Lacoochee, and he measured the distance. About eighty miles.

And now Bobo was slowing down, because there was a sign up ahead on the side of the road, a green metal sign with simple white lettering:

ROSEWOOD

They came to a stop, looked around. Nothing but stands of short scrub pines to the right, second growth come up since the logging crews cleared out. But to the left was thicker forest, the trees larger, older. That's where Rosewood was, back in that forest.

Up ahead, down a dirt lane, under the trees, they could see a few scattered homes, some made of cinderblock, the rest of wood, all small, with roofs made of tin.

Bobo turned there, onto the dirt. Arnett could hear the sand and shells crunching beneath the tires. An old white woman was sitting on a porch swing. When she saw them, she got up and went inside, shut her screen door behind her.

The road forked, and they followed it to another house. Nothing there but some dogs and a dead end, the forest gathering together into a wall of darkness.

They turned back toward the highway, past a house unlike the others, a large, ghostly Victorian place, with stained glass windows and latticed porches, set back among some oaks and fruit trees. It, too, had dogs in the yard, and Arnett and Bobo and George were not about to mess with any dogs, not in a place like this. It was the turn of the '60s, civil rights clashes brewing in cities like Selma and Birmingham, with marchers and megaphones, Freedom Riders and federal troops, newspaper reporters and TV cameras. But back in places like this, there was none of that. Places like this were where black men's bodies still bobbed up from riverbeds and nobody blinked an eye.

Just before they got back on the highway, they passed a small store, no more than a hut, with a couple of gas pumps and four or five white men sitting on stools out front, playing checkers. Arnett watched the group look up, staring at this car of black men, probably the only black men between there and the Gulf of Mexico. He saw a shotgun leaning by the door. And he decided he had seen enough. Fifteen minutes later, he and Bobo and George were back on Route 19, hurtling north to Tallahassee.

Arnett never told his mother about that trip. It had been twenty years now since that day, and he still wouldn't dare to tell her about it. No matter that he was about to turn forty, a middle-aged man. If she knew he had ever been to Rosewood, she would beat him like a child. And if she knew he was considering going up there *again,* and with a white man, no less, well, Arnett could not even imagine what she might do.

But he *was* considering it. He left the reporter that afternoon with the promise he would meet him in the morning at the liquor store, and they would leave from there. He spent the rest of the evening on the telephone, calling his boss to get the day off, calling some friends to let them know where he was going, in case something happened and he didn't come back.

He did not call his mother. His mother would be damned if her boy was going to take a trip like this.

But Arnett would be damned if he didn't.

THREE

"If That Ain't Country"

They call it the Big Bend, the name given long ago to the string of rural counties that curve up the Gulf Coast from Tampa to Tallahassee. This has always been the shadowed side of the sunshine state, a section of Florida frozen in time, dirt poor and barren, a world away from the glitter of Orlando and the gleam of Miami. Even the cabbage palms and palmettos lining the shoulders of State Route 19, which traces the coastline from north to south, look tired.

Hand-scrawled signs nailed to roadside pines hawk fresh-picked corn and okra, pecans and "p-nuts." Plywood placards appear, mounted on twisted oaks, their warnings scribbled in bright red letters:

PREPARE TO MEET THY GOD

Towns pop up along the way, places like Perry, where the Flat Creek Gun Shop shares its front lawn with the Pisquah Missionary Baptist Church, where the Rebel Room Bar & Grill is right up the road from Grady's Feed and Hound Supply.

And Cross City, the hub of Dixie County, where flatbed trucks and railcars

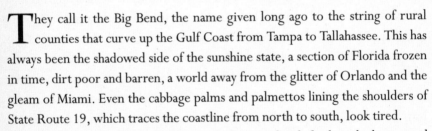

Lelland "Beauty" Carrier and her sister Ruby

loaded with fresh-cut timber rumble past the B&B Ammo store and the Lost in Time Lounge.

And Chiefland, where Elnora's Beds for Less furniture shop and the Bent & Dent discount food store flank VFW Rebel Post 5625.

And Otter Creek, nothing but a flashing orange light in the heart of Levy County, Hershel's Quick Stop grocery on the right and a BP service station on the left. There is no need to slow at Otter Creek, no drop in the speed limit, and most of the traffic shooting south—the RVs and campers with lawn chairs and bicycles strapped to their roofs, out-of-state plates screwed to their bumpers, vacationers bound for Sarasota, retirees headed to Clearwater—they keep going. The few vehicles that stop here are turning inland toward Gainesville, twenty-five miles to the east on Route 24, or out toward the coast, twenty miles west.

Route 24 is the road that runs through Rosewood, two lanes of lonely asphalt slicing straight as a razor into thick hardwood hammocks and marshy swampland, past scattered patches of scrub pines and palmettos and bare stretches of briars and weeds, not a soul in sight save for a smattering of tin-roofed shacks and tree-shaded trailers, rickety roadside stands selling smoked mullet, and rotting outdoor tables stacked with sacks of boiled peanuts.

Traffic is sparse. Small brown lizards skitter across the blacktop as packs of turkey vultures, their tar-like feathers gleaming in the midday sun, alight on the sandy shoulders, picking at fresh road kill, undisturbed by the occasional passing of a pickup truck or logging trailer rumbling east, back toward Otter Creek and beyond.

Now and then comes a car headed west. A couple bound for a cheap weekend bungalow. A family with fishing gear stowed in their trunk. Maybe a van full of college kids, University of Florida frat boys and their dates, cutting classes and taking a road trip to the coast.

Halfway there they pass through Rosewood, but few of them notice. There is little to notice. A couple of rusted gas pumps, a half dozen small cinderblock homes stuck back beneath the pines and palms, a tiny trailer park, and a lone, two-story, tree-shaded house set off down a dirt drive. All just a passing blur.

Ten miles beyond, the road runs out in the fishing village of Cedar Key, a tiny island community ringed by coves and bayous, a town that has tried a long time to tout itself as a tourist resort. Twice a year, during its annual art festival in mid-April and its seafood festival in October, when the narrow lanes lining the waterfront are jammed with thousands of camera-strapped visitors, it actually feels like a booming resort. The rest of the time, the place is quiet, sleepy, the way Key West was half a century ago.

That's how the locals like to think of Cedar Key, as the best of Old Florida. And it does have that air of serenity, its hourly rhythms as gentle as the gulf water lapping at its waterfront wharves. The island's main street is quaint, a collection of small shops and boutiques anchored by the old Island Hotel, a weathered wooden structure built back before the turn of the century. Pelicans perch on worn pilings down at the west end of town, where a string of pierside cafes feature the day's bounty, pulled fresh from the holds of Cedar Key's small fleet of fishing boats.

Some new condominiums have recently risen along that waterfront, a hopeful sign for the chamber of commerce but not for the residents who have been driven off the island by ballooning property values and rocketing tax rates. More than a few of Cedar Key's fishermen now commute to their boats from the shacks and trailers sprinkled back up along Route 24, including the handful of homes that make up what has become of Rosewood.

Visitors curious about the area's history can stop in the Cedar Key Historical Society Museum, a homey, coral-colored house a block off the waterfront, where a random collection of pamphlets and scrapbooks, old snapshots and newspaper clippings tell a sanitized version of how this place came to be, how Seminoles fleeing the white settlers to the north arrived on these islands in the first part of the nineteenth century, how the U.S. Army moved in during its war with the Indians in the 1840s and drove the natives out, and how the town took root with the construction of the first trans-Florida railroad, which ran from the Atlantic coast harbor of Fernandina Beach across the state to Cedar Key.

When that rail line opened in 1861, Cedar Key was poised to challenge Tampa as Florida's premier Gulf port. But the Civil War delayed those plans, as Union troops blockaded the island and tore up the tracks. The museum doesn't mention that more than a few local fishermen made good money during the war by trimming their schooners for speed and slipping out through the bayous at night, skirting the Union ships and carrying contraband to the Confederate forces. Nor does it make much of the fact that some of the local folk fought on land as well. To this day, there are people in Cedar Key who recall with pride how a band of their boys ambushed a raiding party of black Union soldiers on the island's Number Four bridge in February of 1865, recapturing most of the booty the Yankees had seized from the surrounding woods and farmland, including a hundred head of cattle, a dozen horses and about fifty slaves.

Two months after that skirmish, the war was over. By the end of the year the tracks were rebuilt, and the boom Cedar Key had been awaiting began. Wharfs and warehouses went up as steamers arrived from Mobile and New Orleans with goods headed east and south. Ships came up from Havana with cargo headed north. Hotels were built—three of them—along with a string of saloons, dance halls and gambling houses. The island's narrow gas lamp–lit streets were jammed with sailors and fishermen, as well as lumbermen who were now sweeping through the surrounding swamps and forests, cutting cedar and cypress for the sawmills that had sprung up along the tracks. The loggers worked all week, sleeping in remote inland swamp camps, then roared into Cedar Key on weekends, wearing six-shooters and bowie knives, looking for some fun and maybe a good fight. The watermen were glad to oblige, and Cedar Key soon built a reputation to rival the deadliest western frontier towns. Shootouts and "bushwhackings," as the local newspaper called them, were common items in daily news columns. Murders were so routine they hardly rated more than a brief mention.

It was during this time, soon after the Civil War, that a young freelance magazine writer named John Muir arrived in town—on foot. He was at the end of a trek he had begun seven weeks earlier, a thousand miles away, in Indiana. His aim was to chronicle the post-war conditions in the South, and his notebooks were filled. His most recent entries described the "watery and vine-tied land" along the Gulf Coast. He hadn't planned to stay in Cedar Key when he arrived in October of 1867, but he fell sick, so sick he wound up slumped beneath a tree in town, where he was ignored as just another drunk until a passerby finally stopped, shook the body to see if it was alive and discovered the man needed a doctor.

Muir had malaria, a common condition in those parts at that time. He spent that winter bedridden on the island, pondering the wilderness he had passed through, sketching his impressions of the land he had seen as well as the people he had met. He moved on in the spring and eventually settled in California, where he helped create Yosemite National Park and founded the Sierra Club. It was not until 1916, two years after his death, that John Muir's journal of that

1867 journey through the South was finally published, with its descriptions of the "traces of war not only apparent on the broken fields, mills and woods ruthlessly slaughtered, but also on the countenance of the people."

For the people of Cedar Key, however, the years just after the war were the best of times. But the boom was brief, lasting hardly a generation. By the mid-1880s, a rail line was opened to Tampa, sucking the shipping away from Cedar Key and turning the place into a relic. By the 1890s the hardwood in the hammocks between the island and Otter Creek was nearly gone, logged out by the voracious timber companies. A pencil factory, built on the island by a German businessman and fed for twenty years by cedar from those swamps, was now barely running, all but a handful of its employees laid off and most of its machinery inert and seized solid with rust. The final blow was a hurricane that hit the coast in 1896.

The people of Cedar Key were used to hurricanes, lived through a couple every year, boarded up their windows, lit their lanterns and sat out the storm. But this one brought with it a tidal wave, a wall of water twenty feet high, sweeping over the island like the hand of God. And when it had passed, it had taken half of Cedar Key with it. One out of every two buildings had vanished. The island's fleet of sponge boats was smashed to splinters. The population, too, was in pieces. The year before that storm, fourteen hundred people inhabited Cedar Key. The year after, fewer than seven hundred remained. The rest had been washed away by that wave, or had seen all they owned obliterated and had simply picked up and left.

Almost a century later, there are still roughly seven hundred people living in or around Cedar Key, many of them fishermen lounging down at the docks beside their tired boats, bitching about the size of their catch, about the price of gas and the government bureaucrats bound to run them out of business with their laws and regulations. Over at the L&M bar, a block away from the Island Hotel, neon beer logos glow in the windows as they do each day beginning at noon. The stools inside are sprinkled with locals, some watching the TV, others waiting their turn at the pool table. A Confederate flag is draped on the back room wall, the words *The South Will Rise Again* stitched on its border. A David Allan Coe tune is punched up on the jukebox:

> *. . . thirteen kids and a bunch of dogs,*
> *House full o' chickens and a yard full o' hogs,*

He spent the summertime cuttin' up logs,
For the winter.
Tryin' like the devil to find the Lord,
Workin' like a nigger for my room 'n board,
Coal-burnin' stove, no natural gas,
If that ain't country, I'll kiss your ass. . . .

This is, indeed, the Deep South, which did not surprise Gary Moore, the reporter from the St. Pete *Times,* who wandered into Cedar Key in early 1982 while working on a travel story. "It was a way to kill a weekend, to get out of town," recalls Moore. "I just went along the way looking for things. I didn't know anything about Rosewood."

But he knew about places like Cedar Key. There were plenty of them all over the state—tiny towns, insulated pockets of people who had been able over the course of the past century to resist change, to keep things pretty much as they had always been, small hamlets that were somehow able to stand still in the face of the force of time. There was mystery around these places, and menace, the gothic stuff of countless southern novels.

But Moore was no novelist. He was a journalist, and he became intrigued by the fact that there was not one black face to be seen in Cedar Key—this in a town whose population had been one-third black at the turn of the century. It was black labor that had laid the tracks through the swamp into Cedar Key, and many of those men had chosen to stay, settling with their families in the woods between Otter Creek and the coast, hunting, fishing, cutting lumber and tapping turpentine for their living. At the turn of the century, there had been a black school in Cedar Key. Black churches, too. And now there was nothing.

When Moore began asking around, no one said much, not at first. Most simply shrugged, a few pointed toward the section of town where the blacks used to live, a place the locals still called "Nigger Hill," back toward the middle of the island. But no one would say where the "niggers" had gone, not until one woman—Moore visited her in an old church, which was now the woman's home—finally mentioned "the massacre."

And that was how it began, one story giving way to another, a light piece on weekend getaways turning into something deeper and darker. Moore could hardly believe what he heard as some of the townspeople began to talk. Images of torture and immolation, of unholy terror and unspeakable fear, of murder and mutilation, body parts severed and stored in Mason jars, still pulled out with a queer sense of pride sixty years later by those into whose hands they had passed.

So much sounded like myth, so much was mere memory, massaged over decades into odd and outsized shapes, pieces that didn't fit, facts that were flawed, truth faded to fable by the passage of years. Still, a story emerged, began to take shape, of something hideous that had actually occurred in those woods up the road from Cedar Key.

And that is what eventually led Gary Moore to Lundy's Liquor Store on that Friday afternoon in the spring of 1982, to ask Arnett Doctor to go with him, to go up to Rosewood.

FOUR

Ground Zero

A rnett was worried sick as he climbed in the passenger's side of Gary Moore's car that Saturday morning. It was a sunny day, cool, with puffs of clouds rolling in from the coast. Arnett wasn't sure if this thing might not be a con, that somehow someone might still be out to get him and his family sixty years after the fact. But he figured he'd done all he could to cover himself. His friends knew where he was, and if worse came to worst, he had that .357 tucked in the waistband of his slacks.

It wasn't himself he was worried about, it was his mother. Her health had been so bad lately, and it was getting worse every day. Blood pressure, diabetes, glaucoma, gout. Arnett could count on one hand the number of sick days his mother had taken during all the years she'd worked for her living, but now it seemed she was sick all the time. And it was all because of the eating.

In the course of just a couple of years, Arnett had watched his mother balloon before his eyes, from one hundred and sixty to two hundred pounds. Then two-thirty, two-forty, twice what she had weighed when she married Arnett's

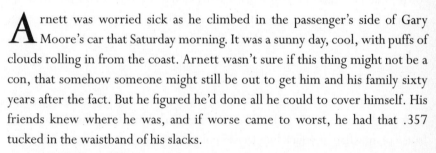

The old Wright house

father. And there was no sign of it stopping. Every day she got bigger, and her health was caving in under the load.

It was hard to watch, hard for Arnett to think that this was what it had come to, that his mother had worked her entire life, from the time she turned ten until she was almost seventy, worked countless hours at thankless jobs, and this was what she had to show for it, a body literally feeding itself on bitterness.

She had washed other people's clothes and cleaned other people's homes for decades before she finally found her first clock-punching job, on an assembly line in an eyeglass factory there in St. Pete. She spent ten years at that, then moved onto another line, this one inside the windowless walls of a missile plant. Arnett never knew exactly what his mother did there—"Defense work," she called it—but he knew she never sat down. Eight hours a day she stood in one spot, sticking the same parts on the same pieces, coming home at night dog tired and aching, her legs still sore when she rose the next morning to go back out to the bus stop and do it again.

It wasn't until she was in her sixties that she found the first and only sit-down job of her life, copying and filing forms for a job-training company uptown, which is where she was when she decided it was time to retire. No to-do about it, no company luncheon. Her last day of work was the same as her first, and when it was done, she punched out, rode home, and opened the refrigerator.

Watch TV and eat, that's all she had done since she quit working—that and attend the monthly meetings of the Quest Federated Social Club, a group of elderly black women who gathered at one another's homes to plan their annual ball, a grand affair at which hundreds of black women from Tampa and St. Pete would convene to see which of them would be crowned Miss Black Federated Woman of the Year. One year—her children say it might have been the happiest night of her life—that crown was placed on Philomena Doctor's head.

Those Federation meetings and church. Nothing else could get Phil Doctor out of the house. Nothing else mattered. Food and her God was all she needed. And family. She never missed a family gathering, no matter when or where it was. A christening, a wedding, funerals, holidays. Relatives were like religion to her, and that's how she raised her children. There wasn't an aunt or uncle alive or dead that Arnett and Yvonne didn't know at least by name. Most of them they knew better than that. Arnett had slept in their beds, broken bread at their tables, bowed his head and held their hands as they lifted their voices to the Lord.

Arnett never knew of a family that prayed like his. Every day of the week they prayed, and not just at mealtime either. When he was grown and on his own, he'd stop by his mother's house to see how she was, middle of the afternoon, and there would be an aunt or two sitting on the sofa, TV on in the corner, and one of them would say, "All right, now, let's have a prayer," and they'd switch off the set and all kneel down together, right there on the living room carpet. Then one of them would get up and go fix him something to eat.

These days that's all Philomena did was eat, and it was killing her. Still, she remained the most powerful person Arnett had ever known, a matriarch who ruled with an iron hand. Every time the family gathered, cousins by the dozen, aunts and uncles by the score, it was Aunt Phil—"Sissy" to her siblings—who held court. Without question. Without dissent. Any decision to be made, whether it was which Bible verse would be read aloud, or who would read it, or when the potato salad should be served, Sissy made it and the others obeyed.

Part of it was her age—once Aunt Beauty passed away, Arnett's mother was left as the oldest female in the family line. But beyond her seniority, it was the sheer force of her will that made Phil Doctor so hard to resist. And the fuel for that force was resentment and rage.

Some of it came from her marriage, Arnett knew that. She had left Arnett's father when Arnett was fourteen. Twenty-four years she and her husband had been together, and she never married again. But long before the breakup— right from the beginning, in fact—there had been a seam of rancor in their marriage. Because Philomena Goins had always wanted to be a singer, and Walter Doctor had made her quit.

She was in her early twenties when they met, during the Depression, and already she was making a name for herself in clubs in Tampa and St. Pete, black night spots where acts like Count Basie, Duke Ellington, Louis Armstrong and Ella Fitzgerald would stop in on their swings through the South. Arnett's mother said she had once shared a microphone with Ella Fitzgerald, a memory Arnett would share as fact all his life, with anyone who would listen.

His mother lived for the sounds of jazz and swing, could hush a whole room with the sweet sadness of the blues, make it feel like Billie Holiday herself was caressing that microphone. Everyone who heard Phil Goins sing could feel it.

They all said she was bound for great things. But when she became a wife, her new husband would have none of it. There were children to raise, a house to keep. And so, beyond serenading herself as she cooked in the kitchen or sharing her voice with the choir on Sundays, the singing stopped.

Arnett knew some of his mother's pain had to come from the career she gave up for a marriage that didn't last. Some of it came, too, from the pride she then had to swallow to keep food on the table. But he knew just as well that beneath it all was what had happened at Rosewood. Everything about his mother, from her seething sense of injustice, to her manic fear for the safety of her children, was rooted in Rosewood.

Arnett hardly heard a word Gary Moore spoke as they drove north that Saturday morning, past the well-heeled retirement resorts of Palm Harbor and Port Richey, Spring Hill and Crystal River, across the Withlacoochee River into the rural woodlands of Levy County. The trip took two hours, and all the way all Arnett could think of was his mother and what it might do to her if she knew where he was.

And then they were there, taking the same turn Bobo had taken twenty years before, off Route 19 onto 24, into the same woods, past the same swamp and the same shacks, finally slowing at the same green sign, across the road from the same cinderblock homes that had been there in 1962. The store was still there, and the pumps. But the store's door was locked and no one was in sight.

The woman was still there, too, sitting out on that same porch swing. Only this time she didn't run inside when they approached. She stayed put as the car crunched to a stop and Moore stepped out. It was only when Arnett emerged that the woman moved, finishing the conversation from behind her screen door as Arnett kept his distance.

This day there were no dogs at the old Victorian house, so they tried there, knocking on the door and getting no answer. Arnett noticed how full the fruit trees had grown, heavy with pears and plums. Pecans, too. There were grapes dangling from an arbor, and beehives off across the side yard, a bank of boxes neatly lined along a pine rail fence. Those hadn't been there twenty years earlier.

They climbed back in the car and turned down a dirt drive Arnett had not seen before. The road, pitted and pocked by recent rains, took them deep into the woods behind the big house, under canopies of old oaks, and finally into a clearing, an open yard where the vines and thickets had been hacked back enough to allow some trailers to be parked.

Out of one of them stepped a small, skinny white man wearing no shirt, no shoes, just a pair of pants and a ball cap, his graying hair hanging in long wet strands, a blue-and-white can of beer in his hand.

The man recognized Moore, offered him a beer. He offered one to Arnett, too, which was surprising. If Arnett had ever seen a redneck in his life, he was looking at one now. But the man seemed pleasant enough, polite even. Moore said he was back again to look around if that was all right, and he'd brought an assistant with him. To sidestep suspicion, that's how Moore introduced Arnett, as his assistant.

Arnett noticed a raised mound of earth grown over with weeds, cutting through the woods, stretching out of sight in a hard, straight line. "That's what's left of the railroad," said Moore. "The tracks were pulled up fifty years ago."

Moore pointed toward a structure off in the distance, beyond a barbed wire fence, back beneath the trees. It was a shack, wet and rotten, sagging with the weight of time, draped in moss from the overhanging oaks. "That over there is where the depot was."

And now Arnett understood where he was standing.

This was ground zero, the place where his mother's Rosewood had stood. That rotting depot had been the center of town, the spot where the trains stopped on their way to Cedar Key. The dirt drive they had just driven down, that used to be the main road through town. The deserted railbed was the path the dogs and the mob had followed the morning they charged up from Sumner.

Arnett approached the shack, stepping over shrubs and briers. He poked at the rubble with his cane, hit something made of metal, bent and picked it up. It was a rust-flaked rod of iron, pointed at one end, pounded flat at the other. A railroad spike. And there was another. And another. The rails were long gone, but the spikes were still there, scattered like seeds.

Moore watched Arnett, studied his face, let the silence sink in. Then he pointed off to the left, deeper into the woods, toward a thicket of palms and palmettos.

"Over there," he said, "that's the graveyard."

Both white men stayed put as Arnett walked that way, pushing through chest-high brush, bending beneath low-hanging limbs, picking his way through thorns and brambles that tore at his trousers. He could hardly see more than a few yards ahead. Sunlight shone down in thin shafts around him. He was sweating. He could hear the buzz of insects, feel them lighting on the wetness of his neck.

Then he stepped on something solid. He bent down, brushed back some leaves and there it was—a headstone, small and smooth, the size of a writing tablet, the shape of an arch. Its inscription was worn away, nothing Arnett could make out. Just a simple piece of carved granite, lying flat in the soft, loamy soil, fallen over or knocked down God knew how long ago.

There were a half dozen more just like it scattered through the brush, some grown over with a thin carpet of soft green moss, the inscriptions unreadable on every one. And then, behind the fronds of a palmetto, Arnett saw one stone still standing, a small obelisk, maybe two feet high. This one he could read:

MARTIN GOINS

BORN JUNE 15, 1842

DIED DEC. 16, 1905

Martine Goins, Arnett thought to himself. Not Martin. Martine. This was his mother's great-uncle's grave, the man she had mentioned so many Christmas mornings. Uncle Martine. The stone had a tiny flower etched on its face, a rose.

Arnett could feel the soft ground sinking beneath his feet. He stepped back, realized he was standing on the bodies of his family, and for a moment he felt dizzy, faint. Then he steadied himself, stepped onto harder ground and circled the stones, seeing if there were any he had missed. There were not. This was it, a plot about ten feet on each side, grown over by forest, smothered by time.

When Arnett got back to the trailer, he asked the man in the ball cap about the cemetery.

"I didn't even know it was there," the man said, " 'til my girls found it one day, playin' back in the woods."

It was getting to be mid-afternoon, time to leave. As they walked to the car, Moore mentioned to the man that Arnett had relatives who used to live around here.

"Is that right?" asked the man. Arnett said nothing.

"So who were your relatives?" the man asked.

"Some of them are buried back there," said Arnett, nodding toward the woods. "The Goinses—they were my family. And the Carriers, Sarah Carrier and Sylvester—she was my great-grandmother and he was my great-uncle."

The man stopped walking. He knew those names. He narrowed his eyes, and pointed his beer can at Arnett.

"So I guess you probably want your land back, right?"

Arnett had no idea why the man would ask that. "I'm just trying to gather some information," he said.

"Unh huh," said the man, squinting and taking a sip from his can. "Information."

By the time they pulled back onto Route 19, the sun was setting. A pickup passed with two white men in the cab and a rifle in the rack. The men stared at Arnett as they went by. Then they slowed, allowed Arnett and Moore to come alongside, and the one in the passenger's seat let loose a rebel yell, a shrieking war whoop.

It was a sound Arnett knew well. He had grown up with that sound in Lacoochee. He heard it from packs of white kids whenever he walked home from the candy store or the movies and he had to go through their part of town to get back to his. That sound was a warning. It was wicked. And it was not a game.

Arnett could still hear it as the reporter let him out in the parking lot of Lundy's. It was evening, Saturday night in the city, and the night was young. The traffic on Tangerine was heavy, the pace picking up by the minute. But for Arnett, the evening was over. He headed home, one hand gripping his cane, the other squeezing a piece of iron tucked in his pocket—a rusty railroad spike.

The Death of a Dog

I t was a family secret that was stirred that spring of 1982, a secret that had been kept for sixty years by a family that included everyone touched by Rosewood, black and white, children and grandchildren, the living and the dead. Over the better course of the century, through twelve presidents, from Warren Harding to Ronald Reagan, the whites of Levy County, as well as the blacks who had fled, had kept their secret among themselves, some out of fear, some out of shame, and all, as the years went by, with the rooted belief that the thing was behind them, done with, a bad memory at worst and at best simply something to be forgotten.

Even those charged with remembering such events—the people who write history—even they had forgotten about Rosewood. There was no mention of it in any book on Florida's past, no record in any account of the region's racial relations. It was as if the historians, like the families themselves, had chosen to leave Rosewood behind, keeping the secret by joining the silence.

But it was far from a secret at the time it took place. Newspapers throughout Florida followed the events of that New Year's week in 1923. After the

(January, 1923, newspaper headlines)

shootout at the Carrier household, the story leaped to the top of every front page in the state.

5 DIE SUMNER RACE RIOT

That was the *Gainesville Daily Sun*'s lead story on Friday, January fifth.

SIX DIE IN RACE CLASHES,
ACCORDING TO TELEPHONE REPORT FROM ROSEWOOD

That was the *Tampa Tribune*'s headline the same morning.

MANY DIE IN FLORIDA RACE WAR,
HUNDREDS OF WHITES BATTLE NEGROES AMBUSHED IN CABIN,
FOUR WHITES, 20 BLACKS DEAD

That was the *Miami Daily Metropolis*'s banner. The *Jacksonvile Journal* head-lined its story in starker, simpler terms:

BURN TOWN OF ROSEWOOD

Eyes beyond Florida were fixed on Rosewood as well, with newspapers across the nation trumpeting the "race war" in this tiny Gulf Coast village. That's what the *Chicago Tribune* called it, taking its information from the wire reports out of Cedar Key. The *Washington Post* did the same, referring to a "negro desperado" whose gunfire from inside his home had sparked the battle. The *St. Louis Post-Dispatch* described "two negresses" dead after an attack on a "barricaded hut" inhabited by a "band of heavily armed Negroes." The *New York Times* ran its version of the story on page one, under a bold black headline:

KILL SIX IN FLORIDA
BURN NEGRO HOUSES

The nation's black newspapers weighed in with their own versions of the at-tack, including the *Afro-American* in Baltimore, which published an elaborate ac-count evoking images of the siege at the Alamo:

FLORIDA MOB USES TORCH,
NUMEROUS INSTANCES OF HEROISM
AS MEN DEFEND HOMES AGAINST SAVAGES

Rosewood, Fla., Jan. 9. (Crusader Service)—Eighteen white and colored men and women are known to be dead and many others wounded in a savage mob bat-tle that has raged here since the evening of January 5th, following an attempt by a mob of lawless whites to take the law into their hands in the case of a colored man accused of attacking a white woman.

Hearing that the accused man, Jesse Hunter, was hiding in the village of Rosewood, whites from the neighboring towns invaded the Negro section and attempted a house-to-house search. They were met with a hail of bullets at the first house they came to. The inmates, recognizing the belligerency and lawless composition of the howling mob did not wait to ask for an explanation of their visit. They opened fire and prepared to sell their lives dearly. They might not have committed any crime but they knew a lawless mob when they saw one.

Two whites were killed outright at the first shower of lead. Four others were wounded, one probably fatally, and the whites retreated to await reinforcements from the surrounding lawless elements.

At this point Negroes from other houses came to the aid of the besieged brothers and a rude barricade was thrown up and loop holes made for rifle fire. Negro ex-soldiers put their knowledge and experience gained in France to use in the service of the Race and an effective defense was soon organized.

The whites, reinforced, came back, 600 strong, and a battle royal developed. In spite of their reinforcements the whites were persistently beaten back by the little determined band within the rude improvised fort. Robbed of their prey and not anxious to face the lions at bay the most cowardly part of the white mob set itself to the safer task of destroying the undefended Negro residences and the village church and lodge buildings.

In the meantime, within their improvised fort the little colored group put up a defense that will bear comparison with many of the bravest feats of the colored soldiers on Flanders fields, and forged another link in the long chain of evidence going to show that the Negro has at last decided he can fight his own battles just as bravely and as effectively as he has ever fought the battles of others.

Finally, their ammunition almost exhausted, the little band decided to emulate the action of the "Guards at Cahill" and with clubbed muskets, made a rush through the besieging forces and, breaking through, sought the refuge of the surrounding woods.

The vacated house revealed the bodies of two victims of the mob, one being that of an old woman.

Another colored woman, apparently 40 years of age, was shot and killed on the same day not far from here. At Bronson, a few miles from here, a colored man was found on the roadway, his body riddled with bullets. On a lonely road an-

other colored victim, a farmer, was found strung to the limb of a tree. Two Negro
women were attacked and raped between Rosewood and Sumner. The sexual lust
of the brutal white mobbists satisfied, the women were strangled. An older colored
woman was severely maltreated on the same stretch of road and forced to submit
herself to the most shameful sexual degradation.

Race feeling is running high as a result of these actual attacks on colored
women and the alleged attack on a white woman. Negro farmers have armed
themselves with rifles and shotguns and are grimly determined to protect their
women and sell their lives dearly if it comes to that. The situation may culminate
in violent race warfare worst [sic] than the terrible night at Rosewood.

Leaders are urging colored people throughout the State to sell their property
and move northward. Every colored home here was set on fire by the mob and
burned one by one. The church and hall also were destroyed.

It was no coincidence that these cities—Chicago, Washington, St. Louis, Baltimore and New York—perked up at news of a "race riot" down south. Each of them had been rocked in recent years by bloody racial clashes on their own downtown streets, attacks that left dozens dead, almost all of them black. They called them riots, but in truth they were large-scale lynchings, sanctioned wildings in which mobs of whites ran rampant through urban black neighborhoods while the authorities looked the other way or in some cases helped out.

It was the end of an era, the turn of the '20s, the climax of a forty-year period that had begun in the post–Civil War South with the backlash against newly freed blacks, had spread north with the onset of World War I and had burst into open combat among white and black workers competing for jobs in overcrowded cities. Those four decades, from Reconstruction through the wake of the first World War, would come to be called the "lynching era" in America. Blacks would continue to be burned, shot and hanged for a half-century more, through the end of the '60s, but the number of deaths during that time would come nowhere near the three thousand men, women and children murdered by mobs between the 1880s and the 1920s.

"The good work of Judge Lynch," as some southern newspapers of the time heartily described it, had been a way of life in America since its creation. The term came from a Virginia magistrate named Charles Lynch, who made a habit in the late 1700s of hanging Tory conspirators without the trouble of a trial. During the next century, as the nation moved west, lynching became the baseline of frontier justice, with the victims mostly Mexicans, Asians and immigrants from southern Europe. Not until their slaves were freed did southern whites have more than an occasional need for the noose, and not until federal troops were withdrawn in 1877, leaving the South to govern itself, were they fully free to use it, which they did with a vengeance.

Beginning in 1883, when the Civil Rights Act of a decade before was repealed, southern blacks who had enjoyed a brief postwar taste of political power and financial success were slammed back into virtual slavery by frustrated, embittered whites. From then until the turn of the century, the nation averaged more than one hundred and fifty lynchings a year, the vast majority of them in the South, some in full view of crowds that numbered in the thousands. The displays were meant to both horrify and delight, to put the fear of God in the hearts of blacks while filling the whites with a sense of power and pride, something they were losing each day as the nation's economy shifted from fields to factories and the curtain of hard times began falling all across Dixie.

Among southern whites, that curtain fell hardest on the working class, the rustic farmers who had become known by a variety of terms over the course of the past century: *rednecks, hayseeds, hicks, piney-wood folks, clay-eaters,* and, most commonly, *crackers.* The poorest of them, with hardly enough acreage to feed their families, were called crackers because of the corn they pounded to make their meals. Those who could afford a little livestock and a couple of slaves preferred to believe the term came from the sound of the whips they used to herd their cattle. For the slaves themselves, who spat the term with disgust, it stemmed from the sound of those whips on their own backs.

Along with their upper-class neighbors, many of these poor and middle-class whites depended on cheap black labor for success. Not only did they lose that labor after the war, but they were forced to compete against it as blacks began growing their own crops on their own land, selling their own harvests at market in quantities and at prices that often outdid the whites. And so, besides protecting white womanhood, which most mobs claimed was their calling—the cry of "rape" guaranteed an enthusiastic posse—or simply asserting the racial superiority they believed had been given them by God and taken away by government, working whites had purely financial reasons as well to reach for the lynching rope.

They called it "whitecapping," the use of terrorism and torture to drive blacks out of their businesses or off their land, and it was openly condoned by officials like North Carolina governor Daniel Russell, who proclaimed in 1900 that for a black man "to get above his ordained station in life is to invite assassination." If they didn't die, whitecapped blacks at the very least lost all they owned to mobs who drove them away, then stepped in and seized the abandoned property at discount rates.

It happened in Tennessee, where a lynch mob chased twenty black families off several hundred acres of land assessed at twenty dollars an acre, then bought the property at auction for less than a fifth that price. It happened in Texas, where a father and his three sons refused to leave their land and were finally hanged, all from the same tree, for the crime of harvesting the first cotton in the county that year—with no one left alive to pay the taxes, their property then went up for sale. It happened in Mississippi, where a white man who owed a black farmer $1,200 led a mob against the black man, running him and his family off their farm forever and erasing the debt in the process.

There were hundreds of cases like these, along with a litany of whippings, knifings, shootings, skinnings, hangings, beatings, burnings, tarrings, dismemberings and desexings too numerous and too often unrecorded to count. The charges, phrases found in official records of the time, ranged from "insulting women" to "annoying white women" to "saying hello to white girl" to "bumping into white girl while running to catch a train." In Paducah, Kentucky, a black rape suspect was lynched by a mob which then murdered a black onlooker for "expressing sympathy" for the first. In Waco, Texas, a mob pulled a retarded black youth charged with killing a white woman from a courtroom, burned him alive, then sold his teeth as souvenirs. In Brooks County, Georgia, a mob enraged by the murder of a white planter stormed the countryside for a week, killing ten blacks, including a pregnant woman who was hanged by her ankles, doused with gasoline and set afire—but not before her unborn baby was cut from her stomach and trampled underfoot. The coroner in that case labeled the victims' deaths, both baby and mother, as coming "at the hands of parties unknown," a phrase repeated in hundreds of official reports written and read by men who not only knew the names of the mob that had done the deed, but were often among them.

"The life of a Negro isn't worth as much as that of a dog," wrote a black minister, venting the despair of the times. "He may be shot down, murdered, strung up to a tree, burnt to death by any white ruffian, or band of law-breakers and murderers with impunity. . . . If he goes to law, there is no redress."

For a time, northerners were able to comfort themselves with the belief that lynching was a southern problem. But it would soon move their way, as Mark Twain predicted in an essay he wrote in 1901 titled "The United States of Lyncherdom." Prompted by the murder of a white girl in his home state of Missouri, a death that led to the lynching of three black men, the burnings of five black homes and the routing of thirty black families who were driven into the woods never to return, Twain warned that this was nothing less than a sickness, "a mania, a fashion; a fashion that will spread wide and wider, year by year, covering state after state as with an advancing disease."

Twain's essay was not published until 1923, the year Rosewood was torched, and by then his forecast had come true. Five years after Twain died in 1910, a combination of the intolerable violence faced by blacks in the South and a devastating boll weevil infestation that wiped out what work was left in the fields caused a northward exodus that came to be called The Great Migration of 1915. Hundreds of thousands of blacks moved north that year, many finding jobs in factories that were gearing up for war in Europe. Agents from those factories swept through the South, tossing leaflets to blacks in the fields, luring them north with visions of wealth and true freedom. Many who knew those promises were too good to be true still made the move. "To die from the bite of frost," wrote one reader of the black *Chicago Defender* newspaper, "is far more glorious than at the hands of a mob."

But the mood of the mob was moving northward as well. That same year, 1915, saw the premiere of a motion picture that would run for a record forty-seven weeks at the Liberty Theater in New York and would continue playing to sellout audiences across the country for the next decade. It was called *The Birth of a Nation,* based on a book titled *The Clansman,* which had been written ten years before. Its portrayal of noble Ku Klux Klan horsemen saving the South from the sinister Negro was "like writing history with lightning," gushed Woodrow Wilson, a southerner himself—a Virginian—who, now that he was president, showed little interest in the subject of lynching.

By the end of that same year, the Klan, which had disbanded during Reconstruction, was resurrected with robes and torches in an eerie ceremony atop Stone Mountain, Georgia, outside Atlanta. Much of the reason for the group's resurgence was a response to the emergence of a stronger, less subservient, more militant black man in America, what many were calling "the New Negro." For decades there had been scattered voices urging black men to fight back if attacked, voices like T. Thomas Fortune's, an early black activist who declared in the mid-1880s, "To be murdered by mobs . . . is not to be endured without protest, and if violence must be met with violence, let it be met. . . . If the white scamps lynch and shoot you, you have the right to do the same."

It was easy for Fortune to talk; he was settled safely in the North. Most southern blacks of the time still leaned toward the accommodationist words of Booker T. Washington, who urged patience and cooperation with whites. But by the turn of the century, patience had run out. Washington was now called "cowardly" for refusing to openly condemn lynching, and a new wave of black leaders was pushing him aside, men like W. E. B. Du Bois, whose defiant attitude was reflected in a 1915 editorial published in New York's black paper, the *Amsterdam News:* "Lynching would cease in short order if the Colored people of this country resented the lawless murdering of friends, relatives and compatriots as they should—with rifles and sword."

The image of black men armed with rifles was unthinkable for most whites, especially in the South, but it became a reality when more than three hundred thousand black men enlisted in America's armed forces as the U.S. finally entered the war in Europe in 1917. By the time those soldiers came home a year later, most of America's cities, north and south, had become cauldrons of suspicion and resentment against blacks. There had been a dozen large-scale outbreaks of violence, capped by a riot in East St. Louis, where rage over black workers brought in to replace striking whites touched off a day-long attack in which thirty-nine blacks were killed and more than ten thousand men, women and children—"truckloads of quivering, bandaged blacks," as one local newspaper account described them; "an exodus of weary, weeping people," as another put it—were chased across the river into St. Louis, never to return.

Nine whites died as well during that attack, and so it was called a riot, a term with clear meaning for black people of the time. If they chose not to resist a mob, their deaths were called lynchings; if they fought back, it was called a riot. Either way they were likely to die, and so now, as never before, blacks were beginning to fight back.

They fought back in Houston, where late in the summer of 1917, a black soldier was shot and killed by a sheriff's deputy. Several days later two black military policemen were beaten by white Houston policemen, prompting more than a hundred soldiers from the highly decorated 24th Infantry, a black unit that had gained fame during the Spanish-American War and was now training in Houston for action in Europe, to grab their weapons and march on the city. It was the white southerner's worst nightmare come true, armed black men on the attack, and before it was done, seventeen whites lay dead, along with two blacks. Sixty-four of those black soldiers were subsequently court-martialed. Thirteen were immediately hanged, and forty-one were imprisoned for life.

That set the stage for the summer of 1919. Cities were swollen with wartime workers who were now left with no war and no work. Bolshevik conspirators were rumored around every corner, organizing labor unions, inciting strikes, fomenting a revolution like the one taking place in Russia. Dispossessed and disgruntled blacks were said to be a prime target of the radicals, and so they became targets as well of fearful, frustrated whites in a climate of racial tension more charged than any the nation had yet seen. With the heat of summer, the tension exploded.

By the end of that "Red Summer" of 1919, twenty-six race riots had left dozens dead on the streets of cities from Chicago to Washington, Knoxville to Omaha. The last of these occurred in remote Phillips County, Arkansas, where a group of black farmers meeting to set the price of their cotton was fired on by railroad officials representing the region's white planters. The blacks fired back, and the result was a slaughter. More than two hundred black people, "many of whom had no idea what the trouble was about," according to an NAACP field report, were, in the words of that same report, "hunted down in the fields and swamps to which they had fled and shot down like animals."

That same summer, a nationwide anti-lynching movement began to stir. The NAACP, which had been created in 1909 in direct response to the problem of lynching, issued a flood of studies and reports detailing the number and nature of the atrocities. By the fall of 1921, a federal antilynching bill made it through the U.S. House of Representatives and onto the floor of the Senate before a filibuster led by Southern Democrats finally killed it. No such law would ever come that close again, but lynch mobs could no longer simply be ignored.

By 1922, the number of lynchings nationwide had dipped to a relatively low total of fifty-seven, almost all of them in the Deep South, where the Klan had reached an all-time peak in membership of three million—some estimates put that figure even higher. Most of these new Klansmen were the same poor and middle-class whites who had been desperate for a sense of power and place ever since losing their hold over blacks a half century earlier. Now, with the "New Negro" rising and society beginning to respond, the rural southern white felt even more cornered, more defensive and desperate than ever, more help-less in the face of blacks who no longer knew their place. The Klan gave these men back some of their pride, and lynching gave them their power.

And so, though the tide was turning, though the number of lynchings that were prevented in 1922 actually outnumbered those that succeeded, blacks in the Deep South, especially in the rural South, still knew there would likely be no one to turn to if a mob attacked. And no one could know when or why such an attack might come.

The people in Rosewood had no way to know, no reason to imagine that when they went to bed that New Year's Eve of 1922, they would wake up to face a crowd of armed, angry white men. Florida had had its share of lynchings during the previous year—a hanging down in Key West, another in Mayo, one out in Kissimmee. Word of those killings might have reached Rosewood. Maybe, maybe not. Surely they knew of the lynching just up the road in Perry. It hadn't been a month since that happened, just before Christmas, three black men killed, one burned at the stake, all after a white schoolteacher was found dead on a lonely stretch of dirt road.

There had to have been talk of those Perry deaths down around Rosewood. The folks in Rosewood knew the people up in Perry. The two towns' baseball teams would often play each other, hooking up for Sunday doubleheaders at one team's field or the other's. They had to know what had happened in Perry, but the men and women of Rosewood had no reason to think it would happen to them.

Not until it did.

And no one else would ever know what it was like, no one but them. Only they could say how it looked from inside their homes, the mob surging up and down their small streets as they hid behind locked doors. Only they could say how it looked from the woods, where they crouched as the sky above them turned orange from the flames of their burning town. Only they could describe what it was like to huddle in boxcars, bringing with them only what they wore, leaving behind all else that they owned, leaving it forever.

Only they could tell that story, but they had no voice. And those who had voices did not speak for them. The day after the attack on the Carrier house, as hundreds of vigilantes poured into Rosewood from across the state and be-yond, Florida's governor, a banker named Cary Hardee, wired the Levy County sheriff from Tallahassee, asking if help might be needed, perhaps the national guard. The sheriff telegrammed back that the situation was "under control," and so, as the town continued to burn and the death toll climbed, the governor took the afternoon off and went hunting.

By the end of that week, in newspapers outside the state, the surge of stories about Rosewood began to subside. It was left to Florida's press to sum up the affair, and although the *Tampa Times* called the attack "a foul and lasting blot on the people of Levy County," such criticism was the exception. The state's general feeling was reflected by an editorial published in the *Gainesville Sun* on Sunday, January 7, the last day of the attack on Rosewood:

> Let it be understood, at the very beginning of what we shall here write, that the racial trouble at Sumner or, more properly, Rosewood, was no "Southern Lynching Outrage." It was caused by the shooting down and killing of two officers of the law and the wounding of another. These law officers were shot down by negroes, barricaded in a house where a brutish beast was supposed to be sheltered and this brute had criminally assaulted a white woman. . . . Preach and admonish and warn as you may, however, the crime of rape will never be tolerated for one single moment. Congressmen may rave and froth and pass laws as they please but the time will never come when a southern white man will not avenge a crime against innocent womanhood. . . . Let it be understood now and forever that he, whether white or black, who brutally assaults an innocent and helpless woman, shall die the death of a dog.

A month later, a grand jury composed of local farmers and merchants, all white, was convened in the county seat of Bronson. Twenty-five witnesses were called, including eight blacks. After three days of investigation, the jury declared the evidence "insufficient" for indictments. None were made, and the case was closed. The alleged rapist, Jesse Hunter, was never found.

And so it was finished. The town was gone, and its memory soon vanished as well. Like the remains of a rock thrown into a pond, the record of Rosewood faded from a single splash, to scattered ripples, to stillness.

It was the last act of an era, the closing chapter, the final "race riot" of its time. It would also be the one that was forgotten, the only one not detailed and documented on library shelves. And perhaps there was a reason for that, because unlike the others, the story of Rosewood did not end in its ashes. Six decades after it happened, in that spring of 1982, those ashes began to stir, and it soon became clear that this was one story that was far from finished.

PART TWO

THE $\mathcal{S}$URVIVORS

SIX

Sweet Potatoes

L ate on a weekday morning, the section of Jacksonville called Lerner's Circle is deserted, like a toy village without people, block after block of squat bungalows painted the bright colors of fruit—lime, grape, raspberry, lemon—their stucco walls blistering in the North Florida sun. The yards are small, some carefully mowed, edged and embellished with ceramic lawn ornaments, others untended, sprinkled with junked automobiles and rusted appliances.

At the end of one lane, beneath the shade of a bent cabbage palm and an old oak, sits a small cinderblock house, painted pink, the color of bubble gum. Beside it runs a culvert, wastewater trickling from an open pipe into a ditch strewn with bottles and beer cans. Insects and sunlight dance off the surface of the green, oily pond.

The home's yard is unmowed, children's toys strewn across the sawgrass—a plastic machine gun, a water pistol, a pair of skates, a go-kart, all circled by a sagging chain link fence. Next to a side door sits a bag of trash torn open by animals, its contents—chicken bones, soiled diapers, a half-eaten piece of fish—spilling onto the dirt driveway.

Minnie Lee Langley

A young woman, gold hoop rings dangling from her ears, lets herself through the fence gate and knocks on the front door, hollering into an open louvered window, a window protected by steel bars. All the windows in this house are barred.

"Minnie!" she calls. "Minnie Lee, you in there?"

No answer.

"I *know* she's in there," the woman says, pushing through the knee-high grass to another window. "She's got to be here. Nowhere else she *could* be."

The woman is a neighbor. She and her mother live two doors down. They keep an eye on Minnie, check in now and then to see if there's anything she needs. This morning they're going out for some shopping and think Minnie might like to come along.

"This is not like her," says the woman. "She's always up by this time of the morning."

The woman taps on a window at the back of the house, and finally, a voice answers. Small, faint, it asks who's there, says to come on around to the front, she'll be there in a minute. And in a minute she is, a tiny face framing a pair of bright, wet eyes, peeking around the doorknob, squinting in the morning sunlight.

It's dark inside, hot and cluttered. A half-eaten pastry sits on the small kitchen table, beside a can of roach spray. Brown sodden newspapers are spread on the linoleum floor by the refrigerator, soaking up a leak. The living room coffee table is covered with vials of medicine. A tube of analgesic cream is by the TV, and half-used bottles of rubbing alcohol are everywhere—on the kitchen counter, atop the refrigerator, on an end table near the sofa where Minnie takes a seat, her thin little body hardly making a crease in the cushion.

She is the color of dark chocolate, her limbs skeletal, her fingers long and gnarled, the nails an opaque, milky yellow. She is wearing a faded pink bathrobe, her tiny feet floating in a black pair of oversized bedroom slippers. Her gray hair is short and wiry, pulled on one side into a small knot held by a rubber band. On the wall above her hangs a plaque:

GOD SEES US AS WE CAN BE, BUT LOVES US AS WE ARE

Beside her sits an ashtray filled with cigarette butts. "Lord yes, I smoke," she says, picking a stray butt off the floor and dropping it in the dish. "Not as much as I used to, but I do. If you're gonna drink that coffee, you *got* to smoke."

The door is still open, and now a figure appears, a man, his face pressed to the screen.

"*Yo,*" he shouts, yelling into the darkness, "can I get a *dollar* from anybody in there?"

Minnie screws up her face, turns her head away, her tiny chin thrust toward the ceiling. "*Hah!*" she says. "I'd like to throw a dollar in a *hole* as give it to you. That's if I *had* a dollar."

The man moves on, and Minnie gets up to shut the door.

"He wants that *dope* is what he wants," she says.

The walls around her are decorated with crucifixes and religious paintings. The Last Supper. The Virgin Mary. A book is propped on a shelf by the window: *You Can Live Forever In Paradise On Earth.*

Minnie decides she'd like to sit outside. It's a nice day. She pushes some toys off the porch sofa, sending a lizard skittering across the cement floor. A small cockroach creeps across the wall behind her as she sits down and sighs.

The toys, she says, are her great-grandsons'. "My children," she calls them, the two little ones living with her right now. They are brothers, Charles and Matthew, one five years old and the other four. Minnie took them in nearly three years ago, after their mother, Minnie's granddaughter, committed suicide. "That hurt me," says Minnie, her eyes welling up. " 'cause I loved that child. She was the oldest grandchild I had."

Minnie has six grandkids, all of whom spent the better part of their childhoods in her care. "Oh, I'm *still* taking care of the children, I sure am," she smiles. "I love my children, I *love* 'em."

She has two of her own, her daughter Dorothy, born in 1930, and her son Anthony, whom she adopted when he was an infant. "He's growed up now, with his big-mouth self," she chuckles.

Anthony was three months old, says Minnie, when she took him in. "This girl where I was working, she was giving that baby *away*. Her husband was in the service, and she was fixing to give her child up. When I heard that, I asked her to give that baby to *me*. She said all right, and that's the way that come along. Went down and had papers drawn up on it, and that was it. He was mine."

Minnie twists a thin wedding band on her left hand. Her husband Clifford gave it to her when they were married in 1936. He died from a heart attack in

'56, the year they bought this house. "That's right," says Minnie. "I moved in here as a widow."

Clifford worked at a filling station most of his life—"Firestone," says Minnie. "Changing tires, changing oil." They met at the start of Franklin Roosevelt's first term and married near the end of it. "Just about the time we started putting in for the Social Security," she says.

Her daughter Dorothy was six by then, born to Minnie and a boyfriend named Curtis Telfer. "I liked him," she says of Curtis, "but he had too many sweethearts, too many outside girls. I wouldn't take him for no husband."

Clifford Langley was a different story. He was loyal, and he raised Dorothy as if she were his own child. "He was a good man, yes *goodness*," says Minnie, her eyes welling up again. "Couldn't find another one like him in a hundred years."

Minnie stopped working in 1980, after more than thirty years on the assembly line at a brush and broom factory. At her peak she turned out fifty boxes of fiber brushes a day. "Fifty-four brushes to a box," she says with pride. For that she was paid seventy-five cents an hour when she began in the late '40s. When she retired, her hourly salary was $3.75.

These days Minnie spends most of her time tending to her great-grandsons. She watches a little television in the afternoons—"'The Young and the Restless' and 'Guiding Light,' that's it." And she spends her Sundays at the nearby Community Faith Baptist Church. "I can't *live* without Him," she says, glancing up at the late morning clouds.

This is as much as most of Minnie's neighbors know about her. Few know anything of Rosewood. Those who do know only what they have heard on television or read in the newspapers. The young woman who has come this morning to fetch Minnie for shopping has never heard of the place, not until now.

"I never talked about it to nobody," says Minnie. "Never told my own children about it. I always said to them, 'I don't want y'all to come up like I come up.' But that's all I told them. Not a word about Rosewood."

She closes her eyes, shakes her head.

"We ain't had no problems back there, not with the white folks, not with no one. Ain't had a *bit* of problems. I don't understand *why* them peoples did us like that."

Minnie was born in Rosewood on the Fourth of July, 1913. Her mother was named Daisy, Daisy Mitchell, but Minnie never knew her. Daisy died during that birth, leaving Minnie and her brother Ruben in the care of their grandmother, Emma Carrier. Emma became "Mama" to Minnie and Ruben Mitchell. Their father Theodore was gone by the time Minnie was born, off making a living diving for sponges, sending home what money he could. Emma occasionally took Minnie to visit him, down the coast at a place called Crystal River, a half day's trip from Rosewood. Minnie would sit by the clear water and watch her father work, see him take deep gulps of air then dive to the river bottom, coming back up after what seemed like forever with a sopping piece of coffee-colored sponge in his huge, hard hands. "Big old pieces," she says. "As big as I was. *Bigger*."

The last time Minnie saw her father was the summer she turned nine, the summer before the attack. "I don't know when he died," she says. "Don't know if he *is* dead. I ain't seen or heard of him since this stuff happened."

The Rosewood Minnie recalls was a happy place, "A good place to be a child," she says. She remembers planting and watering and weeding sweet potatoes with her grandmother, digging them up at harvest time and storing them in piles covered with pine bark to keep them from rotting. Sometimes Emma went to white people's homes in Sumner, to cook in their kitchens and milk their cows, and Minnie would come along. When Emma went down to the Rosewood depot to sell fresh eggs to the trains passing through, Minnie would come along. Before her granddaddy James had his stroke, he trapped for a living, and it was up to Minnie and the Carrier kids to clean what he caught.

There were seven Carrier children and grandchildren in the home, all older than Minnie and Ruben, so Minnie learned early how to hold her own. "Oh, I could fight," she says. "I beat every one that come my way, every one. They was *scared* of me."

She was in second grade at the Rosewood school the winter of the attack, and she remembers the day it began, standing out in the yard with her grandmother, watching "a gang of crackers" charge past with some hound dogs, then seeing them come back to her grandmother's house, pulling her uncle Aaron from inside and talking about hanging him with some rope. It wasn't much later that her cousin Sylvester showed up at the door.

"He told us to come over with him, 'cause he felt like them crackers was going to come our way again and he couldn't take care of both houses. So we went. We didn't carry no clothes or nothin'. We just went. We didn't think we'd be staying long."

Sylvester had been threatened by the mob that afternoon, says Minnie, when they came across him down at the depot. "'Don't let sundown catch you here.' That's what they told him," she says. That is what brought Sylvester to Emma Carrier's door, says Minnie, and that is how both families wound up in Sarah Carrier's house the night of the shootout.

The children were just getting to bed that night, says Minnie, when she heard voices calling from outside the house. "I could hear them out there hollering, 'Sarah! Come on out here! Come on out here, Sarah, you hear me?'"

She heard a blast of gunfire from outside. Then an explosion of shooting. The next thing Minnie knew, her Aunt Honey rushed into the children's bedroom covered with blood and crying. "They done killed Mama! They done killed Mama!" Minnie didn't know it was Sarah who had been shot. She thought it was Emma, and she rushed downstairs, stumbling in the darkness, searching for her grandmother.

"Then Cuz' Syl' grabbed me. He said, 'Come here, baby, let me save you.' And he pulled me back with him, into the wood bin under the steps. Both of us climbed in there, and I got down between his legs and he put his gun up over my shoulder.

"Then they kicked in the front door, *boom,* and that's when my cousin let them have it. Shot two of them dead, right there."

In Minnie's memory, more men died by Sylvester's hand before the night was through: "He could see them crackers running across the yard, and every time he'd see one, he'd shoot them, *BOOM, BOOM!*"

Before long, white men were "piled up on the porch," says Minnie. When the mob pulled back, she says, Sylvester told everyone in the house to leave, out the back and into the swamp. Minnie wound up with some of the other children and her Aunt Beulah, Emma's daughter, the one they called "Scrappie."

"She stayed with us out in those woods for three days, feeding us berries and cabbage root. It was so cold, Jesus it was cold. And we was about naked. We ain't had no clothes. But Scrappie wouldn't let us build but a little bitty fire, because she didn't want them to find us."

By the second night, says Minnie, they could see the flames from Rosewood lighting up the evening sky. "Like Judgment Day," she says.

The third night was when they got word to make their way to the tracks, that someone was sending a train to pick them up. "Captain Bryce," she says, "he sent word through a man that worked up at the turpentine still in Wylly to bring us over and put us on that train and it would take us to Gainesville."

She doesn't remember much about that ride, says Minnie, other than they were fed some fresh fruit and the trip took three hours. When they reached the station at Gainesville, they were met by a cousin who told them Emma was safe in Sumner but Grandpa James was dead, shot to death by the white men.

Emma soon joined them, living with the children in a small shack in the black section of the city. "But she ain't never gotten well," says Minnie. Emma had been hurt in the gunfight, shot in the hand and wrist, but it wasn't those wounds that killed her, says Minnie. "She just took sick over what happened, and she never did get well."

The children went to work, including Ruben, who was left with one eye after the attack. "He found work picking up paper," says Minnie. As for herself, she washed dishes in one white woman's home and helped another milk cows and churn butter. All the children pitched in to put dinner on the table each evening, with Minnie's oldest cousin, thirteen-year-old Lonnie, acting as the father, leading the group in prayer. Late at night, while the others were asleep, Minnie would get up and feed her grandmother her medicine.

But it did no good. Emma died the following summer, in 1924, just after Minnie's eleventh birthday, and the children were on their own. A young aunt came to help out, but left after a few months. "Aunt Rita," says Minnie, with a small smile. "She liked a good time." Another aunt, Ethel, had her own family there in Gainesville. She had no room for the Carrier kids, but she did bring Minnie and her cousins food when she could.

And so they survived. Minnie moved to Jacksonville in 1926 and found work caring for babies in private homes. Four years later she gave birth to Dorothy. Six years after that she married Clifford and she never looked back, never talked about Rosewood to a soul, never had a need to, not until the newspaper reporter from St. Petersburg came to her door in 1982, she says, "right here at this house," and asked her what happened at Rosewood.

"I told him," she says, leaning forward and stretching her thin, bony arms. "I told him everything. He sent me the story he wrote, but I didn't read it.

"Then the '60 Minutes' people came here after that," she says, "right here in my driveway, taking pictures and stuff. They asked if they could carry me down there to Rosewood, me and Lee Ruth. That's all of us that was left. I knowed I had some cousins somewhere, but I didn't know where they was, didn't even know if they was still alive. Ruth was the only one I knowed was alive."

Minnie took that trip, she and her daughter Dorothy, in the fall of 1983.

They drove down to Rosewood, met the television people there, reporter Ed Bradley and his crew. Met Lee Ruth Davis, too, and two other Rosewood survivors as well. One was a man named Sam Hall, who had come down from his home on the Georgia coast. Minnie remembered Sammy Hall as a boy in Rosewood, but she hadn't seen or heard of him since. The other was Lee Carrier, a cousin of Minnie's, settled up in Pensacola now. She hadn't seen Lee Carrier either, not since they were children.

They spent the day with Ed Bradley, walking the grounds of what had once been their home, walking around the yard of the old Wright house, too, the only place still standing from back then, a looming Victorian house. They relived some of the events that had happened sixty years before. They each told their story. Then, at the end of the day, they all went back home.

"I told them everything," says Minnie Lee, standing and stretching before going back in the house.

"Everything you need to know is there on that TV show," she says, pulling open her screen door and moving back into the darkness. "Just watch it."

SEVEN

Hard Dirt

A. T. Goins watched it the night it was broadcast, two weeks before Christmas, 1983. He sat in the den of his St. Petersburg home with his wife Anna Maude and listened to Ed Bradley describe how forty people were killed in the "mass murder" at Rosewood.

Though he hated to admit it, A. T.'s eyesight was even then just about gone, blurred by the glaucoma that had crept up on him in recent years. But he could still make out the figures on that television screen, and he was transfixed as he watched an old white man in a cowboy hat, a man named Fred Kirkland, recall a mob he said grew to as many as fifteen hundred men, and then explain almost casually what drove them toward the slaughter. "Satisfaction," the white man said, chewing on a toothpick. "I reckon that was it."

A. T. could see his cousin, Lee Ruth Davis—"Mossy," they called her—standing by a fencepost, musing about the house and land her family had owned and how they had lost it all, how they had to start over again with nothing. Lee Ruth lived in Miami now, had settled there not long after the attack, but she and A. T. had stayed in touch over the years, meeting up at holidays and funer-

A. T. Goins

als and other family affairs. The same with Lee Carrier, who was up there now on the TV screen, too, talking about Rosewood.

A. T. was amazed to see Sam Hall, limping with a cane across the lawn of the old Wright house. A. T. hadn't seen Sammy since they were both boys, before the attack, and now there he was, so crippled he could hardly make his way from one side of that yard to the other. It made A. T. feel his own age, seeing Sam Hall like that. It made A. T. realize how long it had been.

And by God, there was Minnie Lee Mitchell, as feisty as ever. A. T. hadn't seen her either since the massacre, didn't know she was still alive. They were about the same age, Minnie and A. T. They used to tussle together all the time. She was nothing but a tiny thing, no bigger than a minute, A. T. recalled, but she would not back down from anyone. She had the spunk of somebody twice her size, that's what A. T. remembered most about Minnie Lee. And now there she was, sitting on the porch of a house up in Jacksonville, her little head swallowed by a red knit cap, wrinkles all over her face, telling Ed Bradley how her cousin Sylvester killed all those white men that winter night, "just dropped every one that come to the door."

Lord, A. T. thought to himself, Sissy must be beside herself right now. He knew his sister Philomena had to be cursing all these people at this very minute. He knew how she felt about this whole Rosewood mess, how she squashed Lee Ruth every time she tried to bring it up. And now here it was, going out on the television for the whole country to see.

A. T. felt pretty much the same as his sister, though he wasn't the type to get as upset as her. He never wanted any part of Rosewood after they were all carried away on that train, never talked about it to anyone, not even to Anna Maude. Thirty years they were married before she heard of it, and that wasn't from him. It was from Philomena, who finally saw fit to tell her. Up to then, Anna Maude had always thought A. T. was from Gainesville, and that was the way he wanted it.

It could drive a man crazy thinking about something like that, that's the way A. T. felt. Wondering how things might have been different if it hadn't happened, wondering what life would be like if their family had been able to hold onto their houses and land and make it all grow into something even bigger and better—a man could lose his mind worrying over thoughts like that. And there was the shame of it, too. What man would want to admit that he'd run like a scared animal into the woods, run away from people who had come to burn his home and take his land, run like a rabbit rather than taken a stand? A. T. knew it didn't make sense to think like that, he knew he was just a little boy at the time, only eight years old, but he still felt shame just the same. And so he just didn't think about it. No sense to it, he figured, no sense thinking about things that can't be changed. Just leave it behind. That's what A. T. said when some of the others, like Lee Ruth, got all agitated and tried to stir things up. Just leave it behind.

That's what A. T. had done, and he'd made out all right for himself. It hadn't been easy, shining shoes all those years, twenty cents a pair in the beginning and some of those people so stingy they wouldn't budge from that chair till you made change for their quarter. Some Saturdays A. T. would stay up and shine shoes all night, clear through to dawn, do as many as four hundred pairs of shoes and have them all lined up and waiting for his customers to pick up and wear to church.

That's how A. T. did it for years, and by the time his daughter Annette graduated from high school, he had saved enough to send her to college. Now she was a Ph.D. herself, married to a college president up in Mississippi. A. T. and Anna Maude had Annette to thank for helping them with this nice house they lived in now, a house by a golf course, the same course A. T. caddied on fifty years earlier, in the 1930s, when he first came to St. Pete. Of course he wasn't allowed to *play* on that course back then. No blacks could play that course back then.

By 1983 there were blacks teeing up right alongside whites. But not A. T. His body wouldn't let him. His bones ached day and night with arthritis, and his eyesight was just about gone from glaucoma. He was happy enough just to be able to take his afternoon walk around those fairways, watch the sun set over those sand traps, then come back home to his hibiscus bushes and his lemon trees and his poinsettias. He did love his trees and flowers, had a way with them. Anna Maude marveled at how A. T. could make blooms come up out of nothing but hard dirt.

Some of that had to have come from Rosewood. Their yard was full of fruit trees back then. Pear trees, peach trees, mulberry trees. A.T.'s grandmother Sarah had them all growing outside her windows, and they all bore fruit, all except one, a plum tree, which was her "whippin' tree," the place she'd go to strip branches whenever one of her grandchildren was due for a spanking. Sarah would pull off two or three of those branches, braid them together and just burn their butts up. A. T. never would forget that. Some days Mama Sarah would come home from work, hear about one of the children's transgressions, and she'd just sink into a chair. "I'm too tired to whip you right now," she'd sigh, "but don't think you ain't gonna *get* that whipping." And she always kept her word, even if it meant sometimes saving up two or three into one.

A. T. adored his Mama Sarah, loved staying in her big house when his own mama and daddy were off working for the lumber company. "Harvesting" the logs, that's what the company called it, and the men they sent into those swamps to do it were black men, just like A. T.'s daddy. Five in the morning until five at night they worked, wearing boots and overalls and big-brimmed hats, wading by the dozen into waist-high swamp water, carrying axes and long crosscut saws, saws that were seven feet long, making as much noise as they could so the gators would move over and the water moccasins would move on, seeking out the oldest, biggest trees, virgin cypress and cedar, trees two to three thousand years old, six feet wide in the trunk, some wider than that, notching each one with their axes, then bringing it down with the saws, two men pulling at each end, and once it was down they'd cut off the branches and tie on the ropes and snake the beast back through the thick forest to the train that would haul it to the mill.

It was a hard way to make a living, but A. T.'s daddy did it. George Washington Christopher Columbus Goins, that was his name. His wife was Willie Retha Carrier Goins, one of Sarah Carrier's daughters. When George Goins went to work in the woods, his wife Willie came with him, the two of them living in the logging camp, wherever it was. When they began having children, they'd bring the baby along until it was big enough to stay with Willie's mother. Philomena was their first child, born in 1911. Three years later came A. T.— Arnett Turner. Next came Harold, who lived only two years before he died from the fever. Another brother, George, was born December 24, 1918— "Our Christmas present," A. T. called him. Finally came a baby sister, Vera, born in 1921.

A. T. could hardly remember his parents being home, his daddy was away working so much. It was Sarah's house A. T. would always recall as his own, with its hard wooden floors, rugs in the living room, a piano *and* an organ. It seemed like everybody in the family could play that piano but A. T. He never did have any musical ability, never had any interest in music.

But put a ball in his hands and he became an artist. That's all A. T. cared about: playing ball with his cousins, all those Carrier kids. His great-uncle James had a bunch of boys, and every morning they'd all be out there on the "hard ground," out front of Mama Sarah's house. She'd warn them to stay in that yard, not to go past the fence, but they always did. They knew they'd get a whipping when she found out, but they always did.

What they loved most was to hunt rabbits. A. T.'s Uncle Sylvester kept three dogs in a pen out back of the house. He had a deer dog they called Rattler, a bird dog named Kate and a rabbit dog named Trixie. The boys would take Trixie with them and sneak off into the woods, keeping their eyes peeled for rattlesnakes. Rattlesnakes were the main reason Sarah wanted those boys to stay out of the woods, but to A. T.'s cousins, killing rattlers was as much a game as hunting rabbits.

Trixie would always let them know when a snake was around. She'd stand dead still, bark, then begin walking slowly, in a wide circle. Somewhere inside that circle, in the thick brush, was a snake. The dog would never get within striking distance, but the boys, they would close in, each of them carrying a stick, until one of them spotted the serpent, usually coiled, poised to strike. Then they would kill it, simply beat it to death. They had to kill it. If they didn't, Trixie would not hunt. She would not move on until she saw that that rattler was dead.

A. T. never was much for killing snakes, but when it came to catching rabbits, he was a star. His weapon was a sawed-off broom handle with an iron nut attached to the end. The nut was huge, the size of a baseball. A. T. would find them up by the railroad tracks. Once Trixie flushed a rabbit, the boys would give chase, sprinting behind until the animal hit a clearing. Then they would all heave their weapon of choice at it, mostly rocks and crude spears fashioned from tree branches. A. T. had his club, which he would aim, then hurl, the iron nut leading the stick through the air toward its target. The nut was lethal, and so was A. T.'s aim. By the time the boys returned home, they would have a sack full of rabbits, as many as a dozen, most of them victims of A. T.'s good eye and strong arm.

The boys often returned with just as many gophers, flushed from holes where the rabbits tried to hide, and it was all good eating, the rabbits parboiled then fried just like chicken, the gophers simmered and stewed like beef. Even when he was grown and moved to the city, A. T.'s favorite dish was always gopher stew.

He never did forget how well they ate in Rosewood. Grandma Sarah's smokehouse stayed filled with the ducks and turkeys Sylvester shot in the forest, as well as hams from the hogs they raised. The hogs roamed free through the woods, fattening themselves on whatever they could find, along with the corn and slop they knew they could get at the house. There was no worry of losing them, because A. T.'s Papa Hayward, Sarah's husband, had his mark on each one of them, branded them just like cattle.

They kept a chicken coop out back, and it was A. T.'s job to feed the hens and gather the eggs. He hated that job. As far as he was concerned, chickens were the nastiest creatures on earth, eating anything they could find on the ground and leaving a mess wherever they went. When it was time to have one for dinner, Mama Sarah would carry it in a few days beforehand and keep it in a back room of the house. "Got to let it clean itself out," she'd say.

There was a garden behind Mama Sarah's house, and A. T. remembered it thick with peas and beans. There was a stable, too, for the mule Papa Hayward used for plowing. He used that mule to grind cane, too. A. T. loved to help his grandfather grind and cook that cane. They'd take one of the big iron pots Sarah used for washing clothes, clean it out with hot water, then cook the thick, sweet syrup until it boiled. There wasn't a morning A. T. could recall from his boyhood that didn't begin with a plate of Mama Sarah's hot biscuits, bathed in that home-cooked cane syrup.

That was how the morning began the day the white men came. A. T. was out in the yard that day with his cousins. It was cold, but not too cold to play. When A. T. saw the gang of white men coming up the railroad tracks, he thought it was strange. They were carrying guns, and they had dogs with them, too. But they went right past the house, and so A. T. and his cousins went back to playing. It was not until late that morning that Sissy and Mama Sarah came home and said something had happened over in Sumner.

Still, A. T. didn't know what was brewing, not even the next day when his Uncle James and Aunt Emma and all their boys, and Minnie Lee, too, and her brother Ruben, all of them arrived at Mama Sarah's house, and Uncle Sylvester said they'd be staying there for a couple of days. Even then, the boys went out in the yard and played. But they did not even think about going past the fence. They could see Mama Sarah was more serious than ever about that.

Then came Thursday night. It was around bedtime, the way A. T. remembered it. The moon was shining just as bright as could be, and the kids were all upstairs, horseplaying and staying awake though they were supposed to be getting to sleep. They were making enough noise that A. T. didn't even hear the shouts from outside. The gunshot, though, he heard that, and then it seemed like all hell broke loose, the children diving on the floor, bullets flying through the windows, Aunt Honey rushing into the room with blood all over her, Ruben with blood all over him too. The funny thing was, A. T. didn't feel frightened at all. In fact, the first thing he thought about was his suit.

It was his Christmas present from his daddy, a brand new dress suit. A. T.'s parents had come home Christmas Eve from Otter Creek, where they were staying at a logging camp. They had A. T.'s baby sister Vera with them, and they carried her back with them when they returned Christmas Day after having dinner with the family, leaving Philomena, A. T. and little George with Sarah.

Now, with the window shutters and glass shattering around him, with his aunt and his cousin crying and covered with blood, all A. T. could think was to get downstairs and find his suit. Which was what he did as soon as the shooting stopped. While the other children all rushed toward the back door and out to the woods, A. T. reached the bottom of those steps and turned toward the living room. Then he tripped over something. A body, a dead man. Then another, a woman. And now he was afraid. He left the suit behind and hurried out the back to catch up with the others.

He could hardly remember the next two days and nights. It all seemed like a blur. They stayed in the woods, and it was cold, he remembered that. Too cold to sleep, so they sat up and shivered, leaning close to one another for warmth. He remembered sipping swamp water to quench his thirst.

When they finally got on the train, he thought they'd be coming back. He had no idea this was the last time he would see his grandparents' house. He didn't know what was happening when they got to Gainesville, couldn't understand why his Aunt Rebecca, who lived there with her husband and children, refused to take them in, turned them away, told them she didn't want anything to do with this mess.

A. T.'s mama and daddy got to Gainesville after a couple of days, gathered their children together and left for Tampa, where they found a place to live. They brought Papa Hayward with them, but A. T.'s grandfather was never the same man after what happened at Rosewood, after he'd come back from his hunting trip that week to find nothing left. His wife Sarah was dead. So was his son Sylvester. And his brother James. He had lost his house and his land, lost everything he'd ever lived for, everything he had. He rarely spoke from then on. When he did talk, it was only to himself. If no one was there to stop him, he would wander out of the house and off into the city streets, sometimes without any clothing. Buck naked. No one had to tell A. T. what had happened. His grandfather had lost his mind, gone crazy with grief.

Hayward Carrier died in Tampa in 1925, two years after the attack on Rosewood. A. T.'s mother, Willie, died four years after that, but his daddy George never stopped traveling during all that time, moving from logging camp to logging camp, roaming across the better part of the state, and sometimes he took one or two of his children with him, to fix his meals. That's how A. T. learned to cook, alongside his sister Philomena. Mornings, it was A. T.'s job to get up and fix his daddy's lunch bucket for him, and he'd cook dinner at night, too, after Philomena grew old enough to leave home. When A. T.'s brother George was big enough, A. T. broke him in so they could alternate days, one getting up with their father before dawn while the other slept in.

After A. T.'s mother died, his father remarried and moved to Gulf Hammock. A. T. went to Lacoochee to live with his Aunt Beauty. He was sixteen then, big enough to work for a living, which he did, at a crate factory up in Gulf Hammock, making wire baskets for the people who picked beans and peas on the surrounding farms. A. T. earned a dollar and a quarter a day and was glad to have it, times being as hard as they were.

And they got harder. A. T. worked his way through the Depression digging ditches, laying down sewer pipes, pulling up weeds from the side of the road, any job he could find. Most of them he found down around St. Petersburg. Sometimes he was paid money, sometimes he was simply paid with pieces of paper, scrip redeemable for groceries at neighborhood food stores. Those were hard times for A. T., but then they were hard for everyone. He realized that, so week in and week out he just did the best he could to survive. And weekends, well, weekends were wonderful, because that was when A. T. could play baseball.

He had adored the game from the time he first watched the grownups play back in Rosewood. They had a strong club, the Rosewood All Stars, resplendent in their pinstripe uniforms. Black ball teams would travel down from Perry or Chiefland and play them on weekends. There'd be a big picnic, just about the whole town would walk over to the ballfield to watch, and almost invariably the Stars would come out on top.

A. T. was too little to play with the men back then, too little even to play with the big boys, but he would watch, especially when they went out at night to play a game they called "fireball." There was always plenty of turpentine around, and occasionally a group of the Rosewood kids would grab a bucket, soak a ball in it overnight, and then, the next sundown, they'd head over to the ballfield, carrying some small cans of turpentine gum with them, enough to place one at each base, including home plate, and a couple out around the pitchers mound.

Then they would light the cans. And then they would light the ball. And then they would play, a boy at every position, the infielders' faces glowing from the flames of the flickering cans, the outfielders invisible in the darkness, the pitches lobbed toward home plate, tracing an arc of light against the night sky, the batter swinging, connecting, sending a missile toward the woods, a small flaming comet, the runners circling the bases, stopping only if that flying ball of fire suddenly stopped, because that meant it had been caught and it would be coming back in in an instant because the only way to play fireball was to catch and throw in one motion, get that ball in and out of your hands fast enough so you didn't get burned.

It was a country game, fireball. Nobody had heard of it in St. Pete, where A. T. arrived in 1932. He was eighteen years old by then, big enough to try out for one of several black semipro teams in the city. He was small, five-foot-eight and no more than 130 pounds, but his right arm was like a whip. That and his pinpoint control earned him a spot as a pitcher, and soon he was on the roster of St. Petersburg's best black ballclub, the Florida Stars.

There was a time, during the 1920s, when that team traveled the entire east coast, playing in cities as far north as Philadelphia and Boston. They were called the Sunshine Babies back then, but the Depression did them in. By the time A. T. joined them, the club had changed its name and was playing only in Florida. Still, there were dozens of black ballclubs in cities across the state eager to take them on. Sarasota and Bradenton. Lakeland and Miami. Jacksonville, Sanford, Gainesville. A. T. and his teammates would travel by car, arrive around lunchtime, the hosts would have a homecooked meal waiting for them and then the teams would play a doubleheader, with the winners pocketing sixty percent of the gate.

The Stars offered the same deal when they played at home, and that was where A. T. had the best moments of his life, because that was where he took

the field against some honest-to-God legends, members of the fabled Negro
League professional baseball clubs that criss-crossed the country during the
Depression. Teams like the Homestead Grays and the Newark Eagles, the Indi-
anapolis Clowns and the Chicago American Giants, the Atlanta Black Crackers
and the Birmingham Black Barons. They all stopped in St. Pete during their
Florida swings, they always made a point of playing a game or two against the
local club, and so, during his stint with the Stars in the late 1930s and early
'40s, A. T. Goins played against some of the best hardball players on earth,
black or white.

Cool Papa Bell and Buck O'Neil, Josh Gibson and Satchel Paige, they all
visited St. Pete during that time. Willie Mays's father, "Cat" Mays, he came
through one year with the Black Barons. Not a bad center fielder, as A. T. recalled, though nothing like his son would turn out to be.

One of the strangest sights A. T. ever saw was the Zulu Cannibal Giants,
who took the field dressed in grass skirts and wearing red wigs. They looked
like clowns, he never would forget that. And he never forgot how those boys
could hit the ball. Skirts or no skirts, they put a whipping on the Stars that afternoon.

A. T. pitched against most all of them, but the moment that stood out above
any other occurred the night he played right field against the Grays, and Josh
Gibson came to bat. Gibson—they called him "the black Babe Ruth"—had already hit a home run the day before that was still rising when it cleared the left-
field wall. Rather than see that again, the Stars walked him to get to Buck
Leonard, a monster in his own right. And Leonard proceeded to hit the hardest, longest home run A. T. ever saw. The ball was a pellet as it passed directly
over his head. He didn't bother to move. He simply looked up and watched as it
cleared the wall behind him, cleared the towering oak tree standing beyond
that wall, cleared the street behind the oak, cleared two front yards beyond the
street and finally landed in a vacant lot halfway down the block, a distance of
some five hundred feet from home plate.

People around St. Pete still talked about that home run forty years after it
happened. A. T. still talked about it. He'd take a friend to the south end of the
city, to where that ballpark still sits, Campbell's Park, its sea-green cement out-
field walls now covered with graffiti, the infield swallowed by weeds and
sparkling with bits of broken beer bottles, the wooden bleachers caved in and
rotten, the old stadium gone to seed like the neighborhood around it, and he'd

point toward home plate. Then he'd point the other way, toward a house that now sat on that once-vacant lot where that ball had finally landed that memorable night. And no one would believe him. No man could hit a baseball that far. But Buck Leonard did it. A. T. knew he did it, because A. T. was there.

He married Anna Maude in 1940, Annette was born three years after that, and a year later A. T. was drafted into the Army. They found a spot on his lung during his physical, sent him home to get it checked out, and that's when he learned he had tuberculosis. He wound up in a sanitorium just outside Orlando, where he stayed for nearly two years—twenty-two months, two weeks and two days, to be exact. A. T. could recite those numbers the way a ballplayer recites his batting average.

They weren't sure he would survive when he went into that hospital, but he did. He never played baseball again, though, and his days of hard labor were behind him. When he came out, in the autumn of 1946, A. T. began shining shoes, and that's what he did for the next thirty years, until his eyesight got so bad he finally had to put away his brush.

Yes, he had had a life, and a good one when it was all added up. He was never one for feeling anger, never saw much sense in confrontation. He understood what those marchers were all about in the 1950s and '60s, protesting and demonstrating for civil rights, but that was never his style. He would fight if he had to, but he was never one for the front lines. His way was quiet, gentle, minding his own business, tending his own garden. Nothing like his nephew Arnett, Philomena's boy.

Now there was a fighter. Arnett was like a son to A. T. The boy was named after him, but they were as different as fire and water. A. T. had watched Arnett get in and out of trouble his whole life, always stirring things up. That's the way it was with this Rosewood business. Ever since he was a boy, Arnett had been poking around with questions about Rosewood, and A. T. would shoo him away, ask him if his mother knew what he was up to, nosing around again about that mess.

A. T. was amazed when that newspaper story came out in the summer of 1982. There had never been a word written about Rosewood his whole life, not a word, and suddenly there was this big Sunday spread in the St. Pete paper. Sissy warned him it was coming out and told him not to believe a word of it. The white man who wrote it, he had talked Arnett into going with him up to Rosewood, that's what she said. The man had even tried talking to Sissy herself, she said, till she got sick of his questions and threw him out of her house. Then she got on the telephone and warned everyone in the family not to speak to this man.

The newspaper story came and went, with not much made of it. But about a year later, A. T. got another phone call from his sister, and this time it was about television. She said "60 Minutes" had come to her house, trying to get her to talk about Rosewood. She hadn't given them the time of day, slammed the door in their face, she said. But they went ahead and did their story anyway. Sissy called to warn A. T. it was coming on that Sunday and God knew what it was going to say.

Now it was Sunday, now it was on, and Sissy had to be beside herself. That's all A. T. could think as he sat next to Anna Maude, watching Minnie Lee and Lee Carrier and Lee Ruth and Sammy Hall there on that TV screen, all of them talking about Rosewood. Sissy *had* to be upset now.

EIGHT

No Ear on Earth

"Lies, lies. Nothin' but goddamn *lies!*"

Arnett watched his mother almost leap out of her soft chair, cursing the television set as she saw these people acting like they were the only ones left, talking about her family as if it were theirs, telling her story as if it belonged to them.

Who the hell did they think they were? Sam Hall, he wasn't even *there* when the shooting started. The Halls lived clear across Rosewood, at the other end of town. Lee Ruth? She wasn't there either. She didn't see one person die. She didn't have to sleep in the woods like they did. She was over at the Wright house, hiding in a bedroom with the rest of them till the train came and carried them away. As for Lee Carrier, he should have known better than to get himself drawn into this mess, all these outside people using Rosewood for their own purposes, using *him*. And this Minnie Lee Langley woman? She was nothing but a damn baby at the time, and anyway, where had she *been* all these years? Nobody heard a word from her for a *lifetime,* and now she shows up, putting on this poor pitiful face for the television people, running her sad, sorry mouth about how

Rosewood today

it was like this and it was like that, when she didn't know *what* it was like.

Lies, that's all this "60 Minutes" show was to Philomena. Just like that news-paper story had been nothing but a mess of goddamn lies. She'd given Arnett a beating after that story came out, slapped him like a child for going up to Rose-wood with that man. She thought that was the end of it, and it was, until Arnett called one day about a year later and said, "Mama, Ed Bradley is going to be coming to St. Petersburg to talk to you about Rosewood."

"Who the hell is Ed Bradley?" she asked.

"He's a black guy, Mama," he said, "a reporter for the '60 Minutes' TV show."

"He ain't coming *here,*" she said.

"Mama," said Arnett, "this is a *black* man. His last name is Bradley. *Bradley,* Mama. He might be kin to us."

"He ain't no kin to *me,*" she said. "The only Ed Bradley I know is my cousin Ed Bradley."

"Where is *he* at, Mama?"

"He's *dead,*" she said. "And I don't want to see no other Ed Bradley."

Three days after that conversation, Philomena answered her doorbell and faced two white men. One was the newspaper reporter, Gary Moore. The other said he was a producer from "60 Minutes." They had come to ask Philo-mena if she would be willing to go back to Rosewood with them, to join several other survivors for a taping there.

"No way," said Philomena. "No way in hell am I doing something like that. And you can leave now. Just leave."

When Arnett arrived from work that evening, Philomena was on him be-fore he could sit down.

"Those goddamn sons of bitches came to my house today," she said.

"Who, Mama?"

"You *know* who," she said. "Those damn '60 Minutes' people you was talking about."

"'60 Minutes'?" said Arnett. "'60 Minutes' was *here?*"

She nodded. "And I threw their asses *out,* too," she said.

"Mama, tell me you didn't do that."

"The hell I didn't."

Arnett covered his face with his hands. But Philomena wasn't finished. "*You're* the one started this goddamn shit, you and Lee Ruth," she said. "Now get your ass out of my house. Pick up your shit and get out."

Philomena spent the next several days calling every family member she could, warning them they might be contacted by these television people and forbidding them to take part in the project. But now, as she watched the screen on this Sunday evening, she saw it had done no good. She couldn't stop them all.

Arnett saw it, too, and he hardly knew what to make of it. It had been a year since he had gone up to Rosewood with that reporter, and the subject had become more forbidden than ever. Once that newspaper story appeared, Philomena seemed doubly determined to quash even the briefest mention of Rosewood. It was as if she owned the thing, and she would not allow another soul to touch it.

But Arnett had become just as determined to learn more. Once he sensed the scope of what actually happened that week, what had been a lifelong shadow for him became a burning obsession. He was consumed with Rosewood now, with the need to know who had been there, what they had lost, where they had gone and where they were now.

But the more he learned, the more he felt lost. In the past year he had talked to dozens of relatives, anyone with the least connection to Rosewood. He had begun making a chart, a family tree of sorts, each branch leading back to that town. It was a delicate business, tiptoeing around his mother, trying to find some factual footing in the fog of hearsay, myth and memory, pulling threads of recollections from relatives still reluctant to speak. And when they did, so much of what they said bumped up against what someone else had told him.

So many stories, and how to tell which were true? Everyone had his own truth. If there was one thing Arnett was learning, it was this, that everyone had his own truth about Rosewood.

There were some who said Sylvester Carrier never died in that gun battle, that it was another man they found in that shot-up house, that Sylvester slipped off through the woods that night, his eerie laughter echoing through the trees. Others said he escaped hidden in a coffin, was carried right through that crowd of whites and got away to Texas, then Louisiana, where he lived until the 1960s, mailing cryptic postcards home every couple of years. Arnett's mother said she had some of those cards, though Arnett had never seen one.

Some said Sylvester's wife Gertrude was alive even now, living in Gainesville, where she was married to a minister. But no one knew the minister's name. They said Fannie Taylor was alive, too. Arnett had heard talk about her even when he was growing up in Lacoochee. Four years after the attack on

Rosewood, Cummer and Sons closed its sawmill in Sumner, having already shifted its operation south to Lacoochee. The story was that Fannie and James Taylor moved with the company, that they lived in Lacoochee during the late 1920s until Fannie got in some more man trouble and they were forced to leave. At least that's what Arnett heard. And now he was hearing that Fannie Taylor was still alive, after all these years, staying up around Cedar Key somewhere, though again no one could say exactly where.

The identity of Fannie Taylor's assailant was another misty subject. If he was a white man, why in the world would he have fled to Rosewood, to a town full of black people? That question had nagged Arnett all his life. The answer, he was told, came from the fact that the attacker, whose name no one seemed to know, was a Freemason, a member of the secretive white brotherhood that had met behind locked doors for centuries, swearing allegiances to one another in ceremonies closed to all but themselves. By the turn of this century, there were as many black Masonic temples in Florida as white ones. Before the Civil War, black Masons—freed men—had been a key link in the Underground Railroad, their lodges providing havens for runaway slaves. By the time of the Rosewood attack, Arnett was told, there were white and black lodges that recognized one another, that honored their Masonic bonds like blood. Though they were segregated by race, the brotherhood knew no such bounds—or so Arnett was told. If a Mason was in distress, white or black, his brother was bound to help him.

That, Arnett was told, was why Aaron Carrier opened his door to this white man, why Sam Carter carried the man away, and why neither of them betrayed the man's identity, even in the face of torture—even, in Carter's case, in the face of death. Aaron Carrier and Sam Carter were high-ranking Masons, which apparently meant even more to them than the fact that they were black.

This was hard for Arnett to believe, but then there was so much that was hard to believe about Rosewood. How to believe the tales of the death toll, so many numbers so wide apart, the newspapers at the time saying just two white men died on the front porch that night, while Minnie Lee insisted the white men dropped like flies? The St. Pete *Times* story quoted a white man saying he saw nearly twenty black bodies, including babies, buried in a single mass grave. Ed Bradley stated on TV that a total of forty people died in the attack. Some of the family told Arnett the number was closer to a hundred.

What to believe? Who could believe any of this could have happened in the first place without it becoming a matter of record, something that could be looked up at the local library? Arnett had tried that. He had gone and searched through every text he could find on Florida history. Nowhere was there a mention of Rosewood. Not a single sentence. Yet it had been front-page news at the time it happened. Arnett had seen that for himself, on microfilm in the library's reference room, the headlines in huge black letters stripped across the top of nearly every newspaper in the state. But then nothing. For the next sixty years, nothing.

Now Arnett realized what he was up against within his own family. Now he began to understand the reticence of his relatives. It was more than simple fear that seized their souls, more than the pain of what they had lost or the trauma they had lived through that made them reluctant to even talk about what took place. Now, for the first time, Arnett began to fathom the utter helplessness his family had experienced, not just during that attack but after it as well. In a nation of laws and justice, there had been no law to protect them, no justice to give them back what they had lost. Now Arnett began to sense not in his mind but in his gut, the utter futility his family had felt, the brutal fact that they had had absolutely nowhere to turn for help or for hope, that there was no ear on this earth to hear their pleas, that not only had it been impossible for them to fight for themselves, unless they were ready to die, but that there had been no one to fight *for* them, not even the government supposedly sworn to keep them safe.

That is what it meant to be black in that place in that time. Arnett realized this now, more than he ever had before. As much as he had struggled with and had to swallow in his own lifetime as a black man in America, he realized now how much more his elders had faced. Why should they be expected to believe now in the government that forsook them then? He wouldn't blame them if they gave up on God himself. But none of them had done that. God was all they had had when this thing was over, faith was all they had had to carry them through, faith in something beyond this earth, certainly not in anything on it.

Arnett felt ashamed. He had come to believe that his sense of outrage was somehow stronger than theirs, that his uncles, his aunts, even his mother, they were afraid, meek, weak. But now he knew better. Now he knew they were, in every sense of the word, survivors. When he looked at them now, he felt awe, not anger. And he knew he was going to have to go beyond all of them if he was going to even begin to embrace the extent of this thing. He could not trust them to tell him the story. He could only trust them to tell him *their* story. Neither could he trust the accounts of the institutions ordained by society to record its history. The newspaper reports he had found from that time gave wildly different accounts of what happened, as did the modern journalists who had now come sniffing after this thing. As for the historians, they had never even known or bothered to include Rosewood in their records.

And so, by the end of that December, 1983, broadcast, Arnett understood that nothing he heard could be taken at face value. There was some truth to every story he was told, but no single version had the whole truth to it. The town of Rosewood had been burned, and people—*his* people—had been killed. He knew that much. But how many had been killed, how many were still alive, what they had lost, and what, if anything, they might be owed were questions he realized could not be answered by others—not by his family, not by reporters, not by historians. If he was going to answer any of these questions, he realized, he was going to have to answer them for himself, by himself.

He would continue to talk to the family. He promised himself that. These people were old. Some were dying, and when they died they would take their stories, their own truths, with them. He needed to have those stories, he knew that. But he needed more. He needed facts, numbers, records, the hard stuff of tangible truth. And if those records did not exist after 1923, after Rosewood was effectively erased from written history, then he would go back to before that time, to find clues in this vanished town's past that might help build a bridge to the present.

He would have to sidestep his mother, whose wrath loomed at every turn. He would have to sneak into his relatives' homes, gently probing for whatever their memories might offer. But he also began slipping off to libraries and courthouses, politely asking clerks to pull dusty volumes from backroom shelves, then scanning hundreds of columns of handwritten words and numbers, taking note of any entry connected to the place that had once been Rosewood. Census reports, tax books, property records, deeds, any document related to the inhabitants of that town, that's what Arnett was after. His job, his personal life, it was all going to take a back seat now. If it took him years, nothing was going to come between him and this search.

And it would take years.

NINE

Smoke and Fog

It was a wet morning in the spring of 1987 when Arnett Doctor pulled into the parking lot of the Levy County Courthouse in Bronson, the county seat, twenty miles east of Rosewood, ten wooded miles from Otter Creek. The drive up had been unremarkable, open fields flecked with hay bales and palmettos, ringed by barbed wire and shrouded in mist, clusters of black cattle grazing among flocks of white egrets. Much of that farmland had been sectioned off and sold in recent years, developed into neighborhoods of curving cul-de-sacs and split-level homes inhabited by commuters to Gainesville. But Arnett had seen no suburbs as he passed the green open fields. This part of Levy County was still country, rural and apart, as it had been for centuries, as it had been when Rosewood was a town.

Just south of Bronson, he crossed the Waccasassa River, its waters dark and still, lily pads floating on its unmoving surface. Farther north flowed the storied Suwannee, where Stephen Foster had set his antebellum music about the heart of the southland, his lyrics inked in slave dialect, "Way down upon de Swanee Ribber . . ." In the late 1970s, the federal government set aside thousands of

Downtown Cedar Key, 1920s

acres of Levy County swampland along the Suwannee as a wildlife refuge, and its forests had grown thick with bald eagles, osprey, hawks and ducks, its waters alive with alligators, tortoises, snakes and an occasional manatee wandering upstream from the Gulf.

As Arnett had approached Bronson, he saw swamp ponds swollen by recent rains, the black water rising to the edges of the road, threatening to cover the highway itself. He hadn't been back up this way since making the trip with the reporter five years before. He had spent countless hours since then at libraries in Tampa and St. Pete, studying turn-of-the-century Levy County census reports, taking the information he could find—names, ages, heads of households, occupations, the ability to read or write, whether homes were owned or rented—and using it to construct a skeletal picture of what Rosewood would have looked like in 1923.

Much of the information was sketchy at best. There were names and data that conflicted with what Arnett's relatives had told him. There was information that conflicted with itself. The 1910 census listed "Harod" and Sarah Carrier with a nineteen-year-old son named Sylvester. But in the 1920 census, Sylvester, now married, was listed as age twenty-seven.

That kind of confusion, Arnett knew, had to be at least partly due to the fact that each census was taken by a white man, going door to door on foot in a black community of which he likely knew little, a community he probably had never seen before, asking questions of men and women who were bound to be as uncomfortable with his presence as he was with theirs and who were likely to give him incomplete or downright incorrect information, all of which wound up on the official record, to be taken as truth for all time.

But there remained much that *was* true, much that was familiar to Arnett as he scanned the aged pages of handwritten script. He followed his finger down column after column of names and felt a surge, like the touch of a spirit, each time he came to a name he knew, white or black. It was as if these people, of whom he had heard so much for so many years, were suddenly alive again.

There, on the 1900 census, was the name of the head of the 296th household visited by census taker J. Asakiah Williams—Edward Goins, Arnett's great-grandfather, outlined by government categories: A black male, age fifty-two, married, date of birth unknown, number of years married unknown, place of birth North Carolina, occupation turpentine farming.

And there, on the 1920 census, this one recorded by a man named Alfred

Dorsett, was the name of Dorsett's neighbor down the road in Sumner, the head of the household of the eighth home on the first page: C. P. "Poly" Wilkerson, age thirty-nine, listed along with his wife, two daughters and three sons.

Ten pages later, one hundred homes into the list, up the road in Rosewood now, was the name of Lexie Gordon, a black female, widowed, age fifty-two.

And around her name were all the others, the Bradleys and the Halls, the Colemans and the Carriers, the Davises and the Carters, the Edwards and the McCoys, the Goinses and the Gordons. There was no way to tell exactly where the Rosewood households began and ended on the list, sandwiched as they were between Sumner on one side and the small settlement of Wylly on the other, with no indication where Alfred Dorsett left one town behind and walked into the next.

The entire census for that area for that year listed 638 people—344 blacks and 294 whites—spread among the three communities. Studying the order of households listed, knowing what he had learned from family members about their memories of who lived where in relation to whom, Arnett was able to guess roughly where on the list Rosewood began. From that, he figured there were close to thirty households in the town in 1920, a total of about two hundred men, women and children.

There was other information Arnett was able to glean from the census reports. In 1910, Rosewood's population was nearly seven hundred, and almost one-fourth of those people were white. By 1920 the whites were gone, all except John Wright and a handful of others. It was hard to say exactly why the town had shrunk so severely in such a short time. One reason had to be the depletion of lumber in the surrounding forests, slowing business at the sawmill in Sumner. There was also the departure of Arnett's great-grandfather, Ed Goins. He was listed on the 1910 census as a Rosewood resident, along with about forty men who worked for him. But by 1920 he was gone, along with most of his employees.

Arnett had heard stories over the years about why Ed Goins had left Rosewood, that he was harassed for years by lawsuits from whites who owned their own small lumber and turpentine operations in the area and began filing complaints against Goins and his workers for everything from trespassing to damaging timber. From what Arnett understood, Goins finally decided to move, taking most of what he owned out of his turpentine business and leaving the remains to his sons. Arnett also heard that Ed Goins had, at one time, owned or

leased more than two thousand acres of land around Rosewood. Arnett had always wondered what happened to that land. He still wondered as he read those
census reports.

There was no denying Rosewood was a town in decline by 1923, Arnett
could see that. But it was still a town, nonetheless, with families living in homes
they owned, on land that belonged to them. And this was something the census
did not tell him—how much land these families owned. For that Arnett needed
to see property records, and to see them he had to go to Levy County itself, to
the courthouse in Bronson. Which was how he wound up taking that drive in
the spring of 1987, a drive that carried him past a sign just outside the city lim-
its:

CAUTION

SMOKE AND FOG AHEAD

And then he was there, a string of stoplights to slow the traffic bound south
toward Ocala or north to Gainesville, a couple of service stations, a bank, a
diner, a bar with its door ajar, two men in white T-shirts and ball caps leaning
on a pickup parked on the gravel outside, sipping coffee in silence as Arnett
drove past.

The courthouse was a block off the highway, beside a Methodist church
with a message printed in letters on the signboard out front:

EXPECT GREAT THINGS FROM GOD

An American and a Confederate flag hung side by side by the courthouse
door as Arnett went in and asked a woman seated at a desk where he might find
property records. She asked what he was looking for, and Arnett lied, told her
he was doing a study of the county, a history project. He said he needed to research property records from the turn of the century for his report. She
paused, looked him up and down, then pointed him to a room at the back,
where an old white man approached as he stepped through the door.

"Findin' what you're lookin' for?" asked the man.

"Well, not really," said Arnett. "I've been over in Putnam and Alachua, looking at old property records for a report I'm doing on the growth of these areas,
and I'd like to see those same records for Levy County."

"Aw, well," said the man, stroking his chin, "records that far back aren't out here. They're in the back, but you got to get permission from the supervisor to go back there, and he's off. Won't be in till next week."

"Mmmm," said Arnett. "I really need this today. I drove all the way up from St. Petersburg."

Arnett studied the skin around the man's neck and ears. It was raw and red, scaly, flecking off in spots.

"Is there any way I can get a look at those papers?" Arnett said, reaching in his pocket and pulling out a bill, a fifty. "I'll be happy to pay for it."

The man looked at the money, then glanced back toward the room. No one else was in sight.

"All I really need," Arnett continued, his fingers rubbing the bill, "are the records from, say, 1910 through 1925. If I had those, I'd be in good shape."

The man again looked toward the rear room. Then he reached out and took the money. "Hold on," he said, and he disappeared into the back.

Arnett waited. The woman from the front room peeked in, asked if he was doing okay. Arnett smiled. "Fine," he answered, "just fine." Ten minutes later, the old man emerged, a stack of photocopies in his hands.

"If you tell anyone I gave this to you, I'll call you a liar," he said, passing the papers to Arnett. "I never did a thing for you. I never saw you before."

Arnett nodded, took the material and left. He was sweating. He couldn't believe he was actually sweating. It wasn't until he was beyond the Levy County line that he pulled over at a coffee shop and took a good look at what he had.

He was stunned. There, on the pages of deeds and tax rolls, were his people's names, next to columns of acreage owned and taxes paid. There was Sarah Carrier's name beside two acres of land she bought in 1901. And her husband Hayward's name beside another half-acre. There was Lexie Gordon buying a small piece of property in 1913. And Ransome Edwards, the grandfather who raised Arnett's uncle Willie Evans, he had two acres. The Hall family was down for twenty. Emma Carrier had herself an acre. And Ed Bradley, Lee Ruth's uncle, he owned three.

But the numbers that took Arnett's breath away were Ed Goins's. The deed books were full of transactions with Arnett's great-grandfather's name beside them. Starting in 1907, Ed Goins began leasing land right and left. By 1919 there were thirty-one leases in the Rosewood area with his name on it. The man was a magnate, that's how Arnett felt as he gazed at Ed Goins's name listed alongside the Cummer Cypress company itself, making the same kinds of deals as them, paying the same kinds of taxes.

Then Ed Goins moved away, and his leases expired. The 1921 tax rolls showed him owning a single sixty-five acre plot of land. That year's list was the last that showed any black families in Rosewood owning property. Their names were absent on ensuing lists. Gone. Other names had replaced theirs, the names of white people. Their land had been sold for delinquent taxes, sold, Arnett was certain, to some of the same people who had burned the town down.

But none of the names meant a thing to him. He'd never heard of them. None but one: John Wright, the man who had risked his reputation to save Lee Ruth and her family, who had hidden them in his house till the train came. There was John Wright's name, listed on page after page of the 1927 tax rolls, as the owner of acres of property that formerly belonged to the people of Rosewood.

That was a hard one for Arnett to understand, another twist, one more question with no clear answer.

The old man in the courthouse had been careful. He had picked and chosen what he passed to Arnett. He hadn't pulled everything, but he had pulled enough for Arnett to get a hint of what his people had had. And that was plenty.

Arnett closed the folder of papers, climbed back in his car and pointed it south to St. Petersburg. He'd gotten what he came for, and now he had to get home. There was work to do, a lot of work.

Soul Food

None of his family knew where Arnett had gone that spring of 1987, none of them knew about the documents he had been collecting and studying for the past four years. And when they drove up to Gainesville that summer for the third annual Rosewood Family Reunion, they were not surprised by his absence. He had skipped the first two gatherings as well.

The reunions, spurred by the "60 Minutes" broadcast, had begun in the summer of '85, in Lacoochee, where scattered remnants of the clans connected to Rosewood came together for the first time, the families of the families of the families who had been there. It was a modest event, about fifty people, all told. They rented a tent, set it up in the yard beside the New Bethel A.M.E. church, borrowed tables from the church basement and piled them with steaming pots and laden platters of food, good honest soul food, potato salad and corn bread, fried chicken and collard greens, ribs and ham and gopher, cakes and pies, all cooked in kitchens back home, loaded into bright Buicks and Chevys along with the children and the grandfolks and driven halfway across the state in some cases, the cars arriving Sunday morning, raising dust as they came down

Bernadina "Honey" Carrier

the dirt drives that crisscrossed the section of Lacoochee called Mosstown, where the oaks hung heavy with the green-gray strands that had once provided a living for some of these families back when the moss was pulled from those branches and hung on fenceposts to dry in the sun, to be sold as stuffing for sofas and car seats in upholstery factories up north.

But no one stuffed sofas with moss anymore. Now the grassy beards just waved in the breeze as the traffic streamed past, the vans and station wagons parking in a long line on the sweet green grass of the church lawn, the children spilling out before the engines were even cut off, the older folks moving more slowly, stepping gingerly into the sunlight, some carrying canes, others lifted down into wheelchairs, each of them assessing the scene, narrowing their eyes and taking stock before moving cautiously toward one another, toward faces grown ancient since last they had met, some faces not seen since they had been children, back in Rosewood.

This is what Aunt Beauty had wanted all those years, for the families to come together like this, not just her family but *all* of them, everyone who had sprung from those roots, who had come into this world by way of Rosewood and who had scattered like seeds after the massacre, who had gone on to spawn children and grandchildren and, by the time Aunt Beauty was getting near the end of her life, great-grandchildren. They were all from Rosewood, and Aunt Beauty wanted them to know it, to acknowledge it, to both mourn it and to celebrate it.

Aunt Beauty was the one who would raise the subject whenever her family came together, especially at funerals. Always, it would be after a Sunday service that she would rise to speak. She would pull the grownups and children alike into a group, right there in the church, ask those who were not linked to Rosewood to please step outside, and then she would begin, always the same way, in a soft, almost scolding tone, saying what a shame it was after all they had been through that the only time they seemed to come together these days was for weddings or births or funerals, that the devastation their parents and grandparents had suffered at Rosewood was not something to be forgotten, something fearful, something shameful, but that it should be a reminder of who they were, both then and now, of their connections to one another and to those who had passed on, of what they owed to the memory of the clan and the community they had once been.

It was a speech Arnett heard all his life, growing up in Lacoochee, spending as much time down the lane at Aunt Beauty's house as he did at his own. His mother was a powerful woman, with a will no one could match, but as long as Lelland Carrier Gordine, his Aunt Beauty, was alive, *she* was the matriarch of this family, the trunk that controlled the branches that had spread among the Carriers and the Goinses. As vivid as Arnett's mother's memories of that slaughter might have been, Aunt Beauty's were even stronger. She was twenty-seven when it happened, a grown woman, taking it all in, seeing her brother and mother lying dead on that living room floor as she hurried the young ones out into the night-darkened woods. She could have become even harder and angrier than Arnett's mother. She had every right. But Aunt Beauty was not made that way. Her spirit was different. There was a light in her that refused to grow dim, a glow that infected everyone who came near her. Arnett sensed that glow, could actually feel himself get warmer whenever his Aunt Beauty was around.

When he was still small, he would help her sometimes at bathtime, watching in awe as Aunt Beauty prepared herself, undressing before his eyes, unashamed of her body, the hugest, most massive body Arnett's six-year-old eyes had ever beheld, two hundred and fifty pounds of flesh draped on a five-foot-two-inch frame. They used tin tubs for bathing, galvanized basins filled with water carried in from the outside pump and heated on their wood stoves. The tubs were numbered, from a size one, big enough for a foot bath, to a size two, which could hold a healthy adult, to a three, which was big enough for both Arnett and his sister to bathe in at the same time. A number three tub was like a small swimming pool to the children, but Aunt Beauty's body filled that number three tub from one side to the other, her flesh pressing against the tin in all directions, threatening to burst the whole thing open, flooding the kitchen with gallons of displaced bath water. That's what Arnett imagined each time he watched his Aunt Beauty bathe, and he was amazed each time she emerged, her skin wet and glimmering, ready for drying and powdering and perfuming and, finally, dressing. It was a production, and when she was done, you could smell that powder and perfume all the way up the street and there would be no doubt about it, the entire neighborhood would know that Aunt Beauty had taken her bath.

She sang like an angel, just like Arnett's mother. She was in charge of the choir there at the A.M.E. church and she ran the Sunday school as well. She was a loving, laughing teacher but a stern disciplinarian, too. She busted Ar-

nett's behind more than once, and she busted his mother's, too, when Philomena took to speaking in a way Aunt Beauty thought sassy. That was a sight for
Arnett, to see his mother, a full-grown woman, spanked like a child by his
great-aunt.

Arnett was away in the Army when Aunt Beauty died in 1970. And when
he came home, he could see that his mother had taken hold of the family reins,
her grip growing tighter with each passing year. There were other family members now pushing to do what Aunt Beauty had asked, to reach out and find the
remnants of Rosewood, the relatives who had been lost over the years, but
Philomena would not hear of it. Maybe it was anger, maybe it was fear, maybe it
was the power that came from holding those reins. Maybe it was all those things
and more, but they fueled Philomena's will and allowed her to almost single-
handedly quell the voices urging that the family be found.

Those voices had remained mere whispers until that newspaper story appeared and the "60 Minutes" segment was aired. Neither piece had much effect
on the public—an editorial or two was written and then the subject receded
without notice, just as the stories written at the time of the attack had faded
into silence. But the effect on the families was explosive, stronger than the grip
of any one woman, even Arnett's mother. For better or for worse, and no one
knew which it might be, the silence had been broken. They were a family. Despite the fear and the fragmentation, they were a family, and they extended further than many of them had imagined. Now they felt a need to reach out more
than they ever had. And so a gathering was arranged, a reunion of Rosewood
survivors and descendants.

It was Annie Bell Lee and her sister Altamese, two of Arnett's many
cousins, who picked up Aunt Beauty's old address book, tattered and thick with
names and numbers smudged and yellowed over the years, and began writing
letters and making phone calls. The two women understood what a delicate
business this was, emotional surgery of sorts, probing the edges of the pain,
dread and shame that had silenced so many for so long. Annie Bell was too
young to feel ashamed or afraid, but she knew the hurt, discovering at age ten
that her grandparents' home had been torched in Rosewood and that some of
the people who had lit those flames had been among her neighbors in Sumner,
where she was born two years after the attack.

Annie Bell was living in Lacoochee when she learned about Rosewood, and
fifty years later, in the spring of 1985, as she sat at her dining room table writ-

ing letters and making phone calls to people she had never met, people with the same blood running through their veins as through hers, she was still there. Lacoochee, they decided, was the place to hold the first gathering, and so they came, on a weekend in July, each wearing a nametag, all of them hugging and kissing and crying, praying at a memorial service for those who had "gone on," eating outside under the tent, and laughing, and remembering. Some stayed away, out of fear or discomfort, or, in cases like Sammy Hall's, because they were dead. Sam Hall had passed away the year before.

Though the flush of reunion was buoyant, there was a tension as well, a holding back. The remembering was careful, controlled, the conversations about the attack itself no more open or revealing than those Arnett had over-heard at smaller family gatherings over the years. His mother was there, polic-ing the scene like a sergeant at arms, with a trail of lieutenants behind her, Rosewood survivors like her cousin Eloise King, blind and in a wheelchair, and her cousin Berthina Fagin, who'd driven down from Deland, near Daytona Beach, and Arnett's Uncle A. T., all of them backing Philomena at the hint of an uprising, which there was when Lee Carrier stood up at one end of the tent, the rest of them chewing on their food and chatting about the children, and he stopped them all in mid-bite and mid-conversation with a pronouncement.

"Do you all know what *really* happened at Rosewood?" he said, sweeping the room with his eyes as the place fell silent. "Because I *know!*"

Philomena and Eloise were on him in a second.

"Ya'll let that *alone*," hissed Eloise.

"You shut *up!*" shouted Philomena, and that was the end of it.

Arnett didn't see that showdown, but he heard about it many times over the course of the next year. When the family gathered in Deland in 1986, there were no incidents. But by the following summer, when the group, now grown to more than a hundred, came together in Gainesville, some of the second gen-eration, the children of the survivors, men and women Arnett's age, knowing Rosewood was right down the road, arranged an outing, a Sunday afternoon drive to the site itself.

The idea was appalling to Philomena. Dorothy Hosey, Arnett's aunt, a sur-vivor herself, four years old when the town was attacked, had no interest in going. Arnett's Uncle A. T. stayed behind, too, as did almost all the rest of the men, women and children, gathered at the motel where they were all staying, on the west end of the city. When a van and two cars finally pulled away that afternoon, headed for Rosewood, they carried a mere dozen people, including, surprisingly, Philomena's baby sister, Vera Hamilton.

When it came to the subject of Rosewood, Vera had always stood by Philomena. At the time of the attack she had been but an infant, not yet two years old. She had no memory of Rosewood. The night of the shootout at the Carrier house, she was with her parents at the logging camp in Otter Creek. It was not until six years later, when she was living in Tampa, that she heard a word about Rosewood. That was when she was visiting her Aunt Beauty in Lacoochee, and a cousin named Jimmy Robinson drove her and a couple of the kids up to the town where her Grandma Sarah used to live, the grandmother she had never met, who had died before Vera was born. That's all Vera had been told, that her grandmother had died.

Vera thought she was going to see a town, but when they got there, all there was was woods. They walked back to a clearing, and Cousin Jimmy showed them where their grandma's house used to be. There was nothing but ashes, and a corroded bedstead, and two washtubs, crust-orange with rust as well. There were some crepe myrtles, and it being springtime, they were blooming, pink and white. But there was no house. Just sand, hard white sand.

The place had burned down, that's all Vera knew. That's all Jimmy said. It wasn't until seven years later that Vera was finally told about the massacre. She was a mother by then, with a two-year-old daughter named Juanita. Vera had left school when Juanita was born, still a child herself at fourteen, and Philomena took her in, gave Vera a bed in her home in Lacoochee, where, for the next fifty years, through three husbands, two children, five grandchildren and one great-grandchild, Vera stayed, working for ten of those years at the Pasco Packing plant down in Dade City, the largest citrus packing plant in the world.

Pasco. The company had started out picking and packing whole oranges and grapefruits during the Depression, shipping crates of tissue-wrapped fruit to buyers up north. But soon it shifted focus, finding its niche at the start of the war in sectionized fruit and canned juice, selling millions of khaki-colored containers of orange juice to the military, including the Air Force, which believed the vitamin C helped its fliers' vision during night missions.

It was just before the war that Vera went to work for Pasco, rising each morning at dawn to meet one of the dozens of schoolbuses sent out from the plant into the surrounding countryside to pick up the workers, fifteen hundred workers a day by the mid-'40s. Vera would arrive on her assembly line at seven A.M., walk past the plant manager's office, where a framed motto hung on the wall—*A Quick Nickel Beats a Slow Dime*—and she would spend the next eight hours standing by a conveyor belt peeling grapefruits, seven grapefruits to a tray, fifteen cents a tray.

On a good day she could do a hundred trays, but it was hard. The hot fruit, steamed to make it peel easier, burned her hands as she picked it up. The juice soaked her skin, stinging and swelling her fingers as the acid seeped into the nicks and cuts made by her slicing knife. Her shoulders ached, her feet, wrapped in plastic, ankle deep in sloshing liquid, went numb from cold in the winter. Sweat burned her eyes in the suffocating heat of summer. There were fifty women on the line alongside her, six more lines ahead of them and six be-hind, the building as big as a gymnasium, the fruit rolling past from dawn to dusk, another shift ready to come on when that shift was done, grapefruits by the millions, peeled, sectioned and canned around the clock.

Vera spent a decade at Pasco before she left to get married. For a time, she ran a "jook"—a juke joint, a private club—out of her house over by the railroad tracks, just up the road from where Philomena and her husband and kids, Ar-nett and Yvonne, lived. Vera had the best blues and jazz in town on her juke-box, Erskine Hawkins, Louis Jordan, Lionel Hampton; she even had a couple of country records in that box, "Mule Train" by Frankie Laine. "Something to suit everybody and something to suit me, too," that's what she used to say. Vera served good homecooked food along with the liquor, and she enjoyed it all, the music, the laughter, the dancing, even the trouble her husband and some of the fellows had to break up when the hour got late and the words and the fists would start flying.

Her "shop," that's what Vera called the place. She could have stayed there forever, but she and her husband had to tear it down in the early '50s, needed the lumber to build a bigger house, and so Vera left the bar business and went to work for a family on the white side of town, cleaning and ironing, stirring feed for the chickens, and gathering eggs. She did that for ten years, switched to another family for another ten, then closed out her working days at the Holi-day Inn over by the new interstate west of town, where she cleaned rooms until she retired in 1983.

That was the year the "60 Minutes" show came on about Rosewood, and Vera was beside herself when she saw it. She didn't understand why she was so upset, sobbing the way she did that night. She wasn't there when it happened, never even knew her Grandma Sarah. But she did have a photograph hanging on the wall right above her television set, an old-fashioned tintype, brown and faded, of Sarah Carrier, strong and stern, seated on a chair, surrounded by her children, thirteen-year-old Sylvester standing behind her left shoulder, staring straight into the camera, and a young girl, Willie Retha—Sylvester's sister, Vera's mother, Arnett's grandmother—standing beside him.

Vera never knew her grandma and uncle, but they had always been real to her, and so had the grief she felt every time she thought of them. It was always there, all her life, the thought of what she had lost, the family she had never known, the home she had never had, the course her life had taken and how it might have been different if this hadn't happened. That's why she sided with Philomena every time the subject of Rosewood came up. She agreed there was danger in going too far with this thing, that it could do more harm than good to get into it. Because it just hurt too much.

And yet, when the families met that summer in Gainesville, something pulled Vera toward that van. Though she knew her sister would hold it against her, wouldn't understand how she could betray her, Vera climbed in, along with Lee Ruth and Lee Carrier and Eva Jenkins and Lillie Washington. And Willie Evans, who was blind in both eyes and had no way of seeing the place where the white men had run him and his grandparents out of the home in which he had spent the first sixteen years of his life.

Willie stayed in the van when they got there. He didn't explain why. It's just what he wanted to do. The others climbed out and walked slowly up the drive to the old Wright house, the big Victorian Arnett had seen both times he'd been there. A couple named Doyal and Fuji Scoggins lived in it now, retirees from down in Clearwater who had bought the place in the late '70s, who knew nothing about Rosewood or John Wright until the story surfaced in the early '80s, who tended their fruit trees and grape arbors and beehives, selling jars of honey to passing motorists.

Doyal and Fuji Scoggins were there to greet the group when it arrived, offered them iced tea, asked if they'd like to come inside and see the place. Some did. But most stayed outside, strolling around the yard, looking into the forest, *feeling* the place because that's all they could do was feel it. There was nothing left to see other than this house, nothing left of Rosewood but the swamp around them.

Vera was upset. She thought she would be able at least to see the place where her cousin had brought her nearly sixty years earlier, the spot where her Grandma Sarah's house had stood. But that had long been reclaimed by the swamp, swallowed by six decades of trees and vines and water.

Vera did go in the house to use the bathroom, but as soon as she stepped through the door and saw rifles mounted on the wall in the living room, she recoiled. All she could think was that one of those guns might have fired the bullet that killed her grandmother. It would have done no good to tell her the weapons were antiques, single-shot muskets that hadn't been fired in more than a century, part of Doyal Scoggins's collection. Vera wouldn't have heard that, and no one tried to tell her. She pushed past the others, out to the van, and soon they were all headed back to Gainesville, silent but for the sound of soft crying from the back seat, Vera's tears.

It hurt, more than any of them imagined it might. There was nothing happy or healing about that trip. It was haunting at best, horrifying at worst. But mostly it just hurt.

And that is why Arnett was met with such caution when he arrived at the following summer's reunion in Orlando in 1988 armed with dozens of packets of photocopied documents, the deeds and censuses and newspaper reports he had been collecting for five years, one packet for each family, passing them out in the motel lobby as the relatives arrived to register, asking everyone to take the papers back to their rooms, read them over, and maybe they could all talk about it later. He didn't give a packet to his mother, but someone else did. And at the picnic that afternoon she called him over, pulled out the papers and slapped him across the face.

"What the hell is *this?*" she said, shaking the sheaf in his face.

"It's something I think we should look at, Mama," he said.

"The *hell* we will," she said, and she began tearing the papers, ripping them apart until the ground around her was littered with shreds. "*Nobody* is gonna do a damn *thing* with this," she said, as her cousin Eloise rolled up in her wheelchair.

"Boy," said Eloise, her wizened face turned toward him, her small blind eyes squeezed shut, "you don't know what you're doin'. You wasn't there. You don't under*stand*. Those crackers will *hurt* you, boy, they'll hunt you down, hunt *all* of us down."

"Arnett," his mother said, her voice softened, "I want you to stop doing this."

Arnett said nothing. He didn't argue, didn't fight back. He just left, got in his car and drove home. When his mother came back the next night, he sat her down and told her there would be no more sneaking around, no more hiding.

"Mama," he said, "I can't stop now. There is no way I'll *ever* be able to stop now. I'm going to keep this all to myself as long as you're alive. I'll honor your wishes. But if God sees fit to call you before he calls me, rest assured that I'm going to pursue this with every fiber of my being."

He bent down and kissed her on the cheek.

"Once you're gone, Mama, there is no other survivor that can stop me from doing what I want to do. I'm *going* to go after it."

She heard him. She realized, finally, what this thing had come to mean to her son, that he was as driven now to bring their family's past to light as she had been to hide it. In a strange way, for the first time, she saw something of Sylvester Carrier in her boy, the defiance, the drive, the will to stand his own ground, all of it more likely, she was certain, to lead to self-destruction than to any kind of success. She wouldn't be surprised if this thing killed him just the way it killed Sylvester. But she knew there was nothing she could do. And so, at last, she surrendered, gave her boy her blessing and told the family so, told them to talk to him, answer his questions, share as much of themselves as they could and put the rest in the hands of the Lord.

The next two years were like a whirlwind, Arnett crisscrossing the state, sitting in tiny kitchens and cluttered living rooms with the old ones, the survivors, looking at photographs and letters he had never seen before, hearing stories that had been held back for generations, stories of life in Rosewood that were darker and went deeper than the safe, sanitized accounts he had heard so far. Some of the stories were sad, some were ugly, but Arnett was eager to hear them all because they were the truth, and he needed the truth. He had no idea what he might do with it, but he needed the truth.

He needed to know about the bad blood between the Carriers and the Goinses, about the feud that developed between those families long before the destruction of Rosewood. It was a rivalry rooted in race, the Goinses being a light-complected clan come to Florida from North Carolina, where their African forebears had arrived in the early nineteenth century. They had become indentured servants, mating with the local Lumbee Indians, producing a line of blue-eyed, even blonde-haired blacks, including Martine Goins, whose success and respect among the white men with whom he did business around

Levy County was earned largely by the fact that he looked like a white man himself. It was not until Martine left Rosewood, passing the turpentine business to his darker-skinned brother Ed, that the problems with their white rivals began.

The Carriers, on the other hand, were black as pitch. Their ancestors had come straight from Africa, shipped into slavery in South Carolina. Sarah Carrier had been a Robinson before she married Hayward Carrier, and her roots too went right back to bondage. She had been born a slave, a fact that apparently made her unique by the time she was a grandmother in Rosewood. Arnett's relatives told him the name they used to call Sarah when they were children, a name some used with respect and others with disdain. "Slave Woman," that's what they called her.

They were up against one another in every way, the Goinses and Carriers, competing for control of this small community. The Goinses had their turpentine business, the Carriers their logging. They went to the same churches, the men were Masons together, they even married among one another. But there was always tension among them and sometimes it burst into violence. An argument here, a fistfight there. One memorable Christmas, it came down to murder.

It was Arnett's great-uncle Charlie Goins who pulled the trigger. He was one of Ed Goins's ten children, a brother of Arnett's Grandpa George, a man known for his quick temper. George Goins had married a Carrier, Arnett's grandmother Willie Retha, and Willie Retha's cousin Elias had a problem with George Goins. He didn't like the way this man spoke to his cousin, and finally he told him so, told George Goins he would beat him if he showed disrespect for Willie Retha one more time. Charlie Goins got wind of the threat, shoved a pistol in his pocket and walked across town to the Carrier house. It was Christmas week. Elias wasn't in, they told him. He'd gone over to church, to rehearse with the choir for their Christmas pageant. So Charlie Goins walked to the church, looked through a window, saw Elias Carrier there with the rest of them, singing a hymn, and he shot him. Just like that, right through the church window, he shot him dead.

No one ever saw Charlie Goins in Rosewood again. He left that night, wanted for murder, and no one ever caught up with him. But Arnett knew he survived, because he showed up one Christmas, thirty years later, at the Doctors' house in Lacoochee. He was the lightest-skinned black man Arnett had ever seen, light enough to pass for white, which is how he had managed to get a room in the only hotel in town, a white hotel. Charlie Goins had a pocket full of money, Arnett remembered that, and he passed some out to all of them, a roll of coins each for Arnett and his sister and some paper bills for their parents. Arnett was impressed. His uncle Charlie was clearly a man who had made it. Nice clothes. Pockets of cash. Living in hotels, even ordering room service. He didn't look like a murderer.

That was the only killing Arnett heard of in Rosewood—the only one before the massacre. But he learned there were other petty crimes that occurred, arrests made and jail terms served. He learned that Sylvester Carrier himself served a prison sentence along with his father Hayward, that the two of them spent the summer of 1918 working on one of the state's notoriously brutal road gangs for stealing cattle and changing the brands, a charge the family swore was a setup by whites, another dose of bitterness to shorten Sylvester's temper and sharpen his trigger.

It was hard hearing these stories, of pettiness and anger among his own people, of jealousy and rage. But in the end Arnett found them all beautiful, because they were the truth. Now he was able to see these people, these names he had known all his life, not as myths or legends but as living, breathing human beings, and the town itself, it was no longer an imagined Eden, a place of bucolic perfection. It was real, with shadows as well as light, and that was more gorgeous than any fantasy.

It was also more gut-wrenching. By the end of 1990 Arnett was literally falling apart from the stress, his weight dropping by the week, his vision beginning to blur. He was thirsty all the time, drinking two gallons of water a day and still wanting more. He was working on Rosewood every spare minute he had, but he was working sixty, sometimes seventy hours a week with his own business as well, a janitorial service he had started soon after leaving the liquor store.

He had begun with a contract on one building and was now handling a dozen high-rises and office buildings in the Tampa Bay area. He had more than fifty people on his payroll, and he followed behind them all, staying up until two or three in the morning, checking trash baskets, cleaning toilets, filling paper towel holders, walking the stairwells to make sure the steps were swept, climbing up and down forty-floor buildings, doing the right side one night and the left the next because there were just too many steps to walk them all in one evening.

He had turned forty-seven that year, too young to even think of retiring, but some days he could barely walk anymore. His feet were already bad from the Army, and this work was only making it worse. His body was betraying him now, and he knew some of it had to do with Rosewood.

The thing was eating him up. By that summer's reunion the doctors were telling him he had to slow down, but he couldn't. These people, the survivors, they were old. Some were dying. Some were dead. Lee Carrier had passed away. Sam Hall, whom Arnett never met, he was gone. So many were gone now, with nothing to show for what they had been through, no justice, not even the simple satisfaction of acknowledgment. With each death, Arnett grew angrier. These people were *owed*. That is what it came down to. This thing had affected all their lives, steered the courses of generations, but the survivors themselves, the ones who had actually gone *through* it, they were the ones who were owed first and owed most, because they were the ones whose suffering had been greatest. And they were dying now, dying every year, dropping like leaves off a tree, taking their memories and their grace and their pain and their strength with them. And it just wasn't right. That's how Arnett felt. It just wasn't right. The unfocused rage that had always been a part of his soul now became *out*rage. Someone needed to pay for this. He had no idea who or how, but someone needed to pay.

That's what he was feeling that New Year's Eve of 1990. New Year's was always a hard time for him, its promise of renewal and hope eclipsed by the fact that this was the day it began, the massacre. And that his own birthday, January fifth, was the date Sylvester and Sarah Carrier died in a hail of bullets. Arnett sometimes felt like it was some kind of cruel joke. Other times he was convinced God had piled it all together for a purpose, these January days and all that they meant. He had no idea what that meaning might be, but before this month was over—January of 1991—he would have one more date to deal with. The day his mother died.

It was a Monday, Martin Luther King Day, and she called him that morning, asked him to come over and take her to the parade. He was too busy, he told her, he had too many contracts to check over. Next weekend, Mama, he said, I'll come over next weekend and we'll go out. She sniffed a little bit, but then she was always trying to make him feel guilty. He didn't think anymore about it, was out at one of his buildings until well after midnight, and when he got in, the light on his answering machine was blinking. He punched the button, and it was his niece Gretchen's voice—Yvonne's daughter—sobbing, saying something had happened to Grandma. The next message clicked on, and it was Gretchen again, still crying, saying she was so sorry, that Grandma was gone. And all Arnett could do was stand there and say no. No, No, No, over and over again.

He didn't cry, not yet. He got in his car and drove over, walked in the door and they were all there, Yvonne, her kids, Aunt Vera, Uncle A. T., the whole family. And Arnett came in like it was just another day, hugging everybody, asking how they were doing, seeing his sister break down in tears and telling her to take strength in Jesus, trust in God, moving toward his mother's bedroom even as he spoke, saying he had to go in there, had to see Mama, half of him knowing she was dead, the other half holding out, still believing she was alive in that room.

But she wasn't. Her body was gone. It had happened after dinner, they told him. Fried fish, that's what they'd eaten, fried fish. She'd finished her meal, gone to the bathroom for some Alka-Seltzer, and she never came out. They found her in there, on the bathroom floor. The paramedics tried to bring her back, but she was gone, dead.

It was just words now to Arnett, just noise. He hardly heard it. He closed his mother's door behind him, locked it and sat down on her bed, in the darkness, sat there all night. In the morning he went to her closet, pulled out her housecoat, put it on and sat down again.

He stayed there for four days, sitting, sleeping, rolling on the floor and screaming. They called an ambulance, but he wouldn't let them in. He spoke to the medics through the door, assured them he would not harm himself, and so they left.

Finally, the day of the burial, he came out. The church was wall to wall with people, hundreds of people, a hundred more standing outside. The relatives were there, all of them. Of course. This was a funeral. This was family.

Arnett stepped to the casket, leaned in and put his lips to his mother's, kept them there until he had to be pulled away.

They buried her under an oak, on a knoll by a pond. And when it was done, Arnett drove home, alone. There would be time later for the others, for Rosewood. But right now he needed time for himself.

PART THREE

M OVEMENT

ELEVEN

The Fire This Time

It was May of 1992, one day after a Los Angeles jury had acquitted four white policemen in the beating of Rodney King, and Michael O'McCarthy's car radio was crackling with reports of sniping and looting on the streets of L.A. He was a continent away, steering his small white Toyota into a section of Dade County called Liberty City, a bleak grid of broad streets lined with palms as tall as any in Miami but not tall enough to mask the utter poverty beneath them.

This was not a good day to be a white man in a black place anywhere in America, but that's what O'McCarthy was, hunting among this neighborhood of decaying projects, paint-flaked bungalows and sagging shotgun flats, searching for the home of a woman named Lee Ruth Davis, the address scribbled on the scrap of paper clutched in his hand.

He was surprised his hands weren't shaking. Miami had become a foul stew of racial strife during the past decade, tension among Anglos, Latinos and blacks boiling over into combat on inner-city streets, drug wars and gang battles turning backyard barbecues into drive-by death traps, the Mariel boatlift

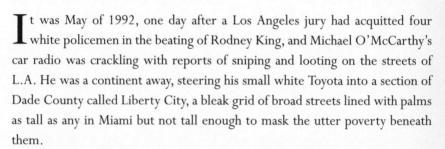

Lee Ruth Davis

upping the ante in the Cuban community, Haitians flooding in as well, facing off with the Cubans, and, always, the dead-end desperation and simmering rage in the black sections of the city, block after block of short-fused dynamite ready to blow with the slightest spark.

They had blown time and again during the previous decade, beginning with an explosion right there in Liberty City in the summer of 1980, after an all-white jury acquitted four white deputy sheriffs in the beating death of a black insurance agent, touching off three days of rioting that left sixteen dead, four hundred injured and more than one thousand residents behind bars. Smaller flareups continued through the '80s, culminating in 1989, on Martin Luther King Day, when the shooting of two black men by a white police officer set off another three days of rioting, this time on the streets of a ghetto called Overtown, to the east of Liberty City. Football fans tuning in for news from the Super Bowl, played that week in Miami, were treated to footage of flak-jacketed police squads patrolling the sidewalks of Overtown and Liberty City, searching for snipers in darkened windows.

It had been three years now since that outbreak, but as O'McCarthy hunted for Lee Ruth's house number, the L.A. updates spilling from his radio gave him every reason to expect it to happen again, here, at any minute. He saw Miami cops on every corner he passed, called out in force in case the lid blew. But they were small comfort. If the shit came down now, in this place, O'McCarthy would have no way out. No white man would.

O'McCarthy had been in situations like this before, but never when he was sober. He'd always had liquor or dope or both to lean on in the past, but now he was straight, no dimmer switch for the fear. And still he kept driving. No way was he turning back from this one. When he had called Lee Ruth the night before, introduced himself over the phone, told her he'd like to meet her, to talk about Rosewood, she said he was welcome to come on over, told him he was *more* than welcome. As a matter of fact, she said, she had been waiting her whole life for him to show up.

The fact was, O'McCarthy had been waiting his whole life for her as well. He would turn fifty that year, Lord willing, and he wanted more to show for it all, more to share with his young son, than memories of modeling gigs and unsold movie scripts, soft news tips peddled to tabloid TV shows like "Hard Copy" and "A Current Affair," the stuff of his life at the moment.

There had been a time when he felt he was at the heart of something that mattered, back in his counterculture days, when he was rubbing shoulders with the Black Panthers, going underground with the IRA, getting laid in Paris and Belfast and writing about it all in radical magazines and books, reporting from the front lines of what looked at the time like an honest-to-God revolution. But that was before the booze wore him down and turned him into a lush, just another leftover from the sad, sorry '60s, holed up in Hollywood, trying to sell his life as a movie and finding no takers, peddling himself and his stories like a carny barker until he finally gave up and came back to the South, the place he'd been running from since the day he was born.

Purebred cracker stock, that was Michael McCarthy—he didn't add the "O" until he was in his forties, marketing himself as a model and needing a gimmick to set him apart from every other McCarthy in the book. His father, an Atlantan by birth, spent the happiest years of his life, including the year Michael was born, killing Japanese in the Solomon Islands. The old man went to his deathbed forty years later, still cursing niggers and Jews. O'McCarthy's mother, born on the side of a steep wooded slope in rural Georgia, left her husband during the war and moved her kids to Miami, where she waited tables in a shrimp shop and fretted that her little boy Michael was getting too friendly with the son of the black woman who kept house for them, a boy named Aubrey. O'McCarthy would never forget the day his mother came home, found him out on the porch with Aubrey, both of them playing the same harmonica, and she snatched the thing away as if it were poison, pushed Aubrey off the porch, told him to get on home and yanked little Michael, all of four years old, into the house, where she washed out his mouth as if there were dirt in it.

He never forgot that, and he never forgave it. He grew up hating the hate he saw in his parents, and he dealt with his hate the same way his father did, by drowning it in liquor. If there was one thing he owed to his father, one legacy the old man left him, it was the bottle. Before O'McCarthy was out of his teens, he had become a drunk, just like his old man. When he was fifteen he quit school, ran away from home, got caught stealing hubcaps and wound up in the state reform school in Marianna, north of Tallahassee, where he was routinely beaten, whipped with a steel strap by "men with taut grins and white Baptist faces, hard Christian men serving the state, steeped in the doctrine of original sin and the swift application of salvation and retribution."

That's how O'McCarthy described it twenty years later, in the mid-'70s, in an essay he wrote for a book about what it was like to grow up in the Deep

South, what it did to a person, black or white. What it did to O'McCarthy was drive him as far away as he could get, clear across country to California, where, on a warm, clear night in the fall of 1962, in an alcoholic haze, with his Jamaican girlfriend asleep back in his apartment, he held up a filling station for six dollars and seventy-four cents and wound up spending the rest of the decade behind bars.

It was there, at San Quentin and Soledad, in cell blocks jammed with Mexicans and blacks, surrounded with books by Trotsky and Marx, that Michael O'McCarthy became a dyed-in-the-wool revolutionary, "the Lenin of western America," as he likes to remember himself. Or another favorite phrase: "the white Eldridge Cleaver."

He rubbed shoulders with Cleaver and Huey Newton, became pals with George Jackson and spearheaded the formation of a racially integrated prisoners' union, the first of its kind in California. He swears he survived two attempts on his life—a stabbing and a shooting—arranged by prison authorities, he has no doubt. The assassination attempts, and that's what he calls them to this day, were like a badge, earning him the respect of his black prison mates. He points with pride to the page in Jackson's collection of prison letters, *Soledad Brother*, where his name is mentioned as a white soulmate, as close to the Black Panthers as any son of the South would ever get.

O'McCarthy was out of prison by the time Jackson was gunned down on the yard at San Quentin in 1970, during an alleged escape attempt. That death only added fuel to O'McCarthy's fire and pages to a manuscript he was writing with some friends on the "police state" of America. But the book, published in 1973 under the title *The Glass House Tapes*, went nowhere, and O'McCarthy dove deeper into the bottle than he'd ever been.

Somehow he was able to keep it going for another ten years, developing documentary-style scripts on subjects ranging from the death penalty in Florida to uranium mining in Virginia, while ingesting insane amounts of cocaine, mushrooms and booze. In 1981, a year before Arnett Doctor took his drive up to Rosewood, Michael O'McCarthy's photo popped up in *Rolling Stone* magazine—bushy hair, beard, backpack and peace button—for his part in organizing a hunger strike among a group of L.A. Vietnam Vets.

But that was his last hurrah. Not long after, his string finally ran out. He was picked up for a DUI in West Hollywood and tossed in the drunk tank, the first time he'd been behind bars since emerging from prison in 1969. The shock

pushed him into AA and, finally, out of Hollywood. In 1987 he moved back to
Florida, found an apartment in Coconut Grove and cashed in on the one thing
he had left—his good Irish looks. Somehow his body had not betrayed him. He
had aged well, a little gray in the temples but that only added to the corporate
cachet his clients were looking for. Soon O'McCarthy's fortysomething face
was on TV screens and billboards all over Florida, hawking pizzas and fabric
softeners, telephone companies and banks. He even did a little stand-up com-
edy on the side. Met a flight attendant from Costa Rica, had a baby boy, and
now he was a family man.

But he couldn't shake the part of him that needed to make news. Or find
news and make it into a movie. He was still sniffing around for stories, something true-life, with a nice edge to it. Something like serial killer Aileen
Wuornos, a Florida prostitute who was arrested in January, 1991, for the murders of seven men. O'McCarthy perked up at that one, tracked down a cop
who had investigated the case, signed him to a book-and-movie deal and now
he was back in the business.

A month later, he was up in Gainesville, poking around for something on
the grisly deaths of five University of Florida undergrads. He wasn't sure what
he was after—a book, a movie, maybe a tip for one of the tabloid TV shows,
anything he could dig up. He got on the phone with a producer friend in Hollywood, told him where he was, what he was up to, and the friend asked if he'd
ever heard of a place called Rosewood, said it was right down the road if he remembered right. O'McCarthy had never heard of the place, never heard of the
story, but it sounded like it had potential. So the next morning he rented a car
and drove on down to Levy County.

It was a wet, eerie day—primordial is the way O'McCarthy recalls it. Dark
sky, a steady rain, old oaks and thick moss, all of it sodden and dripping. He
came to the sign for Rosewood, saw nothing but mud and trailers, and so he
drove on to Cedar Key. Went to the library and asked if they had anything on
the shelves about this massacre. The two librarians, both elderly women,
looked at each other, then eyed him, then hesitantly pulled out a tattered newspaper clipping, the St. Petersburg Times story from 1982.

Before O'McCarthy was halfway through it, he was on fire. This was a story
that encompassed his entire life, a parable of the breed to which he belonged,
the strain of white working-class southerners that produced his parents, a tale
of the twisted blend of religion and violence that created the Messianic Baptists

who ran that Marianna reform school. When O'McCarthy read the account of the mob ravaging Rosewood, all he could see were the faces of the men who had beaten him at that school. He saw the death of George Jackson, too, lynched on the yard at San Quentin just as surely as Sam Carter was lynched under a tree in this Gulf Florida swamp. There might have been fifty years between the two, but to O'McCarthy they were the same story, the murder without penalty of black men in America. He'd done all he could about the death of Jackson, but there was still something O'McCarthy felt he could do about this. So many things: stir up some social justice, assuage some of his family ghosts, and maybe get a movie deal in the bargain.

He called back his producer friend and was told that the story, optioned a while back by the St. Pete reporter, Gary Moore, had been shopped around L.A. for a couple of years with no luck. Everyone in town had passed on it, the producer told O'McCarthy. It was old news, they said, a period piece. By the time O'McCarthy hung up the phone, he knew he had to have some kind of modern hook, something to bridge those seventy years, to carry the story into today's world. Something like a lawsuit.

He spent the rest of that summer calling, writing and faxing every civil rights agency he could think of—the NAACP, the ACLU, the Southern Poverty Law Center, Klanwatch, Jesse Jackson's Rainbow Coalition—trying to find anyone who would take on this case, take on this cause, help him find survivors and pursue restitution. They all either turned him away or passed him along to someone else. Most had never heard of Rosewood. The few who had said there was nothing to be done, not now.

"Your objectives are laudable," the NAACP's national deputy executive director wrote O'McCarthy that October, "and we believe the truth should be pursued. Unfortunately, our limited resources both in financial and staff terms rule out our active participation."

He called Moore as well, who was then living in Seattle. O'McCarthy described his idea for a film, built around current-day courtroom testimony of aged Rosewood survivors. Moore backed off, telling O'McCarthy no such testimony had ever occurred. Moore was interested in fact, not fiction.

So O'McCarthy was left with nothing but names, the names he'd read in Moore's story. He had no faces, no flesh and blood, no survivors. He had no addresses, no phone numbers; Moore wasn't about to share that information, though O'McCarthy did his best to pull it out of him.

A year came and went, and O'McCarthy kept modeling, kept developing movie deals, kept passing tips to the tabloids and kept trying to track down one living person connected to Rosewood. Finally, that summer, after all the long-distance phone calls and faxes, he found what he was looking for in his own backyard, there in the Miami telephone directory—Lee Ruth Bradley Davis, of Liberty City.

And so, on this bright morning in May, as Los Angeles burned, Michael O'McCarthy pulled up to a faded green cinderblock house, parked his Toyota at the curb, and walked in to see if Lee Ruth Davis was ready to make a deal.

TWELVE

Eat What You Kill

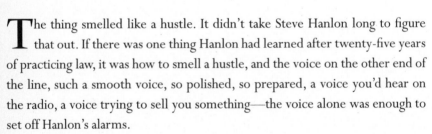

The thing smelled like a hustle. It didn't take Steve Hanlon long to figure that out. If there was one thing Hanlon had learned after twenty-five years of practicing law, it was how to smell a hustle, and the voice on the other end of the line, such a smooth voice, so polished, so prepared, a voice you'd hear on the radio, a voice trying to sell you something—the voice alone was enough to set off Hanlon's alarms.

And then there was the man's name. O'McCarthy. Now why in hell would someone stick an "O" on a good Irish name like that, hang it out there like a stolen hood ornament? Hanlon was Irish himself, a "recovering Catholic," as he liked to put it, and if he had a nose for hustlers, well, he had an even better nose for Irish hustlers. It didn't surprise him one bit when this man said he was in the movie business. Of *course* he was in the movie business.

Still, the guy could tell a story. Hanlon had to give him that. He could tell a story, and that's what kept Hanlon from simply hanging up.

On the face of it, the tale was preposterous. Two women, elderly, poor, black, the sole survivors of a town that was wiped off the map seventy years

Rosewood, January, 1923

ago, and now they wanted to bring a lawsuit against the state of Florida, a lifetime after the fact. Preposterous. But then that was Hanlon's job, to pursue the
preposterous. That's why the largest law firm in the state had hired him, put
him in charge of its new pro bono division, set him up in a swank suite in its
Tallahassee high-rise headquarters and given him carte blanche to call on any of
the firm's four hundred attorneys for some free, non-billable hours. Go out and
represent the poor, he was told when he was hired. Go out and represent the
preposterous.

    And so he had. In the three years since he had joined the hallowed Florida
law firm of Holland and Knight, he and his colleagues—they called themselves
the Community Services Team—had tackled almost two dozen cases, ranging
from civil rights transgressions to consumer fraud. With Hanlon at its helm,
the team had filed a class action suit on behalf of several hundred low-income
women in the Tampa area who had unwittingly signed a form during their
pregnancies allowing doctors from the University of South Florida to perform
medical experiments on their high-risk fetuses. Hanlon's group had filed a
housing discrimination suit against a Miami apartment complex that had
turned away thousands of prospective black tenants over the course of the
1980s. It had filed a civil suit on behalf of a lesbian couple who had become foster parents to a six-year-old boy only to see the boy removed from their home
by state authorities after it was revealed they were gay.

    These were David and Goliath cases, the huddled masses versus the powers
that be, high-profile battles guaranteed to make headlines if not money, and either one was fine with Hanlon. By the time he arrived at Holland and Knight,
he had made plenty of both.

    The headlines had come first, back in the mid-'70s, when he moved south
from his home town of St. Louis to join the staff of a nonprofit legal services
team in Tampa, representing the underprivileged of that community. He was
paid twelve thousand dollars a year, a salary his law school classmates would
have laughed at, but he was making a reputation as well, as a gladiator for the
underprivileged. Rent disputes, food stamp cutoffs, tenant complaints, migrant worker rights—whatever walked in the door, Hanlon took it, and those
being the Carter years, the glory years of legal services, there was plenty walking in the door.

    But Hanlon and his partner, a fellow named Robert Shapiro, weren't con-
tent to just take what came to them. They were out to stir the pot themselves.

Each morning they'd open their small rented office there on the east side of the city, across the street from a bar, with spent bullet casings from the night before sprinkled on the sidewalk outside, and they'd look out their window toward the distant skyline of downtown Tampa, turn to each other and ask, "Who should we go after today?"

They went after them all. They took on church and state. They battled the bishop of the Roman Catholic diocese of St. Petersburg over back pay for a former nun. They forced a local school system to allow a teenage girl to play football with the boys. They represented a woman whose charges of sexual harassment against a community college president eventually led to the man's dismissal. All those cases were covered by local and state newspapers and television, of course, and when Hanlon stepped into the arena of racial issues, challenging Florida's functional literacy test as being culturally biased against black students, he was given a national stage, arguing his case against "funky lit"—as the black kids called it—on "Nightline" and the "Donahue" show, as well as in front of the U.S. District Court in Tampa, which handed down a four-year injunction against the test while a new one was devised.

This was heady stuff, the kind of law Hanlon had imagined practicing when he was fresh out of the University of Missouri Law School in the late '60s, he and his wife camped in a small St. Louis apartment, the two of them young and poor and happy, surrounded by neighbors just like themselves, Jewish couples, Italian couples, black couples, all of them fresh and full of faith, talking politics and the war late into the night over potluck dinners and bottles of cheap wine, gorging themselves on *The Greening of America* and *The Making of the Counterculture*, quoting Baldwin and the Berrigan brothers, believing they were all going to go out and make a difference, that every one of them would make some change for the better in the dominant culture.

The dominant culture. Hanlon adored that phrase from the moment he first heard it. He was still using it long after he had become part of that culture himself, after he left his little office in Tampa to join the corporate world. It was the looming specter of his kids' college years that did it, he says, prompting him to set social justice aside and start earning a serious salary. It was a tough decision, he says, but his daughter had her heart set on Yale, his oldest son on Swarthmore, and there was no way he could afford that on the thirty grand a year he was making in Tampa at the time. So in 1980 he shaved his beard, left legal services, signed on with a large corporate firm and stepped into the world of lean, mean billing machines, where a man eats what he kills.

Hanlon ate plenty. He spent the rest of that decade "rearranging the assets of the upper class," as he puts it, and watching his own income swell to three hundred thousand dollars a year. By the time his two kids had gotten their diplomas, and the third was about to get his, Hanlon was deep inside the belly of the corporate beast. And he was miserable. Not miserable enough, however, to go back to making a tenth of the salary he was now earning.

It was a quandary, comfort calling from one side and conscience nagging from the other. Hanlon had always said there was no thrill in life like walking to the courthouse with a poor person. He had shared that quote with more newspaper reporters than he could count, shared it so often it began to sound canned. But he meant it, he really did. He needed that feeling, just as much as he needed his six-figure salary. He wanted to have it both ways, and eventually he figured out how. In 1989 a couple of lawyers with Holland and Knight, knowing Hanlon's sense of social commitment, approached him about running for office. He laughed. Politicians spend more time raising money to keep their seats than making real changes, he said. But he countered with an idea of his own. Pro bono, he said. Let's talk about pro bono.

The legal profession has long considered pro bono work—from the Latin *pro bono publico*, meaning "for the public good"—as part of its social duty, giving a voice to those who would otherwise have none. Not all lawyers buy into the notion, by any means. Traditionally, most law firms have always left it up to the attorneys themselves to volunteer whatever hours, if any, they would like to work for causes in the community. A few firms, however, have long required their attorneys to participate in a measured, accountable, obligatory pro bono program. Hanlon's idea was to turn Holland and Knight into one of those firms.

The firm, chaired by a former American Bar Association president named Chesterfield Smith, a maverick of sorts who made a name for himself in 1974 by publicly calling for Richard Nixon to resign, considered Hanlon's suggestion. Holland and Knight, whose clients included most of the largest corporate interests in the state of Florida, surprised Hanlon by agreeing to create a division that would likely wind up turning many of those clients into defendants. By the following year, the Community Services Team had been created, with Steve Hanlon as its quarterback—its well-paid quarterback.

He brought the same game plan to Tallahassee that he had used in Tampa, a laid-back, what-me-worry demeanor comfortably cloaking a strategic, calculating mind. His weary, heavy-lidded eyes, his unruly salt-and-pepper hair—more salt than pepper—his unknotted neckties and wrinkled shirts, his loafered feet propped on his cluttered desk, a framed portrait of Sir Thomas More gazing down from the wall behind him—a gift from the nun he represented in that back pay dispute—all of it was meant to disarm the most skeptical onlooker.

And almost always, it worked. Hanlon knew how to play an audience, be it a jury or a television camera, and he understood how thin the line between the two had become. He constantly referred to the "court of public opinion," where the outcry of newspaper readers and TV viewers on an issue could affect judges and politicians just as much as any attorney's well-reasoned argument. Hanlon had turned to that court more than once in his career. That's what all those headlines had been about. That's why he went on "Nightline" and "Donahue."

And that's why he was willing to hear this O'McCarthy character out. So what if the guy had an angle? Everybody has an angle. All Hanlon cared about was the question of whether this was the kind of case he wanted to take. It sounded crazy, which he liked. It sounded implausible, which was true of almost every case he represented. It sounded like it couldn't possibly be true. But there was only one way to find that out.

He buzzed his secretary and asked her to book a flight to Miami.

Tiny Island

$\mathbf{A}$ rnett Doctor felt lost, dead in the water. It was May of 1992, more than a year since he had buried his mother, and months since he had finished mourning and begun throwing himself headlong into Rosewood, into *doing* something about this thing.

But nothing was happening, nothing was moving. He had called or written every black attorney he knew of in the state of Florida. Tampa, St. Pete, Orlando, Miami, even Atlanta—he'd gone to them all, sat in their waiting rooms, his briefcase perched on his lap, watching the doors open and close, people coming and going, shadows crawling across the carpet, until finally a secretary would emerge and tell him he'd have to try another time, that Mr. Jones or Ms. Williams was just too busy to fit him in today.

They were all too busy, even the ones who saw him, who listened to his story and looked politely at the papers he pulled from his case. They nodded with interest, agreed how awful this was, but they all wound up saying the same thing. They had no time for it, and time was money, and Arnett had no money,

Arnett Doctor

so, well, they hoped he understood: It was very nice meeting him, they would say, and they would wish him the best of luck as they showed him to the door.

Arnett could not understand it. These were black people, his people. The Rosewood story was *their* story. That was how he saw it. He had no doubt when he began looking for a lawyer that they'd be lining up to take this case. Righteousness. Outrage. Injustice. The eternal themes of the black man in America, they were all there, right in his briefcase. How could anyone turn away from that?

But they did. Most didn't even bother to take a look. Business, they told him. This was about business, and that meant money, in this case at least fifty thousand dollars up front, for a retainer. That's the number he kept hearing. Fifty thousand dollars. Arnett had twelve thousand to his name, his entire life savings, all he had to live on now that he wasn't working anymore.

He had left his job in October, when the doctors told him he had a choice: He could quit working or die. The circulation was gone in his feet. His legs were shot. He could hardly haul himself up the steps of his own house anymore, much less climb the stairs of those skyscrapers. His strength was sapped, and his weight was dropping like the autumn temperatures outside. By Christmas his body had shrunk from 230 pounds to 170. He was so weak he could barely pull himself out of bed. He could hardly even breathe anymore.

Grief. That had to be part of it, he figured. The madness he'd gone through with his mother's death had given way to an emptiness that lasted for months, a kind of walking coma. From that January of 1991 through the spring and on into the summer, he did nothing, saw no one, left his business to his employees and went off alone, north of the city about twenty minutes, to a little fishing spot on a creek off the Hillsborough River, a quiet place he'd been escaping to for years, whenever he needed to be alone.

Now he went there for days at a time, set himself up on an empty dock, tossed out his line, leaned back and watched the wildlife go past. Turtles and egrets. Deer and wild hogs. And gators, lots of gators. Sometimes he'd grunt those gators up, just the way his Uncle Ernest had taught him back in Lacoochee. He'd make a high-pitched, screechy sound, the sound of a baby alligator in distress, and the grown females would rise up from the river bottom, swim straight toward that sound like a fish to bait.

Grunting gators. For Uncle Ernest, it had been a way of catching dinner. He'd skin the creatures, chop up that meat, sprinkle it with salt, pepper, a little vinegar, slice up some onions, garlic, cloves, a few tomatoes, wrap the whole thing in aluminum foil and bake it in the oven. That was some of the best eating Arnett ever tasted, though food was the last thing on his mind as he sat on the dock that spring. All he wanted was to watch those animals. There was something soothing about them, the way they slid through the water.

But the monkey, that was something else again. There was nothing soothing about the monkey.

Arnett had heard about the monkey long before he actually saw it. A park ranger had told him about it. There was a small wooded island out in the river, about twenty-five yards offshore, and one day the ranger happened by, pointed at the island, and told Arnett an ape lived out there, a chimpanzee of some sort. Right, said Arnett. The ranger shrugged, left, and Arnett went back to baiting his line.

A few weeks passed, and one morning Arnett was sitting out on the dock's edge, nearly asleep, when he heard a commotion in the treetops out on that island, a violent heaving among the branches. And then he saw it, hanging among the cypress and myrtles and weeping willows, leaping from limb to limb. A monkey, small, maybe two feet tall. It couldn't have weighed more than twenty, maybe thirty pounds, but it was shaking the trees like something twice that size. It was going berserk.

Arnett couldn't imagine where it came from. The zoo, maybe. Maybe the circus. How it got onto that island was anyone's guess, but it soon became clear how badly the thing wanted to get off. Arnett began looking for it every time he came out to fish, and sooner or later it would always appear. There was a tide to the river, and when it was low, the monkey would climb down from the trees and creep out across the mud, tiptoeing toward the edge of the water on all fours, as if it were looking for some way to get across, to reach the shore. But there was no way. And the tide would rise. And the monkey would retreat from the riverbank, back into the trees, back to life on its tiny island.

That was the way the summer went, Arnett spending his days by that creek and his nights at home, in his small pale blue bungalow, with its fruit trees—plums and papayas, bananas and oranges—shielding it against the surrounding squalor, the decayed trailer park a block down the lane, the half-naked Hispanic kids playing in mud puddles in the street out front, the pawn shops and prostitutes and pink rent-by-the-hour motels over on Hillsborough Avenue, where the Saturday night shouts and gunshots were loud enough to keep Arnett awake, the Cuban flea markets and sandwich shops selling their *empanadillas* and *alcapuras* in the shadows of billboards pointing the way up the interstate to Busch Gardens, or down to the dog track, or out to the new gambling casinos at the Seminole Reservation.

Arnett would shut all that out, blockade himself in his tiny office, no bigger than a closet, pull the shades, turn his TV up and pick through the piles of papers he had amassed on Rosewood. Mountains of paper, hundreds of pages of notes, interviews, records, charts, old newspaper clippings, everything that remotely had anything to do with what happened to his people. Sometimes he'd fall asleep right there in that room, in that chair, with those papers all over his lap.

Another reunion was approaching, down at Deland this time, and Arnett wasn't sure he even wanted to go. His mother's death had taken so much out of him, and so many others were dying now, too. They'd lost eleven family members since the summer before, including a couple of survivors. Leroy Smith, from Tampa, one of the oldest—he was eighteen years old when the attack happened—Leroy had passed away that year from a brain tumor. And Eloise King, Philomena's right hand, she had just died that very week. In fact, they were going to bury her the following Wednesday, three days before the reunion, right there in Deland.

That was the reason Arnett finally decided to go, because of Eloise's funeral. And after they put her in the ground, he did what he'd done just about every day lately, grabbed his tackle box and poles and went off to do some fishing. The family could use some extra food for the weekend, and he'd heard there was a nice spot just up the road, on the St. Johns River, where a man could catch more fish than he could carry. Bluegill, shell cracker, speckled perch, all good eating, great on the grill. His cousin Albert Edwards saw Arnett loading the trunk, asked if he could come along, and so they both went.

Albert was a big man, bigger than Arnett, about the same age, with a bad shoulder that left his right arm hanging limp at his side. His father was Earl Edwards, another Rosewood survivor who had passed away. Arnett had never met Albert until the family's 1986 reunion. There was no mention of Rosewood at that gathering, and now, as they pushed their boat out into the river, settled back and began baiting their poles, Arnett was shocked to discover Albert knew nothing at all about the massacre. Here it was, the summer of 1991, and this man, a direct descendant, knew nothing at all.

"You're kidding me," said Albert when Arnett mentioned that he was thinking of finding the family a lawyer. "You mean these reunions we been having are because we were all chased *out* of that place?"

"They killed us, man," said Arnett. "They came in and killed our people, burned the houses down, took our land and refused to give it back."

Albert's face was flushed.

"*All* our people?" he asked.

"Yes," said Arnett. "Your father, too. Your father and his family had to leave their land."

"My family owned land in Rosewood?"

"Five and a half acres," said Arnett. By then he had memorized every name and number on those pages of property records stacked back in his house.

Albert had never heard of any land owned in Rosewood. He'd never heard of the massacre. His father, like so many others, had mentioned the place only as the town he came from, nothing more. Not until this moment did Albert realize there was more to these reunions than spare ribs and cole slaw.

"Those crackers," Albert said, staring at the water and shaking his head. "Those goddamned crackers."

"Yeah," said Arnett, "but I think there's something we can do about it."

"Go get some *guns* is what we can do about it," said Albert.

"No," said Arnett. "I'm thinking about a lawsuit. A class-action lawsuit." Arnett paused, tugged on his line. "If we did sue," he asked, "how much you think we should ask for?"

"I don't know," shrugged Albert. "Millions, probably."

"I don't think so," said Arnett, smiling now. "I'm thinking more like billions."

"*Billions?*" Albert snapped back his neck. "Are you serious?"

"Hey," said Arnett, "have you ever heard of the Japanese-American Reparation Act? Just a couple of years ago. They gave those people twenty thousand dollars each, a billion and a half dollars in all. A billion and a *half.* And all they did was intern those people, put 'em in prison camps. They *killed* us, man. They eradicated us, burned our property, terrorized us, took our land, took away our whole *livelihood*. That's got to be worth at least a hundred times more than what they gave those Japanese."

Arnett paused, gazed at the ripples around his fishing line.

"I think five billion would be more like it."

"Five billion?" said Albert. "At that rate, everybody in this family would be a millionaire."

"So?" said Arnett. "That's the idea, to break the whole cycle of poverty in our entire family, the cycle that goes straight back to Rosewood."

Now it was Albert studying the ripples.

"If I'm not mistaken," he said, "we'd have to go through some white people to get anything out of this."

"That's right," said Arnett.

"Uh huh," said Albert, giving his reel a spin. "I can see trouble down the line any way this thing goes."

And that was it. The fish began biting, and the men stopped talking. They came back with a cooler full of bass and bluegill, and everyone ate well that weekend. Arnett didn't mention the lawsuit, not yet. But he wasn't surprised when Albert pulled him aside on Sunday, as everyone was saying their good-byes, and told him he was going out and buying himself a rifle. "Just in case there comes a time I might need it," he said.

And so that summer and fall came and went. By the winter, even with his body falling apart, Arnett had begun looking for a lawyer. His weight loss and weakness kept getting worse, and now he figured it was the stress added to the grief that was doing him in. He hated hospitals, had never trusted a doctor since the time he was a soldier. He had always blamed those Army doctors for letting his feet go so bad in boot camp. But now, as Christmas turned to New Year's, he couldn't even get out to take care of his yard.

Finally, one afternoon in early January, on the verge of fainting, he had a friend drive him to the hospital, where they pricked his finger, checked his blood sugar level, read the result and rushed him straight into the emergency room, put an IV needle into his left wrist and the thing popped back out like a bullet, his blood pressure was so high. He wouldn't know it until a day later, when he woke up in a hospital bed, but Arnett had gone into diabetic shock.

He should have known. Lying there in that hospital bed, he thought about his mother and her diabetes. Uncle A. T. had it. Aunt Vera, too. Come to think of it, almost all the old folks at the Rosewood reunions had diabetes, every one of those families. *That* was their legacy, Arnett smiled to himself. That was something they'd been allowed to keep.

So now he had insulin to carry him through his days, and his days became better. He had the energy to write letters and make phone calls, to drive to those lawyers' offices. He was eager, hopeful, certain his story would light a fire under the first attorney who heard it.

But January turned to February, and February to March. Winter turned to spring, and the doors kept closing. And now it was May, 1992, and Arnett felt the way he'd felt the summer before, dragging himself home each night to that back room and those piles of papers. And those kids out on the street. And the gunshots from over on the Avenue, everything the same as it ever was. And he felt lost. Dead in the water.

FOURTEEN

Original Sin

By the time Steve Hanlon returned from Miami after spending a day with Lee Ruth Davis, and from Jacksonville, where Davis sent him on to see her cousin, Minnie Lee Langley, he was pumped. These two women and the story they shared represented everything Hanlon liked to think he believed in, both about himself and his profession.

He always told people there were two ways in which he ultimately measured every case he took. One was what he called its "wonderfulness scale"—how inspiring, noble, dramatic, even romantic a situation and its circumstances were. And the other was its "impossibility index"—the odds against winning the case, which, being a man who relished a challenge, Hanlon preferred to be high, very high. These two graceful, elderly women with their mixture of beautiful and horrific recollections of this vanished village were off the chart on both counts.

Hanlon had always been a self-confessed bleeding-heart liberal, embracing that label like a badge of honor in a time and a profession where it had become an object of ridicule. Issues of race had always been close to his heart, even

Walter H. Pillsbury

though he was raised in a suburban, middle-class world as white as milk, a world of cul-de-sacs and country clubs, of Catholic nuns and Jesuit priests, a world where he and his buddies would choose up sides for pickup baseball games by counting, "Eeny, meeny, miney, moe, catch a nigger by the toe," and none of them even knew what a nigger was. Hanlon's father, a prestigious St. Louis attorney and a liberal Democrat, applauded the Supreme Court's *Brown v. Board of Education* decision the day it was passed in 1954, to the chagrin of his Republican clients and friends, yet he continued to use the phrase "a nigger in the woodpile," and meant no harm by it.

Young Steve Hanlon had no idea what that expression meant. He was thirteen at the time, and the only black person he had ever met was his grandmother's maid, Mildred. He never even knew her last name. Holidays he would sit in his grandmother's kitchen with Mildred and listen with fascination as she talked about her family, about how her daughter was studying to be a nurse. He'd watch how Mildred swelled with pride when she talked about her girl and it would make him swell with pride, too. There were marches and protests going on all over the country by then, demonstrations for civil rights, a bus boycott in Montgomery, Martin Luther King making newspaper headlines. But Mildred didn't talk about any of that, not there in that kitchen, nor in Hanlon's family car when he grew old enough to drive it and would often carry Mildred home to her apartment in a black section of the city Hanlon had never seen before.

That was when he began to think about race. He and his buddies, their hair slicked back in ducktails just like James Dean's, would listen to black music on the radio—Chuck Berry, Jackie Wilson, the Isley Brothers—and they'd talk about how unfair it was that you had to hunt so hard to find those songs in the record stores and then you'd turn around and see some white guy doing a lame imitation of the same stuff and his watered-down sound would be everywhere. It just didn't seem right.

By the time Hanlon had finished high school and gone on to spend a year in the seminary, he had formed a personal philosophy about racism in America. To him it seemed much like original sin—an apt analogy for a former altar boy. White people in America, he believed, would never escape the taint of their treatment of blacks during the first two centuries of this nation's history. It was a sad, sorry fact that could neither be changed nor denied. It could only be acknowledged, with amends made whenever possible.

Hanlon carried that conviction with him into college, where he and his classmates at St. Louis University would take weekend excursions across the river into East St. Louis, sampling the delights of that city's Harlemlike Saturday night scene. His racial sensitivities were further galvanized in law school, where his favorite professor was an outspoken liberal who had actually had a cross burned on his lawn back when he was teaching at the University of Mississippi. By the time Hanlon emerged from law school in the spring of 1966, his heart was set on doing wonderful, impossible things, and he vowed that some of those things would involve racial justice.

He learned a lot during his legal services stint in Tampa during the 1970s, both about black culture and about the most effective ways to take racial cases through the legal system. He continued handling a few civil rights cases even while practicing commercial litigation in the '80s, and what he saw during that time was the increasing uselessness of federal courts for rich and poor people alike. As far as he could see, the field of commercial disputes had evolved into six-year paper wars in which only the lawyers came out ahead. Everyone else, plaintiffs and defendants alike, were simply financing the furniture and artwork in the attorneys' offices. That, figured Hanlon, was why, by the end of the decade, there was already a movement away from the courtroom, toward mediation and arbitration.

As for poor people, the thrill of walking toward the courthouse doors had been dampened by the fact that now, when those doors were reached, they were almost impossible to pry open. The federal court system had been dramatically altered during the decade, first by Ronald Reagan, then by George Bush. By 1990, the federal benches were filled with phalanxes of judges who were white, conservative, and male—three strikes against Hanlon's clients. Blacks. Females. The elderly. The disabled. AIDS patients. These were the people Hanlon represented, and it became rapidly, painfully apparent to him that they were simply not wanted in those courtrooms. He was facing barrages of pretrial hindrances now that he had never encountered before—federal preemption, the abstention doctrine, webs of technicalities and piles of paperwork that made actually getting a case onto the courtroom floor almost anticlimactic.

And so, by the time he came to Holland and Knight, he was looking for alternative arenas for his civil rights cases. One was the state courts, where he had more control over the agenda. Another was the state legislature.

He considered both options as he mulled the story these two women had told him. Their details differed, as did the specifics in the old newspaper clippings O'McCarthy had shared with him. But the basic, essential facts were clear. A town had been burned, people had been killed, the government knew about it and did nothing to stop it, and that's just not supposed to happen in America. To Hanlon it was that simple. *All those in favor of burning towns, raise your hands. All those against . . .*

Simple. Everything else was just details, tangential material, mere static. The fogginess of the facts—exactly how many people lived in this town, how many homes were there, how many businesses, how much land, who owned what, who lost what, how many people were killed—those were for the journalists and historians to sort out. The essential facts were clear, and these two women, the only survivors left, were living witnesses to those facts—powerful, compelling, heart-wrenching witnesses. Hanlon's favorite kind.

As for Michael O'McCarthy and his movie deal, that meant nothing to Hanlon. O'McCarthy had both Lee Ruth's and Minnie Lee's signatures on contracts for the film rights to their stories, signed for a thousand dollars each, and that was fine with Hanlon. Let this guy go and make his movie. All that mattered to Hanlon was making a case, and he had a pretty good idea which direction he would take this one. If there was ever a situation made for the court of public opinion, this was it, and there was no forum more sensitive, more *answerable*, to public opinion than the legislature.

The Florida House of Representatives and the Florida Senate, they would be both the target and the arena. A claims bill filed against the state of Florida itself, for damages done to these two women, these two American citizens, seventy years ago—that's how Steve Hanlon shaped the case as he began drafting a memo that summer of 1992 to send around to his colleagues. The first step would be finding a sponsor for the bill, a champion, a man or woman willing to carry a cause layered with controversy into the political thicket of a southern state legislature. And there was no mistake about that. This was, as ever, even at the tail end of the twentieth century, the South, with all the pride and pain, stain and shame, hope and hurt that that implied, especially when it came to matters of race.

Wonderful. Impossible. Steve Hanlon was pumped.

FIFTEEN

A Delicate Dance

On the face of it, it would have been hard to find two men on the planet more unalike than Miguel De Grandy and Al Lawson. One was Cuban-American, born in Havana, raised in Miami, urbane and even-keeled, respected by friends and foes alike, a compact presence at five-foot-eleven inches, and a Republican. The other was African-American, with rural roots, from a panhandle farm family, a fiery man, outspoken and quick-tempered, courting controversy at every turn, a looming giant at six-foot-eight, and a Democrat. There were no two more improbable allies to be found on the floor of the Florida legislature, but Steve Hanlon needed them both. If the Rosewood claims bill he had in mind was to become anything more than a notion, these two men would have to make it so.

There were reasons Hanlon believed they could. Despite their differences, both were members of a minority, politically as well as racially. On the crowded floor of the Tallahassee statehouse, the black and Cuban-American caucuses were little more than upstart seedlings among the implanted, overwhelming forest of their non-Hispanic white colleagues. Both De Grandy and

Miguel De Grandy and Al Lawson

Lawson knew what it was to be outsiders. They also understand dispossession. De Grandy's family had lost all they owned when Castro took power in Cuba. Lawson's family, with its roots in slavery, owned little to begin with. If these men could not relate to what happened at Rosewood, no one could—which was what Steve Hanlon was counting on when he contacted them both in the fall of 1992.

Hanlon knew he had no hope if this bill were presented as strictly an African-American issue. The Florida legislature was too thick with born-and-bred good old boys, North Florida lawyers and Big Bend businessmen who proudly referred to themselves as crackers with neither shame nor apology. To ask them to pay for the sins of their fathers, to compensate a pair of elderly black women for damages done seventy years in the past, was like asking them to turn their backs on those Confederate flags flapping outside their county courthouses. Hanlon knew he needed to broaden the issue, to pull in moderate Democrats and even Republicans with concerns that went beyond mere moral obligation, and he knew he could do it with the Cuban-Americans by plucking that chord of dispossession, of people run out of their homes and off their land, losing everything they owned, including their sense of place, of belonging.

That was the story of almost every Cuban-American family in Florida, and that was why almost every one of them had voted Republican for the past thirty years, ever since the aborted invasion of the Bay of Pigs, when John Kennedy's scheme to retake the Cuban expatriates' homeland unraveled into a laughable travesty. Kennedy had destroyed their hopes, let them down, and they never forgave him. Kennedy was a Democrat, and so, for that reason alone, from 1961 onward, almost every Cuban in Florida could be counted on to vote Republican.

Miguel De Grandy's parents certainly did. Theirs had been one of the more fabled families on the island, a clan of stage stars—singers, dancers, actors. De Grandy's grandmother was known as the Shirley Temple of Cuba, the island's most famous child actress in the 1920s. His grandfather was a tenor featured on opera stages across Latin America. His mother was a soprano and, when television arrived, she became a staple on variety shows and Spanish soap operas. De Grandy's father, also an actor, was a favorite among the Cuban-Jewish community—"Jubans," they were called—for his role as Tevye in Spanish versions of *Fiddler on the Roof.*

Miguel was born one month before Fidel Castro took power in 1959. His family fled to Mexico, where they became thespian gypsies, traveling by bus from town to town, staging comedies, dramas, musicals, whatever could pull in a crowd and a check. In 1963 they moved to Miami, where Miguel grew up among a transplanted Cuban middle-class community that would transform the face of southeast Florida, both economically and politically. By the time he graduated from law school in 1981, a year after the Mariel boatlift, he was among the generation of "Yucas"—Young Urban Cuban-Americans—who were replacing their parents not as adjuncts to American society, but as Americans through and through, here to stay, to make it in this country on this country's terms.

De Grandy's first job was as a prosecutor in the Dade County state attorney's office, one of a hundred and fifty young lawyers working for a hard-driving boss named Janet Reno. Seven years later, at the age of twenty-nine, he made his first run for political office, campaigning against a fellow Cuban-American for a state House seat. When all eight thousand votes were counted in that election, the two men were tied. A recount gave the seat to De Grandy's opponent—by one vote. That story was front-page news across the state, as was De Grandy's election a year later, in 1989, when Florida's fabled U.S. Senator Claude Pepper died and a state legislator ran for his open seat in Washington, opening a seat in Tallahassee, which De Grandy filled.

He arrived as one of a mere seven Cuban-Americans on the floor of the Florida House of Representatives, and like his Hispanic colleagues, though Republican by party, he was far from conservative, especially on social issues. Hispanic rights were of course his priority, but he also sponsored a bill for homeless assistance in Dade County; he pushed an environmental amendment that killed plans to build a jetport near the Everglades; and, in probably his most visible act, he sponsored a bill to allow breast-feeding in public. That got him national headlines, as well as a tour on the talk show circuit.

So he and Steve Hanlon had at least one thing in common—they had both been on "Donahue." They also both knew how to use the press. By the time Hanlon called him in the fall of 1992 about Rosewood, De Grandy was chairman of the Cuban-American caucus, savvy enough to understand exactly why this attorney was approaching him to help sponsor a bill aimed at black people, and skeptical that such a piece of legislation stood more than a snowball's chance in hell of passage.

But he went ahead and met with Hanlon, had lunch, took the inch-thick package of material Hanlon left him—copies of sworn statements from these two women, assorted newspaper clippings, excerpts from the "60 Minutes" program—looked over it all, and when he was done he still felt this thing was politically hopeless.

But he felt some other things as well. He felt depressed. He felt ashamed. He felt the same rage about these people's uprooting that his own people had felt about theirs. And, though he was convinced the bill was a long shot, he felt there was no way he could turn it down. When he called Hanlon back to say he'd give it a go, he also suggested the obvious choice for a co-sponsor—Al Lawson.

Lawson was chairman of the legislature's black caucus—no more a position of overwhelming power than De Grandy's. The caucus numbered nineteen members at the time, up from the ten who had been there when Lawson arrived in '82, and they were generally considered a cautious group, struggling to find their footing, rarely willing to stick their necks out on any issue that might offend their white colleagues and hurt their careers. Their timidity was no secret. One state newspaper columnist wondered in print "if they would ever stop begging for political crumbs and take their rightful place in the political buffet line." One of the caucus's own members criticized them as a group that was "just happy to be here." That member was Al Lawson.

Lawson was not the most beloved leader the black caucus had ever had, but he had, during his decade in office, pushed the group to become bolder, fighting for money to shore up the state's two leading historically black universities, Florida A&M and Bethune-Cookman, which had begun to decay from neglect. Under Lawson's leadership, the group had pushed the state government to do more business with minority firms, and it had put pressure on the state to hire blacks in key positions. Issues like these were unthinkable when Lawson arrived in Tallahassee in 1982. But then so was his arrival itself.

He came out of a district that was seventy percent white, a North Florida panhandle region of farmers, loggers and fishermen that hadn't elected a black to the state legislature since Reconstruction. These people were, in Lawson's own words, "poor, rural, redneck." He could pronounce each of those terms with an odd sort of affection, the way only a poor black who has grown up among poor whites in the poor Deep South can.

Only those who have lived it can fully comprehend this curious coexistence, the blend of fondness and fear, of endearment and revulsion that evolves from black and white lives shared on the same land, under the same conditions, flowing from one generation into the next, the bond of something close to affection that develops even in the context of rooted resentment, rivalry and racial dis-ease. The fact that the people who burned Rosewood were essentially the same people who elected Al Lawson could not be explained simply by the passage of time and the shift of circumstances. There is a delicate dance that has gone on between poor blacks and whites in the South for well over a century, an intricate *pas de deux* that continues to this day. Some partners are clumsy, some are smooth, toes get stepped on, faces are slapped, punches are thrown and guns sometimes pulled. The tune changes, but the music never stops. And neither does the dance. And Al Lawson was a man who learned to dance early and to dance well.

He was born in a place called Midway, a dozen miles west of Tallahassee, on land his father's family had bought out of slavery. Lawson's great-grandfather Eugene had come down to Florida from Alabama before the turn of the century, found work as a miner, digging what they called *fill-o'-de-earth*—phosphate. Day and night Eugene Lawson's life was defined by the land—on it, in it, under it. Land was holy to him, like religion. His father had taught him that. To own a piece of land was to have a small part of heaven right there in your hands.

And so he bought some of that north Florida soil as soon as he could. Even when he couldn't afford to do anything with it, when he had to go under it to earn his living and feed his family, he still bought land. And his son Solomon bought some more. And by the time Al Lawson was born, the family had a couple of hundred acres to its name.

Lawson's father built a house on that land, farmed as much of it as he could plant and plow by himself—about forty acres—selling what he grew off a truck he drove to the market in town. But when Al was four, the house burned down. The family had no insurance, the corn and tomatoes his father grew couldn't cover the cost of rebuilding, and so Al's father found better-paying work in town, hiring on as a maintenance man over at Florida State University. They were poor, dirt poor, but they rebuilt their house, and they still had their land. They would never give up their land.

The little town of Midway was a black island in the white sea of Gadsden County, a poor county lorded over by a handful of millionaires whose families had made their fortunes buying Coca-Cola stock back in the early part of the century. The place was all tobacco farms by the early '60s, with white schools and black schools. The black schools would let out early during harvest time so the children could get out in the fields and help pick those leaves. "It was almost still like slavery," says Lawson, who was one of those children.

He was always big for his age, strong, and so he went into the fields earlier than most—he turned eight the summer he first started picking in 1956. A dollar a day, that's what they paid him. He was allergic to tobacco, bad enough that his parents sometimes had to take him to the doctor when his rashes flared up. But worse than the rashes was the coughing. That happened whenever the cropdusters flew over. They didn't bother getting the workers out of the way. They just dumped those clouds of pesticides right on the pickers, sent them all home that night with their lungs full of poison. Some would complain, say this stuff was making them sick, and the boss would say, Fine, go ahead and quit, there's plenty of others waiting to take your place.

Years later, Al Lawson would visit some of the older folks, his neighbors, people he had worked beside out in those fields, and they'd be lying in their bedrooms, hooked up to oxygen tanks because they could no longer draw a breath on their own, and he knew, he had no doubt, it went straight back to those tobacco fields. He often wondered why he'd gotten out healthy and they hadn't. Fate is all he could figure. Just fate.

The thing was, he never felt as much anger as he might have, as so many did. He saw racism every day, had a white boss in those tobacco fields who liked to pair the pickers up during water breaks, pick out two of the biggest, strongest men and make them go at it, fight each other just for a show, for his amusement. The boss would sit back under a tree and watch until it was time to get back to work. Al Lawson was young, but he was big, and more than once he was forced to join one of those contests—that, or lose his job.

It was humiliating, demeaning. So was going to the doctor and having to come around through a back door, sit in the waiting room for hours, watch white people come and go until there weren't any white people left, and then the doctor would start seeing the blacks. Lawson's parents always taught their children to love everybody, even those who did you wrong, because hate was something that ate you up inside, that hurt you just as bad as it hurt whoever you hated.

But sometimes it was hard for Al Lawson not to hate. It was hard not to hate the colored and white bathrooms they had all over Quincy, where the Midway kids went to high school. Or the water fountain at the truck stop Law-

son and his buddies would walk past every day on their way home from basketball practice, a fountain with a dipper hanging on a hook for the black people to
draw their drinks with. One day Lawson stopped at the fountain, started to
take down the dipper as usual, looked at how filthy the thing was and said, no,
he wasn't doing this anymore, he was going to take his drink straight from that
water cooler just like the white people. And when he bent to take a sip, an old
white man sitting on a bench nearby stood up, said, "You trying to be *funny*,
nigger?", walked into the store, came back out with a pistol, fired it into the air,
then pointed it their way. Al and his friends took off running, found a police officer, told him what had happened, and the cop just laughed. Shrugged his
shoulders and laughed.

It was hard not to hate after things like that, but when Al got home that day,
when he came home every day, it was as if he'd been out in a foreign world and
now he was stepping back into the real one, a warm haven filled with family
and friends, familiar faces, comfort, protection. This was home, and this was
his. Even with all the ugliness outside, this was a beautiful place, and it belonged to him, him and his family. Every year that passed, he understood better
why his father held onto that land at all costs, even when there was nothing to
do with it but to have it, simply to have it.

That was the chord that struck deepest when Lawson learned about Rosewood. That visceral, inviolable link to the land that meant so much to his people, and the soul-stripping devastation that would be wrought if that land and
that link were lost. Until he learned about Rosewood, he could only imagine
what a loss like that might be like.

But it would be a long time before Al Lawson learned about Rosewood.
Meanwhile, he made his way through high school, continuing to grow until he
was pushing seven feet tall, won a basketball scholarship to Florida A&M, entered college in 1966 wanting nothing more in life than a good job, a nice
home, a nice new car every couple of years, maybe a Cadillac. That's how he arrived, but he left wanting a lot more.

He had never paid much attention in high school to anything beyond sports
and his studies. The civil rights movement was something the folks in Midway
read about. They watched it on television the same way they watched footage
from the war that was heating up over in Vietnam—as something happening
someplace else, far away. There were NAACP meetings down at the church,

but they were always hush-hush affairs. Al Lawson always wondered what was going on in those meetings, but he never wondered enough to join them.

It wasn't until he got to Florida A&M that his eyes were, as he says it so simply, opened. Suddenly he was learning there were black leaders out there besides Martin Luther King, black organizations besides the church and the NAACP. Stokely Carmichael. Eldridge Cleaver. SNCC. CORE. The Muslims. Even a country boy couldn't help learning these things at that time in that place.

Even a jock couldn't help it, and Al Lawson was a jock, running track and playing basketball, putting up numbers gaudy enough to draw professional scouts. By the time he graduated in 1970 with a degree in government, the offers were good enough that he took one, signing with the Indiana Pacers of the American Basketball Association, an upstart league on the last legs of its quirky existence. Lawson played with and against the likes of Julius Erving and Moses Malone, Rick Mount and George McGinnis. He played *for* Wilt Chamberlain during a brief, bizarre stint with the San Diego Conquistadors, a team as destined for obscurity as Lawson's own short career.

By the mid-1970s he was back in Tallahassee, coaching basketball, getting a graduate degree in public administration, selling life insurance to some of the professional athletes he had played against, and building a base to launch a political career. In 1982 he made his move, running for a state seat from a district of Gulf Coast counties that flanked the one in which he was raised, down along North Florida's Apalachee Bay. The voters were predominantly blue-collar and white, loggers and oystermen who were used to seeing black candidates on their ballots and who had always voted for someone else.

But that year came a shock. Out of a five-candidate primary election emerged two choices for the final runoff race, and both were black: Al Lawson and a woman named Bette Wimbish. While Wimbish, with years of local and state government experience and connections behind her, took a polished, refined approach to the campaign, aiming at the more elite among the electorate, Lawson went door to door, pounding the pavement, rubbing shoulders with the common man, white or black, eating more raw oysters and barbecue at more shucking houses, flea markets, picnics and pig-pickings than he could count.

He touted himself as the poor man's choice, and there were more poor men in those counties than rich ones. He even met with some of the Klan, at a campground back in the woods, where he parked his car pointing out the way he'd come in. He half-jokingly asked if they wouldn't mind taking a bite of some of that fried chicken before he did, just to make sure they hadn't put something evil in it. He glanced kind of nervously at the hunting rifles they had propped against their pickups. And when it was over, he came away with enough of their votes and the votes of people just like them to push him over the top. No one expected Al Lawson, a man with no political experience what-soever, to beat a veteran like Bette Wimbish. But he did, thanks largely to hair-sprayed women in polyester pantsuits and burly white men in fishing caps and wading boots—"Rednecks For Lawson," as the newspapers called them.

And so here he was, ten years later, reelected twice, keeping his con-stituents happy the way any politician does, by tending to their interests, fun-neling state money their way, pushing laws that protected their livelihoods, getting himself named to committees that mattered to his people, which, with all those shrimpers and farmers back home, was why he had focused on the state's Committee on Natural Resources, of which he had risen to chairman.

Keeping himself in office, that was Al Lawson's priority, just like every other legislator around him. Yes, he had pushed his black colleagues to be more aggressive on black issues, but he understood their caution as well, their sense of self-preservation, and their ambition. No one was more ambitious than Al Lawson, and no one understood better than he the juggling act of balancing his conscience as a black man with the demands of a white constituency. He was no good to anyone, black or white, if he didn't keep his seat. And so, although he had been urging his colleagues to step out front on issues of race, he was still prudent enough to pick his battles. And this Rosewood thing, at first glance, did not look like a battle worth fighting.

Lawson had no doubt that something like this could have happened in Florida in the 1920s. He *knew* things like this had happened back then. He had studied about them back in his undergraduate days at Florida A&M, about all the lynchings, and the riots, and he wasn't surprised. There wasn't much that could surprise him after what he'd experienced himself during the time he'd grown up, and those were "modern" times.

But politically this thing was dynamite, and it had all the looks of something that would blow up in his hand. There was no question how an issue like this would divide the people in his district, as well as polarize the entire state.

Florida had more than it could handle at the moment in terms of racial problems, from its seething inner-cities to its poverty-riddled rural areas. Did it need to dredge up something that happened seventy years ago? And besides, this thing happened halfway down the coast, five counties south of Lawson's own district.

The issue looked like a loser all the way around. But like De Grandy, Lawson took home the package of stuff Steve Hanlon gave him and he read it, read about a somewhat independent, relatively prosperous community of property-owning black people—a community much like the one he was raised in, the one in which his family still lived. These two women, and all those who had died before them, had lost their community, lost all they had, and that hit too close to home for Al Lawson to turn away. If he stepped into this fight, he had a lot more to lose than Miguel De Grandy. So did his colleagues in the black caucus. No matter how it was packaged, this was a black issue. It would be their fight, and the price would be theirs to pay.

When Lawson called back Steve Hanlon, he couldn't speak for his colleagues, but he could speak for himself, and his answer was yes, count him in.

And so, as the year moved toward its end, the Rosewood claims bill began to take shape.

SIXTEEN

Road Kill

It began as just another winter morning for Arnett, his legs cold and numb as he rolled out of bed. This had become his daily routine now, rubbing his calves to get the circulation going, to get a glimmer of feeling back, knowing that what he'd be feeling the rest of the day would be pain. It was the diabetes, and there was nothing he could do about it, nothing but live with it, throw on a bathrobe, cut on the heat and wade into another day. The newspaper was out on the porch, as always, and he'd get to it soon enough. But right now he needed to wake up, get warm, have a little breakfast.

And then the telephone rang. Odd. Kind of early for a phone call.

"Arnett?"

It was one of his cousins, the daughter of one of the survivors.

"Arnett," she said, "have you seen it?"

"Seen what?"

He moved to a chair, sat down, still kneading one of his legs, trying to get the blood moving.

"The story in today's newspaper, did you see it?"

Cummer and Sons sawmill, Lacoochee

No, Arnett said, he hadn't read the paper yet.

"Well you *better* get it and read it, because Lee Ruth is in there, and Minnie Lee Langley, and they've got themselves a lawyer, saying they're the only survivors of the Rosewood massacre. *The only ones left*. That's what it says right here."

Arnett listened, tried to keep himself calm. He couldn't afford to get worked up these days, not with his blood pressure the way it was.

"Let me look into it," he said.

"Well, *somebody* better damn well look into it," she said, "because this Minnie Lee woman knows damn *well*, and so do you and so does Lee Ruth, that my father was there, and your mother, and all the others, and I don't know what kind of *shit* these two are trying to pull, but they're not going to get *away* with it."

Arnett tried settling her down, told her not to get excited, said he'd take care of it. Then he hung up and dialed his Uncle A. T. over in St. Pete.

"Yeah, I saw it," said A. T., his voice as soft and steady as ever.

"You okay?" asked Arnett.

"Why *sure* I'm okay," said A. T., sounding like the question made no sense at all. And really it didn't. Arnett had never seen his uncle upset, not once in his life, not about anything.

But Arnett's sister, Yvonne, she was another story. No sooner did he finish with Uncle A. T. than Yvonne was on the line, and Arnett could have sworn he was listening to his mother, raging from the grave.

"What the *hell* does Lee Ruth think she's doing?" Yvonne yelled. "I'm going to write that bitch a letter and I'm going to give her a piece of my *mind*. This is *crazy,* Arnett. Do you hear me? *Crazy*."

And then Aunt Vera called from up in Lacoochee. And Eva Jenkins from over in Orlando. And Lillie Washington from Gainesville. And on and on, the phone ringing and ringing until finally Arnett pulled the plug, fetched the paper off his porch and sat down in blessed silence to read this story himself.

And there it was, dateline December 29, 1992, from the Associated Press, out of Miami:

Two survivors of a racial rampage that destroyed the all-black Florida town of Rosewood 70 years ago will ask lawmakers to reimburse them for property loss and memorialize the New Year's Day massacre.

That was the lead. Arnett read on.

> . . . . *Lee Ruth Davis, 77, of Miami, and her cousin, Minnie Lee Langley, 88* [sic], *of Jacksonville, say they are the only people left who witnessed the violent chaos. . . .*

Now he couldn't help himself. He could feel his pulse racing, his blood pressure rising, that familiar, lethal feeling of fury. He read the rest of the story in a blur, set it down, shut his eyes, collected himself. Then he called Lee Ruth.

"*Hey*, honey!" sang the voice at the other end of the line. "How you doin'?"

Arnett had always been Lee Ruth's favorite cousin, almost like a son. And he'd always adored her right back, lived under her roof for a time when he was in the Army, stationed at Homestead, near Miami.

"I'm doin' fine, Ruth, just fine," he said. She sounded the same as always. Bright, upbeat, unbothered by a care in the world. No different today than yesterday or last month or last year. No mention of any lawyers, or newspaper stories. Or lies.

"Ruth," said Arnett, "I been getting phone calls all morning from family members about an article in the newspaper today concerning Rosewood."

Silence.

"You and Minnie are quoted in here as saying you're the last two survivors."

Now Lee Ruth spoke.

"I ain't said *no* such a lie as that."

"You didn't say that?"

"No, I didn't say any such a lie as that. I told that reporter I don't know where they all *live* at, that's all I said. Now Minnie *Lee* might have said that they was all dead, I don't know. But Arnie, I could never say that there was only two survivors, because I *know* where you all are at."

She had already gotten other phone calls that morning, Lee Ruth said. Ugly calls. Upsetting calls, from various members of the family. Arnett's sister was the worst of them, she said. Lee Ruth said she almost didn't pick up when Arnett rang, but she was glad she did.

Arnett didn't push her any further. It was pretty clear Lee Ruth had played this thing halfway at best. Maybe she hadn't come right out and claimed she and Minnie were the only ones left, but she hadn't pointed to the other survivors either. She had let the reporter *believe* there was only Minnie Lee and her. If she hadn't lied, well, she certainly had not told the truth—the whole truth. Maybe that was her decision, maybe it was Minnie's, maybe it was their lawyer's. All that mattered to Arnett now was calling this lawyer, the name there in the newspaper story, an attorney named Manny Dobrinsky, with the Miami office of the law firm of Holland and Knight.

It took Arnett a while to get through, and Dobrinsky sounded skeptical to Arnett, cautious. After several phone conversations and a couple of days, he told Arnett he would talk with Holland and Knight's Tallahassee office. They were the ones who would have to make any decisions about representing any additional survivors, said Dobrinsky. And so, a week into the new year, Arnett got a phone call from a man named Steve Hanlon.

If Dobrinsky had seemed cautious, Hanlon sounded downright disbelieving. When Arnett told him he was a direct descendant of a Rosewood survivor, that his mother had been in that house at the time of the attack, Hanlon chuckled. When he asked Arnett where his mother was and Arnett answered that she was dead, Hanlon said nothing. When Arnett said the only reason any of this was happening at all was *because* his mother was dead, Hanlon remained silent.

Arnett could hear doubt in that silence. But he kept talking, and Hanlon kept listening. And when Arnett was done, Hanlon said, "Look, can you prove this to me? Can you arrange for me to meet face-to-face with these people? Can they bring documents with them, birth certificates, deeds, something to show me they're who they say they are?"

"You got it," said Arnett. "Name the time." Hanlon checked his calendar, saw he had a partner's meeting coming up in the middle of the month down in Tampa, asked if they could all meet sometime that weekend, and Arnett said that would be fine. He suggested Sunday, the seventeenth, the day before Martin Luther King Day. At the New Bethel A.M.E. church, in the town of Lacoochee.

And so that Sunday arrived. Hanlon and his wife Fran got an early start, driving north from Tampa on Interstate 75, passing rest stops marked by newly installed signs:

THIS AREA PATROLLED
BY 24-HOUR ARMED SECURITY.

A recent spate of carjackings and killings across South Florida had the whole state on edge, fanning the festering image of the Sunshine State as a feeding ground for madmen and murderers. Racial violence was in the air that

month as well, after the shocking New Year's Day attack on a black man in
Tampa by three whites who kidnapped and robbed the man, then doused him
with gasoline and set him on fire, leaving his body to burn in a wooded field on
the outskirts of the city.

Like everyone else in America, Steve Hanlon was disgusted by the torching
of Christopher Wilson, and he couldn't help thinking how it connected to
Rosewood, a modern-day mirror of the same sort of hate that swept through
that town back in 1923. Hanlon was thinking about that that morning, as he
and his wife approached the Interstate exit toward Lacoochee.

Lacoochee had made its own lurid splash four years earlier, in 1989, when
Esquire magazine published a story about a grisly murder that had taken place
there a decade before. A rancher searching for some of his lost cattle in the
summer of 1979 had come across the charred remains of a human body in a
stand of trees near the Withlacoochee River, just east of town. Two local white
men, members of a biker gang, were subsequently arrested and sentenced to
death for raping, then beating and burning a white woman they had met at a
party—it was her blackened body the rancher had found. Nine years later, the
pair were freed from death row after a key witness recanted her original testimony under questionable circumstances. That brought on *Esquire*, whose
writer found the essence of Florida's seedy side on the streets of Lacoochee.
"The town that eats road kill," he called it. "In Lacoochee," he wrote, "roads are
dirt, cars are dented, teeth are missing."

A pretty fair description. This was a place beyond decline, with its best days
far in the past. A century earlier, the town of Lacoochee had sprung from the
fields beside the Withlacoochee River, the rich soil producing orchards thick
with oranges and strawberries. Fortunes were made from that fruit, and opu-
lent homes were built on the banks of that river. But a freeze in 1895 so devas-
tated the crops that the fields were abandoned, as were most of the homes. Not
until the early 1920s was Lacoochee reborn, when the grandsons of a Canadian
timber tycoon named Jacob Cummer moved their largest sawmill operation
from a small Gulf Coast town called Sumner south to Lacoochee. Some sources
say that move was made in 1922, others say 1923. None give a reason for it.
None mention anything about a place called Rosewood.

By the late 1920s, Lacoochee had established itself as one of the busiest logging towns in the nation, boasting the largest electric sawmill in the South.
More than two thousand employees worked the 83,000 acres of timber owned

by the Cummer and Sons Cypress Company. The company's saws turned twenty-four hours a day. The town's main street had a thirty-room hotel, two movie houses, four churches, two bakeries, two drug stores, three barber shops, a pool room, a couple of gas stations and public boxing matches every Saturday afternoon on the town square. Housing was plentiful, with the company renting homes for twelve dollars a month and rooms for fifty cents a week. A company store was provided for mill employees, and a company doctor was available as well.

Timber, specifically cypress, was Lacoochee's lifeline. Its homes were built from cypress. The furniture inside those homes was fashioned from cypress, as were the sidewalks outside them. Even the town's heat came from cypress— the fine wood was so plentiful Lacoocheeans used it to feed their fireplaces.

Those were Lacoochee's high times, the 1920s and '30s, but the Depression took its toll, and by the early 1940s—around the time Arnett Doctor was born—better-paying wartime jobs elsewhere, coupled with forests thinned out from twenty years of logging, drained off the town's work force, and Lacoochee began to wither away. Businesses closed. The mill downsized. Finally, in 1959, Cummer and Sons closed up, and the town became what it has remained to this day—a decayed, hollow shell of its former self, a company town without the company.

Its main street now runs past little but boarded-up buildings. The mill is a massive ruin, its sloped tin roof, the size of a football field, rusted and riddled with holes, its windows shattered by rocks and gunshots, pigeons fluttering in and out of its interior darkness. Across a muddy dirt lane, in a field where the company homes once stood, now sit rows of beige concrete duplexes— government-subsidized housing inhabited by families from Haiti, Cuba, Mexico and Vietnam. In one way or another, through migrant field work or government assistance, these families have wended their way here, to Lacoochee.

There are still whites and blacks here as well, among the town's population of about three thousand, almost every one living in poverty. And there remains racial tension among them, sporadic outbreaks of violence. A beating here, a shooting there. And the occasional cross-burning, most recently in the fall of 1993.

This region—Lacoochee, Dade City, all of Pasco County—was once known as the heart of Florida's Klan country. A 1965 series of investigative newspaper articles examining the extent of Ku Klux Klan activity in Florida featured a segment on the Dade City area, including a photograph of the La- coochee Klavern, a decrepit, tar-papered shack perched beside a remote two- lane highway. The chapter's treasurer, according to the story, had recently emptied the group's bank account and skipped town.

One of Steve Hanlon's partners in the Holland and Knight offices up in Tal- lahassee, a woman named Martha Barnett, was from Dade City. She never said much about the place, just that it was *real* country. And now, on this January morning in 1993, Hanlon was driving through it, past Dade City's small, quaint downtown district with its dress shop and department store, and on toward the north side of town, where the looming water tower of the Lykes Pasco citrus processing plant threw its shadow over rows of brick buildings inside which hundreds of workers cranked out the FLORIDAGOLD line of cartoned orange juice and frozen concentrate. Hanlon had heard of this plant, recalled that at one time it was said to be the largest such factory in the world. He had never heard of Vera Hamilton—not yet—but these were the same buildings in which Arnett's aunt had spent the 1940s peeling grapefruits.

Fifteen minutes north on Route 301—the same roadway on which that Klavern had been photographed nearly thirty years before—Hanlon slowed, took a right onto a narrow asphalt lane called Cummer Road, and then he was there, in Lacoochee. He passed the abandoned mill, the government housing, and turned down a dirt lane into a tree-shaded section of small homes, some solid and neatly-tended, others no more than shacks, with trash and animals sharing space on rotting porches, each inhabited by a black family. The whites, as ever, lived on the other side of the tracks, but in this case their homes were no better than the blacks'.

Hanlon followed the directions Arnett Doctor had given him, turned one corner, then another, and finally came out from the shadows of the overarching oaks and up to the sunny, front lawn of the A.M.E. church—a lawn covered with lines of parked, empty automobiles.

In front of the church stood a single figure, a tall black man wearing a white dress suit, his hair shaved close around his large, blocky head, a goatee framing a polite smile, one hand leaning on a walking cane, the other raised in a gesture of welcome.

"Hello," he said, approaching Hanlon and his wife as they climbed from their car. "I'm Arnett Doctor."

An impressive man, thought Hanlon. Pleasant. Polite. Low-key, even. But there was nothing low-key about the number of cars parked out on that lawn. The sheer size of this gathering was more than Hanlon had expected. And when he stepped into the church itself, packed wall-to-wall with nearly two hundred people, including a television news crew from the ABC affiliate in St. Petersburg and a reporter and photographer from the St. Pete *Times*, Hanlon recoiled. This was *definitely* more than he'd expected.

He pulled Doctor's sleeve, leaned toward his ear with the eyes of the entire room upon him. "You didn't tell me we were going to have *television* here," he hissed, hoping his whisper hid his distress.

"Well," said Doctor, smiling like a cat enjoying his first bite of canary, "we want to ensure that our efforts are known."

Hanlon drew a deep breath.

"Well," he said, forcing a tight smile as he turned toward the audience, "I just wish you would have let me know."

And so they walked side by side up the red carpeting to the front of the church, this odd couple, facing what would become a familiar task over the coming months—answering the many questions of these hopeful, expectant people. But first Hanlon had some questions of his own, such as who these people were.

Arnett turned toward the families and asked the survivors among them to please stand. Seven elderly men and women rose from their seats, and Arnett introduced each one. Willie Evans. Arnett Goins. Dorothy Hosey. Eva Jenkins. Lillie Washington. Vera Hamilton. And Berthina Fagin. All the survivors but four—Lonnie Carroll, who was in a nursing home, Thelma Hawkins, who was sick in bed in her home just next door to the church there in Lacoochee, and Lee Ruth Davis and Minnie Lee Langley, who simply hadn't shown up.

Hanlon looked out at the scene, at the sunlight washing through the windows of this old church, at the dozens of black faces gazing up at him, some with suspicion, some with hope, young faces, old faces, the oldest of them, the seven survivors, up on their feet, gripping the pews in front of them to stay steady, all waiting to hear what he had to say, this lawyer from Tallahassee.

And Hanlon had no doubt now, no question about the truth of what this man Arnett Doctor had first told him on the telephone. He felt none of the skepticism he had harbored right up until the moment he had entered this church. These people's validity was no longer an issue for Steve Hanlon. He was looking at the truth, and the truth, two hundred pairs of anxious eyes, was looking right back at him, waiting for him to speak.

And he did. Two survivors. Twenty-two survivors. It made no difference how many they were, he told them. As long as they could pull together and stand united, his firm was willing to represent them all, from now till the end of time. That's what he said. But they had to be *together*, he said, and they had to be happy. There was a lot of work ahead of them, a lot to do, but he and his firm were ready to do it, he said. They were ready to spend time, money, whatever it took, and there was but one condition—that everybody stay *happy*.

Everyone in that church knew what this man meant with his "happy" talk. He was talking about Lee Ruth and Minnie Lee. He was talking about deception, about the families' anger. He was telling them they had to put that anger aside, work out their differences and make some sort of peace with Lee Ruth and Minnie Lee, that they didn't stand a chance if they went into this thing fighting among themselves. The fact was, and most of them knew it, they didn't stand much of a chance anyway.

By the time the afternoon was done, after Hanlon had finished fielding questions, after Arnett had delivered his message from the pulpit, speaking for and to the gathered families, raising the issue of compensation, not just for the survivors themselves but for everyone in that room, for children and grandchildren, for "all the generations who have suffered," as he put it, and after Hanlon had dealt with the reporters, facing their cameras and notebooks, after all of that, Hanlon and his wife climbed back into their car, watching the Rosewood families climb into theirs, and the lawyer smiled.

Keep it simple, he thought to himself. That had always been Steve Hanlon's cardinal rule. But it was going to be tough keeping this thing simple. If there was one thing that had become abundantly clear to him by now, it was that there was nothing simple about the subject of Rosewood.

SEVENTEEN

Three More Names

None of the Rosewood family members were surprised when Minnie Lee Langley and Lee Ruth Davis missed that Sunday afternoon meeting in Lacoochee. Most figured the two women had stayed away from fright, that they were avoiding the wrath of their relatives, which may have been so. But Minnie Lee and Lee Ruth had another reason as well to skip that gathering—they were scheduled to appear on national television the following day, as featured guests on the "Maury Povich" show.

After six months of striking out in Hollywood, Michael O'McCarthy had finally scored in New York. He had left the legal side of things to Steve Hanlon, as well as the task of hunting down other survivors, if there were any. "I didn't give a fuck *who* he found," recalls O'McCarthy. "He could go find *all* of them, for all I cared. I was going on with what *I* was doing."

For the previous half a year O'McCarthy had not been doing well. Los Angeles was still reeling from the Rodney King riots, and so were the Hollywood dealmakers who showed him the door each time he ambled in with his tale of this mass lynching in Florida. "They told me, 'You've got to be fucking *crazy*.

Wilson Hall

The last thing we want to make right now is a movie about white people killing niggers.'"

Finally he had turned to television, calling the Povich people in New York and pitching the Rosewood story as a natural for Martin Luther King Day. When a Povich producer called back and said they liked the idea, O'McCarthy leaped. He booked Minnie Lee and her daughter on a flight from Jacksonville to New York, arranged for Povich to do a videotaped interview with Lee Ruth in a Miami hospital, where she had been admitted with stomach pains, and he caught a red-eye flight himself from L.A. back to the east coast, arriving in New York the night before the taping, just in time to get himself a haircut before taking the stage with Maury and Minnie Lee. "The ball was rolling," recalls O'McCarthy. "Hollywood wasn't biting, but the ball was finally rolling."

The broadcast, on Monday, January 18, 1993, was vintage talk-tabloid-television, opening with taped footage of the Cedar Key waterfront, moody shots of the highway to Rosewood, images of rural shacks and the thick palmetto forest of Gulf Hammock. Povich's grave voice-over described the murder of "nearly one hundred women, children and men" that January week of 1923. Then the cameras cut live to the program's New York studio, where Minnie Lee Langley, dressed in a bright red suit, and Michael O'McCarthy, with his hotel haircut ("Just horrible, man. The guy gave me whitewalls. I looked like Jack Nicholson playing Hoffa"), sat on the stage with Povich, facing a studio audience encouraged to react audibly to each revelation.

They gasped as Minnie Lee described the shooting of Sarah Carrier. They grumbled as she told how the children hid in the swamp, wearing nothing but nightclothes. They shook their heads as Minnie detailed her escape by rail. They drew their breaths as Lee Ruth appeared on a video screen, propped in a hospital room chair, wearing a bathrobe, plastic tubes running from her nostrils, telling Povich her account of the rampage. "They was killing everything breathing that was black," she said.

Finally, after fielding questions from the audience, Povich turned to Minnie Lee and asked how she felt about white people today. "Well," she said, pausing for several long seconds. "*Some* of 'em is real nice." Another pause as she stared hard at her lap. "Too *good* to be white." And the audience erupted into laughter and applause.

More than two million Americans watched that broadcast, including one with more than a passing interest, a man named Wilson Hall, the owner of a small nightclub in a north Florida hamlet called Hilliard, above Jacksonville, just seven miles from the Georgia state line.

Actually it's generous to call Wilson Hall's place a nightclub these days, and he's the first to admit it. "Yes," he says, pulling a chair across the plywood floor and taking a seat at one of the room's three tattered booths, "it's been hard staying open anymore. The drug peoples, that's what did it, with their guns and their fussing and shooting. They done drove all the *decent* people away."

A juke box by the back wall blinks red and orange. A pool table in the corner is bathed in the glow of the shaded lamp above it. Other than that, the room is dark, even at midday. The neon beer signs in the tiny front windows are turned off, and the bar, its refrigerator stocked with food Hall cooks for himself and his wife, is locked behind a wire cage door.

He calls his place the "705 Club," after its address on Oxford Street, the only paved road in or out of the black section of Hilliard. Most of the town's population of twenty-five hundred live on the other side of the tracks, where Hilliard's main street features a hardware store, a taxidermist, and the Dixie Motel. The rest live here, in an assortment of small clapboard houses, some saved by aluminum siding, others decaying into shacks. There's a ballfield and a swimming pool just down the way from Hall's place, both built a few years back for Oxford Street's children. The pool is bone dry and abandoned. The ballpark is grown over with weeds, stray dogs asleep on its infield dirt.

It wasn't always this way, says Hall. When he first bought his place in '84, the front dirt parking lot was clean, not littered with broken glass and torn lottery tickets like it is now. Back then he didn't need the barbed wire fence that encloses his long, gray stucco building. "Had to put that up when the cars kept driving around back, dealing their drugs and shooting their guns. I walked out there once, and one man had a gun stuck in another man's mouth, robbing him. Can you believe it?"

Wilson Hall didn't used to have to hire security guards at thirty-five dollars an hour each, but the town began cracking down a few years ago, closing a half dozen other clubs in the area for drug and disturbance violations and threatening to close Hall's if he didn't do something about the "bad elements." Never mind that the county sheriff himself had a healthy little cocaine business of his own going on the side, for which he is now doing time in federal prison.

Hall shakes his head and chuckles at that one. He's eighty-one, but still built like a block of granite. Stout, barrel-chested, strong enough that he doesn't bother hiring bouncers on the rare nights when he still opens his bar for business. He can take care of trouble himself, just like he takes care of his forty-four-year-old wife Stephanie, who lives with him here at the club. He takes care of his eighty-six-year-old sister Margie, too, who lives just up the street in the same rickety, tin-roofed cottage she's called home for the past thirty-six years.

Margie was one reason Wilson moved here from Chicago in the spring of 1984. The other was that this remote, wooded corner of Florida reminded him more than any place he'd ever seen of the town where he was born and raised, a little village over on the Gulf side of the state, he says, a place called Rosewood.

Wilson Hall was seven years old when he last saw Rosewood, but not a day has passed since then that he hasn't thought of it, of the forty acres of land his granddaddy started with just after the Civil War, and the hundred his daddy added to it, clearing the trees, pulling the stumps, growing sugar cane and sweet potatoes in that soil, building the biggest smokehouse in all of Levy County, bigger than the nightclub Wilson owns today. "People would bring ten cows to my daddy to butcher, and he'd take some of that meat in payment, smoke it and sell it in his store."

Charles Bacchus Hall, that was Wilson's daddy. He ran the only general store in Rosewood other than the one owned by a white man named John Wright. Charles Hall's store took up the first floor of the family's two-story house. They had a corral out back, with pens for their animals and a grinding machine to squeeze the juice from their sugar cane. Come cane season, farmers would arrive from miles around, hauling wagonloads of sugar stalks to Charles Hall's grinder. Wilson's earliest memory was riding the back of his daddy's mule as it circled that machine, turning the gears of the grinder as the farmers fed the sweet stems into the machine.

Charles Hall was a blacksmith, too, along with Sam Carter. He was a Mason as well—"Thirty-second degree," says Wilson, "just about as high as it got." Sundays Charles Hall preached at the AME church, says Wilson, and he was a principal for a time at the Rosewood school. "Everything that needed doing, my daddy did," says the son, still swelling with pride more than seventy years after his father died.

That was in the winter of 1920, when Charles Hall took sick to bed and never got back up. After that the family had to shut down the store. Wilson's mother Mary went to work over at the sawmill in Sumner, "dogging" logs—rotating the tree trunks with metal tongs each time the saws sliced off a plank. "Lord, she was strong," recalls Wilson. "She worked for a while on the railroad, too, stripping crossties."

With their mother off working, it was left to Wilson and his brothers and sisters to tend to the house and themselves. They each had their duties, and Wilson's was cooking. His mother taught him how to make fried chicken and bread pudding, grated potato pone and sweet potato pie. Seventy years later, he was still using her recipes. When his club was thriving, he'd throw open the doors at holidays and lay out a spread for his customers, treat them to a free feast. But it's been a couple of years now since the last one.

"People have changed so much," says Wilson. "You do a favor for someone now, not only do they not do one for you back, but they expect *another* from you. And they gets *angry* with you if they don't get it. It's not like it used to be, no, not at all."

That was the thing about Rosewood, says Wilson. "Everybody helped everybody there," he says. "You didn't want for nothin'. You didn't *need* for nothin'. If I didn't have no flour or bacon, I came to your house. If nobody was home, I'd come in and take what I need and leave a mark, and you'd do the same with me. That's the way it was, the way it *should* be."

But it all ended that cold January night in 1923, when Wilson's mother shook the children awake a little past midnight. "Get *up*, we got to *go*," Wilson remembers her saying. "I can hear 'em comin'." The family didn't know about any shootout earlier that evening at the Carrier house. Sarah Carrier lived clear at the other end of town. But everyone knew about the killing of Sam Carter early in the week, they knew trouble had been brewing ever since then, and now they could see car headlights bumping up the road through the woods, coming straight toward their house.

Mary Hall and her children barely made it out the back door before the white men got to the front. Wilson remembers slipping through the corral, under the fence and into the woods. They spent two nights there before making their way to Wylly, then boarded a train that was stopped and searched twice on its way to Gainesville. "Women and children were safe," he recalls. "They were looking for *men*." He remembers lying on the floor beneath the railcar's bench seat, watching mud-covered boots go past. "Mama didn't want us to look in those white men's faces, no how," he says.

Wilson turned eight that April in Gainesville, in a two-room shack behind an ice house near the railroad station. That's where he and his mother and brothers and sisters lived for the next seven years, finding work wherever they could, all of them. "Gathering trash, cleaning yards, shaking pecans out of trees," says Wilson. "We picked up some coins any way we could."

He was big for his age, and at thirteen he got a job sparring at a local gym, five dollars a session. He'd bring that money home to his mother, never told her where it came from, because he knew she'd never approve. She was a devout woman, and boxing, well, that was the devil's work. One day, the Jewish man who owned the gym came to her door and told Mary Hall he wanted to turn her boy into a professional prizefighter, that Wilson was a better boxer than the men he'd been sparring against. She sent the man on his way, then sliced a switch off a nearby tree and gave Wilson the worst whipping of his life. "That," he says with a smile, "was the end of my boxing career."

When he was fifteen, he moved to Miami, where he lived with his older brother Steve and found a job cleaning and maintaining cars for a local cab company. People would ask where he was from, and he'd say Rosewood. They'd say they never heard of the place, they'd ask where it was at, and then he'd tell them about the attack. "No one ever believed me. They couldn't believe nothin' like that ever happened. Pretty soon I just stopped tellin' the story. It wasn't worth the bother."

But he never stopped thinking about it. And he never felt anger. Nostalgia, yes, but never anger. "What could I do with anger? Where could I put it? A black man in the 1930s and '40s didn't have no place to put any anger. And my mama explained to me early that I didn't have no reason to be angry, that I didn't have no one definite to be angry *with*. There was no one individual to put a finger on. I didn't have a name, I didn't have a face. So I just pushed the bad part to the side. Not to where I ever forgot about it, but to where it didn't worry me."

He moved to Chicago in 1945, after getting a telegram telling him another older brother, Charles, was dying, and he wound up staying. He made a good life for himself there, working as a janitor for the Universal motion picture company, cleaning the two warehouses the company used to produce its newsreels. He bought a home, moved his mother up with him when she took sick in 1950, and that's when he found out what had happened to Dosha and Sammy. His mother wasn't real specific, but she knew Sammy had settled in a place in

Georgia called Brunswick, out on the Atlantic coast, and Dosha had moved with her husband to a little Florida town called Hilliard, someplace just below the Georgia line.

Wilson decided to find Sammy first.

It was August of 1955 when he climbed in his DeSoto with a buddy and headed south. That same month a fourteen-year-old boy named Emmett "Bobo" Till was lynched near the town of Money, Mississippi—pistol-whipped, shot through the head, strangled with barbed wire and dumped in the Talla-hatchie River for calling a white woman "baby." Wilson Hall drove through that very county mere days after the killing, stopped for gas at a small service sta-tion and was turned back to the road by a raised shotgun. "The same thing hap-pened again just before I got to Brunswick," he says. "That stuff was everywhere then, it was all over."

Sam Hall had been working in Sumner the week of the attack on Rose-wood, says Wilson, and wound up cut off from his family. That was the first thing Wilson says Sammy talked about when Wilson arrived at his door. "He told me that was the worst mistake he ever made, the only thing in his life he was sorry about, that he left Mama with us little children out in those woods. He felt bad about that, right up to the day he died."

It was two years after finding his brother that Wilson took a train from Chicago to Miami, got off in Hilliard and bumped into a local church deacon who took him straight to Dosha's house, there on Oxford Street.

"She came to the door, and this deacon says, 'You know this man here? Be-cause he *think* he know *you*.'

"She eyeballed me up and down and said, 'No, I don't know him.' Said, 'He kind of *favors* one of my brothers, but I don't got no brothers this large.'

"Then she looked hard at me and said, 'Who *are* you?'

"I said, 'I'm Wilson.'

"She weighed about three hundred pounds, and she musta' jumped high as my waist. '*Wilson! My baby brother!!*' She damn near killed me, but I wiggled out of that."

And he visited her every year thereafter. Bought some land in the process. Then he bought his club. And finally, in 1984, the year Sammy died, Wilson Hall moved to Hilliard. His mother was dead by then. All Wilson's siblings were dead by then, too, except Dosha, Margie, and their baby sister, Mary, who lived down in Jacksonville. They all watched Sammy on that "60 Minutes" show in 1983, but none of them heard of any Rosewood reunions after that. They didn't know about any Arnett Doctor. And he didn't know about them.

Dosha passed away in 1991, leaving Wilson, Margie and Mary as the last living Rosewood Halls. None of them saw the story in the newspaper about Lee Ruth and Minnie Lee's lawsuit. But by the time the "Maury Povich" show was rolling its credits that Monday afternoon in January of 1993, Wilson Hall was on the telephone. And before that month was out, Steve Hanlon had three more names to add to his list of Rosewood survivors.

PART FOUR

THE CLAIM

EIGHTEEN

"Attention White People"

The auditorium was filled, aisle to aisle and front row to back, every seat taken, the room pulsing with the grassroots black power of the state of Florida. Black mayors and black city councilmen, black school commissioners and black board members, black principals and black professors, black businessmen and black businesswomen, black ministers, deacons and elders, the NAACP, the Urban League—they were all there, more than three hundred leaders of every black social, political and religious organization between Pensacola and Key West, gathered on this sweltering Saturday in September of 1993 on the campus of Florida A&M University in Tallahassee to see for themselves what this Rosewood matter was all about.

It was Al Lawson who had issued the call, and now he stood on the stage, surveying the scene, beholding a sea of curious but suspicious faces—not unlike the faces Steve Hanlon had stood before in Lacoochee eight months earlier. Lawson knew a moment of truth when he saw one, and this was most assuredly such a moment.

Skepticism about Rosewood, about the validity of this claim by the scat-

The lynching of John Evans, St. Petersburg, 1914.

tered survivors of a sketchily documented racial attack seventy years in the distant past, had soared since the start of the year. What had begun as a noble crusade had rapidly dissolved into a quagmire of doubt and dissension, beginning
with the very filing of the claims bill itself, which was late. Lawson and Miguel
De Grandy had stumbled out of the starting blocks by missing the January 1 filing deadline for that year's legislative session, and only the forgiveness of
Florida's House Speaker Bolley Leroy "Bo" Johnson had saved the bill from
a stillborn death. Johnson's leniency was surprising on the face of it, considering his white North Florida background and his brittle relationship with Al
Lawson.

Bo. The name itself fit the timeworn tradition of the shrewd, savvy political
kingpins who have long carved up and controlled small chunks of the Deep
South as if they were their personal fiefdoms. Bo Johnson was bred to inherit
that tradition, born into a family of local politicians up around Pensacola, raised
on a steady diet of after-dinner cigar smoke and deal-making among his father
and grandfather and their friends. Sometimes, after the smoke cleared, there
lingered the scent of scandal. The scent was there when Bo's father Leroy, who
held local office up near the Alabama border during the '60s and '70s, died in
1984—not a week after he was arrested on a murder-for-hire charge. A police
informant had taped Leroy Johnson offering $10,000 to have a political critic
killed. Six days after his arrest, he dropped dead of a heart attack.

By then, Bo Johnson was nearly a decade into his own career as a state legislator, well on his way to the most powerful seat in the House, and—not coinci-
dentally, according to his critics—also amassing a personal fortune in real
estate. By 1993, his net worth had ballooned from $28,000 the year he was first
elected to the House, in 1977, to more than $800,000—not bad, said skeptics,
for a man whose annual salary as Speaker was $31,000. Johnson claimed that
his wealth came from astute real estate deals. Doubters said those deals were
steered by political clout. They pointed to a bridge-building bill he pushed
through in 1984, the same year his father died. Was it coincidence, they asked,
that the proposed bridge over Pensacola Bay would bring a new highway—and
rocketing property values—directly through waterfront land owned by Bo
Johnson's family? A decade later, Johnson would shake his head about the
"grief" that bridge deal brought him. But it also brought him nearly half a million dollars when he sold the property in 1991.

Bo Johnson admitted early on in his career that he was from the Old Testament school of politics, where friends are rewarded and foes are punished, where favors are remembered and betrayals never forgotten. When he became Speaker in 1992, he wasted no time acting on that edict, passing out the key positions of House committee chairmen to his buddies—an all-male group led by a disproportionate number of North Florida lawmakers. In the process, Johnson removed several veteran chairmen, including Al Lawson, who wound up in a shouting match in Johnson's office after he was stripped of his chairmanship of the Committee on Natural Resources.

"It was a slap in the face," says Lawson, whose wounds were still fresh when Rosewood came into his life. His war with Bo Johnson made even his colleagues in the Black caucus reluctant to support *any* Al Lawson–sponsored legislation, much less a bill laced with the racial controversy of Rosewood.

"They didn't want to do anything to piss off the Speaker," says Lawson of the caucus. "They went, 'Omigod, *Rosewood?* You don't get along with the Speaker *now*, and you think he's gonna let *you* lead this damn thing?' They knew where I stood with him. *Everybody* knew. Word had gone out among every lobbyist in the state, 'If you've got an issue, *don't* bring it to Al Lawson, 'cause he's not going to get anything out of there for the next two years, not as long as Bo Johnson is the Speaker.' Still, the way I saw it, what did I have to lose? I'd already made the decision this was a horse I was going to ride."

As the 1993 legislative session convened, it quickly became clear that Lawson and De Grandy were riding that horse virtually alone. The only reason the Rosewood bill was even allowed to continue breathing was because Bo Johnson recognized the volatility of the topic and the public stink that would surely be raised if it were dismissed on grounds of mere tardiness. Better to let it die a natural death than kill it, and the bill indeed looked doomed when eleven *more* Rosewood survivors surfaced even as Lawson and De Grandy were trying to get the legislation on its feet. Here they were, seeking compensation for two women who were supposedly the only survivors left alive, and suddenly there were eleven more people creeping out of the woodwork, people Lawson and De Grandy hadn't even known about. How many *more* would there be?

What little credibility the bill might have had took a nosedive. Even Lawson's black colleagues began publicly bailing out. Cynthia Chestnut, a caucus member from Gainesville, told the *Miami Herald* she had serious reservations about this bill. "I have no idea of the cost, of what this bill would entail," cautioned Chestnut. "A claims bill takes money from the general revenue fund.

That's money for education, health and everything else. You have to have good supporting data to get that money."

That theme became the drumbeat among Rosewood's doubters—the lack of good supporting data, the fact that there was scant evidence to support the reliability of these people's claim, the haze of speciousness that infected this whole affair.

By early April, as the legislature moved toward the end of its session, it was clear the 1993 Rosewood claims bill was defunct. Lawson knew that. He and De Grandy were already looking ahead to the next year's session. The original bill, on behalf of Minnie Lee Langley and Lee Ruth Davis, had been obsolete even before it was filed. So much had changed since the start of the year, so much had been discovered, not the least being the fact that there were thirteen survivors now, not two, and each of them would hopefully bring a wealth of evidence and information to bolster a new bill. Rosewood's opponents wanted more supporting data? Lawson and De Grandy would *give* them supporting data. Between that spring and the end of the year, they planned to amass more information than anyone could imagine—along with a bigger, better bill, nothing so flimsy as the piece of legislation they filed the first time around.

And so Al Lawson proposed that spring that the state fund a study to determine what exactly happened at Rosewood. It wouldn't cost much, maybe $50,000 or so. The governor, Lawton Chiles, liked the idea. "There should be a full accounting and investigation into the incident," said one of Chiles's spokespeople, putting the pressure on Bo Johnson to come up with the money. There were murmurs of protest that spending even that small sum on Rosewood—a sliver of the state's $35 billion budget that year—would be a waste. But it was worth it to Johnson, who announced in July that the money had been found and the investigation would be launched.

"At the least," said the Speaker in a prepared statement, "this study is sure to teach us something about our past so we can use the knowledge to guard against anything like it in the future."

That was Johnson's public posture. But there were those who believed his real reason for relenting was less lofty. "That's one of the easiest ways in the world to kill something," says Lawson. "Send someone to go off and study it, and hope the thing just fades away."

But Rosewood was not going to fade away. Lawson believed it, and Arnett Doctor and Steve Hanlon were going to make sure of it. Even as the state began putting together a research team of university history professors, Doctor and Hanlon were pulling together the Rosewood families, healing the rifts, bringing Lee Ruth and Minnie Lee into the fold as well as the newcomers—Wilson Hall and his sisters. Hanlon told them all they had no hope if they did not form a united front.

Doctor reminded them that Lee Ruth and Minnie Lee had done a brave thing by stepping forward, that despite their neglect of the others, these two women were the catalyst for all that was happening now. The message to Minnie Lee and Lee Ruth was that they needed the families as much as the families needed them, that there was even more at stake now than there had been when they first filed their claim. The bill that died that spring was in essence a test run, what the golfers A. T. Goins once caddied for down in St. Pete would call a mulligan. A free swing. The state was now giving the Rosewood families a chance to tee it up one more time, and they were preparing themselves to make the most of it.

While Hanlon worked the halls of Holland and Knight, gathering the firm's legislative resources, the families convened in Orlando to elect a committee, a group of four family members to represent them with the law firm and the legislature. The chairman of that Rosewood Advisory Committee was a natural choice—Arnett Doctor. He would be the spokesman for the more than four hundred survivors and descendants of Rosewood, and he took to the task with relish, spending the spring and summer of 1993 talking to every reporter who would answer his telephone calls, speaking to every group that could find a place for him on its calendar.

And they answered those calls, and they opened their calendars. A year earlier Arnett Doctor couldn't get the time of day from these people, but now they were throwing open their doors to him, and he burst through with a vengeance, wearing his dark purple suit with the gold Lion of Judah pin on its lapel—a family award, he explained to those who asked. "For leadership," he would add, swelling with pride. The NAACP asked him to address its state conference in Fort Myers in April, and he did. He made more television appearances than he could count. The TV news people loved him, this strong bold black man with a hint of anger in his eyes, articulate, almost poetic, with a heart-rending tale to tell, and he told it with such a perfect blend of empathy and outrage.

Arnett Doctor made for great television, and he made great copy, too, feed-

ing the newspaper reporters the kinds of quotes their editors savored. He knew
how to tell a story, and if it needed some embellishment here and there to dress
it up just a little, well, he was glad to gild the lily. If it took hype to get this story
in the papers, Arnett Doctor would give them hype. He would make the people who inhabited Rosewood, as well as the place itself, as mythic as he had
imagined it when he was a little boy. Sylvester Carrier was no longer simply a
crack marksman; Arnett turned him into a Winchester-wielding superman
who, with a slug from his .30-.30, "could drive a nail into a tree one hundred
and fifty feet away." There were no longer just two white men shot dead by
Sylvester that fateful night; Arnett solemnly told reporters his uncle was "responsible for nineteen deaths." The town of Rosewood was no longer a tidy village of twenty to thirty homes; Arnett fudged the figure to "sixty or seventy,"
and, in a rush of excitement, he described the place as a "Black Mecca . . . what
Atlanta is today."

All these depictions were dutifully rushed into print. No matter that they
weren't quite true. That wasn't the point, not to Arnett. The point was to keep
this subject in the public eye, to make people aware of Rosewood, to stir the
pot while the state did its study. If there was backlash, arguments, debate, so
much the better. Anything to keep Rosewood in the news.

And there was backlash. Letters of protest began flashing on editorial pages
of newspapers across the state, questioning the validity of this claim and asking
why, even if it were true, people today should pay for a crime that took place
seventy years earlier. Even the Ku Klux Klan climbed into the act, sending two
of its members to Rosewood to do some research of their own. They wound up
at Doyal Scoggins's doorstep, on the porch of the old Wright house.

"Two guys in a pickup truck," recalls Scoggins. "They were very polite. I had
no idea they were Klan till they said so. They started asking if I knew anything
that had not been in the newspapers. I think they wanted somebody to say this
had all been an invented story. After about ten minutes, they left."

The Klan then issued its own press release, picked up by the Associated
Press and printed in newspapers across Florida. "Things can always be fabri-
cated," said a man who identified himself as H. Jobes, one of the pair that had
visited Scoggins. "I don't think it did happen. I can't in my mind believe that
these people have such great memories after all these years."

Fliers began appearing around Levy County and on the fax machines of
news organizations throughout the state. "ATTENTION WHITE PEOPLE,"

the notices blared, and they went on to alert Florida citizens that their tax dollars were being spent on a sham. "It's like being sued without due process and YOU are the victims of this scheme," the leaflets proclaimed. There was a phone number at the bottom of each one. Those who dialed it heard a recording by a group called the "Collective Action Network." At the end of the recording, another number was given. Dial that, and a man named John Baumgardner answered from his home in a small town south of Gainesville, where he still lives today.

Baumgardner is a forty-one-year-old "housedad," he says, home-schooling his two children while his wife works. He is also the former Florida Grand Dragon of the Invisible Empire Knights of the Ku Klux Klan, a position he held at the time those fliers went out in the summer of 1993. He directed that campaign, he says, as well as a subsequent demonstration at Rosewood, in which twenty Klansmen outfitted in robes and hoods paraded along Route 24 near Doyal Scoggins's house, waving at passing motorists.

Baumgardner says there were about six hundred members among the state's twenty or so Klan chapters at that time. "But only about a hundred of those were hard-core, active people," he says. Those figures are all about the same today, he claims, although the Florida Klan technically disbanded in 1994 in the wake of a successful lawsuit brought against the national organization by the Southern Poverty Law Center after a lynching in Alabama. Some saw the splintering as a sign of the Klan's decline, but Baumgardner says it's actually made the group stronger. "It's harder," he says, "to kill a snake with many heads."

Baumgardner says he is now retired as Grand Dragon, but he still edits and sends a monthly newsletter titled the *Florida InterKlan Report* to those six hundred names on his mailing list, and he still quotes Bob Dylan and Che Guevara on his newsletter pages—unlikely touchstones for a Klansman.

"Hey, I was a hippie in the Sixties," says the bespectacled south Georgia native. "I was in the SDS, a left-winger. 'Don't trust leaders, watch your parking meters.' I've *always* been a radical. I've never believed solutions are found in the middle of the road. Solutions are found out on the edges, on one side or the other, and I've been on both."

He can't quite explain how he came to the Klan thirteen years ago—"I've been asked that a hundred times, and I don't know the answer"—but he says racial hatred was not a reason. He says he's more concerned about homosexual-

ity and crime than race, and he says the Klan should be, too. He says he trea-
sures his memories of the black nanny and black cook who helped raise him in
Georgia. "I considered those people part of the family," he says. "I loved 'em."

The Florida Klan's opposition to Rosewood, says Baumgardner, was focused on the claim, not the claimants. "Even if this thing occurred," he says,
"and I'm not convinced we'll ever know what happened, we just thought it was
a shame that the state would pay money to these people without knowing exactly what took place. To us, it was an issue of justice, not race. What's right
and what's wrong? That's what this was about."

That was the question Al Lawson hoped every person in that Florida A&M
auditorium was asking themselves as they listened to him speak that Saturday
afternoon in September. The state's study team had finally been selected and
they were there, four history professors and one graduate student, beginning
their research that week by interviewing the survivors themselves. The setting
for those interviews, Florida A&M's Black Archives Research Center and Museum, provided a powerful backdrop, its rooms filled not only with testimony
to the achievements of African-Americans, but also adorned with artifacts of
slavery, segregation and Jim Crow, evidence of what the museum's curators
label "The Black Holocaust."

Signs for "Whites" and "Coloreds," pulled from old bathrooms and water
fountains, are mounted on the walls. Glass cases display vintage Florida postcards from the 1930s, '40s, and '50s, images of black cartoon figures eating
watermelon, stealing chickens, being swallowed by alligators—keepsakes
white tourists could pick up along with a sack of oranges, something to give the
folks back home a chuckle. Mid-century magazine ads, sheet music, toys and
souvenirs abound with the unabashed language of the time: "coons" and "niggers," "mammies" and "Sambos," "black crows" and "pickaninnies."

All artifacts now, remembrances of things past. But for the Rosewood survivors, those were pieces of their lives on those walls and under that glass,
painful yardsticks by which the years since their childhoods could be measured.
Some broke down. Others pulled back. Minnie Lee refused to talk to the study
team member who wanted to interview her, a young white man, until Steve
Hanlon drove over from his downtown office and calmed her, assured her these
people asking all these questions were good people, decent people, that they
weren't going to hurt her. No one here was going to hurt her.

The survivors were in the auditorium that Saturday morning, all but Lonnie

Carroll, who lay in the nursing home in New Smyrna, and Lee Ruth Davis, who had passed away the month before. The stomach pains that had brought Lee Ruth to the hospital in January had turned out to be cancer. Her death added the element of urgency to the bill, the fact that these men and women were all in their twilight years, that time was not on their side. Sympathetic editorials in newspapers around the state noted Lee Ruth's death, the sadness of the fact that she would not be alive to see her day of justice, if indeed that day was to come.

They sat in the front row that morning, the survivors along with Arnett Doctor, who, at Al Lawson's request, stepped forward and introduced them, one by one. As they stood, slowly, with both effort and grace, eleven ancient figures, each turning to face these hundreds of strangers, Al Lawson could see the awe that washed through the room. He felt that awe himself. The sheer sight of these living, breathing beings, the power of their presence, was so much stronger than words, or debate, or doubt.

And Lawson knew right then and there that he would have what he hoped for, that when this crowd dispersed that day and went back to their classrooms and congregations, to their boardrooms and businesses, they would bring with them a commitment to make the Rosewood claims bill black Florida's top priority come 1994.

Now it was up to him—and the families, and Miguel De Grandy, and Holland and Knight—to put together that bill.

And it was up to the study team, they all prayed, to back up the bill with its blessing.

NINETEEN

Doc Willie's Little Girl

It was autumn now and Tallahassee was teeming with college students, the massive campus of Florida State University swarming with tens of thousands of undergrads, a sea of Seminole-shaded shorts and tank tops—garnet and gold—spilling from tree-sheltered dorms and Georgian frat houses, sleepy-eyed students hustling to make it to another Monday morning class. A half-mile south, on a smaller scale, wearing their own school colors of green and orange and scurrying to their own labs and lectures, were the students at Florida A&M.

Downtown it was getting toward lunchtime, the sandwich shops and cafes surrounding the high-rise state capitol building doing a decent business with lawyers and bankers and the occasional tourist, but counting the days until January, when the 1994 legislature would convene, when politicians and staffs and lobbyists from across the state would converge and the cash registers would truly begin ringing.

Steve Hanlon was counting those days, too. He had been in over his head the first time around with the Rosewood bill. He admitted it. He knew the court system inside out, could litigate with the best of them in front of any

William Walters ("Doc Willie") in Lacoochee, 1940s

bench, federal or state. But the labyrinthine rules and procedures of the legislature, not to mention the webs of personal and political relationships among the men and women sitting in those House and Senate seats, could be grasped only with time and experience, and Hanlon had had neither.

He was new at this, and that's why the first bill had fallen apart. Lawson and De Grandy were happy to sponsor it, but they had more than Rosewood on their agendas. It had been up to Hanlon and his crew to write the thing, then nurse it through the elaborate maze of hearings and committees that would finally culminate in a vote. They had gotten no further than filing the first time around, and Hanlon took the blame for that. He simply wasn't ready. But then neither was the bill.

This time would be different. The smoke had cleared in terms of the number of survivors. No more surprises there. As for the veracity of the claim itself—the facts surrounding the 1923 attack—the state's fact-finding team would return with its results in December, and Hanlon could only hope those results would be positive. If not, the whole thing was over. Close the books and go home.

But assuming that first hurdle was cleared, that the study team's report supported the claim, Hanlon had to prepare his plan of attack, and he knew he needed help, more than he had thought he might need it the first time around. That's why he asked one of his partners in the Tallahassee office, an attorney named Martha Barnett, to join him for lunch on this autumn afternoon.

While Steve Hanlon was a relative newcomer to Holland and Knight and an oddity of sorts in his role as head of the pro bono division, Martha Barnett had been with the firm for twenty years—nearly half her life—representing the moneyed, powerful clients who had made Holland and Knight the most moneyed, powerful law firm in the Southeast. From the environmental tangles faced by Florida's phosphate mining industry to the franchise squabbles troubling Kentucky Fried Chicken, from antitrust legislation to tax laws, the twenty-six attorneys staffing Holland and Knight's Tallahassee headquarters were there to roam the corridors of the state capitol two blocks away, to shepherd and shape the state's laws as best they could to suit the interests of their corporate clients.

They were lobbyists, Holland and Knight's best and brightest, scurrying up and down the halls of the sixth and seventh floors of the Barnett Bank Building there in downtown Tallahassee. And the best and brightest of them all—the best of any lobbyist in the entire state of Florida, according to some observers—was Martha Barnett.

She rolls her eyes at that accolade, shifts with discomfort at newspaper articles that describe her as "tough." She looks anything but tough, camped behind her walnut desk in her homey, tasteful office, surrounded by photos of her family—her husband and two children, and her parents. A pink "I Believe Anita Hill" button sits on a side table. A personal secretary is stationed at a desk outside her door, screening calls and visitors. Barnett is forty-eight years old, but she still looks like the high school cheerleader she once was, her round brown eyes bright as a doe's, her straight dark hair trimmed shoulder-length, her tan suit, white stockings and print scarf as comfortably elegant and impeccably arranged as her office furniture. She could easily be one of the local television news anchors with whom she has done so many interviews.

Some say that's part of the reason for her success as a lobbyist, that the good old boys over at the Capitol are charmed and disarmed by a woman, especially one as youthful and attractive as Martha Barnett. Her low-key, relaxed demeanor doesn't hurt, and neither does her accent, the lilting Deep South twang that tells the Big Benders she's one of them—which, in a sense, she is.

That's what she was chatting with the firm's new receptionist about that Monday afternoon in September of 1993, making small talk while waiting for Hanlon to get off the phone so they could leave for lunch. She wasn't sure exactly what Hanlon wanted from her, just that it had something to do with this Rosewood bill he'd been working on. She didn't know much more about the case than what she had seen in the office memos Hanlon had been circulating for months. She had read a couple of newspaper articles, and she knew Hanlon had missed the boat the first time around. But she was too busy with her own legislation to pay more than passing notice. Now he wanted to pick her brain a little bit. That was all she knew as she stood by the elevators, waiting for him to get off the damn phone.

"So where are you from?" asked the receptionist.

"Oh, a little bitsy place called Dade City," said Barnett, watching the elevator doors open and close. "Small town, simple Florida. You know."

Hanlon walked up.

"Now don't you listen to her, Joanie," he said. "Next thing you know she'll be telling you she's just a li'l ol' country lawyer. And then you better hold on to your wallet."

Barnett grinned, cocked her head.

"Steve Hanlon," she said, "you don't even know how small-town I really *am*. Dade City's where I *say* I'm from, but I actually grew *up* in a little place you never *heard* of."

"Mmm, hmmm," smiled Hanlon. "And where might that be?"

"A place," said Barnett, "called Lacoochee."

Hanlon nearly fell over.

"Martha," he said. "Do you know where half the Rosewood survivors are from?"

She shrugged, shook her head.

"They're from Lacoochee. They all moved to *Lacoochee*."

"You're kidding," she said. "Steve, I spent the first nine years of my life there. My dad *died* in Lacoochee."

"Did you ever hear of a man named Arnett Doctor?" asked Hanlon.

Now it was Barnett's turn to almost fall down. What she had heard and read of Rosewood till now had not mentioned a word about Lacoochee. And nowhere had she seen the name Doctor.

"Arnett *Doctor?*" she said. "My father *delivered* Arnett Doctor. I grew *up* with Arnett."

"Just a minute," said Hanlon. And he reached for the phone.

Arnett Doctor. Martha Barnett couldn't believe it. Arnett and her big brother Will had been good friends growing up in Lacoochee, as close as a black and a white boy could be back then. Martha was the tot, four years younger, trailing behind the big boys whenever they'd let her. Arnett used to hoist her on his back when the summer sun baked the schoolyard sand so hot it burned her bare feet. "Baby Martha," he called her.

They all went barefoot back then, the black kids who lived across the tracks in Mosstown and the quarters, and the children like Martha and her brothers, who lived on the same side of town as the Cummers, the white side of Lacoochee. Martha had grown up with the Cummer kids, eaten plenty of meals at their dinner table and they at hers. It was the Cummers who had brought Martha's father to Lacoochee in the first place, to be the mill town's doctor.

Doc Willie, that's what his patients called him, black and white alike. William Walters. He wasn't Cummer and Sons' first doctor, but he would be its last. The company brought him down from Jacksonville in the late 1930s to set up his office in a long wooden building there by the sawmill. He was still

there when the mill closed in 1959, and he kept his office open for his Lacoochee patients until the day he died in 1983. Even after he moved his family
down the road to Dade City in 1957, Doc Willie still made the daily trip to his
old wood-framed office along the dirt drive at the edge of the Mosstown section of Lacoochee.

Martha Walters just about grew up in that office, its wood floors and walls
rough-hewn and smooth, carved from some of that sawmill cypress. Her
mother Helen was there just about every day, too, to take care of the records
and paperwork. Helen Walters never liked the fact that her husband kept separate waiting rooms for the whites and the blacks, but that was the way of the
times and there was nothing she could do about it. She could, however, see to it
that the blacks had a few more comforts, something to compensate for the separation. She got them a brand-new TV, for example, while the snowy set in the
white waiting room went wanting for repairs. And when color television came
along, she bought one for the blacks long before the white patients got theirs.
"That was just her way," says Martha. "You know, social equity."

Social equity was not a major concern for young Martha, though she saw in-
equity all around her every day. The black children she played with went to a
different school from hers. When she went to the movies, the black kids had to
sit up in the balcony while Martha stayed on the floor level with her white
friends. The only black people she saw when her family went out for a meal
were the cooks and waiters who served them. She and her brothers would play
with kids like Arnett, but always outdoors. The only times black children came
inside her house were when they were with an adult like Arnett's Aunt Rebecca,
who cleaned and washed for the Walters just as she did for the Cummers.

When Martha went into her black friends' homes, it was always with her father, who made his house calls at night. Martha loved to tag along, and she was
always struck by the size of the homes, so small compared to hers, so crowded,
even with hardly any furniture. And always the smell of cooking, something
frying. Night or day, the air in those homes was thick and sweet with the smell
of fried fat. To this day, when Martha Barnett passes a frying pan, it takes her
right back to one of those Mosstown cabins, her daddy in a back bedroom with
his medicine bag while Martha sat in the front room playing on the floor with
the kids, the hum of crickets and the croak of frogs drifting through the open
windows, the air inside warm and soft and safe.

Martha knew almost every family in Mosstown, and they all knew her, Doc

Willie's little girl. Even when the Walters moved to Dade City when she was nine, Martha kept coming back to Lacoochee, making the rounds with her dad. It wasn't until she began high school in 1961 that her visits became less frequent. That was the year the Freedom Riders came south, young protesters rolling into Georgia and Alabama and Mississippi, beaten by mobs in Birmingham and Montgomery, their bus set afire in Anniston, just a taste of the clashes and killings to come.

But Martha Walters knew about none of that. She was a Pasco High cheerleader—a co-captain. She was on the yearbook staff, the student newspaper, an officer in the arts society, head of the Beta Club. "That was my whole life," she says. "I was the typical middle-class kid."

She knew that some of the boys she dated were in the Klan, just like their fathers. To this day she says she wouldn't be surprised if her own brothers had been in the Klan, though she has no doubt her father was not. Back then Dade City had the largest Klan membership in the state. It was almost like a club, as socially acceptable as the Kiwanis. If some of those boys Martha dated were Klansmen, they didn't talk about it, they were never ugly or racist, at least not around her. They were nice boys, good boys, nothing like the "rednecks," as Martha calls them, the ones who swaggered down Dade City's main street, hooting, shouting "nigger" this and "nigger" that, taking weekend joy rides into the black sections of town, heaving beer bottles and jars of mustard at black homes, then driving off into the night, their drunken laughter trailing behind with the exhaust fumes from their hot rods.

Martha Walters knew about them, but she didn't know about the murder of Medgar Evers, or the bombing of Birmingham's Sixteenth Street Baptist Church, or the beatings at the base of Selma's Edmund Pettus Bridge in the spring of 1965. That was the spring of Martha's senior year at Pasco High, and all she knew about the world beyond Dade City was that she wanted to become a part of it, to leave this little town behind and make something more of herself than the nurses or teachers or housewives the women in Dade City were allowed to become.

So she went to college at Tulane, shared classrooms for the first time with blacks and Jews. The only Jewish people she had ever known until then were the Weitzenkorns—Otto and his wife Elaine, who ran a little department store back home. Theirs was the only Jewish family in Dade City. Martha worked summers for them as a clerk.

Now she was surrounded by Jewish students from cities like Chicago and New York, and black students come all the way from Africa. She shared classes with Asians and Europeans, young men and women with wondrous accents and urbane ideas. This was New Orleans in the late 1960s, more than a world away from Dade City, where everything was simply, rigidly black or white.

Martha got married in 1969 and graduated that year with a degree in American Studies, after writing her senior thesis on race relations in America. She watched her husband, a Marine, leave for Vietnam, then she entered law school at the University of Florida, thinking she might make a career working for the rights of underprivileged children. She came out with an offer from Holland and Knight, and she took it, joining the firm in 1973.

Twenty years later she was still there, among the shining stars of Holland and Knight's more than two hundred partners. She billed her clients a top rate of two hundred and eighty-five dollars an hour, a fee they were happy to pay for the services she provided. She was a busy woman, which was part of the reason she hadn't paid much attention to Rosewood. Another was that the case had nothing to do with her, no connection to any aspect of her life.

Until now.

"Arnett?" Hanlon asked, keeping his eyes on Barnett's as he spoke into the telephone. "Hey, this is Steve Hanlon. Listen, do you know a woman named Martha Barnett?"

Silence. Hanlon knotted his eyebrows.

"*Walters*," whispered Barnett. "My name was Martha *Walters*."

Hanlon nodded.

"I mean *Walters*," he said. "You know a woman named Martha Walters?"

Barnett could hear a small yelp on the other end of the line. She reached for it, excited, amazed. Arnett sounded pleased, but not particularly surprised. She exclaimed what an incredible coincidence this was, and he chuckled, as if it were the most natural thing in the world. Wasn't he amazed? she asked him.

No, Arnett told her, actually he was not amazed at all. "This is growing beyond us now," he said. "It's in bigger hands than ours. It's in God's hands. If it was time for you to be a part of this," he said, "then you would be. And it looks like it's time."

Martha Barnett didn't know about all that, but she did know one thing. This was personal now. And she was absolutely going to be a part of it.

TWENTY

Satisfaction

There are things Maxine Jones remembers about her father, and there are things she simply knows. She remembers her father was always around the house when she was little, fixing things, horsing around with her and her brothers. But she knows he never lived there, not before she was born and not after. She remembers her mother would cook dinner for the family then carry a covered plate up the street to the room where her father lived. They took care of each other like that, Maxine's mother and father. Sometimes they even acted like they were in love. But they were never married, Maxine knows that. Her mother eventually took another man for a husband, but even then Maxine kept carrying dinner up the street to her father. And sometimes he would come down and join them for a meal at their house, sitting at the table alongside Maxine's mother and stepdad, just like family.

Maxine remembers how awfully old her father was. It always seemed that he should have been her grandfather, he was that old—fifty-five when she was born. He died before she was grown enough to ask many questions, but she knows his name was Unis McCloud, that he was born in 1898 up around Geor-

Maxine Jones, William Rogers and Tom Dye

gia, and that his parents were slaves, a fact which astonishes Maxine to this day, that a woman as young as she is can say that her grandparents were slaves.

Maxine's father owned his own home for a while, there in the St. Petersburg neighborhood where Maxine grew up. But he got behind in his taxes is the way she remembers it, and he had to give the place up, go back to renting a room. Maxine remembers helping him the day he moved out. She was six or seven at the time, and they were hoisting a wardrobe down the stairs when one of the doors swung open and its mirror shattered.

"Oh Daddy," Maxine said, "you're going to have seven years bad luck."

"Baby," her father told her, "it can't get any worse than this."

Maxine's father was a painter by trade, and sometimes she would go with him on jobs. He didn't have much education, quit school in the third grade, could sign his name and that was about it. But he always told Maxine she was going to be something more, she was going to be something special. She was going to be a teacher, he told her, and she believed him. Maxine believed everything her father told her.

He died when she was twelve, but by then Maxine was already on her way to making her father's vision come true. She was always near the top of her class, came home every afternoon and went straight up to her room to read. She devoured books as if they were candy. Her family didn't live far from 22nd Street, the heart of black St. Petersburg, and there were plenty of kids in Maxine's neighborhood who spent their afternoons and evenings roaming over to those bright lights and loud sounds, seeing what kind of trouble they could get into, what excitement they could find. But Maxine wasn't interested in any of that. The swirl of 22nd Street may as well have been on the other side of the world as far as Maxine cared. Her life was bounded by her books, her school, the church, the playground, her mother and brothers and sisters, and, for the time he was alive, her father who lived up the street.

Maxine Jones is forty-two years old now, an associate professor of history at Florida State University. Of her nine brothers and sisters, and her parents, and their parents, Maxine was the first in her family to graduate from high school, the first to attend college. And now she has become the teacher her father told her she would be.

Her specialty is African-American history. She has written books on the subject, of course, and she keeps a file cabinet full of folders in her tiny office tucked at the end of a narrow hallway in the high-rise history building on the FSU campus. Each folder contains clippings on a topic she might like to write about someday, newspaper and magazine articles that have caught her eye over the years. She never picks up a newspaper or magazine without a pair of scissors by her side.

One of those files is marked ROSEWOOD. She began it in 1982 with a single clipping, that Sunday story in the *St. Petersburg Times*. "I remember saying, 'Hey, this is something I might be interested in.' It didn't shock me. I know my black history, and there's *nothing* that shocks me. But it piqued my interest. I thought it might be something I'd get around to someday, but then I've got a file cabinet *full* of things I might get around to someday."

She fidgets when she talks about Rosewood. She taps a pencil on her desk, squeezes her eyes shut, chooses her words with care. She is an exceptionally tall woman, six-foot-two, dark-skinned, a commanding presence. But she seems to shrink when she talks about Rosewood. And she winces.

"It was not," she says, pausing and drawing a deep breath, "anything like the experience I thought it would be."

Jones remembers the flush of excitement she felt in the summer of 1993 when she first heard that the state was forming a fact-finding team to investigate the circumstances surrounding the attack on Rosewood. She had followed the demise of the first claims bill, adding the clippings to her folder. Now she had a chance to actually become involved, and she leaped at the opportunity. She could think of no one better suited for this study than herself, and the state's Board of Regents, which selected the team, apparently agreed. When the academic political smoke had cleared, after a month or so of behind-the-scenes elbowing and jostling among history departments across the state, five names emerged to form the group, with Maxine Jones's at the top.

It was an impressive lineup, but not without controversy. Besides Jones, there was Bill Rogers, sixty-four, a venerable elder statesman among Florida's historical scholars and an authority on the Old South. From Gainesville came David Colburn, a fifty-one-year-old professor of history at the University of Florida and an expert on the state's racial and civil rights history. Representing Florida A&M was forty-one-year-old Larry Rivers, whose current research focus was slavery in Florida and who was the only black member of the team besides Jones. And then there was Tom Dye, a doctoral student at Florida State who had spent almost a year researching Rosewood's history after stumbling across the subject while writing his master's thesis on the fishing industry in Cedar Key.

There had been some questions about selecting Dye. Compared to the others, he was just a kid, still in his thirties, not even done yet with his dissertation. There were full professors across the state, department heads with pages of publications and awards on their resumes, who had been passed over for this team, and here was a *student* in line for a slot. But Jones, the team's director, and the others insisted Dye be included. He knew more about Rosewood than any of them, and more importantly, he knew his way around the docks and fishermen of Cedar Key. His in-laws had a summer home there. He had spent years in those woods and wetlands, as well as along that waterfront. The team would need someone like that when they began poking around down in Levy County itself.

By the time they first came together that August, the group was well aware of the political freight they were taking on, the firestorm of controversy that was certain to swirl around their findings, and the impact those findings would have on real lives. Before they even began, Florida State's dean's office sent over a public relations expert to give them a crash course in dealing with the media. But there really was no way to prepare for what lay ahead of them. "This was so different from anything any of us had ever done," says Maxine Jones. "We were used to studying history, not becoming a *part* of it."

They faced an ungodly deadline as well. The state had to have the report by December, for the start of the 1994 legislative session. That gave the group four months to conduct the kind of investigation that, under normal academic circumstances, would take three or four years to complete.

But then there was nothing normal about Rosewood. The team soon learned that as they launched their study in late August, beginning with a day trip down to Gulf Hammock, an excursion intended to give them a feel for the place. The outing in itself was odd for scholars more accustomed to searching among library shelves and sifting through archival collections than climbing over barbed wire fences, hacking through briers, swatting at swarms of mosquitoes and dodging the occasional rattlesnake—which pretty much summed up their visit that day to what was left of Rosewood. They scrounged around the woods behind Doyal Scoggins's house, came across a pile of old bricks, one of which Maxine Jones took home with her, "as a souvenir." Other than that, the highlight of the day was the barbecue lunch they stopped for on their way through Chiefland.

Their real research began with the September gathering of Rosewood survivors and their families at Florida A&M University. Tom Dye used his connections with the Tallahassee Radisson, where he once worked, to get a discount rate for hotel rooms for the families. Minnie Lee Langley, for one, had never stayed in a place like that. She'd worked in some, but she'd never stayed in one.

The team spent two days interviewing the survivors over at the A&M campus, sitting down one on one, taping the witnesses' remembrances of the town and their accounts of the attack. The details were vivid, the emotions palpable. Maxine Jones had never experienced anything quite like it, nor had her colleagues. "We knew then that we were dealing with something special," says Jones. "Not just tombs and cobwebbed documents, but living breathing human beings."

Documents, as the team soon found, were maddeningly scarce. Through September and October, Jones and her colleagues fanned out in search of any records they could find related to Rosewood, any shreds of paper that might shed some historical light on this extinct little village.

Larry Rivers flew up to the Tuskegee Institute in Alabama to search the NAACP records stored there, especially the lynching files, and was disappointed to find only one reference to Rosewood, in a tiny newspaper story. Newspaper stories were the last thing the team needed. They had dozens of those already. What they were after, like any good historians, were primary sources, official records and reports. And what they found, which did not entirely surprise them, was that when it came to a black community in the rural Deep South in the early part of this century, nobody seemed to bother much with records and reports.

Still, the team's job was to find what it could. Tom Dye went to Washington, D.C., where he waded into the Library of Congress, sifting through west Florida post office records, federal marshal's reports, Masonic society listings, the congregational records of black churches that existed in that region of the state at the time—he even rode a bus to a distant annex building where old state health department records were stored, hoping to find some reference to Rosewood. His efforts yielded a few scattered sightings of the town's name on this list or that, but nothing that helped sharpen the picture of what the place was like at the time of the attack or of the attack itself.

For that, the team searched closer to home, hoping the state's archives collection in Tallahassee would give them more than the census and property records they already had. Tom Dye's previous research on Rosewood, culled mostly from records stored in the Levy County courthouse, established the basic history of the village, its beginning in 1845 with the opening of a post office, its growth during the next half century, the existence of the black-owned M. Goins & Brothers' Naval stores company, which did a big business after the turn of the century distilling turpentine and rosin from the surrounding pine forests, the decline of the town's population by 1920, and the general layout of the village in terms of homes and churches at the time of the attack in 1923.

Unfortunately, the archives yielded hardly anything beyond what the team already knew. The state of Florida did not even begin keeping an archives until the late 1960s. "History," sighs Jones, "was apparently not a top priority down here."

The archival material concerning Rosewood was spotty at best. There was, for example, no correspondence from Governor Cary Hardee concerning Rosewood, no letters that might have fleshed out and verified newspaper accounts of the telegram he sent to the Levy County sheriff during the week of the attack. In fact, none of Hardee's correspondence during his term as Florida's governor from 1921 to 1925 could be found in the archives. "If those papers exist," says Jones, shaking her head, "they're in someone's attic or basement."

The county's grand jury records of the time were gone, destroyed in a fire. The attorney general's records for that year made no reference to Rosewood. The archives did contain old state prison records, which revealed the arrest of twenty-five-year-old Samuel Carter in 1900. The charge, according to the hand-written one-line entry on the brittle, yellowing ledger book page, was *assault to murder*. Carter was sent to prison that November, according to the entry, and was released in October of 1901—twenty-one years and three months before he was lynched in Rosewood.

On another page, written in the same florid script, were the names of Sylvester Carrier, age 26, and his father, Hayward, age 50, both *brown*, both from Rosewood, Fla., and both sentenced on April 2, 1918, to six months in prison for *fraudulently changing marks*—cattle rustling. They came back home that fall, September 20, according to the record.

As for the 1923 attack, however, there were no records at all. No sheriff's papers. No state militia entries. Nothing from the national guard. Nothing from the governor's office. All the team had to go on were newspaper accounts and the survivors' testimonies. And if those testimonies were to be trusted, the team felt it needed to hear the other side of the story as well, the white side. Which was what Tom Dye and Bill Rogers spent most of that autumn trying to find.

They were the natural choices to try penetrating the close-knit circles around Cedar Key, Rogers with his country lawyer demeanor and his seersucker suit, and Dye with the boyish eagerness that had served him so well during the months he had spent researching his thesis. "I had really gotten close to the guys down there," recalls Dye. "They took me out fishing, shared their beer with me, shared their *homes* with me. I figured I'd just put the beat-up ball cap back on, wouldn't shave for a couple of days, and could go back on down there and get right in some doors."

He figured wrong. The previous year had seen Cedar Key overrun with newspaper, magazine and television reporters nosing around about Rosewood, hunting for evidence of racism past and present, and the town was sick of it. Cedar Key felt it was getting a bad rap, along with a bad name. Dye himself had become something of a celebrity around the Florida State history department when he popped up in a *Washington Post* story that summer, quoted as an expert on Rosewood. A copy of that story was still tacked on the department chairman's door when the fall semester began. "I guess it *was* sort of a big deal, for a graduate student to be quoted in a national newspaper like that," admits Dye. "Shit yeah, I was flattered."

The people of Cedar Key were not. Doors that had once been opened to Dye were slammed in his face when he and Rogers came knocking that fall. "They treated me like I was a traitor," he says. "I understood how they felt, people being stigmatized for something they weren't even connected to. But I was hurt, too. I felt like I'd lost some friends."

The best Dye and Rogers were able to turn up was a tape recording Dye had discovered at the Cedar Key Historical Society Museum during his thesis research, and an interview Rogers was able to finagle with an old man in a nursing home in Chiefland.

The tape was a cassette, unlabeled, tossed in a drawer in the museum's back storage room. It contained an interview done in the early 1980s by a local historian with an old fisherman named Jason McElveen, who died not long after the tape was made. Most of the recording consisted of McElveen's memories of logging and fishing around Cedar Key during the first half of the century. But at one point the old man suddenly turned to the subject of the "riot" at Rosewood, and Tom Dye realized he was listening to an eyewitness account of the slaughter he had heard only rumors about until then. The scratchy voice, hardly intelligible at times on the dusty tape, told a tale of carnage tinged with the bluster of a braggart:

> It jus' rolled on three days. We surrounded the mill with guards and tried to keep the niggers working. We knew if we could keep them niggers in the mill we could keep 'em straight. But we knew if we let 'em out of there the farmers would get 'em. Every nigger had jumped up and run out of there whether it was a coon dog or what.
>
> So that rolled on for three days. In three days they sent word that the one we wanted would be in a certain building, an old school building right beside the depot. Said that they had 'im and that if we thought we could, to come get 'im. That be just about like throwing gasoline on fire, to tell a bunch of white people that.
>
> So it turned my blood red and all of the others. A bunch of us gathered up and went up there. I didn't have anything but a twelve-gauge gun, a pump gun. Plenty of buckshot. And most of them had the same thing. So we went up to the niggers and come back about midnight, and everything was quiet when we got back.
>
> The next day, they went up there and buried seventeen niggers out of the house. I don't know how many more they picked out the woods and the fields 'round about there. It was stated several times that there were ten more.
>
> But Ol' Man Sumner was the yard man around there and he done the burying. They jus' laid 'em in a row and plowed two furrows with a big field plow. Plowed two big furrows there and put the niggers in the trench.
>
> There's no marker or anything. Don't know who they was or why they was. They said there was twenty-six in there. After that, for the next four or five years, they picked up skulls and things all around there, in the woods and up the creek.

The volunteers manning the museum wouldn't think of letting Dye borrow the tape when he returned that fall, but they reluctantly allowed him to listen to it again in the back room. He had a recorder of his own in his pocket and used it to surreptitiously tape the tape. "I guess it was a little dishonest," he admits, "but it was the only way to get the information."

McElveen's account became part of the team's final report, as did Dye and Rogers's encounter with Fred Kirkland, the same man who had appeared on the 1983 "60 Minutes" broadcast. A former Levy County game warden who knew the Gulf Hammock swamps like his backyard, Kirkland had been an old man when he appeared on "60 Minutes." Now he was ancient, living in a nursing home in Chiefland, where Dye and Rogers arrived on a late October afternoon.

They asked a nurse where they might find Mr. Kirkland, and she pointed toward a ring of rocking chairs set out under a tree on the side lawn, four or five old men rocking silently in the shade. "That's him right there," she said, pointing to a huge, white-haired figure filling one of the chairs.

"He must have been six-three, six-four," recalls Dye. "You could see he had been a big, powerful man at one time. Now he was bent over a little bit. Big hands, big thick glasses. His eyes were real bad. Cataracts. And he was a little hard of hearing. You had to talk real loud to him."

Dye let Rogers do the talking. The professor was at his porch-sitting, iced-tea-sipping best among old folks.

"Why, are you Mr. Kirkland?" asked Rogers, sidling up to the circle.

"Why, yes I am," said the big man.

"Well, Mr. Kirkland, I am so *happy* to meet you. I'm Professor Rogers from Florida State University, and I understand you used to be sheriff here in Levy County."

"Well, yeah, sure," said Kirkland, puffing up with just a little bit of pride. He motioned toward an empty chair with one of his huge hands. "Sit down."

They chatted for a while about this and that, then got around to the subject of Rosewood. Rogers asked if he could use his tape recorder, and Kirkland said he'd prefer not. So the professor simply took notes. The old man said he knew James Taylor, was there the day it started, when Taylor's wife was "raped by a nigger," as Kirkland put it. When Rogers asked him about the lynching of Sam Carter, Kirkland backed off.

"I'm not gonna talk about that," he said. "We got this one boy. We got him. That's all I'm gonna say about it."

"Fine," said Rogers, and he moved on to the shootout at the Carrier house.

"I don't want to talk about that part of it," said the old man.

Rogers nodded. Then Dye stepped in.

"Well," he asked, "how did everybody feel when it was all over?"

The old man looked off in the distance.

"Well," he said. "After it was over, James Taylor said he was satisfied."

"What do you mean?" asked Dye.

"Just that," said Kirkland. "When it was all over, James Taylor was satisfied."

They chatted a while longer, then bid Fred Kirkland goodbye. The old man smiled and leaned back in his rocker, with his friends, quiet again in the October afternoon.

TWENTY-ONE

Backwoods Folks

So this was what the historians had. A sheaf of seventy-one-year-old news-paper clippings and a smattering of official documents. They had a dead man's voice on a dusty tape and the coy recollections of an old man in a nursing home. They had the testimonies of the survivors, filled with vivid, wrenching details—but those details diverged as often as they overlapped.

All in all, Maxine Jones and her colleagues were on shaky ground, far from the solid footing of fact to which they were accustomed. Still, it was November now, the deadline approaching for the report to be written, and if this was all they had, well, it had to be enough. And they felt it was—not nearly enough to satisfy their own standards as historians, but enough to give the state what it had asked for, an objective basis on which to judge the validity of this claim.

"We would have liked to have had a lot more, of course," says Jones. "But we had the basics. It would be impossible to recreate exactly what happened, but we felt we had come pretty close. Especially considering the constraints of time."

The attack on Rosewood occurred, there was no doubt about that. It lasted

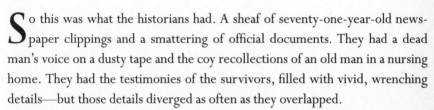

Sumner baseball team, 1922 (Ernest Parham, second from right)

a week, and at least eight people were killed—six blacks and two whites. That much was documented, as was the fact that property owned by blacks in Rosewood prior to 1923 was vacated that year and acquired by local whites soon thereafter. The state government was aware of the activity that week in Rosewood, and although it had time and the resources to respond, it did not. Nor was an effort made to protect or restore the property that was destroyed and the land that was subsequently sold. These, concluded the team, were facts. Finally, the failure of the grand jury to issue a single indictment was evidence of nothing less than "the abandonment of the American justice system," as the team described it in their report.

But even as they began shaping that report in November, the five historians were nagged by the fact that so much of it—especially the description of the town of Rosewood as it existed at the time of the attack, and the specifics of the attack itself—was based almost exclusively on the testimonies of the Rosewood survivors, who were all children at the time, whose memories could well have shifted over the course of seventy years, and who were the claimants in this bill, a fact which might affect their objectivity—or at least be conceived that way.

Total objectivity. That was what was missing from the reconstruction of what happened that week. The witnesses found by the team so far, black and white alike, had reason to be biased, as did the newspaper accounts of the time, which were almost entirely second-hand elaborations of sketchy wire service reports. Few, if any, of the journalists who wrote those articles were actually at the scene. Most of their information came from the Levy County sheriff's department or was relayed through rumors and word of mouth among the area's whites. These "facts" were then filtered through the interpretations of each newspaper's editorial staff, which—black journals as well as white—all had their own social, political and racial agendas.

Just one detached, disinterested witness, one man or woman who was there, who was neither among the attacked nor the attackers that week, but who simply saw what happened and who now, seven decades later, could recount it, clearly, lucidly, unburdened by the yokes of fear, shame or guilt—that is what the study team needed. That is what the Rosewood families themselves would need, when their claim faced the scrutiny of a skeptical legislature.

And that, remarkably, is what fell into Maxine Jones's lap late that month. She won't say who gave her the man's name—"It's a small, small world," is all she will offer. That, and the fact that the man's name came from "a friend of a friend," via Jacksonville, who pointed Maxine down to Orlando, where an eighty-nine-year-old widower named Ernest Parham lived by himself on a tree-shaded street in a quiet neighborhood called College Park. Ernest Parham had never talked about Rosewood to anyone—"No one ever asked," he says—until David Colburn, prompted by Maxine Jones, drove down from the University of Florida on a Wednesday afternoon two weeks before Thanksgiving and knocked on the old man's door.

Ernest Parham answers that same door today, a couple of years older but still remarkably fit. The tiny lawn in front of his house, mowed smooth as a putting green, Parham cuts that himself. The Buick parked in his carport, sparkling alabaster in the midday sunlight, he washes it by hand every week. Waxes it, too. The small, cozy living room into which he hospitably invites visitors is immaculate, kept that way by Ernest ever since his wife Sophia passed away seven years ago. He offers a cup of coffee, tea, maybe a glass of something cold, then settles his soft ninety-one-year-old body into a seat.

His cheeks are pink and his thinning hair is snow white. His eyes smile calmly through a set of wire-rimmed glasses. He moves without effort, rising several times from his easy chair to fetch an old photograph or a scrapbook, nothing hurried or labored about his movements or his speech, everything about him as steady and serene as a monk. His light cotton shirt and khaki slacks are perfectly pressed and creased, fitting for a man who worked almost fifty years in the laundry business. He owned his own company by the time he retired in 1976—Acme Cleaners and Laundry, "the biggest in Orlando at the time," he says, not boasting, simply stating a fact. He sold the place to a nephew that year, and he remembers the specifics of the deal as if it were yesterday. He remembers the specifics of his entire life that way, including the details of what he witnessed that winter's week in 1923, when he was living in a small Gulf Coast village called Sumner, just down the road from a place called Rosewood.

He was twelve when his family moved to Sumner from Cedar Key in 1916, after Ernest's father, a logger, "took tuberculosis" and died. Ernest's mother and stepfather owned the Island Hotel in Cedar Key for a time, and Ernest and his two brothers made good money carrying bags for the steady flow of "drummers"—salesmen—who stepped off the Seaboard train every night looking for the best room on the island. The boys were disappointed when their parents told them the sawmill company up the road in Sumner had hired them to come run the hotel there. Cedar Key was like a city compared to where they were headed, but Ernest and his brothers made the best of it.

"Sumner was strictly a sawmill town," says Parham. "About three hundred and fifty people. Those who worked for the Cummers, blacks and whites, lived in furnished homes provided by the company. Down toward the train depot there were farmers and lumbermen living in homes of their own. There was a post office, two grocery stores, the hotel, and that was about it."

Ernest and his family lived in the hotel, and when Ernest got a little older, he went to work in the commissary owned by the Cummers. The other store in town, a much smaller operation, was run by a man named Poly Wilkerson.

"A big, blustery fellow," recalls Parham. "He was the quarters boss for the Cummers for a time, but they let him go, I presume because he was carrying liquor into the quarters to sell to the black people. At least that's what I was told. There were several other incidents, too. Walter Pillsbury, the general superintendent, finally let him go and hired Clarence Williams, the deputy sheriff, as quarters boss, and Wilkerson was real upset with the mill people after that."

Parham shows no trace of emotion as he tells his story. Occasionally he lifts his hand, ever so slightly, to make a point. But other than that, he simply measures his words and speaks.

"One day Wilkerson came up to the hotel," he continues, "where Clarence Williams stayed. It was a Sunday afternoon, and he called Clarence Williams out. He told him he was gonna kill him.

"Well, Clarence came out. And Wilkerson drew his gun. But Clarence drew his at the same time, and he poked his gun right in Poly Wilkerson's stomach, and he said, 'Well, now. You pull your trigger, and I'm gonna pull *mine*.' And Poly Wilkerson backed down.

"Now that was not the only incident like that that involved Wilkerson, but it was the only one I actually saw."

Though the blacks and whites worked and lived alongside one another in Sumner, their lives were lived apart, says Parham. "My mother's cook had a boy, and we played with him, but that was it. We never played with black kids from the quarters. We called them 'nigras,' and if you were upset with them, you called them 'niggers.'"

As for the blacks in Rosewood, they seemed a world away. "They had a very good baseball team, that's something everyone knew. We used to go up there to watch them play. Whites would come and watch as well as blacks. Sumner had its own team, a white team, but we didn't play Rosewood. You just didn't do that in those days. Or you weren't *supposed* to. The fact of the matter is we used to slip off sometimes and go up to Rosewood to play them, and they would let us win. But they were better than we were, no question about it."

It was in the summer of 1919, after he turned fifteen, that Ernest Parham got to know Rosewood well. That was the summer he began driving his stepfather's ice wagon, making a circular route that took him to houses throughout Rosewood as well as Sumner. He rarely went inside the homes—one of his stepfather's black employees actually hauled the blocks of ice off the wagon, while Ernest did the driving—but over the course of the next couple of years, Parham became familiar with almost every family living in Rosewood. And he respected what he saw.

"These were very progressive black people. They had their gardens and their homes, and they kept them in real good shape, above the average for blacks at that time. No one lived in that settlement but black people, except for Mr. Wright, who had a store there. He was the only white in that area that I knew of."

Parham pauses, takes a sip of water, then goes on.

"They were high-type people, houses kept up real good, white picket fences around some of them. They didn't have lawns. The yards were dirt, and they swept them with big brushes. They had flowers, too, and some fruit trees.

"Some grew vegetables and sold them to people around the mill. Some of the men in Rosewood worked at the mill, and some of them worked at a turpentine still over at Wylly. Almost all of them worked somewhere, and they worked hard and seemed to do fairly well for themselves. The families that stood out, as I recall, were the Bradleys and the Carriers. Sarah Carrier, Sylvester Carrier's mother, was educated, I think, because she had a piano in the front room. They kept that house looking very good, a two-story house. As I said, these were high-type people."

And that, as Parham sees it, was the root of the trouble that erupted that week in 1923.

"Basically there were no problems at all between the people in Sumner and the Rosewood people," he says. "None at all. There was a local Klan group in

Sumner, plenty of Klan people in town, and *they* had no problems with the blacks. The blacks took care of their own business, stayed on their property, and the whites stayed on theirs.

"But there was a certain amount of jealousy among what you called the 'outback' people, the whites who didn't live in the town itself. They lived out in the woods. There was some resentment among those backwoods folks because of the fact that the Rosewood people were more aggressive than they were, selling vegetables and such in Sumner. To tell the truth, they just didn't like to see black people doing better than they were.

"And there was a lot of them that didn't think too much of Sylvester Carrier. He was not as polite as the rest of the blacks. He worked away from Rosewood a lot. Where, I don't know. He'd come home and be there awhile, and then he'd be gone and you didn't know where he was. He was aloof, distant, and there were some who didn't like that attitude. It wasn't the Cummer people who didn't like it. It was those white people who were more out in the woods who didn't like it. The outback people."

Parham stops, takes another sip of water.

"All I can say is they didn't think too much of Sylvester Carrier. They felt like he was *uppity*."

And so arrived that New Year's morning, 1923. Parham remembers how cold it was. "Awfully cold," he says. "There was frost that morning, and we didn't have frost that often."

Normally Ernest would have been off to school. He was eighteen, in his junior year at Cedar Key High, and he drove the school's bus, picking up his classmates on the way in each morning and dropping them off on the way home to Sumner each afternoon. But this being the holidays, Ernest was working at the commissary that morning, punching in at five-thirty, as always. It was midmorning, as he recalls, when he first heard of the "rape situation."

"Everyone coming into the store was talking about it. First they were saying Fannie Taylor had been attacked. Then somebody said they were pulling bloodhounds together. All day long, I kept getting updates like that."

By the time Ernest locked up at seven, it was dark. His boss, the commissary manager, had left hours earlier to join the group that was following the dogs. "Johnson was his name," says Parham. "Albert Johnson."

Ernest walked on over to the hotel, where he saw Clarence Williams's car parked out front. Someone said the deputy sheriff had gone to Rosewood, so

Ernest decided to bring him his car. "The keys were in it, sure," he says. "You never took a key out of the car in those days."

Parham took a short cut to Rosewood, a dirt road, then circled back onto the "hard road," the highway of crushed limestone that eight years later would be paved and labeled Route 24. There, about a hundred yards from the western edge of the village, sitting on the running board of another man's car, was Clarence Williams. In the distance, in the darkness, Ernest could hear the barking of dogs and the muffled voices of men. He gave Williams the car keys and walked toward the commotion.

"It was a group of about twenty-five, maybe thirty men, not a mob yet," recalls Parham, "in front of Sam Carter's house."

Ernest Parham knew Sam Carter, says Carter often came to shop at the Cummer commissary. "Sure I knew him. He was a large fella, a blacksmith, very humble, like most of them were in those days. I remember the thing about him is he was always immaculate. He wore overalls, what we called a 'jumper' in those days. They'd be blue when you bought them brand new, but they bleached out to almost white after you washed them. And Sam Carter always stood out that way, in this bright white jumper."

Parham pauses a moment, taps the arm of his chair with his fingers.

"When I got there they had him stretched up, trying to make him talk. It was his wagon tracks they'd followed, and they assumed he had picked this black man up, which I'm reasonably sure he had.

"They had him stretched up there and he couldn't talk even if he wanted to. Someone said let him down, and when they did, he said, Yes, he'd tell them where it was. And this one fella who had a hold of the rope, he also had a double-barreled shotgun, and he said, 'Now if the hounds don't pick up that trail, I'm gonna kill you.'

"There'd been some drinking. You could smell it. And this fella with the shotgun, he had been doing some drinking. It was obvious by the way he acted.

"There's no need telling you who he was. I knew him, but he still has family around. I'm sure there are others can tell you who he was. But I won't."

The rope was untied from Sam Carter's neck, and he led the mob about a mile into the woods, says Parham. There were no homes in sight. The only light came from their lanterns.

"They got to where they couldn't go any further. The bloodhounds ran around but couldn't pick up the trail. So this fella stepped up, called Carter a black so-and-so, and then he pulled the trigger. Just like that. Held the shotgun right against his head, and he pulled both triggers."

Parham taps his fingers again.

"I'd never seen a man shot before."

He folds his hands together.

"You could hear the gasps. I think most everyone was shocked. Mr. Pillsbury, he was standing there, and he said, 'Oh my God, now we'll never know who did it.' And then everybody dispersed, just turned and left. They was all really upset with this fella that did the killing. He was not very well thought of, not then, not for years thereafter, for that matter."

Clarence Williams, the only arm of the law within reach, was still up the road at the time, says Parham, waiting beside his car.

"There wasn't a whole lot Clarence could do about this group," says Parham, "and he knew it."

The next morning, "Rosewood was all anybody was talking about," says Parham. The mill was still operating, people were still going to work, black and white. "But there was a lot going on, people coming in from up in Taylor County and Gilchrist County, rushing into the store, getting shells, buying ammunition. We had to finally hide the guns and shells 'cause the people weren't paying for them."

It went that way Wednesday as well, and Thursday, too, strangers streaming into the store, looking to buy weapons. There was no word of anything actually happening in Rosewood, not until Thursday night.

"It was late," says Parham, "probably close to about ten o'clock. It couldn't have been after that because the electricity was always cut off at ten. The hotel was one of the few places in town with electric lights, and they'd flash 'em a couple of times just before ten, from up at the mill, to let us know they were cutting them off. And I know the lights were still *on*.

"We were sitting in a circle around the living room fireplace, there by the lobby. Clarence Williams came up and took a seat. The fire was popping and crackling, like it would, and Clarence sat down and said, 'All hell is taking place up at Rosewood.' He said something about a group getting set to go up to Sylvester Carrier's home.

"And it wasn't much after that, the lights were still on, and in comes one of the fellas that was stayin' at the hotel, and he had four bullet wounds through his arm. He was all bandaged up. He didn't stand around and talk too much. He was headed up to his room. But he did say there'd been some men killed over in Rosewood."

That was all Parham saw that night, but the next morning there was a crowd at the door when he came to unlock the commissary.

"Lots of unfamiliar faces, people I'd never seen before, coming in and asking for shells and guns. We sold them to those who could pay. Sold a lot. That Friday was a busy day."

Parham didn't see what was happening at Rosewood. He was too busy behind the counter. But he heard reports all afternoon from the people passing through his store.

"Word was they were shooting the whole town up, setting fire to houses, shooting people that ran out, just shooting everything they could, which was more or less the elderly men and women."

By the time he closed the commissary that Friday evening, Parham understood that Rosewood had been essentially emptied, that most of the townspeople had fled to the woods, those who hadn't been killed. He went home to the hotel, and not long after, W. H. Pillsbury, the mill superintendent, burst into the lobby.

"He said he wanted as many of us as had guns to come with him. He'd gotten word that these out-of-town people were going to come try to burn the quarters in Sumner, burn down the black section of town. 'We got to stop this mob,' he said. 'They're coming this way.'

"Well, every one of us had guns. That was the way it was back then. You carried a pistol from the time you were fifteen years old. You didn't necessarily carry it on you, but you had it in your car or someplace nearby. Guns were just a part of the way of life in those days."

Parham grabbed his gun and joined the group.

"It was a cold night. Gosh, it was cold. We all went out to the edge of town, the east end, closest to Rosewood. There was a spur at the railroad track there, and we lined up across the road right at that spur, about twenty of us.

"We could hear them coming. They were talking loud. You could tell they'd been drinkin'. It was dark, about nine-thirty. Mister Pillsbury had us lined up from one side of the road to the other, and when they come up to that spur, about a hundred feet away from us, he called out to them, told them that the first man sets foot on that rail, he would personally shoot him. He said he had orders to shoot anybody that came across that track.

"Well, that stopped them. There was a lot more of them than there was of us, and this one fella that killed Sam Carter, he was heading it up.

"They stood there and talked it over among themselves a few minutes. I didn't know what was going to happen. I don't think anyone did. Then they turned and went back. And they didn't come our way anymore."

In the meantime, says Parham, some of the women and children of Rosewood were hiding in Sumner, taken in by sympathetic whites.

"Most of us had taken in some of them. Liza Bradley, she worked for my mother, and she was at the hotel the day after the shootout. When word came about what was happening, she stayed with us. I don't know about her family, but Liza stayed with us. We protected her.

"I know the Pillsburys—they lived right close to us—they did the same. The rest, I don't know. I guess they were out in the woods."

It was W. H. Pillsbury, says Parham, who arranged for the Bryce brothers to bring a train from Cedar Key to pick up refugees from the swamp.

"Mr. Pillsbury was good friends with the Bryces. They were conductors on the train. Everybody thought they *owned* the trains, because they always had a good amount of money, and everyone knew they lived in good homes up at the other end of the line. They were fine people, well-to-do, but they didn't own the train."

Nevertheless, the Bryces were able to bring a train through that weekend, says Parham, and that, he says, is how most of Rosewood's population wound up in Gainesville.

"By the end of that weekend, all the homes in Rosewood had been burned down. There wasn't anything left. After that, every once in a while, when we'd go up to Gainesville for one reason or another, we'd see one of the Bradleys sitting around the courthouse square and they'd come over and talk to us, wonder how things was down home. But they were afraid to go back. In fact, none of them ever did go back."

Ernest Parham left Sumner in 1925 and wound up in Orlando, where he went to work for a laundry company, the same company he eventually owned. Two years after he left, the sawmill in Sumner burned down. By then, most of its workers had already moved to another Cummer mill town, a place called Lacoochee.

"I don't really know how it burned," says Parham, "but you know sawmills had a habit of burning when the timber got all cut out. Just like orange-packing houses would catch fire after all the citrus was frozen."

A pause, and a small smile.

"Funny how that happens."

Now and again over the years, Parham would hear tell of this person or that who had been involved in the affair up at Rosewood. One was a man named Elias Roland.

"He was a high school boy at the time, just like me," says Parham. "That night they killed Sam Carter, he went up and cut off one of Carter's ears. I didn't see him do it, but he was showing it around town for a couple of days, till he finally got rid of it because he wasn't sleeping at night.

"The last I heard of him, they said he was in a bar in Cedar Key and a man shot him, killed him. That was sometime in the early thirties."

Another name Parham heard was John Wright's. Some said Wright was often seen in Gainesville during the years after the attack, talking to some of the Bradleys and other residents who had fled Rosewood, trying to convince them to move back. Wright had bought some of the Rosewood land that went up for sale after it was vacated, and some said his purpose was to return it to its original owners. But no one took him up on the offer, if indeed the offer was actually made.

In any event, John Wright's life was never the same after the attack. When word got out that he had harbored some of the blacks from Rosewood, he was vilified. "Nigger-lover" was one of the kinder things he was called. There were threats on his life, and he took to arming himself wherever he went. At home, they said, he kept a pistol on every table. His wife Mary died eight years after the attack, and they said Wright developed a drinking problem after that. He was drinking the night he died, they said. It was the dead of winter, he'd been at a bar over in Cedar Key, he was nearly passed out and so some locals carried him home in their truck, dumped him off in front of his house and drove off. He never made it to the door. The next morning he was still there, on the ground, dead of exposure.

They buried John Wright in the old Shiloh Cemetery, back behind Sumner, in a grave with no markings. No headstone. Not even a wooden cross, like most of the graves around it. Just a mound of broken clam shells under an old moss-hung oak.

A final name Ernest Parham kept up with, for personal reasons, was W. H. Pillsbury's. Six years after the attack on Rosewood, Parham married Walter Harlow Pillsbury's oldest daughter Sophia. By then, Pillsbury was three years dead.

"He had moved down with the rest of them and taken over the operation in Lacoochee," says Parham. "But it was hard. That group down there did not get along well with him because of their animosity about what happened at Rosewood. A lot of the people that were involved had moved to Lacoochee, white people, and they resented Pillsbury, called him 'nigger-lover' and stuff like that. He never fit in down there, and so the company retired him. He went home to Jacksonville, and he died not long after that, in 1926."

Parham has a photograph of his father-in-law, taken when Pillsbury was a young man in Jacksonville, before he came to work in Sumner.

"He was born up in Michigan," says Parham, opening the frame that holds the photo. "He was Indian, though I can't honestly say what tribe."

The man in the photograph looks stern, strong, tall. He is wearing a dark wool suit and a white shirt, its starched, stiff collar rising to his chin. His black hair is thick, combed straight back. He resembles, in size and stature as well as facial appearance, another Native American of the time, the athlete Jim Thorpe.

"He was a tough man," says Parham, running his fingers across his father-in-law's photo. "He *had* to be tough."

He shuts the frame and sits back in his chair with a soft sigh.

"It was an awful thing, all of it," he says. "You can just imagine being burnt out, run off your home, for no reason whatsoever. None of them had anything to do with it. I doubt very seriously if Sylvester Carrier had anything to do with hiding the man. He could have, I don't know, but I doubt very seriously if the man who did the raping was in Sylvester's home that night."

Parham has no doubt that Fannie Taylor was raped. The story that she had a white lover is, in his opinion, just that. A story.

"I doubt very much that she had a lover," he says. "Because James Taylor and Mrs. Taylor seemed to me to be very nice people. They came from a good Cedar Key family. At least *he* did. Where she came from, I don't know. But some of James Taylor's sisters were in my class in school. I knew that family, and they were good people.

"Besides, if it was a white man, why would he run to *Rosewood*? And why would Sam Carter help him get away?"

The theory of Masonic loyalty brings another small smile to Ernest Parham's lips.

"I think it was a black man," he says, lifting that right hand ever so slightly. "I really do."

Then he leans back and lets out a deep breath.

"But really, it's going to always be just like Walter Pillsbury said when this fella shot Sam Carter."

One more tap on the chair.

"We'll never know."

TWENTY-TWO

Special Master

I t was three days before Christmas, and Richard Hixson was lacing up for his early evening run, a five-mile loop that wound through the hilly tree-shaded Tallahassee neighborhood where he lived alone with his pet Pomeranian, Jennifer, in a brick two-story ranch overlooking the Florida State campus, just a few minutes from his office at the State Capitol.

His nightly run was like a sacrament to Hixson. Sometimes it seemed like the only thing that kept him sane, and this was one of those times. The fact-finding report he'd been waiting weeks for had finally landed on his desk that day: *A Documented History of the Incident Which Occurred at Rosewood, Florida, in January 1923.* Ninety-three double-spaced pages, benignly bound with a powder blue cover, along with more than four hundred additional pages of appendices, including charts, graphs, statistics and verbatim transcriptions of every interview conducted by the study team over the course of the previous four months.

Hixson had skimmed those pages that afternoon, and could already see the minefield of issues contained in them, questions that would have to be an-

Richard Hixson

swered during the legislative hearing session that lay ahead, a hearing Hixson knew would be unlike any over which he had ever presided.

Richard Hixson had pretty much seen and heard it all during his ten years as "special master" for Florida's House of Representatives, a position in which he acted as an appraiser of sorts, a quasi-judge whose job was to provide an initial assessment of the two dozen or so claims bills filed each year with the legislature. In each case, the special master's job was to listen to evidence by witnesses and attorneys, then recommend to the House whether and why it should award the claim, and if so, how much that award should be. The hearing was in essence a gateway, the first hurdle a claims bill had to clear on its journey to the floor of the legislature.

The vast majority of those claims bills—roughly ninety percent—were personal injury cases, lawsuits against the state that had already been tried in a court of law. A teenager run down by a school bus; a woman drowned at a public beach; a young girl decapitated by a state highway sign blown off an overpass by a gust of wind—these were the kinds of cases in which the state, or more precisely, one of its agencies, had been sued for negligence and taken to court.

The question of whether the suit ended there, with a jury's verdict, or whether it went on to the legislature as a claims bill depended on dollars and cents—how much money the jury awarded the claimant. If the verdict was for $100,000 or less—$200,000 in the case of a group claim—the state simply paid. If the jury awarded more than those amounts, the case was passed up to Tallahassee, where it became a bill for the lawmakers to consider, to decide for themselves whether the case in question warranted the payment they were being asked to pull from the state's coffers. In those debates, practical concerns could often become as critical as legal or moral issues.

"Unlike a trial," explains Hixson, "a government agency can step up in this situation and talk about the consequences of the payment it's being asked to make. For instance, a school board that's been sued can come in and say, 'Hey, wait a minute, if we have to pay a million or two million bucks here, we're not going to be able to fund certain programs out of our budget.' There are impacts with judgments like this, government agencies are affected, as is the public, and that's something the legislature has to consider.

"To tell the truth," says Hixson, brushing a lock of thick brown hair away from his eyes, "the members of the legislature don't particularly like having to do this. It's different than any other part of their job. Essentially they have to look at these things like jurors, and they don't enjoy that."

Hixson had played the role of judge to the legislators' jury ever since the position of House special master was created in 1983. Before then, Florida had always hired private attorneys to come in and conduct each claims hearing. Deciding it would be both cheaper and more consistent to have a hearing master on staff, the House had turned to Hixson, who already had a reputation among Florida's legal circles as something of a boy wonder.

A Clearwater native, he had come out of the University of Virginia's law school in 1973, clerked for a federal judge in Tampa for two years, then spent five years in the state's Attorney General's office, where he was put in charge of the civil litigation division. His rise was meteoric, to say the least, a tousle-haired kid of thirty suddenly in charge of fifteen of the state's most seasoned attorneys. In 1981 he became staff director of the House Judiciary Committee. Two years later, when the House went looking for a special master, it didn't look far.

That Christmas of 1993, Hixson was forty-three, still working for the Judiciary Committee. He was a government employee, but when he stepped into the master's role, he was no longer an advocate of the state. In fact, he often became its critic.

"I was basically an independent appraiser," he says, and the costs of the cases he appraised were sometimes dizzying. The teenager run down by the school-bus won a $5.5 million verdict in a Dade County courtroom. The family of the young girl killed by the highway sign was awarded $9 million by a Palm Beach jury, the largest judgment against the state in Florida's history.

"Of course these cases were appealed," says Hixson, "but in Florida, jury verdicts are pretty sacrosanct, and appellate courts are reluctant to change them."

So they wind up in Tallahassee, where the hearing master decides what size *he* thinks the verdicts should be. He looks at precedents, studies similar cases across the state, listens to the testimony of witnesses and the arguments of attorneys, searching for a footing to make his own judgment. Often, that footing remains slippery.

"Take the decapitation case," says Hixson. "Here you had the wrongful death of a child, and that's pretty much the same situation in Pensacola or Miami or Tampa. You have a dead child and grief, which are basically the same anywhere.

But when I began going into other jury verdicts dealing with deaths of children, the awards were all over the ballpark. They ranged from $127,000 all the way up to that nine million. You look at the variety of these judgments, and it's very disconcerting. You try to figure out what makes one jury come back with one figure and another come back with one so completely different, and you can't. You'd like to think there's a better, more consistent way of addressing these issues, but there isn't."

As troubling as such personal injury claims can be, they at least have the basis and context of prior court proceedings to help guide the hearing master. But besides these "waiver statute" claims bills, as they are called, the state faces about four or five claims each year that have not been considered in any court of law. These "equitable" claims arrive in Tallahassee untried, untested. And they are, says Hixson, the most difficult to decide.

"They can come from almost anywhere," he says. "Basically you've got someone who has been aggrieved by some form of state action for which there is no legal remedy, no legal redress. There's no court the person could walk into, and so they come here, to the legislature."

The first question in any such case, says Hixson, is whether the claimant could have brought his case into a courtroom. If he could have and did not, says Hixson, "that's his fault, not the state's."

"Some people simply let time expire without taking their claim to court," he says, "and then they show up at the legislature, trying to bring a suit here after they've had the opportunity to bring the suit into court and simply didn't do that."

Most of these equitable claims involve situations in which years have passed since the case could, if possible, have gone to court. A schoolteacher asking for retirement benefits not paid when he was teaching in the 1930s; a man who charges that his property was improperly seized by the sheriff's department back in the '60s; a woman who was committed by the state to a mental institution when she was a child in the 1950s. In each of these cases, the hearing master's first question is whether the claimant could have taken his case into a courtroom at the time it occurred, and whether he could have received a fair hearing if he had done so.

"That," says Hixson, "was one of the first questions that came up with Rosewood."

There were others as well, all tumbling through Hixson's head as he took off for his run that December evening. Who was in charge of enforcing the law that week in Rosewood? Did they respond? If not, why not? How many people were killed or injured? How many people lost property? How much did they lose? How did the grand jury arrive at its finding?

All these questions would have to be explored, as well as the issue of payment if the state was indeed found to be at fault. Payment, however, was a question still far down the road.

"I wasn't even thinking of the compensation part," says Hixson. "I wasn't going to even begin looking into the issue of who would get what until I was satisfied about what had *happened*."

That satisfaction would not come from the study, but the study was the starting point. "Without it we could not have gone forward," says Hixson. "The study was the line in the sand, the demarcation of issues and facts against which the witnesses' words would be measured."

And the attorneys' words as well. Hixson already knew who would be representing the claimants. He had watched Steve Hanlon in action years before, down in Tampa, and he knew Martha Barnett as well. As for who would represent the state, the special master had no idea.

That was one more question to ponder as he jogged off into the night.

TWENTY THREE

The Eleventh Hour

H ow much? And how many?

Ever since the legion of Rosewood survivors and descendants—more than four hundred of them—had surfaced at the beginning of the year, those two questions had hovered at the edges of the public debate, beating their wings like two bothersome birds. How much money would the state be asked to pay, and how many claimants would be asking?

For almost a year, Steve Hanlon, along with Arnett Doctor, had been able to keep those questions at bay. With all that had been written and reported about the attack itself and the impending bill, there had been no mention yet of specific numbers, no reference to what exactly might be the price tag of this claim. One reason Hanlon had sidestepped such questions was a simple matter of strategy, a lesson he had learned during years of courtroom litigation.

"You never mention numbers in your opening argument," he says. "You want the jury to hear the story first. You want them to identify with your people, be angry, be upset. *Then* you hit them with a number."

The jury in this case was essentially the entire population of Florida, four-

Steve Hanlon

teen million men and women, represented by their legislators, which meant there was the media to consider as well—another reason, according to Hanlon, to keep money out of the matter for as long as possible. "As soon as you mention money," he explains, "that's all the press is going to focus on, the only thing they're going to cover."

But beyond simple strategy, the fact was that even if it had wanted to, the Rosewood group—the attorneys, the families, and the bill's two sponsors— had no numbers to share. As late as Christmas Day, with the fact-finding team's report freshly in hand and the final draft of their bill due to be filed at the end of that week, they still had not decided on the amount and terms of the compensation they sought. Their focus up to that point had been on shaping the language and issues of the bill, understanding full well the implications of this claim, not just for Florida but for the entire nation. There was no doubt the debate would be fierce when the bill arrived before the legislature. Its ramifications, in terms of the volcanic issue of reparations, were immense. This proposed law was bound to open some of Florida's—and America's—deepest, most sensitive wounds, picking at the raw nerve endings of the nation's racial history.

The Rosewood group realized this, and so they had spent months trying to anticipate every possible issue, hoping to address and clarify each one, in preparation for the hearing process, where their claim would get its first taste of scrutiny.

The language of the bill was no small matter. The distinction, for example, between the terms *compensation* and *reparation* was enormously important. Compensation, as Hanlon made painstakingly clear to every reporter he faced, is a strictly judicial term, involving payments for specific losses or damages identified and measured through legal procedure. Compensation is what is paid each time a lawsuit is won in court or a claims bill is passed by a legislature. Reparation, on the other hand, is a much broader "extra-judicial" concept, extending beyond the strict bounds of law. Reparation involves payments to make amends for more general wrongs and injuries, such as the devastation done during a war or the suffering inflicted by a system such as slavery.

The Rosewood bill sought compensation, not reparation. But that distinction was already becoming lost in the clamor of alarm that had begun rising around Rosewood that summer and fall, fears about the door this claim would open for every group with a historical grievance against the government. Native Americans whose ancestors had been slaughtered and whose land had been seized. African Americans whose forebears had suffered as slaves. What, critics asked, was to keep tens of thousands of these people from stepping through the door opened by Rosewood and draining the nation's treasuries with claims of their own?

The answer—and Steve Hanlon knew it would need to be stated again and again in the coming months—was that the losses suffered by Native Americans and slaves, as grievous as they were, were suffered under circumstances that set them far apart from Rosewood. America was at war with the Indians. And slavery, as heinous as it was, was legal. The people of Rosewood, on the other hand, were United States citizens, entitled to the same personal and property protections as any American—protections they did not, according to this claim, receive. And so they were seeking compensation.

Beyond that issue, the Rosewood group also knew it would face the argument that the attack on the town, as horrible as it might have been, was not extraordinary, that this was, after all, the lynching era in America, that there were literally thousands of cases all across the country in which people—full-fledged United States citizens just like the residents of Rosewood—were killed and their property taken. Were all those families, too, now entitled to step forth and claim compensation?

Steve Hanlon knew this was a stickier question to answer, because even if in principle the answer was yes, in practical terms he realized the bill would be torpedoed if the lawmakers saw it as a precedent for a torrent of claims just like it from every corner of the country. Again a distinction had to be made, and Hanlon and his team were ready to make it. In every other case of lynching that they knew of, whether it was an isolated killing or a large-scale "race riot," the incident took place over a relatively short period of time—a day or two at most—and the authorities could conceivably claim that they did not have adequate time to respond before the deed was done. The attack on Rosewood, on the other hand, lasted an entire week. The nation watched while it happened, as did the governor of Florida and local law enforcement agencies in and around Levy County. That fact alone, Hanlon was prepared to argue, set Rosewood apart from any other lynching in American history.

As for the veracity of the claim itself, the questions surrounding the circumstances and actual extent of the attack on Rosewood, the fact-finding team's report was a godsend, better than anything Hanlon or the Rosewood families could have hoped for. Not only did its detailed, day-by-day description of the events of that week support the claimants' own accounts, but its conclusions included precisely the points Hanlon intended to make during the hearing.

"Rosewood was a tragedy of American democracy and the American legal system," wrote the study team. "By their failure to restrain the mob and to uphold the legal due process, we can only conclude that the white leaders of the state and country were willing to tolerate such behavior by white citizens."

This was a gift that could not have arrived at a more appropriate time. With Christmas lights twinkling outside the Capitol building, the spearheads of the Rosewood claims bill—Arnett Doctor, Steve Hanlon, Martha Barnett, Al Lawson and Miguel De Grandy—came together in a House committee room to answer the only questions left before the bill would be launched.

How much, and how many?

Doctor had actually begun toying with numbers back in October, during a weekend stay at Hanlon's Tallahassee home. The two had become surprisingly close friends over the previous months, considering Doctor's initial suspicions about this white man from a conservative law firm, a firm founded by a politician whose name was synonymous in the Doctor household with racism itself.

Spessard Holland had been the governor of Florida when Arnett Doctor was born in 1943 and became a U.S. Senator for a quarter century thereafter. He was a man who was proud of his Dixie roots—both his father and grandfather fought for the Confederacy. A self-professed "hopeless reactionary," Holland had dug in his heels against the civil rights movement and Great Society reforms of the Fifties and Sixties. In a household like the Doctors', he was considered as close to an antichrist as a human could get.

"He put the black man through hell," says Arnett. "That's all I knew about Spessard Holland. He used the word 'nigra' like you would chew chewing gum. When I heard the name Spessard Holland, it was like hearing the name Theodore Bilbo up in Mississippi. The racist Bilbo. In our house, Spessard Holland was in that same category."

In truth, Spessard Holland, who died in 1971, was more complex than that, more multi-dimensional than most of his political colleagues in the mid-century South. He was an avowed segregationist, but unlike most Dixie legislators, for whom "separate but equal" meant "separate, period, and the equal be damned," Spessard Holland truly believed that blacks deserved the same protections and benefits of the law as whites. He backed that belief by fighting for thirteen years to get the U.S. Senate to pass a constitutional amendment outlawing the poll tax, one of the South's most precious weapons to keep blacks from voting. When the 24th Amendment finally became law in 1964, it bore Spessard Holland's name, to the confusion of many of his critics.

His critics would have been surprised, too, to learn that twice in his life Spessard Holland personally prevented a lynching. The first was in Lakeland in the mid-1930s, when Holland, who was a state senator at the time, happened upon a mob at the city jail while driving home from his law office. Two men inside—white men—had been imprisoned for killing a pair of police officers who had tried arresting them for drunkenness at a party. By the time Holland came upon it, the mob had reached the men's cell and were banging on the bars with bricks. The senator pushed his way through the crowd and was able to quiet the mob by promising to prosecute the prisoners himself. True to his word, he helped convict both men, getting the death sentence for each.

The second case, in the early 1940s, happened in Quincy, the same town where Al Lawson would eventually attend high school. Three black men had been captured and accused of raping a young white woman, then cutting her throat and leaving her for dead. When Holland, who was now governor, got word that a mob was forming in Quincy, he ordered the prisoners transferred to the Tallahassee city jail. The mob followed, and were met outside the jail by the governor himself, who ordered the crowd back while he talked to the prisoners. The three men told Holland they were indeed guilty, that they expected to die, but they begged him to protect them from this horde. Again, Holland talked the crowd down, promising full and fair prosecution, and again he kept his word. The three prisoners wound up dying in Gainesville State Prison's electric chair.

But none of that mattered to Arnett Doctor. He didn't know any of these things, and he didn't care. The only truth he knew was the truth he got from his parents, and that was the truth that counted. His parents had told him Spessard Holland was a dyed-in-the-wool racist, so that's what he was.

Nevertheless, Doctor eventually warmed to Steve Hanlon. It took some time, but he came to trust Hanlon, then to actually like him. At least once a week throughout that summer and fall, the two men met either in Tampa or in Tallahassee, and they found they had a lot in common. They were about the same age. They both liked to fish. They even shared the same medical condition: glaucoma. Doctor had begun taking early morning walks for his diabetes, and when he was in Tallahassee, Hanlon would join him, the two of them rising early, before six, and hiking the hills at the edge of town, talking about themselves, their families, and about Rosewood.

That weekend in October, for the first time, they talked about money. Hanlon had been telling Arnett and the families for months to "start dreaming." Don't think about dollars and cents, he had told them, but just about what they'd like to include in this claim. Education. Scholarships. Maybe a memorial. Things like that. A list had evolved, and most of those items had become part of the bill Hanlon and Barnett were drafting. A college scholarship fund for students descended from Rosewood. Money for scholars to study the attack on Rosewood and other such incidents in Florida history. Inclusion in history books, so no one would ever forget that this attack took place. These were all now part of the claim.

But no one had been allowed to mention money. Arnett wouldn't permit it, on advice from Hanlon. Now, though, Hanlon was asking Arnett to name a figure, privately, to give him something to begin batting around with Lawson and De Grandy, "to get a sense of the size of the ballpark," as Hanlon put it. Martha Barnett had said she knew of very few waiver statute claims bills that came in for more than a couple of million dollars and almost no equitable claims for anything higher than a half-million or so. But then again, there had never been an equitable claim like this one.

"Twenty-six million," said Arnett.

Hanlon coughed. He'd asked for a nice round number, and Doctor had given him one.

"Twenty-six million," Arnett said again. "We've identified twenty-six families that were living in Rosewood at the time of the massacre and that have family members still alive today, either survivors or descendants. That's a million dollars for each family, for each estate."

Hanlon listened.

"Look," said Arnett, "*any* number I give you is going to be too low, as far as I'm concerned, as far as most of the families are concerned. But twenty-six million. I think that's fair."

When Hanlon called Lawson with that figure, Lawson exploded. "He went through the ceiling," says Hanlon. "He said I was out of my mind. He would never submit a number like that. So now we had a read on where Lawson was."

De Grandy was just as shocked.

"He told us one million dollars was doable, two million at the most," says Hanlon. "Anything higher than that, and he was going to back out. He wouldn't have anything to do with it."

And so Arnett spent the next two months talking with the committee, meeting with family members, shuttling back and forth between them and the law firm, trying to whittle down the figure as best he could. By that December evening, when Doctor and the lawyers walked into the committee room to meet with Lawson and De Grandy, they had hammered the amount down to $270,000 for each family—a total of just over seven million dollars. That figure would be divided in various amounts among the fifty-six claimants named in the bill, with survivors each receiving a full share while descendants split theirs.

The mood in the committee room was initially merry, the good news of the study team report still filling the air. But then it was time to talk dollars, and the bubble burst. Lawson and De Grandy waited to hear what Hanlon had now. When he laid seven million on the table, Lawson didn't blink. But De Grandy backed off. No way was he going beyond two million. He had said it before and he was saying it now. Bring the number down, or he was gone.

Lawson understood his colleague's position. De Grandy was a Republican up for reelection. He couldn't afford to be labeled tax-and-spend, and that was the word already going out about this bill.

What Lawson didn't know was De Grandy had no intention of running for reelection. He was about to be married, and had decided to return to private practice in Miami after the upcoming legislative session. His personal political stakes were not a factor in his position. He simply didn't believe the bill would survive at seven million. And he was also playing hardball with Lawson for control of this thing. One of them would be lead sponsor, the man who would run this train, and De Grandy intended to be that man.

Doctor didn't know or care about any of that. All he saw was that here, at the eleventh hour, one of his patron saints was about to turn his back on them all. He was furious. He felt betrayed.

Hanlon and Barnett just watched. They were here for their clients. This was as low as their clients would go. Seven million.

Lawson tried convincing De Grandy to stay in. If the bill's got to be cut, he said, let the legislature do it. *We* shouldn't cut the thing, he said. Make *them* cut it. We owe it to this family, he said.

But De Grandy shook his head. He was sorry, he said, but he could not back this bill for that amount. Then he left the room.

"Hit him."

Hanlon could hardly believe what he was hearing. Then Lawson said it again.

"Hit him. Don't let him get away with that shit. *Hit him.* Go with the seven million."

Barnett, unlike her partner, was not surprised. She'd seen enough back-room legislation to know how it worked. Lawson was ready to force De Grandy's hand. The black caucus, he said, the same group that had basically abandoned this bill the first time around, now had its honor on the line.

"We've been stepping out on this thing," said Lawson. "We've been saying what a great harm was done here. We can't ask for an outrageous amount, but we can't ask for peanuts either. That would be an insult. Anything less than what you're asking here would be an insult."

And so they hit him. Lawson phoned De Grandy and told him they were going ahead with this bill whether De Grandy was in or out. The family, said Lawson, refused to reduce the amount of their claim any more than they had. De Grandy listened, considered, then played his own card. There was no love lost between the Cuban and black caucuses; they were in the midst of a battle to decide where the state should place a new law school—at predominantly black Florida A&M University or at Florida International University in Dade County, whose population was sixty percent Hispanic. If De Grandy was not out in front on this bill, the Cubans were going to bolt. Lawson knew that, and he knew he needed them.

So when De Grandy told him he'd stay in at seven million *if* his name was listed at the top of the bill, as lead sponsor, Lawson said fine. He knew his black caucus colleagues would be irate if an outsider wound up with top billing on this, of all things. The *Rosewood* bill, with a *Cuban* leading the way? Unthinkable. Unthinkable, too, that Al Lawson would step back and let someone else take the lead. That wasn't like him at all. He admitted it himself. He had never been a man who would give up credit if he could claim it himself.

But this was different. That's what Lawson told the black caucus, and that's what he told himself. This was bigger than who got to be the hero. This was more important than politics, he said, though the fact was that this decision, like anything that passed through a legislator's fingers, had indeed become political. It was politics that lost Lawson the lead sponsorship of the Rosewood bill, and it was politics that gave it to De Grandy.

And so another call was made, announcing a press conference for Thursday, December 30. That morning, with Arnett and the family's committee members standing beside him and Hanlon and Barnett watching from the back of the room, Al Lawson announced that the Rosewood claims bill had been filed. It would seek seven million dollars for fifty-six family members, "a small penance," said Lawson, for the state to pay for its role in this "shameful" chapter of Florida history.

"For those who say that's a lot of money," he told the roomful of reporters, "it's really not. If we were in a court of law and the state had to pay restitution to these families, it would be an amount you couldn't add up on paper."

The next day, newspapers across the state ran those words, along with photos of Lawson and Doctor and details of the historic bill. Missing from the rostrum was the proposed law's lead sponsor, Miguel De Grandy, but he had a valid excuse for not being there. He had had to fly home to Miami that day for a wedding—his own.

TWENTY-FOUR

One Last Matter

It was early February now, a week into Florida's 1994 legislative session, bill after bill—more than three thousand proposed bills—already cascading into committees while the Rosewood group sat on the sidelines, awaiting their turn at the end of that month, when their hearing before the House special master was scheduled to begin.

Steve Hanlon was ready to go. He had his arguments prepared and his witnesses lined up, ranging from a psychologist who had interviewed several of the survivors and would testify that each showed symptoms of post-traumatic stress disorder, to an economist whose specialty was translating "value of living" losses from years into dollars and would testify that the amount the survivors were asking in this claims bill was a pittance compared to what his calculations would yield in a court claim. And finally there were the survivors themselves, four of whom Hanlon planned to put on the witness stand.

Choosing those four had been a fairly simple process of elimination. Mary Hall would do little good, since she was only three years old at the time of the attack and had no memories to share. The same was true of Dorothy Hosey,

Willie Evans

who had turned only four that week. Then there was Margie Hall, who was fourteen in 1923. While the others were too young, Margie was now too old. She had begun slipping into senility; her recall was shaky at best. Lonnie Carroll, who was twelve when the massacre occurred, was incompetent, bedridden in the New Smyrna nursing home where he had lain for the past eight years and where he would lie for the rest of his life. As for Lillie Washington, Berthina Fagin, Thelma Hawkins, Eva Jenkins and Vera Hamilton, doubts had already begun stirring about whether those women's names would still be on the bill by the time the hearing was done, since none of them were actually living in Rosewood at the time of the attack, although each had been born and raised there.

That left four: Willie Evans, who was sixteen at the time of the attack and who, unlike Margie Hall, had lost none of his memory; Wilson Hall, who was seven at the time and could speak vividly of what the town had been like before it was destroyed; Arnett Goins, who was eight and was upstairs in the Carrier house the night of the shootout; and finally, Minnie Lee Langley, who was downstairs that night, in the actual line of fire, huddled between Sylvester Carrier's legs. Minnie was nine at the time.

So Steve Hanlon was set, and Martha Barnett, too, was busy. While Hanlon would carry the ball through the critical phase of the hearing, it was Barnett who would usher the claim from that point on, carrying it into the maze of the legislature itself. She was already working the one hundred and twenty members of the House, making phone calls, dropping by their offices, getting a read on where each of them stood on the issue of Rosewood, leaving packets of news clippings and the study team's report, urging them all to give it a read, sowing her seeds now so she'd have a head start when this bill finally arrived on the lawmakers' desks.

She was doing the same with the forty-member Senate. She couldn't afford to wait until the hearing was done to begin her work. The entire legislative session lasted but sixty days, and they were already ten days in, with two more weeks to go before the Rosewood hearing would even begin. The clock was ticking. Barnett had to start now, not knowing what Hixson's decision would be, but assuming—praying—it would give her the boost she needed.

Just before Valentine's Day, Hanlon and Barnett arrived at Richard Hixson's office for a meeting. There were still a few things left to go over. Hixson told them the Senate's special master, an attorney named David Kerns, would be sitting in on the proceedings. Since this bill had been filed with the House and would begin its passage there, Hixson would take the lead, with Kerns essentially looking on and weighing in with any questions he might have.

Hixson stressed, as he had during several meetings he had already had with the Holland and Knight team, that this was an "evidentiary" hearing, that it was not the kind of adversarial proceeding they were used to in court. Hixson had never handled an equitable claims bill with the stakes as high as this one, both in terms of money and moral issues, and he wanted to make the rules of this hearing process absolutely clear.

This was not about lawyers arguing with lawyers, he explained. This was an arena in which each side would simply present the evidence it had to support its position. But they all knew it could never stay that simple, that there was no way to keep a lawyer from being adversarial. It was in his blood. It was what he was trained to do. Asking a lawyer to make a case but not to argue was like asking a boxer to step into a ring but throw no punches.

Which raised one last matter that was still unresolved. Who, Hanlon and Barnett wanted to know, would the other boxer be? Who was going to represent the state?

They'd been asking the state that question for weeks, pestering Pete Antonacci, the state's deputy attorney general, about how the AG's office was going to handle this case. Each time Barnett had called, Antonacci had told her the state was staying out of it. There would be no defense. Hixson could have his hearing, write his recommendation, and the legislature could vote on this thing. But the state was not getting involved.

"'Get a life,' that's what I told them," recalls Antonacci. "We had *never* defended ourselves in one of these types of claims, and we weren't going to start now."

Hixson had gotten the same response, and he didn't like it any more than Hanlon or Barnett. There *had* to be a defense. That's how Hanlon and Barnett felt. The hearing, Hixson's decision, the very bill itself would all lack legitimacy if the state stayed out of it. Even if they won, under these circumstances, if the bill were passed, it would appear that the skids had been greased, that the law was a gift. They didn't want a gift. The essence of this claim was the issue of responsibility, the assertion that the state had shirked its duties seventy-one years before. Hanlon and Barnett were not about to let it happen again. They were not about to allow the state to sidestep yet another responsibility it owed to the people of Rosewood—the duty of answering to these charges now, today.

Hixson had his own reasons for dismay. If the state had no representation in this case, Hixson would wind up in the uncomfortable position of being the only voice critiquing this claim. He would appear to be representing the state, and that was not the role of the special master. That was not his job.

Barnett left the meeting and immediately phoned the Attorney General's office yet again. Antonacci took the call. "No way," he repeated. "We are *not* going to do this, especially not at the eleventh hour like this. That's ridiculous. Forget it."

Hixson then made a few calls of his own. He met with the chairman of the Judiciary Committee—his boss, Robert Trammell—and with the House Speaker, Bo Johnson. The entire process was in danger of losing legitimacy, Hixson told them. The state had to defend, he said. Al Lawson weighed in as well, as did Miguel De Grandy.

Finally, Johnson paid a visit to the AG's office. He closed the door behind him, sat down with Antonacci and Antonacci's boss, Florida Attorney General Robert Butterworth, and said, "Boys, this is how it is. . . ." The state was holding this hearing, Johnson said. And the state was going to *be* at this hearing. Period. End of meeting.

"It didn't take thirteen seconds," says Antonacci.

Bob Butterworth now had some phone calls of his own to make. All right, he said, he would fight this thing. But he was not going to fight it halfway. There was going to be no charade here, he said. If they wanted him to play, he was playing to win. He was going all-out, putting his best man on the case. And so, a scant ten days before the Rosewood hearing began, Assistant Attorney General Jim Peters's telephone rang.

Remarkably, Jim Peters had never heard of Rosewood. At least that's what he says today.

"Not a word," he says. "I didn't know where it was. I didn't know *what* it was."

It's hard to get Peters to open up about his experience with this case. But then he's not the type to open up easily about anything. His answers to questions are as clipped as his haircut, which resembles the actor Steve McQueen's in his prime. In fact, Jim Peters looks a lot like Steve McQueen did, from the laser-beam squint of his eyes to the ropy leanness of his forty-nine-year-old body. The barbell sitting on his cluttered desk is more than a bookend.

"Nautilus, swimming, and rowing machines, I do them every *day*," he says. "That's good stuff. Keeps you from going crazy."

He seems, at first, an impatient man, edgy, at least with an inquisitor. Maybe it's because he is so accustomed to being the inquisitor himself. Maybe it's just the way he is. Or maybe it has something to do with Rosewood.

"This is something I'd just as soon *not* revisit," he had said when first asked to sit down and talk about this case. "There are some things you just have to put behind you," he said. "You just have to get on with life."

Nonetheless he agreed to meet, and after a short time he loosened up a bit. He never stopped twisting the pen gripped in his right hand, and his left eye had a nervous tic to it, but a disarming openness began to shine through the cracks of his military demeanor as he explained some of the souvenirs arrayed on the walls of his cramped, cluttered office in a nondescript corner of a non-descript building located off a parkway just east of downtown Tallahassee.

There is a black-and-white photo, for example, perched on his windowsill. The two men in the picture, one in a sleeveless T-shirt with a Harley-Davidson tattoo on his bicep, thumbs hooked in his belt loops, the other a steely-eyed blond with a thousand-yard stare, are standing by a river. They look like killers, which a jury concluded they were, when the two were sentenced in 1980 to die in the electric chair.

Their names are Earnest Lee Miller and William Riley Jent—the two bik-ers found guilty of the murder down in Lacoochee, the one in which the woman's charred body had been found in the woods near the Withlacoochee River, the murder written about in *Esquire* magazine. When they were released from death row in 1988 on new evidence, Jent and Miller sued the state's attor-ney who had put them there. It became Jim Peters's job to defend the state, and he did it well. The suit was dropped, though Miller and Jent still wound up walking. "Yeah," says Peters, flashing a tight smile toward the photo, "I like to keep mementos of some of my fun cases."

He's not your run-of-the-mill, off-the-assembly-line attorney. He came to law late, after earning an M.B.A. degree and working for the Florida state gov-ernment's consumer protection office. That job was actually what he did be-tween weekends, when he turned to his true passion, racing sports cars. He's got a poster of the Sebring raceway front-and-center on his office wall. MG's, he says, that's what he's into. He actually worked for a sports car dealership for. a time before he decided, at the age of twenty-eight, that law school might give him a step up in life. He didn't have the pedigree or credentials of a white-collar attorney. Basically he was a working stiff. But he wasn't intimidated either. "These guys put their pants on one leg at a time, just like I do," he says. "That's the way I approached it. If they could do it, so could I."

So he got his law degree from Stetson University down in Deland and went to work for the attorney general in 1977, at age thirty-one. Seventeen years later, he was one of two hundred and fifty assistant attorney generals in Florida. Twelve of those assistant AG's were in the state's civil litigation division, and Peters was the senior attorney among them, the best, as Bob Butterworth had said, they had.

Steve Hanlon, for one, was elated when he heard Jim Peters would be doing this case. Hanlon and Peters had locked horns several times over the years and Hanlon had nothing but respect for an attorney he considered much like himself.

"I don't generally have many good things to say about most lawyers these days," says Hanlon. "I think we have a profession of people, too many of them, with seriously unresolved adolescent conflicts, just horrendous individuals. We don't have trial lawyers anymore. We have litigators who don't really go to court at all. They write memos, file frivolous motions, and accuse each other of being assholes. They're a bunch of yuppies, firing off faxes to each other. I can't stand these kids. I don't even want to be in the same room with them.

"When I heard it was Jimmy who would be doing this hearing, I said great, now here's a *real* lawyer. This is gonna be two old guys who love to try cases, rolling up their sleeves and going kick-ass against each other. This is gonna be fun."

That was hardly the non-adversarial approach Richard Hixson was urging, but Jim Peters's attitude was the same. He was a fighter all the way, a man who had been known to fling a chair across a courtroom in a fit of anger, to get in a witness's face and scream, a passionate man if not always a prudent one. And he was, beyond all else, a loyal man, the state's man, whether prosecuting a case or defending one.

Jim Peters might never have heard of Rosewood, but he knew Levy County. One of the oddest cases he had ever been involved in had come from down around there, in the early 1980s, when the state's Department of Law Enforcement had used an undercover agent to bust a Big Bend cocaine kingpin named "Bubba" Capo.

"The godfather of Dixie County," smiles Peters. "That was Bubba Capo." The FDLE got its bust by having its agent order several thousand pounds of mullet from one of Capo's fishing partners, a man named Buck Sheppard. The government had no intention of actually buying the fish, and after the bust, when Sheppard found himself holding a couple of tons of mullet stored in frozen lockers across north Florida, he sued the government for the price of the fish.

"They popped Bubba," chuckles Peters, "and Buck comes right in and says, 'Hey, wait a minute, what about these *mullet?*' The Great Mullet Caper, that's what we called it."

Again Peters defended the state, and again he won. Poor Buck Sheppard wound up with nothing to do with his fish but eat them.

Peters knew Levy County, and he knew the members of the black caucus, too, as well as Miguel De Grandy, all of whom he had represented when Florida went through a laborious reapportionment process after the 1990 census. Jim Peters went to an NAACP conference in Atlanta that year to help shape the redistricting requests of Florida's black legislators.

"I *knew* these guys, okay?" he says, rankled again at the wounds incurred by Rosewood. Peters won't admit the wounds even exist. Like a good soldier, he saw—and still sees—his role as the state's advocate in those hearings as nothing more nor less than his duty. Some saw that role as thankless. They say Peters was a straw dog, a sacrificial lamb set up to take a hit for the higher-ups. But Peters will hear none of that. He won't complain that he had only ten days to prepare for the most visible—and volatile—case of his career. His upper lip remains stiff.

"It was never a question of sacrifice," he says. "It was my *job*. We're trench-level lawyers here, that's all. We do what we can with what we've got. We do it all the time."

At the end of the interview, as he walks toward the door, he almost relents. Almost, but not quite.

"It was a draining experience," he says of the Rosewood hearing. "But it doesn't *matter* how I felt about it. It was my job, and I did it."

PART FIVE

REDEMPTION

TWENTY-FIVE

Like an Ant

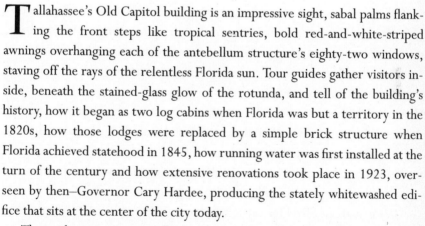

Tallahassee's Old Capitol building is an impressive sight, sabal palms flanking the front steps like tropical sentries, bold red-and-white-striped awnings overhanging each of the antebellum structure's eighty-two windows, staving off the rays of the relentless Florida sun. Tour guides gather visitors inside, beneath the stained-glass glow of the rotunda, and tell of the building's history, how it began as two log cabins when Florida was but a territory in the 1820s, how those lodges were replaced by a simple brick structure when Florida achieved statehood in 1845, how running water was first installed at the turn of the century and how extensive renovations took place in 1923, overseen by then–Governor Cary Hardee, producing the stately whitewashed edifice that sits at the center of the city today.

The guides point out proudly that this was the only Confederate capitol east of the Mississippi not seized by Union troops during the War of Northern Aggression. They do not mention that Tallahassee, being part of the cotton belt, was the center of Florida's slave trade, and that rumors persist that some of those slaves were auctioned off the back steps of this very building.

Minnie Lee Langley

Nor do the guides speak of the two dozen lynchings that occurred in Florida during Cary Hardee's four-year term, including the attack on Rosewood, which took place the same year that the silver-domed cupola, frosted glass skylights, double-curved staircases and marble wainscoting were added to embellish this seat of the state's law.

The Old Capitol is now used only for occasional bill-signings and, every four years, to swear in the state's governor. The actual business of lawmaking now takes place behind it, in the *new* capitol building, a twenty-two-story monolith of steel and cement, constructed in 1977 to house the offices and chambers of Florida's House and Senate. Day and night a constant stream of legislators, lawyers and lobbyists pushes through its ground floor glass doors, nodding to the pair of security guards stationed inside.

But on the last Friday of February, 1994, there were guards stationed outside those doors as well, and at the rear of the building, and up on the third floor, where the Rosewood hearing was scheduled to begin. At eight-thirty that morning, a full hour before the hearing was set to start, packs of reporters and camera crews were already punching the elevator buttons, asking which way to Room 317.

Richard Hixson had never seen anything like it. The most media attention any of his hearings had ever had was a disciplinary proceeding a few years back, on sexual harassment charges brought against a representative named Fred Lippman. But that was nothing like this. This was national. All the networks were here. Cable, too. Magazines and wire services.

Hixson had reserved the largest hearing room in the building, knowing there would be a crowd. But the room was hardly large enough. By nine o'clock, all seventy seats were filled, and three dozen more onlookers, mostly television camera crews, stood shoulder to shoulder, squeezed along the room's mahogany-paneled walls.

Hixson had not asked for the extra security. That was mainly Martha Barnett's doing. But he was glad the guards were there, for the same reasons Barnett was. This hearing was open to the public, and Hixson had imagined what kind of maniac might show up to make a point, maybe make a name for himself. Arnett Doctor had received enough threats during the previous months, both through the mail and over the telephone, that the FDLE had provided periodic patrols past his home in Tampa. Al Lawson had also gotten several "hate calls," as he put it. Probably just cranks, Lawson said, but Hixson believed they could not be too careful.

Most of all, Hixson was concerned about the witnesses, the survivors. He knew how frightened these elderly men and women were, simply appearing in a setting like this. This was the very thing they had avoided for more than seventy years. This was why they had kept their silence for so long. They did not want to be hurt again by the law, the government, the white people who had punished, then forsaken them so long ago. Hixson wanted these people to know they were safe. He hoped the guards would give them that feeling, but he couldn't be sure. In fact, he realized armed guards might well have just the opposite effect, that they might seem more a threat than a comfort. The sight of white men with guns meant something to the people of Rosewood that no one else could possibly fathom. If there was one thing Richard Hixson understood, it was this.

The witnesses were already upstairs when Hixson arrived, waiting in a private room, along with about a dozen family members. They had all gotten to town the day before, Wilson Hall driving over from Hilliard with his wife and his sister Margie, A. T. Goins coming up from St. Petersburg with his wife and daughter, Willie Evans traveling from Sanford with his son Donnell, and Minnie Lee Langley arriving from Jacksonville with a niece and one of her grandsons.

They stayed at the Radisson, meeting briefly with Steve Hanlon in the afternoon. "This is going to be a long process," he told them, "but I want you to keep in mind, to always remember, that *you* are not on trial here. *They're* the ones who are on trial."

Most of the family took their meals in their rooms that night, avoiding the reporters who had found their way to the hotel and were roaming the lobby. Minnie Lee spent the night at Hanlon's home. She had been hospitalized just the month before with double pneumonia, and she was still weak. There remained a tinge of tension between her and the other survivors. They would always consider Minnie an outsider, not truly a member of the family circle. They had forgiven the claim she and Lee Ruth had filed without them, but they had not forgotten it.

As far as Steve Hanlon was concerned, however, Minnie Lee was going to be the star of this show. He planned to put her on the stand first, to set the stage for the others. If he had a key witness that first day, it was going to be Minnie, and so he took special care of her. His wife Fran made dinner, and when the meal was done Minnie turned to Hanlon and told him he better not leave this woman, because he'd never get cooking as good as this anywhere else.

And now, Friday morning, they were all here, Willie Evans huddled in his wheelchair, and the others, Minnie Lee and A. T. and big Wilson Hall, each perched on the edge of a cushioned waiting room seat, lost in their thoughts, shaking just a little, listening to the hum of the crowd on the other side of the wall, watching Arnett crack open the door every couple of minutes to take a peek and each time he did, hearing the cascade of clicking camera shutters snapping like a swarm of cicadas.

Jim Peters stopped in, introduced himself to the family and survivors, then left to go over his opening statement one last time. Miguel De Grandy came through, told the family how proud he was and what an important day this was, not just for them but for the entire state of Florida. Then he, too, left to go over the remarks he would make as the bill's lead sponsor.

Al Lawson was not there. This time it was *he* who had been pulled out of town by a personal matter. His father, who had battled lung cancer for years, had suddenly died the day before, apparently of a stroke. Lawson had left almost immediately for Midway, where his father was to be buried that weekend.

Before he left, however, Lawson had issued a statement to the press, returning a volley from Jim Peters's office, which had issued a prehearing statement of its own, claiming that Governor Cary Hardee could not be held responsible for trusting the word of the Levy County sheriff after Hardee sent the telegram offering help toward the end of that horrible week. If the sheriff told Hardee that no help was needed, the governor had no reason to doubt him. If anyone was negligent, Peters argued, it was the local authorities, not the state.

Lawson shot back, likening Hardee's lack of response to a modern-day Florida governor sitting back and doing nothing while a hurricane bore down on the state's coast. "How," asked Lawson, "is a governor not responsible when you have a major disaster that you *know* is about to occur, and he does nothing?"

But all the statements and counterstatements were mere preamble. Now it was time for the hearing to begin. The witnesses, surrounded by their relatives, came through the door and the room exploded with flashing camera strobes and the whirr of motor drives.

They took their seats in the front two rows, a mahogany and metal railing separating them from the long hearing table, where the two special masters sat in the center, facing them. Across from the masters, with their backs to the audience, sat the attorneys, Peters and Hanlon. Stationed at one end of the table was a court stenographer, and beside her, the empty seat that awaited each witness.

Hixson called the hearing to order, introduced himself and David Kerns and the attorneys, then invited Miguel De Grandy to step up and make his opening remarks. De Grandy was brief, addressing the main fear of most of his colleagues.

"I have heard that to compensate the victims of the Rosewood massacre would open a Pandora's box," he began. "I have heard arguments, for example, that need we not compensate the Indians for the taking of their lands if we compensate the victims of Rosewood?

"I submit to you that however wrong people may believe those acts were, we were a sovereign nation at war with another sovereign nation and we owed them no legal duty as we owe to our own citizens.

"I have heard," he continued, "that if we compensate the victims of Rosewood, must we not compensate every black citizen in the state of Florida for the crimes committed during slavery? As atrocious and repugnant as you and I and every member of the legislature find slavery to be, there was a time when it was legal. When a human being could be considered property, there could be no deprivation of human or civil rights of that individual.

"There came a time in this country when we as Americans became enlightened. It took a civil war to reread what was written hundreds of years ago, to realize that all citizens *are* created equal and that all citizens are entitled to due process and equal protection of the law.

"And so today, the citizens named in the Rosewood bill come to us as a legislature, either personally or through their descendants, to seek justice—justice not because of the color of their skin but because of their condition as proud, free and equal citizens of this nation and of the great state of Florida. I am convinced as a legislator that when we as a body evaluate the facts and weigh the equities, we will be compelled to find that their cause and their claim is just.

"Thank you, Mr. Hixson."

Then it was Steve Hanlon's turn to speak. Relaxed, conversational, he sounded as if he were chatting with friends in the living room of his own home.

"This is a good day for Florida," he said, addressing the audience as much as the hearing masters. "The old bromide 'Better late than never,' if it was ever applicable, is applicable here today."

Hanlon outlined the briefs both he and Peters had filed, noting that although they might differ about details, he doubted there was any disagreement that this town was attacked, wiped away, and that his clients suffered serious harm. It was the extent and complexity of that harm that Hanlon then honed in on.

"The damage these folks suffered," he said, "is similar to the damage that Holocaust victims suffered and that has endured with them throughout their lives, down to the present day. The Rosewood massacre, from my clients' point of view, is *not* some long forgotten, ancient, unfortunate chapter in Florida's sometimes violent and racially troubled past. It is, and I am convinced you will be convinced of this, a deep, dark present reality in my clients' lives today, tomorrow, and the next day, as it has been for this entire period of time. It has brutally disrupted their lives, and it has changed those lives in ways we will never really fully understand."

The issue, said Hanlon, was not the actual property that was destroyed, the buildings that were burned or the land that was lost.

"The real damage was the loss of that *community*," he said. "It had its ups and downs, economically, just like everybody else did, but this was a remarkable African-American community, an intact, industrious, self-sufficient community.

"To lose the continuity of that community and be scattered throughout the state and the nation, as these people were, is the core of this damage claim. Literally, as I have said before and I will say it again, the property damage is a pebble on that beach. We will present testimony from an economic expert next week that the amounts sought by the claimants here are remarkably low in terms of the true value of these claims in any American courtroom today."

Hanlon made a point of referring to the Japanese Reparations Act, which had become the basic model for this bill. Then he came to his conclusion.

"Governments which come forward and acknowledge problems in their past, as the United States government has done before and is doing right now with radiation experiments, are *good* governments. It's difficult, but ignoring the problem and pretending it did not exist and hoping it will just go away instead of creatively devising a remedy, which is really what I am urging you to do here in this case, is a serious mistake.

"We *can* devise a remedy here," he said, turning to Hixson and Kerns, "and you *can* make findings about the uniqueness of this situation which will not open the Pandora's box that people have expressed concern about.

"Thank you."

Now it was Jim Peters's turn. He stood, walked around the table and faced the family, the two dozen Rosewood relatives filling the room's front three rows.

"Notwithstanding our differences," he said, "this really *is* a good day for the state. Notwithstanding our differences, I was pleased to be able to meet the claimants today."

Then he turned toward the hearing masters.

"Make no doubt about it, this is a claim about a societal wrong, one of too many such wrongs. I recall approximately fifty or sixty lynchings, violence in which towns were affected, included in the team report, and I will admit that this was a sorry damn period in Florida's history, no doubt about it. Deaths of innocent citizens occurred, property was destroyed, and families were displaced by violence. We should be ashamed of that, and we are.

"I respectfully disagree, however, that insofar as entertaining a claims bill process, Rosewood is really that unique. Whatever damage and trauma were visited upon the claimants—and we'll have the opportunity to prove that later—I respectfully submit that that damage, that trauma, is no greater than the damage or trauma that *other* families of any race who were lynched or murdered or felt that the state's law enforcement powers didn't do justice to them have suffered. It's sad, it's sorry, it's tragic. But I disagree that Rosewood is really unique."

Then he turned back and spoke directly to the families.

"With my apologies," he said, "and I met some of you this morning—Ms. Langley, Ms. Jenkins, Mr. Hall, Mr. Goins, Mr. Doctor, Mr. Evans—I respectfully submit to the special master that you are asking too much of the claims process, too much of the state of Florida, to come forward after over a generation, seventy-one years, and ask this from the state, based upon what we all have to concede is hearsay evidence—family stories revisited in good faith, no doubt—and in the absence of the state officials and county officials who are ei-

ther implicitly or expressly accused in this claims bill of these wrongs. On behalf of the state, I would say that's not fair.

"The passage of time," he continued, "has precluded the state from being
able to respond to your assertions—made in good faith, I am sure—as to what
happened.

"I can't," said Peters, turning back toward Hixson and Kerns, "speak
through the lips of dead officials."

Then he, too, concluded.

"As a matter of fairness to the claimants, I request that what evidence there
is, as flawed as it is, be objectively reviewed today. I welcome the opportunity
for the claimants to have a fair hearing. And I am certain this forum will enable
the state to have the *same* fair hearing, notwithstanding the emotional appeals
with which I sympathize in this case.

"Thank you."

Hixson thanked both attorneys, then asked Hanlon to call his first witness.
Gingerly, with gentle pats on her back from family members as she made her
way down the front row of seats, Minnie Lee walked to the witness chair. She
had on a bright red dress—the same dress she'd worn on the "Maury Povich"
show—and her hair was tucked beneath a wig of short silvery curls. Her hands
trembled slightly as Steve Hanlon helped her into the seat. He held her shoulder and leaned toward her ear.

"Are you ready?" he whispered. "Are we gonna *get* 'em?"

Minnie nodded slightly, pursed her lips and stared straight ahead. She was
sworn in, then Hanlon began, first asking her age, where she was born, who her
parents were, her grandparents, what kind of house they lived in, what kind of
town Rosewood was. The pace was leisurely, the questions and answers paint-
ing a portrait of a serene village, which made it all the more startling, as Hanlon hoped it would, when the subject turned to the night of the shootout at the
Carrier house.

"Well," said Minnie, wringing her hands, "I was upstairs with the other children. We was *all* upstairs under the bed."

"Why," asked Hanlon, "were you and all the children upstairs under the
bed?"

Minnie paused. For sixty years she had told this story to no one. Then, once
she did tell it, it seemed like it never stopped. Lawyers. Television people.
Newspaper people. Those college history professors. Everyone asked her to

tell the story. Now they were asking again. But this time, she knew, was the one that would matter the most.

"People were shooting at the house," she began, drawing a deep breath, "and they told us to go, brothers and sisters, told us to go under our bed."

It wasn't long after that, she said, that one of her aunts ran up the stairs to say Sarah Carrier had been shot. The hearing room fell dead silent. No clicking of cameras, not even the rustling of reporters writing their notes. They had all stopped writing. They just listened. The only sound was the drone of the air conditioning and Minnie Lee's voice.

"She told us Mama is *dead,* they done *killed* Mama. So we got up, and I crawled up from under the bed, and I went down looking for Mama. I couldn't find Mama, and then Syl grabbed me and said, 'Come on baby, let me save you.'"

Hanlon paused, steering the pace, working the drama.

"Then what happened?" he asked.

"I went in the wood bin with him."

Another pause.

"Then what happened?"

"This old cracker comes looking . . ."

A ripple of titters ran through the audience. Hanlon loved it. It wasn't often that the term "cracker" came up in a setting like this. Hanlon milked it for all it was worth.

"When you say this old *cracker* comes looking through," he said, "are you talking about Poly Wilkerson?"

"Yes," said Minnie Lee. "*All* the crackers come up there looking in, saying 'Come on out of there.'"

"Were there a *lot* of crackers there?"

"Yes, a lot of them out there."

Another pause.

"What happened then?"

" 'Come on out of there,' that's what they said. Syl got up under the wood bin, put the gun on my shoulder, told me to lean this way. I leaned over, and then Poly Wilkerson, he kicked the door down. And when he kicked the door down, Cuz' Syl let him have it. He shot him."

"Did he kill him?"

"Yes, he killed him, right in the door."

"What happened next?"

"Another one jumped up there, and Cuz' Syl killed him, too."

Hanlon then turned to the escape, the image of frightened children fleeing into the swamp.

"After Cuz' Syl shot Poly Wilkerson and the other man," he asked, "what happened next? Did you all get out of there?"

"Yes, we had to leave. We wasn't going to let nobody kill us in there."

"Was the gunfire still coming?"

"Yes, it was still coming."

"What did you all do?"

"Jumped and hid, jumped down on the edge of the porch and hid underneath the thing until we can get out of there."

"The *back* porch?"

"Yes."

"How long was it before you ran out of that house?"

"About fifteen minutes."

"About fifteen minutes?"

"Yes, until it got quiet with the bullets."

"It was January of '23?"

"Yes."

"Was it cold?"

"Oh, yes."

"How were you dressed?"

"Naked."

"You don't mean *naked?*"

"We didn't have no clothes."

"Did you have a nightie on?"

"No, we had a gown on, that's all."

"Just a little gown?"

"Mmm-hmmm."

"Now, who all got out of there?"

"All the children did."

"Okay, who was 'all the children'?"

"Twelve of us, about twelve."

"About twelve children?"

"About twelve or thirteen of us was together."

"Did you have an adult with you?"

"Not then."

The reporters were writing now, taking down every word.

"Were you walking through any swamp?" asked Hanlon.

"Yeah. We had to go through the swamp. With the crackers down there shooting, we couldn't walk on no road."

Three days and nights, Minnie said, they hid in the woods. Her Aunt Beulah found them the first night and stayed to take care of them as best she could.

"Did you get some clothes on by this time?" asked Hanlon.

"No, we didn't have no clothes. She covered us with weeds and leaves and stuff. But we didn't have no clothes."

"Did you see these crackers keep coming by those three days?" asked Hanlon.

"Yes. Those crackers were on the road just like an ant."

Another wave of light laughter ran through the room.

"Just like an ant?" asked Hanlon.

"Yes."

Hanlon then took Minnie through her escape by train to Gainesville and through her life over the course of the next half century. Her eyes moistened several times, and Hanlon would stop while she wiped them.

"Did you ever talk about this to anybody?" he asked.

"Unh-unh," she said, shaking her head. "I ain't *never* talked about it."

"Why not?"

"It hurt me. It was just building up in me to just think about how my folks went down and how they killed them and everything. Took everything we had."

Again she wiped away a tear. This time Hanlon did not pause.

"Have you ever talked about this with anybody where you didn't cry?" he asked.

"I don't talk about it to *nobody*."

"Do you talk to your daughter about it?"

"No."

"You have a daughter, don't you?"

"Yeah. She never heard me say a word about it, not to nobody. Never mentioned it to nobody."

"Why not?"

"It *hurt* me. It hurt me because I loved my grandmother and all my grandparents. They was nice to me, would see we were going to school and being clean. Yeah, I *loved* my grandparents. I really do. I love them up until now. I really love them. And I don't want . . ."

Minnie took a breath.

"I *didn't* want nobody to hurt them. Them crackers . . ."

Hanlon glanced over at Peters as he asked the next question.

"I think one thing Mr. Peters is going to ask you and that people would want to know is why didn't you come forward until now to file a claim against the state?"

"I didn't know how to file no claim," said Minnie, lifting her chin. "I am going to tell you, I didn't know *how.* And I wouldn't try to file no claims because I am scared those crackers might come up there and find me and *kill* me up there."

She shook her head.

"I ain't filed no claim. I ain't *tried* to. I just went to work for my living."

Perfect. Steve Hanlon couldn't have asked for anything more perfect than the testimony Minnie Lee Langley gave on the witness stand that morning. By the time she stepped down, Hanlon could see that Hixson and Kerns were both mesmerized. The entire room was entranced. Jim Peters's cross-examination of Minnie Lee was cursory, half-hearted at best. There was nothing he could take her to task for, little he could question without appearing to be a heartless villain.

It was the same with A. T. Goins, who testified next. A. T. talked about the white man his sister Philomena saw rushing from the Taylor house the morning of the alleged rape. He described bumping into dead bodies as he came downstairs to search for his Christmas suit the night of the shootout at the Carrier house. He told of his uncle James coming out of the woods two days later, being seized by the mob, and having to dig his own grave before he was shot to death. And he talked about his life after Rosewood, shining shoes and storing quarters so his daughter could go to college. Again, there was little for Peters to confront.

When Willie Evans was wheeled to the witness table, sunglasses covering his sightless eyes, one hand gripping his cane, his wavy white hair swept back as if the wind were blowing through it, the image alone was as powerful as his testimony. And when Wilson Hall took the stand and described what a heaven on earth his village had been before it was burned—"All we needed was God," he declared, "and God was all around us"—a chorus of *Amens* and *That's right*s burst from the family members.

Then Hanlon brought on his psychologist, a black University of Florida professor named Carolyn Tucker, who detailed the symptoms of post-traumatic stress syndrome shown by each Rosewood survivor she had interviewed, their lifelong struggles with "flashbacks," "emotional numbness," "hypervigilance," and submerged feelings of "stress, fear, terror and helplessness"—all terms Tucker said come straight from the texts.

Finally A. T. Goins's daughter Annette took the stand, testifying to the effects Rosewood had on her father's relationship with her and her mother, how it affected his friendships, how he protected himself and overprotected her throughout their lives. She was never allowed, for example, to spend the night at a friend's house when she was a girl, and she never understood why until she learned about Rosewood. "Even in college," she said, "I couldn't go home with people, like roommates. I could visit, but I couldn't stay for weekends, like roommates do."

There was nothing Jim Peters could do, not on this day. When the session concluded late that afternoon, the hallway outside was filled with hugs and hallelujahs. The family had won, that's how they felt. It was as good as over. Even Steve Hanlon felt that way. He had never seen testimony as compelling as what he witnessed that afternoon. "The greatest day in court in my life," he said.

Jim Peters stopped Hanlon on his way out to acknowledge how strong the survivors' testimonies had been. "Riveting," he said to Hanlon. "Absolutely riveting."

But it was not over. Jim Peters knew it was far from over. This had been Hanlon's day, no doubt about it.

But it was only the first day.

TWENTY-SIX

Ambush

Saturday morning, newspapers throughout Florida displayed the drama of the Rosewood hearing across their front pages. By now most of their readers were familiar with the story of the attack; thousands of words had been written about it over the previous year. But Arnett Doctor and Steve Hanlon had been the sources of almost all those stories, making a point of shielding the family members from the press. And so, for most Floridians, this morning gave them their first look at the actual faces of the Rosewood survivors themselves.

The power of those photographs—the frailty of Minnie Lee Langley, the tears of A. T. Goins, blind Willie Evans being wheeled toward the witness stand—was as strong as the headlines and stories that surrounded them.

Jim Peters hardly glanced at the papers. He had more important things to do. He had taken all the punches that first day, and now he was preparing to punch back. Already the answering machine in his office was filling up with phone messages from Levy County, angry calls from white residents demanding that their side of the story be told. By the time Peters arrived at his desk Monday morning, more than a dozen messages were on the machine.

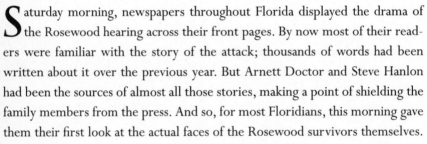

Willie Evans

As it stood, Peters had just two days to counterattack. The hearing's second session was scheduled Tuesday, with the final session set for Friday. Tuesday was a wash as far as Peters was concerned; the only witness scheduled to testify that day was the economist Hanlon had lined up to calculate the claimants' losses—a mere nuisance, in Peters's eyes. He would cross-examine the man and be done with it. His entire focus was on Friday, when he planned to thrust at the heart of the claimants' case, the study team's report. That was his primary target from the beginning.

But now, with those messages on his machine, he realized he might have more ammunition than he thought. Most of the calls were probably dead ends, he knew that. But if there was one voice on that tape that could lead to an actual witness, it was worth extending the hearings to track it down. And so that's what Peters planned to ask for on Tuesday, an extension. Meanwhile, he began returning those calls.

Tuesday's hearing paled compared to the opening session. Gone were the survivors, who had all returned to their homes over the weekend. Gone, too, was the national press; they had gotten the story they came for. What remained were a sprinkling of reporters from state newspapers and television stations, a handful of Rosewood family members, and a couple of dozen curious onlookers, all gathered into a room much smaller than the one Hixson had reserved for the first day. And still there were empty seats.

The session lasted a mere hour and a half. The economist, a man named Stan Smith, whom Hanlon had flown down from Chicago, explained how his company calculates what it calls the "loss of quality of life" for victims of catastrophes. Those calculations, Smith testified, had been used by his company in nearly a hundred court cases, including an ongoing case in California, where four thousand people in a neighborhood near a toxic waste dump site were suing for damages—"A Love Canal–type situation," explained Smith.

In that case, Smith explained, as in every other, he used a formula he had developed himself—based on a combination of property value, wage growth rates, interest rates, ages of each individual and rates of life expectancy—to arrive at a dollar figure for losses suffered over time. In the case of Rosewood, he said, he applied his formula to each survivor listed on the claims bill, as well as to the deceased head of each Rosewood household from which there remained no survivors. His results ranged from a high of $3.1 million for Mary Hall to a low of $423,000 for a deceased Rosewood resident named Queen Pollard, whose offspring were listed on the bill as descendants. Smith's combined calculation for the entire list of Rosewood claimants totaled more than $55 million.

Hanlon felt his point was made. The $7 million his clients were asking was a pittance, he said, and Peters hardly bothered to argue. His cross-examination, again, was cursory. What mattered now was time. His phone calls had already turned up one witness willing to testify, a woman named Margaret Cannon, whose father had been a Levy County deputy sheriff at the time of the attack. There were surely more, but Peters needed time to follow up on them all. And so, after the economist had finished his testimony and Hixson had begun wrapping up the day's proceedings, Peters dropped his bombshell.

"I have another . . ." He paused to pick through his papers. "I have another problem that I can't quite put a finger on right now."

Hixson looked up. So did Hanlon.

"I have received probably a dozen telephone calls from north Florida since the media coverage began," Peters continued. "I'm attempting to make a responsible effort to cull out folks who might have something to say of personal knowledge, and I may be needing to amend my witness list after I meet with these folks."

Hixson paused, said he would decide on Friday, but left Peters with some encouragement. "If we need to take a few more people the following week," Hixson said, calling the day's session to a close, "we'll accommodate you."

Arnett was irate. He saw this as nothing but a stall tactic. Martha Barnett was alarmed. The longer this hearing lasted, the fewer days the bill would have to wend its way through the legislature, and each day was precious at this point. Hanlon, for his part, figured Peters was grasping at straws. The guy was desperate. Let him do what he wanted. This thing was in the bag, that's how Hanlon felt. So he wasn't particularly upset or surprised when Hixson opened Friday's hearing with the announcement that the State's Attorney had submitted a new witness list for that day's proceedings and that Peters had also asked that the hearing be continued for an additional week to contact possible witnesses. Both requests were granted, and then the day's fireworks began.

Peters went straight for the study team's throat, first by getting Eva Jenkins, one of the claimants who had spent her childhood in Rosewood, to acknowledge that a photograph of a burning shack, included in the study team's report and identified as a Rosewood home, was no such thing.

"There was nothing like that home in Rosewood," said Jenkins, studying the photo and shaking her head. "That looks like an *outhouse*. That's not a Rosewood house. No house *like* that in Rosewood."

Doubt. The more doubt Peters raised, the better. When the study team itself took the stand following Jenkins—all of them except David Colburn, who was in Spain at the time—they looked uncomfortable, nervous, out of their element, which they were. Maxine Jones's jaw was clenched as she walked toward the witness table. She hadn't expected anything like this. She thought the team's work had been finished when they turned in their report in December. She was stunned when they were called actually to testify.

And now, as she watched Peters leaf through his copy of their report, its pages bristling with bright yellow Post-It notes, she was terrified. It was clear her work—*their* work—was about to be attacked, lacerated, dismissed as shoddy, sloppy, incomplete. Page by page, paragraph by paragraph, Peters intended to do just that, dissecting the team's methods, their sources, even their choice of words.

He began with the photograph of the burning shack, asking them to respond to Eva Jenkins's assertion. Bill Rogers answered that the photo had been found in a news magazine from the time, that the magazine had identified the shack as a house in Rosewood, and that the team had assumed that identification was correct. "We were really pressed for time," noted Rogers. Peters nodded. *Assumed.* He liked the sound of that word.

Peters spent a full fifteen minutes asking the team to explain its use of the word "posse" in reference to the mob that captured and killed Sam Carter. He noted the legal definition of the term, the fact that men must be legally deputized to become a posse, and he pointed out that there was no indication in the report that anyone was deputized in this case, or that there was even an officer of the law present at the lynching of Sam Carter or at the gun battle at the Carrier house.

"How do we know," said Peters, poking a finger at the report, "if that was a posse, or maybe just a bunch of mad white people?"

It went on like that for more than an hour. Several times Tom Dye almost came out of his seat. He had a temper, and his colleagues knew it. That's why Rogers and Larry Rivers had put Dye between them when the team took their seats at the witness table, so they could hold the kid back. It was Rogers, with his cool, courtly, southern gentleman demeanor, who took the lead in responding to Peters. And it was Rogers who answered when Peters stunned the room with a question no one expected to hear.

"What," Peters asked, focusing on the night of the Carrier house shootout, "if there was a living witness in Levy County today who could testify under oath, with cross examination, that he—he and another white gentleman— were *asked* to come to the Carrier household, because they were trusted, that they were told that a black prisoner was in custody in that house and that there were arrangements made to hand over the suspect to them to put in safekeeping because there was trust between the Carriers and these two gentlemen, who were then killed? What if that person was here to testify? Would that change your conclusion?"

The wave of shock that ran through the room was almost palpable. Even the unruffled senior professor looked at a loss for words. When his answer came, it was halting, almost confused.

"It would be new evidence," said Rogers.

"New material," he added.

He paused.

"It would be important."

Peters had hardly made a dent in his dog-eared copy of the report. He had hours of questions still left for the study team to answer. But when Hixson looked at his watch, then dismissed the professors, explaining that there were other witnesses to get to that day, Peters only mildly protested. He sailed through the remainder of the session, throwing a few jabs at Arnett Doctor, who had little to offer as a witness beyond his mother's memories and the things he had learned about Rosewood from talking to his relatives—all secondhand information. As was the testimony of Margaret Cannon, who followed Doctor to the stand to share the story her father had told her years after the attack of how he had been summoned to Rosewood toward the end of that week and had helped some of the women and children hiding in the woods get aboard the train that would take them to Gainesville.

That was fine as far as it went, but what mattered most to Peters was the bomb he had planted that morning. The fuse was now lit, and it was his turn to open the next day's newspapers with an apparent upper hand.

An ambush. Innocent whites lured to their death. That was the stunning scenario replayed by reporters, the revelation that the destruction of Rosewood might possibly have been brought on itself. That was what Peters's inference boiled down to, and he backed it up by blasting the study team's report in interviews with the press. The document might be fine for historical purposes, said Peters, but it "ain't worth a damn," he said, for determining whether the state should pay this claim. As a matter of fact, he said, the claim itself was hugely inflated, an overblown sack of unsubstantiated exaggerations.

"We're dealing with the *myth* of Rosewood," he told reporters. "I use the word 'myth' not to denigrate the tragedy, but a lot of this myth is just not true. There were deaths at Rosewood, but there was *not* a seven-day reign of terror."

The professors' protest that it was "highly unlikely" that black people in a southern town in 1923 would invite aroused whites to their home in order to shoot them was lost in the furor over Peters's charges. So was Steve Hanlon's attempt to remind reporters that what he called "the core issue here" remained unchanged.

"These people were entitled to police protection and didn't get it," said Hanlon. "Even if the men were invited to the Carrier home and shot, you can't burn down the town and run around shooting people. That's not the remedy."

But Hanlon's words were buried far beneath the headlines and Peters's accusations. All anyone wanted now was to see who this "surprise witness" would be and hear what he had to say. And so Jim Peters packed his gear for a drive down to Levy County to meet the family he was counting on to win him this case.

The family of Poly Wilkerson.

TWENTY-SEVEN

"He Didn't Have a Holster"

J im Peters headed out that Monday afternoon, after a brief hearing session in which he put a psychologist of his own on the witness stand to counter Carolyn Tucker's opening-day assessment that the Rosewood survivors were suffering from post-traumatic stress disorder. After a quick hour, with Steve Hanlon's short cross-exam, the psychologist was dismissed, the day's session was adjourned, Hixson announced they would reconvene Friday, and Peters rushed home, where he changed into a pair of jeans, grabbed a bag of quarters, tossed a video camera into the back seat of his white Miata and pointed the car south on Route 19, toward the green swamp air of Gulf Hammock.

On the seat beside him sat a list of more than two dozen phone numbers, Levy County callers he hadn't been able to contact yet. Since the hearing's first day, messages had continued flooding into his office, every caller claiming to have the true lowdown on Rosewood, and Peters was determined to follow up on each one. "A living witness," he says, "that's what I wanted."

Short of that, he'd take what he could get if it brought him as close to the truth as a man named Herb Wilkerson claimed he could take him. Wilkerson

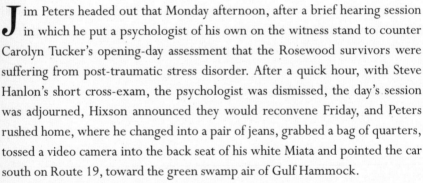

R. L. "Pink" Wilkerson, the brother of Poly Wilkerson, in 1924.

had been cautious when Peters first returned his call. He said he was the grandson of Poly Wilkerson, that his father James—Poly Wilkerson's son—was a boy at the time of the massacre, that James knew the whole story of what happened that night at the Carrier house, and that he might—*might*—be willing to testify.

The family was upset about what they'd been reading in the papers, said Herb. The stories these black people were telling was not the way it happened at all. He gave Peters a quick sketch of the account his daddy had always told him, how his granddaddy was lured to his death that night, murdered by those black people. But like he said, he wasn't *sure* his daddy was willing to come up to Tallahassee to testify. Their family were private people, Herb said, and they just didn't know if they wanted to be dragged into this mess.

So Peters asked if he could at least come down and meet them, there at their home. Wilkerson hesitated, then said he didn't see why not. When Peters asked for directions, Wilkerson paused again. "Just give me a call when you get down here," he said, "and I'll tell you the way to the house."

It was nighttime, darkness swallowing his headlights, by the time Peters reached the intersection of Routes 19 and 24, a place called Otter Creek. There was a tiny grocery store there, with a pay phone outside. Peters pulled into the gravel lot, got out and dialed Wilkerson's number. Herb answered, said he wasn't far from there, not far at all, but it was getting late and he'd rather they meet in the morning. So Peters found a motel, got to chatting with the desk clerk, said what he was doing, and the man got excited, gave him a few more names to add to his list, people he ought to call if he wanted to know what *really* happened at Rosewood.

First thing the next morning, Peters pulled up to the front porch of a place just off the highway, a tidy, gray woodframe house tucked back among the trees. An aged man, big, with thinning white hair and thick eyeglasses, sat in a rocking chair. He couldn't see too well, he said, as he introduced himself.

"James Wilkerson," he said, extending a large, heavy hand. His son Herb emerged from the house, offered Peters a seat, and they chatted a while, long enough for Peters to feel comfortable asking if the two men might be willing to make a sworn statement right now, this morning. They said they would. Then, as he sat on this porch, at the edge of this swamp, in the middle of this forest, miles from anything resembling a town, Jim Peters realized he needed a notary public.

"Just a minute," he told the Wilkersons. "I'll be right back." And he sped off, back to the grocery store, where the clerk behind the counter shook his head, said he knew of no such thing around those parts, then said Wait a minute, there might be someone over at the phosphate mine, just down the highway a little bit.

Peters floored it, pulling into the company's dirt drive and up to a trailer just as a man was locking up for lunch. Yes, said the man, one of the women working there had a notary's license, but she had just left to go home. Peters asked what kind of car she was driving, which direction she'd gone, then he shot back on to Route 19, raced south, spotted the woman's car up ahead, pulled alongside and waved her over. Ten minutes later, they were both in the Wilkersons' front yard, Peters with his video camera loaded and ready to roll, and the woman, slightly disheveled, standing on the grass, set to swear in the state's witness.

The tape is strange, almost surreal, the sounds of swallows chirping in the treetops as the notary stands awkwardly on the lawn, looking straight at the camera and identifying herself. She is Pamela L. Owens. This is Tuesday, March the 8th, 1994. Sworn testimony is about to be given by Mr. James E. Wilkerson.

Then the lens turns toward the old man. He sits, short-sleeved, in the sun, where his rocking chair has been moved so the camera will have better light. The roar of trucks sweeping past on the highway occasionally interrupts the old man's answers. His voice is gravelly. It quavers slightly, not from nerves but simply from age.

He was born in 1915, he says, in Sumner. His father was named Poly Wilkerson. His name is James. He was the youngest of his family's five children. They called him "Monkey" when he was growing up.

He was seven years old the week the trouble started in Rosewood, he says. He remembers it was a Thursday, early in the afternoon, when "a colored woman come to my daddy's house."

"I was in the yard playin'," he says. "My mother told me to leave."

He doesn't know exactly what transpired that afternoon—"Nothin' but what I was told," he says. But he knows his father met with the woman. Then she left. The family had dinner that night, he says, and then he went to bed. The next time he saw his father was the following evening.

"He was laid on the cooling board in our house, in the hallway." His father was dead, James says, with three loads of buckshot through the head. He had been killed early that morning, he says, but the body wasn't driven back until that night. "By three niggers," he says.

Actually, says Herb, it was a hand-pumped railroad utility car that was used to carry his grandfather's body back from Rosewood. That's part of the testimony the younger Wilkerson gives on the videotape, once he is sworn in after his father is finished. Again Peters remains behind the camera, his voice guiding the interview.

Herb Wilkerson was born in 1941, he says. His grandparents' names were Poly and Mattie. Poly was a "deputy," he says, "a quarter boss" in charge of the "holding cell" at Sumner. "He had the authority," says Herb, with a bit of pride, "to arrest anybody and put them in that holding cell."

Herb says he grew up asking his grandmother Mattie again and again to tell him about Rosewood. "She always told me she'd tell me when I got bigger," he says. "I think it was a bad memory for her."

When he was a teenager, says Herb, he finally heard the story, how his grandfather went to Rosewood that night to bring back the suspected rapist— "To get him out and avoid anyone else getting harmed," says Herb—and how both his grandfather and a deputy from Otter Creek, a man named "Doc" Andrews, were bushwhacked on the steps of the Carrier house. Andrews, says Wilkerson, "took a load of buckshot in the chest." His grandfather took three loads, "in the side of his face."

"But that's not what killed him," says Herb. "He fell backwards, and his neck went over the edge of the front porch, and it broke his neck, and that's what killed my granddaddy."

His grandfather's pistols were still in his pockets when his body was laid out in the hallway of their home, says Herb. "He didn't have a holster," he explains. "And those pistols had never been fired. That's what my grandmother told me."

Herb Wilkerson's grandfather was buried that Saturday, he says, nearing the end of the tape. Jim Peters asks who attended the funeral. As Wilkerson begins to respond, he is cut short by the sound of a screeching cat. Wilkerson is startled. He glances off camera, in the direction of the shriek.

And then the tape is done. Seventeen minutes of testimony from father and son.

Jim Peters had dozens of phone calls yet to make and two days to make them, but he doubted he'd get anything stronger than what these two men had given him that morning.

He just hoped it would be strong enough.

TWENTY-EIGHT

Hands Unknown

While Jim Peters was pouring quarters into the pay phones of Levy County, the Rosewood forces were busy back in Tallahassee, mounting yet another offensive of their own. Arnett Doctor, doing what he had learned to do best, began working the reporters. He called a press conference to cry foul about Jim Peters's tactics, claiming the state's attorney was simply stalling, using the clock to kill the bill.

"If he can postpone it long enough or get enough extensions," Arnett announced, "then time will run out and, for all intents and purposes, this claims bill will die."

Martha Barnett realized how critically true that might be. Assuming the Rosewood claim made it out of this hearing with Hixson's recommendation, it would then have to weave its way through a tangle of committees, each of which would have to approve the bill before it could finally arrive before the legislature for a vote.

The problem was that most of those committees had already finished their scheduled hearings for that year's session. They were done. Of the three thou-

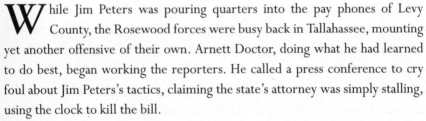

Ernest Parham

sand bills filed that January, almost every one had already either been passed or killed by committee. The few that remained to be heard would need special arrangements by the Speaker, and there was no guarantee he would give them. Which was why Barnett went to talk to Bo Johnson that week.

"I wanted to know that we'd be given a chance," she says. "That's all we wanted, was a chance for a fair hearing. And he assured me we'd get it. He made no commitment about his own stand on this bill, but he assured me he was not going to let the clock run out on us. He told me he'd made that message clear to his lieutenants, the committee chairmen.

"He did not want the House of Representatives to be criticized for killing the Rosewood bill on procedure. No matter how long this hearing took, he told me, we were going to get into committee. After that we were on our own, of course, but he assured me we'd get that. We'd get a fair hearing."

Meanwhile, Al Lawson made a move of his own. Jim Peters's suggestion that the Rosewood massacre might have been triggered by the victims themselves had stirred more outrage among the black community than Lawson had seen during his entire career in public office. He wasted no time using that anger to put Peters's feet to the fire.

"We *had* to put him on the spot," says Lawson. "We respected Jim Peters. Still do. But he was bringing up all *kinds* of stuff. We just had to make him back up and think. What are you gonna do? He was putting the heat on us, we had to put the heat on *him*."

So Lawson called in some of those chips from the meeting he'd staged the previous September with the state's black leaders. He sent out word for them all to respond. He asked for a backlash, and he got it. The strongest, most visible blow came from the state chapter of the NAACP, whose president, T. H. Poole, fired off a letter to the attorney general, with copies sent to the press, calling Peters's tactics "totally indefensible" and his accusation "absolutely ridiculous."

"This position," wrote Poole, "is an affront to the memory of the victims of the Rosewood Massacre in particular and the African-American community in general."

Meanwhile, Steve Hanlon sat back and smiled. He was far from alarmed about Peters's counterattack. In fact, he had little doubt that the bomb Peters planted was going to blow up in his hand.

"I actually thought of going up to him and saying, 'Jim, I don't know if you want to go down that alley.' Going out and getting some witnesses to try to prove that black people egged this on, well, when the headlines came out about that, I think it incensed the average American here in this state, black *and* white. And I think it really put the pressure on Jim. I think it really turned things bad for him."

Still, Hanlon was not about to simply wait for his counterpart to self-destruct. Peters was rooting around for new witnesses, so Hanlon got together with Barnett to do the same. Was there anyone they had missed, anyone they could put on the stand to counter whatever Peters might manage to pull together? They talked it over with Arnett, combed through everything they had, searching for a jewel they might have overlooked. Nothing.

Then they picked up the study team's report. Nothing there, either. They had read the thing more times than they could count, all ninety-three pages. But the appendix, that thick stack of census data and genealogical charts, lynching statistics and interview transcriptions, they had only cursorily looked at that before now. They had assumed all they would need was contained in the main body of the report. And most of it was. But now, as they looked again at the appendix, really *looked,* they realized they had a bomb of their own right under their noses, buried deep in those pages—on page 351, to be exact. The testimony of a man named Ernest Parham.

Hanlon and Barnett knew Parham's name from the main body of the report, where he was mentioned several times. But somehow, through sloppiness or sheer oversight, they had missed the man's significance, the fact that here was an eyewitness to the attack from the attackers' point of view. Hanlon and Barnett's focus had been almost entirely on the survivors. They had never considered the need for this witness. But they needed him now.

Hanlon immediately called Maxine Jones, who had hardly slept since she and her colleagues had been raked over the coals four days earlier. It wasn't Peters's assault on their report that had kept Jones awake. That was upsetting, having her capabilities questioned, her abilities as a historian impugned, but it was Peters's suggestion that the people who lived in Rosewood might have caused their own destruction that tore at Jones's gut. That accusation swept beyond who she was as a historian and cut to the core of what history itself was, what *black* history was in this country.

"My stomach was in knots," says Jones. "I just could not believe that Jim Peters was doing precisely what so many whites have done throughout this nation's history, which is rewriting it in their own terms, either ignoring the victims or making the victims at fault. That didn't sit well with me. It just ate me up that this was happening *again,* that black history was being rewritten yet again at the expense of the victims."

Jones gave Hanlon David Colburn's phone number, since Colburn had been the study team member who had interviewed Ernest Parham. Colburn then called Parham and asked if he'd be willing to meet with this attorney. Parham said sure, and Hanlon caught the next flight down to Orlando. When he returned to Tallahassee that afternoon, it was with a promise from Parham that he would be at the capitol Friday morning, ready to testify. No, Parham told Hanlon, he didn't need a hotel room. He'd just as soon stay with his brother, who lived up around there.

True to his word, Ernest Parham was there that Friday morning as Richard Hixson called the fifth session of the Rosewood hearing to order. Jim Peters had his videotape in hand. His interview with the Wilkersons had indeed been all he was able to bring back from his three-day sojourn to Levy County. He began the morning by asking the masters to view it. He also offered to bring James Wilkerson himself up the following week to testify in person. Finally, he noted that the study team was not off the hook, that he had eighteen pages of interrogatories he expected them to answer in writing.

Hixson said he'd look at the tape later. The study team questions would be taken care of as well, he said. But right now they had a witness to hear. And so Ernest Parham, wearing a light tweed sportscoat, a soft sweater vest and a neatly-knotted necktie, was called to the witness chair.

Again, Steve Hanlon began nonchalantly, asking Parham his age, and how he spent his time these days. Parham responded just as casually. He talked about his yardwork, about the occasional hand or two of blackjack he played with friends, and the baseball games he enjoyed taking in every now and again.

Then Hanlon turned to Parham's boyhood, beginning with his birth in 1904 in a town called Oxford, then on to the death of his father in Cedar Key in 1912, his mother's remarriage, and the family's move to Sumner in 1914. Hanlon asked about the hotel in Sumner, and the company commissary where Parham went to work as a teen. Then he asked Ernest Parham to recount what happened that week in 1923.

Still casual, totally relaxed, Parham described that first day, the rush of customers charging into the store to ask for shotguns and ammunition. His manner was so low-key, so matter of fact, that by the time he came to the events of that evening, when he drove the deputy sheriff's car over to Rosewood, no one was prepared for the impact of what they were about to hear, what no witness in this hearing had described until then, what few people in that room, or anywhere, would expect to hear in their lifetime—an eyewitness account of a lynching.

"What time of day was it now?" asked Hanlon.

"This was approximately eight o'clock," Parham answered.

"Pretty dark out in January?"

"Pretty much, yes."

"When you were there by Deputy Williams's car, did you know—could you *hear* a crowd ahead, a quarter mile, a half mile away?"

"Yes."

"Did you know something was going on up there?"

"That's right."

"What did you think was going on up there?"

"Well, I assumed it was the group which was following the dogs."

"Did you say anything to Deputy Williams then?"

"Yes. I told him I had driven his car up and told him where it was."

"Did you then go up ahead to where the crowd was?"

"Yes, I did."

"Did you have a sense, when you were back there with Deputy Williams, that there was anything wrong going on up where that crowd was?"

"Why, sure."

"Why did you have that sense? What was going through your mind at the time?"

"Well, at the time I really didn't know *what* was going on up there, but I knew that there was a crowd up there."

"You heard a lot of noise?"

"Of course."

"So you wanted to go up and find out what was going on, is that right?"

"Right."

"And you did that?"

"I did."

"And you walked up there?"

"That's right."

"When you got up there, what was going on?"

"Well, they had Sam Carter strung up on a tree limb."

The room tensed. Richard Hixson leaned closer, as if he weren't sure he was hearing this. He hadn't expected to hear this.

"Now Sam Carter," said Hanlon, "who was he?"

"Who *was* he?"

"Yes, sir."

"Well, Sam Carter was a black man that lived in the neighborhood, and this was across the street from—across the *road* from—his home."

"Did you know Sam Carter?"

"Yes, I did. Not personally, but I knew who he was."

"What did you think of him?"

"Well, he was a very fine fellow. Everybody thought real well of him."

"When you say he was strung up, was there a noose around his neck?"

"That's true."

"And a rope over the limb on the tree?"

"That's true."

"And was he pulled up in the air?"

"Well, he was pulled up, but his tiptoes was still on the ground as I came up."

"And the deputy sheriff was still sitting back about a quarter to a half-mile away?"

"That's right."

"Did he ever come up to find out what was going on here?"

"Did he find *out?*"

"Yes."

"Well, now, that I couldn't say."

"Well, while you were there, did you ever see the deputy get off of the running board of that car and come up to see what was going on with that crowd?"

"No, I did not."

"When you got up there to where the crowd was, and you saw Sam Carter hanging there kind of on his toes with the noose around his neck, what was the next thing you saw or heard?"

"Well, I happened to walk right into it, and they had Sam strung up and they was asking him questions."

"What were they asking him?"

"Asking him where he put the fugitive—the black man—out of his wagon. Apparently he had refused to tell them up to that time. And I understood later that they had strung him up about three times, and then they let him down, and he would not tell them. So this particular time when I walked up, I didn't realize I was right into it. And this particular fellow had him strung up, and he was choking, and this fellow was beating him on the chest trying to make him talk. And I said, Well, how can he talk when you're *choking* him? So he let him down. And when he let him down, he kind of fell to his knees. And then he got up, and he said, Yes, he'd tell them."

"Now, was there a man there that had his hand on the rope?"

"That's true."

"Did that man have anything else in his hands?"

"Well, he had a shotgun."

"When he let him down, did he say anything to Sam Carter?"

"Yes, he said, If the dogs don't pick up the trail where you put this fellow out, I'm going to shoot you."

"What happened next?"

"Well, we went about a mile from there, following through the woods, following this man Sam Carter and the fellow who had the gun, to where Sam Carter said, This is where I put him out of the wagon."

"And then what happened?"

"Well, the dogs did not pick up the trail. So he shot him."

Richard Hixson almost came out of his seat. It had been one thing to hear the survivors, who were small children at the time, describe the chaos, confusion and killing that swept through the Carrier house the night of that attack. But this was different. None of those children could name their attackers, none of them knew who was shooting to kill them. They were inside the storm. But this man was outside it. This man was a witness to murder. He watched a killer, and he watched a killing.

Hanlon went on.

"Was Mr. Pillsbury there?"

"I was standing beside him."

"What was Mr. Pillsbury's position?"

"He was general superintendent of the Cummer Lumber Company."

"Were you surprised when this man shot . . ."

"Well, we were *all* surprised. Had no idea. We thought it was just threats. We had no idea he was going to shoot him."

"Did the crowd disperse after that?"

"It did, yes."

"Do you know if the deputy sheriff came up and did anything?"

"I did not see him."

"Was there a coroner's verdict the next day or two?"

"Yes, there was."

"And what was the coroner's verdict?"

"'Killed by hands unknown.'"

"And what was your reaction when you heard that?"

"Well, we were surprised."

"How many people were in that crowd?"

"At the time of the shooting?"

"Yes, sir."

"About twenty-five or thirty."

Richard Hixson did not move back from the edge of his seat for the remainder of Parham's testimony, which went on for two hours more. Beyond compensation, there was now a new aspect to this claim, to the state's responsibility in this matter, and that was the issue of criminal investigation. The fact that there was a witness to murder here, and that the murderer—or murderers—might possibly be out *there,* was something Hixson had not considered until now.

When Parham mentioned that the Florida Department of Law Enforcement had recently sent two agents to his home to interview him, Hixson jolted. And when, near the end of Hanlon's interrogation, Parham again mentioned the inquest conducted the day after Sam Carter was shot, Hixson stepped in.

"Let me understand something," said Hixson. "The very next *day* you heard there was an inquest?"

"Yes," answered Parham.

"But no one talked to *you,* no law enforcement official?"

"Right."

"You witnessed a killing, right?"

"Right."

"And no one talked to you from law enforcement over all these years, until two weeks ago?"

"No."

"You were never contacted by a state attorney, a deputy sheriff, a policeman, *nothing* in regard to this killing?"

"No."

"Not until two weeks ago?"

"That's right."

And that was that. Three hours had gone by like three minutes. Not only had Ernest Parham's testimony bolstered the families' claim for compensation, with his depiction of Rosewood as a healthy, viable community, but he had added the dimension of murder, something neither the claimants nor the state had considered. It was possible that the men who committed this crime and other killings that week might still be alive, and if they were, it was the state's duty to pursue charges against them.

It had been only three years since the conviction in Mississippi of Byron De La Beckwith, the man who murdered Medgar Evers back in 1963. That case had reminded the nation that there is no statute of limitations on murder. Medgar Evers was dead almost thirty years before his killer was brought to justice. It didn't matter that that killer had become a frail old man. Neither, knew Richard Hixson, did it matter in this case that it had been more than twice that long since the killings at Rosewood occurred. Though there was little chance that any of the assailants were still alive, if the possibility existed that they were, then the state was bound to pursue it.

Hixson watched Jim Peters's videotape that afternoon. And, a week later, he listened to James Wilkerson share from the witness stand the same story he had told on the tape, the story his mother had told him from the time he was a little boy.

And then it was over. The study team's responses to Peters's questions, said Hixson, had yet to be completed and would have to be dealt with by whatever House committee cared to look into them. There was no more time to wait. Friday morning, March 18, the final session of the Rosewood hearing was adjourned. The special master's report was due on the Speaker of the House's desk Monday afternoon. That gave Richard Hixson three days to write it. One weekend, really.

He had a lot of running to do.

TWENTY-NINE

A Moral Obligation

~~~

R ichard Hixson had no doubt he was going to recommend that the legislature pass the Rosewood claims bill. He had been as thunderstruck by the
emotional impact of the survivors' testimony on the hearing's first day as
everyone else who was there to witness them. Beyond the drama of the stories
told by Minnie Lee, A. T. Goins, Willie Evans and Wilson Hall, Hixson was ut-
terly convinced of their sincerity.

"I'd read the testimonies in the report," he says, "but reading the words is
one thing, and seeing them spoken is another. There's nothing quite the same as
seeing living, breathing human beings tell their stories. How a person says
something—not just *what* he says, but the *way* he says it—goes a long way toward judging a witness's credibility. It's like old Justice Potter Stewart put it:
'You know it when you see it.'

"You could see it in each of these people. There was a dignity to all of them,
a grace, and an obvious honesty. When they were talking about their lives, they
spoke as adults, but when they went back to describe Rosewood, they began to
speak as *children* would speak. The terms they used changed. Even the way they

---

Arnett Doctor and Al Lawson

spoke, their inflection. It was as if they were *there* again. You can't coach something like that."

Hixson thought about that that weekend. And he thought about motive.

"There was no doubt in my mind that these people were not here for money," he says. "I truly don't think they cared about compensation. I think they simply wanted the truth to be known about what happened to them. That was very clear to me that day. You can get a sense of people who are trying to tell you what they think you want to hear, to better their case. But that was not the case here. I truly think they didn't care whether they got fifty cents or a hundred and fifty million dollars. It didn't matter."

As for the factual basis of the claim, the doubts surrounding the details of the events that took place that week, Hixson was convinced, despite the flaws that might exist around its edges, that the heart of the study team's report was reliable. It was true. The town had been savaged; people were killed—at least eight, perhaps more; the state was aware of the events as they transpired and did not respond to prevent them; and after the attack, the state neither pursued prosecution—beyond the cursory grand jury investigation—nor did it protect and attempt to restore the property to its owners. It was the issue of law enforcement and prosecution, raised most of all by Ernest Parham's testimony, that hit Hixson hardest.

"You try to be detached and objective," he says, "to simply listen carefully and show no visible reactions. But sometimes it's hard. The point when Mr. Parham began describing the lynching was one of those times. It came in a such a manner that I wasn't quite sure I was hearing what I was hearing. I had *expected* the other witnesses' descriptions, the survivors', to be about what they were about. But Mr. Parham was so low-key, so reasonable. He was just going along, and I was just making notes, and then, suddenly, he was describing this killing. I remember rising up in my chair and saying, 'Wait a minute, are you telling me you observed a *murder?*' That was one of those moments you never forget. It will always stand out in my mind."

Parham's reference to the inquest of Sam Carter's death was supported by a copy of the coroner's verdict, dated January 2, 1923, produced by the study team:

> *In the peace of God then, we the Jury, after the Examination of the Said Sam Carter, who being found lying Dead, find that the said Sam Carter came to his Death by being shot by Unknown Party so say we all.*

Incredible, thought Hixson, as was the fact that no charges were ever brought by the state for the other killings that occurred that week—the deaths at the Carrier house the night of January 4, and the deaths of Lexie Gordon, James Carrier and Mingo Williams. Nor was there any investigation into acts of arson or theft.

Ernest Parham testified to the study team and at the hearing that he would rather not identify the man who shot Sam Carter. Nor did he name the other members of the mob he saw that night. Some of them might still be alive, he explained—though he doubted it—and he said he would just as soon not disturb them or their families after all these years. What would be the point? But of course, he added, that was only if the choice were his. If the law required, he said, he would certainly name everyone he could remember. Hixson was determined that the law require it, that an order for a criminal investigation be included as part of the Rosewood bill. "Regardless of how anyone feels about compensation," he explains, "no one would think a crime should be left unprosecuted."

The issue of the passage of time, the question raised by Jim Peters as to why these victims had waited seventy years to file this claim, why they had not pursued their case at the time, when the crimes occurred and the accused could defend themselves, was, in Hixson's opinion, no issue at all.

"Civil rights laws were effectively on the books beginning after the Civil War," he says, "but they were never given any real meaning as far as claims and causes of action, by Supreme Court decisions and such, until you saw the Warren Court come forward beginning in the 1950s. Those laws *certainly* had little meaning back in the 1920s.

"And besides," he adds, "these people were *children* at the time."

There was, concluded Hixson, undeniable damage suffered by the people who survived the attack on Rosewood as well as the descendants of the survivors and the dead. The state, he concluded, had been negligent and now had a "moral obligation" to compensate the victims.

And so, the final issue Richard Hixson had to grapple with that weekend was the same one faced by the claimants themselves when their bill was written.

How much? And how many?

The Rosewood bill as filed was by far the largest equitable claims bill Hixson had ever faced. No such claim in the history of Florida came close to the seven million dollars the Rosewood claimants were asking. Hixson knew the legislature would never seriously consider, much less pass, this bill for that amount. Most House members he had spoken with, as well as his boss, Robert Trammell—whose Judiciary Committee would be the Rosewood bill's first stop on its journey through the legislature—had made it clear this bill would almost certainly sink if it stayed at seven million. Hixson had to somehow slice that figure down to an amount the legislature could swallow, while still honoring the claimants with an amount of compensation that adequately reflected and respected the damage they had suffered.

He began by dividing the claimants into two categories—the actual survivors, and the descendants of victims or survivors who were now deceased. For those descendants, the only tangible loss from the attack on Rosewood was the property that their forebears had owned. The precedent Hixson looked to to compensate such a loss was the same model Hanlon and his colleagues had used to write their bill—the Japanese-American Reparation Act of 1988. That law directed that each Japanese-American citizen who lost his home and land during the internment that occurred during World War II would be given an apology and twenty thousand dollars by the federal government.

Using that figure and the fact that there were roughly twenty-five households identified in Rosewood at the time of the attack, Hixson came up with a round number of $500,000. He recommended that a fund of that amount be included in the bill, from which payments would be made to each family that could prove its relatives lost property during the 1923 attack. Those payments would be $20,000 apiece, with the state authorized to increase that amount up to $100,000 for each claim in which the value of the lost property was shown to be higher than twenty thousand.

As for direct compensation, Hixson decided it should be paid only to the survivors, with survivors defined as people who were physically present—actually living in Rosewood—at the time of the attack. That meant that Lillie Washington, Berthina Fagin, Thelma Hawkins, Eva Jenkins and Vera Hamilton were out as survivors. They would now be considered descendants.

To decide the amount of compensation for each survivor, Hixson again searched for a precedent, a similar situation, something that could give him a fix on how much to award in a case like this. But there was no other case like this. Rosewood was spectacularly unique, not only in the annals of Florida's legal history but in the nation's legal history as well. There was no model to which Hixson could turn to answer the issue of money. "This was the most difficult question I faced," he says. "What number do you come up with, and how do you defend it?"

He decided to go back through every claims bill he had ever judged, looking hard at those that involved injuries to children. "Because that's what these people were," he says again. "They were *children*."

He finally found what he was looking for in a claims bill from the early 1980s, filed by the guardian of a young girl in Tampa who had been removed from her home by the state when she was three years old. The reason she had been removed was physical abuse. For the next five years, until she was eight, the girl lived in a series of foster homes where further abuse occurred, causing permanent physical and psychological damages. The girl was twelve when the bill was filed and the claim came before Hixson. It charged that the state social services agencies responsible for monitoring the girl's care in those foster homes had been derelict in their duties. The claim asked for fifty thousand dollars, which Hixson approved. When the bill then went before the legislature, the lawmakers not only passed it, but they tripled the amount of compensation to one hundred and fifty thousand dollars.

"That happens," says Hixson of the increased award. "It doesn't happen often, but it happens."

One hundred and fifty thousand dollars. That was the figure Hixson decided to write in for each of the Rosewood survivors. By Sunday afternoon, Hixson had finished the basic draft of his report—"The guts of it," he says—including the stipulation that a college scholarship fund be established for Rosewood families and descendants.

Monday morning—March 21, the first day of spring—it was done, the House special master's final report, fifteen single-spaced pages ending with the conclusion that "a moral obligation exists on the part of the State of Florida to remedy this matter" and recommending a total payout of $2.1 million. The report was addressed to the Honorable Bo Johnson, with copies made for Al Lawson and Miguel De Grandy, Steve Hanlon and Jim Peters.

Hanlon rushed to Hixson's office to pick up his copy, sat down right there to read it, and by the time he turned to the last page, he felt like a hole had been blown through his gut. On the one hand, he was awash with elation. This was a victory, a tremendous step toward winning the claim in the legislature. In Hanlon's opinion, Richard Hixson had shown the wisdom of Solomon. But the family. Hanlon could only imagine how they were going to respond. And Arnett. He didn't even *want* to imagine what Arnett might do.

He didn't have to. Arnett showed up with Martha Barnett while Hanlon was on his way out of the building. Hanlon handed him the report and held his breath. Arnett read it, standing there in the hallway, and when he finished, he exploded, his voice careening down the Capitol corridors.

"Take it, *take* the goddamned thing," he shouted, thrusting the paper back at Hanlon. "This is *your* goddamned bill now, not mine. You do what the hell you want to do with it. I'm *finished*. I'm *through*."

And he stormed out.

But he wasn't finished. Hanlon was in De Grandy's office that afternoon, talking to some of the newsmen who had already gotten their own copies of the report, when he got a phone call from his office telling him he might want to know that Arnett was over there, that he had prepared a statement blasting Hixson's decision, and he was getting set to fax copies out to the press.

"Put him on the phone," said Hanlon.

Arnett came on the line.

"Look," said Arnett. "I'm not gonna take this. *We're* not going to take this. We've watched this thing get chopped down and chopped down, and now we've got people getting cut *out*. My *family*. Aunt Vera and Eva and Lillie Washington, what am I supposed to say to *them*? How am I supposed to tell them they don't *count*? We've already compromised, we've compromised more than we should ever have to. This isn't about money, it's about justice. And *respect*. This is an insult. That's what it is, an *insult*. Two million dollars? People get more money than that for spilling a cup of coffee on themselves at a *McDonald's*."

Hanlon heard him. He understood. But the first question he asked was whether that fax had gone out.

"Not yet," said Arnett.

"Okay," said Hanlon. "Now listen. I know how you feel. We all do. But I'll tell you this right now. If you send that thing out, we're dead. We can all just go home. And you can tell your uncle he's not getting his hundred and fifty G's. If that's what you want, if you want to go back to him, to all the survivors, and tell them you've taken that away from them, that you've taken away any justice they might ever hope to have, then go ahead. If you want to live with that, go ahead. Do it."

The line was silent.

Hanlon went on.

"Or you can suck it up, Arnett. You can praise what Hixson's done here, and we can all go forward and we can *win* this thing."

The line was still silent. But Arnett had listened. He hung up and began calling the family. The survivors were fine. Richard Hixson had been right. Money was not the issue for them. Two hundred and seventy thousand dollars. A hundred and fifty thousand. Either was fine with them. But the younger generations, the descendants, some of them were as furious with Arnett as Arnett had been with Hanlon.

For many of them, it *was* the money. This had become something that could make a difference in their lives, more money than most of them had ever imagined having. They *hadn't* imagined it at first, hadn't believed it could actually happen when this whole thing began. But once they heard the numbers, saw them in the newspapers, had neighbors and friends asking about it, as if they'd won the lottery, it had become real. Arnett had warned them, and Steve Hanlon, too, that there was a long road ahead and a lot could happen, but still, it seemed real.

And now, just like that, it was gone. Just like that, something they felt was theirs had been snatched from their hands, taken away, *again,* just the way it was taken away in Rosewood.

And they blamed Arnett.

"That was when it started," he says. "The whispering. The finger-pointing. I'd sold them out, that's what some of them started saying. I hadn't stood my ground. I'd given up. That's the way they saw it. No matter that I didn't have anything to *give* up, that the state held all the cards. Some of the family were telling me I should've negotiated, when I had nothing to negotiate *with.*

"Take it or leave it, that's what I ended up telling them. We're going to try to get the most we can out of this for the *survivors,* if no one else, that's what I said. This started with the survivors, the ones who were *there,* and that's who we are all responsible to in the end. If in the course of pursuing justice for them, we can get any benefits at all for ourselves, the direct descendants, then that's gravy. That's what I told them. That's what I told everyone."

That, essentially, is what Arnett wound up telling the reporters that Monday afternoon. And when Tuesday's newspapers came out, with Hixson's decision in the headlines, and quotes of gratitude and praise from Steve Hanlon and

Martha Barnett, Arnett Doctor was right there as well, weighing in with his own kind words for the special master.

Steve Hanlon's work was essentially done. It was up to Barnett now to carry the ball into the legislature. And Richard Hixson's work was done as well. He came home that Tuesday evening exhausted, slumped into a chair and punched the button on his answering machine. He always had two, maybe three calls waiting when he got home from work. Rarely were there more than that.

But this night, the tape was filled. And the calls were ugly, strangers' voices telling Hixson how they felt about what they'd read in that morning's newspaper and how they felt about him. Some of the calls came close to threats, but only one really disturbed Hixson—the one that mentioned his dog, Jennifer. How would someone even *know* about Jennifer?

There had been a newspaper story written just the week before about the hearing and about Hixson, and about the thirteen-year-old Pomeranian he'd inherited from a friend, how he'd fed his pet carryout ribs and Chinese food till it had gotten too fat to join him any more on his evening runs. That was Jennifer. That must have been where this caller learned her name.

His colleagues at the Capitol were amazed Hixson still kept his number in the book. He'd never thought twice about pulling it, getting an unpublished listing. But he was thinking about it now.

THIRTY

Good Friday

The waning weeks of a state legislative session resemble a battlefield in the times of trench warfare, an ugly landscape littered with the carcasses of lobbyists and laws, some mortally wounded, moaning with the last gasps of life, others nothing but corpses, limp casualties to be tossed aside or simply stepped over as weary waves of survivors rise again and again, day after day, over the top and into the breech, a blizzard of bodies and bills, lawmakers and lobbyists alike surging down corridors, shoving into committee rooms, launching salvos of faxes and phone calls, cornering one another in offices, in lunchrooms, on the toilet if that's what it takes, anything to get a minute or two to bend a vote their way.

So many votes, on so many bills. That spring of 1994, more than three thousand proposed laws washed through the halls of the Florida capitol. Some stood out more than others, foaming whitecaps bursting above a roiling sea of more mundane matters.

There was a bill to castrate convicted rapists, and one to ban nudity on public beaches. There was a proposal to pay women on welfare to use birth con-

A. T. Goins with daughter Annette Shakir

trol, and another to bar protesters from blockading abortion clinics. A bill to allow prayer in public schools was filed alongside a bill to allow paddling as well. There was a bill to punish people who spread lies about Florida oranges. And a bill to clean up the Everglades. And a bill to build more prisons. And one to ban assault weapons. There was a bill to honor the Florida State Seminoles for winning the 1993 national collegiate football crown and a bill to designate Collier County the "Purple Martin Capital of Florida."

This was the tempest into which the Rosewood claim was tossed that first day of spring. Compared to the $700 million asked to clean up the Everglades, the $300 million it would take to build the proposed prisons, or the $821 million insurance subsidy plan that was at the heart of the Governor's massive health-care proposal, the $2 million asked by the Rosewood claimants was a mere speck in a sandstorm—one two-hundredth of one percent of the $38 billion proposed budget on the table that March.

Not that two million dollars was irrelevant, especially in committees, but on the basis of money alone, Rosewood would not seem a priority. Beyond that, the bill had already gone through the scrutiny of a hearing master, which typically meant a rubber stamp from the legislators. "Members have told me that in the past," says Richard Hixson, "that their policy is generally to vote whichever way the master's recommendation comes down, favorable or unfavorable."

But this case was clearly different.

"I was stunned by how many members came to see me about this, to ask, 'How could you *write* this?'" says Hixson. "I'd say, 'Read it. Just *read* it.' And they did. Almost all of them actually read the report, which is not always the case."

And they talked about it.

"They weren't talking about anything *else*," says Al Lawson. "With health care, the prisons, the environment, all those things in the air, all you heard people talking about was Rosewood."

Martha Barnett had more than a little to do with that. From the day the bill was filed in December, she had been sowing Rosewood's seeds, planting the issue with every lawmaker she could corner, beginning with the governor himself, Lawton Chiles. Chiles, who was hand-picked by none other than Spessard Holland back in 1970 to fill Holland's vacated seat in the U.S. Senate, had a long history of support for civil rights issues. But at the time the Rosewood bill was filed, there was no telling which way he might lean.

Late that January, one of Barnett's partners at Holland and Knight hosted an evening cookout. "Nothing fancy," says Barnett. "Blue jeans, real casual." Among the four or five couples there were Lawton Chiles and his wife Rhea. "Naturally the subject of Rosewood came up," says Barnett. "Everybody wanted to know about it, Mrs. Chiles in particular. The governor was pretty quiet, but she was asking a lot of questions."

Two weeks later, before Hixson's hearing had even begun, the governor issued a letter to the president of the Senate and the Speaker of the House endorsing the Rosewood bill, saying he would sign it if the legislature passed it.

So Barnett had a bit of momentum as she hit the capitol corridors that March, joining the mob scene that began each morning at eight. "I made a list, mostly of leadership people" she says, "and every day I'd mark six to eight names and say, Okay, these are my Rosewood contacts today. I couldn't wait until the committee meetings were scheduled. I had to lay a lot of groundwork beforehand. If I was lucky, I'd get ten, maybe fifteen minutes with each person, just enough time to touch base and maybe do a little educating."

In his own less polished but just as determined way, Arnett Doctor became a self-styled lobbyist, a daily presence in the halls of the capitol. Holland and Knight footed the bill for his room at the Radisson, and each morning he would rise at five, take a short stroll, grab a whirlpool, get dressed, be at the door to the hotel's restaurant when it opened at six, and swallow his breakfast while rifling through a stack of the state's newspapers, scissors in hand, clipping every item he could find about Rosewood. Then he'd head over to the capitol, where his day, like everyone else's, began about eight and lasted till midnight, when he would return to the hotel, catch a few hours' sleep, rise the next morning and do it all over again. Nobody knew who he was at first, this tall, intense black man stalking the halls of the capitol. But they learned.

"I had to be there," says Arnett. "They needed to *see* me. I needed to be on the scene, physically present, every *day*. Even if I didn't talk to them, if I didn't talk to *anybody*, I was going to be *seen*, to remind them of Rosewood, to let them know they were not going to be able to just forget about this. They were going to have to face it. They were going to have to deal with it. I was there to be a reminder, a committed African-American individual, in the flesh, in their faces, every day."

They noticed. There was no way they could not notice.

"Arnett was squaring off against *everybody*," says Al Lawson. "People were coming up to me and saying, 'Al, keep this guy Doctor away from me, get him off my *back.*' Arnett definitely tested people's patience, but he was also a reminder of the personal side of this bill, that this thing was about living breathing people. That was important."

In the early going, Martha Barnett was hardly more welcome than Arnett. Mostly she got cold shoulders and the waves of impatient hands, which didn't put her off in the least. That was what she expected. She smiles even now, recalling the brushoffs from conservatives like Everett Kelly, from down in Tavares, and Fred Dudley, from Cape Coral.

" 'Martha, I love you,' they'd say to me, 'but there isn't any way in the *world* I'm voting for this bill.' All of them were against it at that point. They just couldn't see spending money on something that happened seventy years ago. They just didn't want to open that can of worms. The best I'd get was, 'Let's wait and see what the master says. I always go along with the master.' "

More disturbing to Barnett was the lack of support, or even interest, shown by the black caucus. If there was one base of strength Barnett thought she could count on, it was the black leadership, but when she arranged a breakfast meeting with the group a week before Hixson's hearing began, to go over their plan of attack, a mere four members showed up.

"Four out of nineteen," says Barnett. "I was shocked. I couldn't believe it."

So Al Lawson had to weigh in again, gathering the group and delivering the message that had become almost a mantra during the preceding year. "I told them it was time," he says. "Till then we'd always been Democrats first and blacks second, and we went along with the Democrat agenda whether we believed it or not. We were afraid to step on toes, and they knew that. They figured the caucus was in their pocket, that blacks didn't even need to be consulted. And they were basically right.

"I said if we don't change and focus on an issue like this, then we're failing the people who *put* us here, we're failing the NAACP and the purpose of reapportionment, which was to make a difference in our people's lives instead of just getting by and going along. If there was ever a time for us to earn respect as a force to be reckoned with, it was now."

By the time Hixson's report was issued, the black caucus was on board. And they had to be, because what Barnett had been told by so many of the lawmakers she'd met with—that they would take the master's recommendation and vote his way—turned out not to be so. The day the report came out, the voices of opposition were loud and harsh.

"This is a very, very sad part of Florida history, just as the Civil *War* is a very, very sad part of United States history," said Charlie Williams, an insurance salesman whose district included Levy County and the man who would spearhead the fight against Rosewood if it made it to the Senate. "We can't just back up and make everyone whole who's been hurt by injustices," he said.

"I simply don't want today's taxpayers to be responsible for something that happened decades ago," said George Crady, a fifty-two-year-old veteran legislator from Yulee, up near Wilson Hall's home in Hilliard. Crady was one of the first people Martha Barnett had talked to about the Rosewood bill and now he had become one of its chief critics.

Randy Mackey, a real-estate developer from Lake City, who would also become one of the leaders of the opposition, was as succinct as possible. "I'm not supportive of giving the survivors of Rosewood *anything,*" he said.

Dozens of voices echoed the same feelings. Beryl Burke, an attorney and female black caucus member from Miami—one of two blacks on the crucial twenty-four-member Judiciary Committee—tried to counter by arguing that, far from asking too much, the Rosewood families had already sacrificed more than they should by watching their claim sliced to $2 million. "When it comes to minorities," said Burke, "we always seem to be looking for an avenue where, instead of giving people what they rightfully deserve, we try to justify just a little bit here and there."

But Burke's words were lost among howls of protest from many of her fellow legislators. So were the sentiments of newspaper editorials across the state, which generally supported the bill even as their readers overwhelmed the letters to the editors pages with complaints against it.

"For the state of Florida to compensate survivors of Rosewood for something that happened seventy-plus years ago," wrote a reader of the *Orlando Sentinel,* "is comparable to reimbursing my family because our family home was burned down a hundred and thirty years ago by Quantrill's raiders during the Civil War. Sounds dumb, doesn't it?"

"Rosewood wasn't the bleakest chapter in Florida's history," wrote another, "because before Rosewood were the Indians of Florida. Maybe Florida should make Rosewood a reservation for the survivors like they did for the Indians. Just a thought."

One reader linked the killings at Rosewood to the recent spate of murders on Florida's interstate highways:

If that bill is justified, then I propose that the same legislature enact similar bills
to compensate white victims of black crimes, such as the British man who was shot
and killed at the rest stop on Interstate 10, or the German family whose
wife/mother was brutally murdered in Miami. These crimes, or "massacres," were
committed by blacks on whites. Is the state only responsible for protecting blacks
or other minorities?

This was going to be a dogfight, no doubt about it. And the toughest road-block was the first one, two days after Hixson submitted his report, when the Rosewood bill went before Robert Trammell's Judiciary Committee, generally regarded as the most conservative committee in the House. Trammell, a North Florida attorney and former college basketball coach, had already made it clear he was against this bill. Normally that would have been enough to kill it right there. Committees basically belong to their chairmen, which is why Martha Barnett went to Trammell the day before the Wednesday hearing—the sixth time she had seen him in the past month—to plead her case yet again.

"I told him I knew he was going to vote against it," she says. "Fine. But I asked him not to leverage his power with the other members. I asked him to let them vote on their own, to at least give us a chance to make our case."

Trammell told her he would, which guaranteed only a fair hearing, far from success. Tuesday morning's newspapers proclaimed the Rosewood bill was already in "deep trouble." By that afternoon, Al Lawson could count only eight votes among the two dozen Judiciary Committee members. Miguel De Grandy, who was himself the lead Republican on the committee, had only three of the five Republican votes he knew they needed to win.

Late that night, with a committee roll-call sheet clutched in his hand, Lawson stalked the blue-carpeted aisles of the House chamber, cornering Judiciary members and reminding them, in no vague terms, that they were each up for reelection that fall, and they might want to think twice about risking the wrath of the black voters in their districts. Even Robert Trammell had to think twice about that proposition. "He had thirty-seven percent blacks in his district," says Lawson. "I reminded him of that."

One card Lawson knew he now had, which he would not have dreamed of a year earlier, was the support of Bo Johnson. The two had been forced to spend hours together during the previous months, arranging the logistics of this touchy bill's strange path, and the animosity between them had faded. Martha

Barnett had helped as a peacemaker of sorts—she and the Speaker had always been on cordial terms. And it didn't hurt that Bo Johnson's chief of staff, Theresa Frederick, was African-American, providing Johnson with some perspectives on the issue that went beyond the purely political.

Johnson had helped nurse the bill through Hixson's hearing, had waited for the results of that hearing to decide how he personally felt about this bill, and had been convinced by those results to back it with everything he had. He had his doubts about this thing when it was first filed more than a year earlier. He still had his doubts when the hearing began. But now he was a believer. And so, the night before the Judiciary Committee was scheduled to meet on Rosewood, with the eyes of the nation watching, with "Dateline" and "60 Minutes" on the scene, and *The New York Times* and the *Wall Street Journal* and the *Washington Post,* with Florida's national reputation on the line, the Speaker took Al Lawson aside and told him he was going to "try to help turn some people around for you."

When the committee convened the next morning, not only were its twenty-four members present, along with an audience of reporters and Rosewood family members, but two wild cards were in attendance as well, and they weren't there just to watch.

One was Elaine Bloom, a college fund-raiser from Miami Beach who, as Speaker *pro tempore,* had voting rights on every committee. The other was Peter Wallace of St. Petersburg, chairman of the powerful Rules Committee and the Speaker-designate, next in line to succeed Bo Johnson at the helm of the House. True to his word, Bo had sent in his troops—Bloom to cast her swing vote if it was needed, and Wallace to remind the members by his mere presence that he would be the man passing out committee memberships next year.

It was going to be close. The members were caught in a tight squeeze, with their chairman pushing from one side and the Speaker's office pushing from the other. Steve Hanlon and Jim Peters testified first, summing up the cases they had made before Hixson. Then came De Grandy. Then Lawson put a fresh spin on the claim, explaining that it was not so much an issue of race as of property rights. "I was not being sincere," he admits now, "but I had to get the Republican members to see this thing in a different light, one they could relate to."

Martha Barnett stepped up and chided the state for its "collective amnesia." "The simple truth," she told the committee, "is that the whole world knew what happened at Rosewood."

Committee member John Cosgrove, an attorney from Miami, agreed. "We have the power today to right a wrong," he said. "This is, in effect, from the people of Florida, a public confession."

The vote was by voice, *yeas* and *nays,* and when it was done, Arnett Doctor, sitting near the back of the room, had lost count. He had to ask Steve Hanlon the total. Fourteen to eleven, in favor of the claim. Bloom's vote hadn't been needed, but she had cast it anyway.

Arnett leaped from his seat, let out a whoop, and Trammell quickly called for the next item on the committee's agenda. In the hall outside, Arnett was beside himself, hugging Hanlon, high-fiving De Grandy and holding court with a small circle of reporters.

"We buried them," he crowed. "We *buried* them."

But Martha Barnett knew better. Next up was the Appropriations Committee, where the focus would be simply and solely on money. Stung by their defeat in the Judiciary, the Rosewood opposition was already shifting its strategy. If they couldn't outright defeat this bill, they would gut it, strip away its payments and reduce it to something symbolic—a formal proclamation of regret and perhaps a plaque.

"I object only to the money," said Robert Trammell the day after his Judiciary Committee passed the bill on to Appropriations, of which he was also a member. "But a recognition that something terrible happened," he added. "I could support that."

Trammell said he might allow the property payments and perhaps the scholarships, but the direct payments to survivors had to go and he was going to do his best to amend them out. Daryl Jones, the member of the black caucus who would lead the Rosewood fight if the bill made it out of the House and into the Senate, called Trammell's suggestion "totally unacceptable." Pulling the payments from the bill, he said, would render it meaningless. De Grandy preferred the term "hollow" and threatened to use a rare parliamentary ploy—a "point of personal privilege"—to withdraw the bill entirely if the money was siphoned out. That would leave the legislature to answer to the kind of public indignation expressed in an editorial published that week in the *Tallahassee Democrat,* after Trammell announced his intentions.

"This is ill-advised, and almost insulting," wrote the *Democrat.* "It would transform an overdue but heartfelt gesture to a mockery of an apology."

Stepping in to help Trammell lead the fight was fellow Appropriations member Allen Boyd, from Monticello, up near the Georgia state line. The forty-eight-year-old Boyd was born in Georgia, grew up on his great-grandfather's hundred-year-old farm and still listed farming as his profession. Levy County was in Boyd's district; just like the black caucus was defending their people, well, these were *his* people he was standing up for.

Like Trammell, Boyd was a big backer of the school prayer bill written by Randy Mackey, another Appropriations member who had already come out strongly against Rosewood. Al Lawson decided it was time to take all three of them—Trammell, Boyd and Mackey—to task for their piety.

"These people say it's going to make kids more morally fit to pray in schools," Lawson told reporters. "But the same people who are talking about what's morally right are the people who are voting against Rosewood."

Lawson had his staff do some hurried homework, then distributed a list of what he called "frivolous" items passed by the legislature in recent years—a million dollars for a tennis center in Tampa, a quarter-million for a Florida Sports Hall of Fame in Lake City, another quarter-million for a stock car racing promotion—all of which were close to the hearts of conservative whites and all of which the black caucus had supported. Now, said Lawson, those same whites were turning their backs on Rosewood.

"The issue is race," he said flatly. "A lot of racism is still prevalent in this state. What's wrong with our race relations in Florida is this thing right here."

If money was the issue, he continued, why had the state approved more than fifty million dollars in claims over the previous decade with none of those bills facing the heat Rosewood was getting?

He got no answer, but he was feeling that heat. They all were. The day before the Appropriations Committee was scheduled to hear their claim—the last day of March—the Rosewood forces were still at least three votes shy of the number needed to pass the thirty-eight-member committee. Taking a cue from Lawson, Alzo Reddick, a college administrator and black caucus member from Orlando, stepped up and made the same threat Lawson had made on the eve of the Judiciary vote. If Rosewood went down, Reddick promised, the state's black leadership would target the reelection campaign of every legislator responsible. "The process of politics," he proclaimed, "allows for retribution as well as repatriation."

Something was stirring here, a boldness neither Florida's House nor its Senate had ever seen from its minority members. The call to arms issued to the black caucus at the beginning of the session was finally being answered.

But the fact was that it might be too late. The Appropriations Committee seemed dead-set on gutting the bill at best and simply voting it down at worst. Martha Barnett had met with every member, she had counted the votes, and it looked bleak. That Wednesday afternoon, the day before Appropriations would decide Rosewood's fate, she went to see John Long.

Long was the Appropriations Committee's chairman, arguably the most powerful position in the House. It was the Appropriations chairman who held the purse strings, who was responsible for putting together the state's multibillion-dollar budget and who essentially decided how every one of those dollars would be spent. Long was an even-tempered man, forty-eight years old, highly respected by his peers—a *Miami Herald* poll of the legislature conducted that spring rated him third among the state's 120 representatives.

When he wasn't in Tallahassee, Long worked as an assistant school superintendent down in Pasco County, which included the schools of Lacoochee and Dade City—a fact both Martha Barnett and Arnett Doctor reminded him of each time they ran into him, which was as often as they could. Barnett had been knocking on John Long's door for weeks, and each time she did, he told her to come back later. Talk to me when the hearings are over, he told her in February. Talk to me after you get past Judiciary, he told her in March.

Now it was almost April, nine days until the 1994 Florida legislative session would draw to a close, fewer than twenty-four hours until Long's panel would meet to decide whether the Rosewood bill would finally move out of committee and onto the floor for a vote by the entire House of Representatives. Now, Barnett told him, it was time to talk.

This time Long did not send her away. He invited her in, told his staff to hold his calls, and asked Barnett to take a seat and tell him everything she knew about Rosewood. An hour later, she was done. An hour with John Long. The man had more lobbyists lined up outside his door than any legislator in the Capitol. If they got five minutes with him they were lucky, and Martha Barnett had just been given an hour.

Long was glad to give it. Now that this issue had reached his doorstep, he needed to know the specifics. He hardly cared about the money aspect of this bill—"In terms of dollars and cents," he said, "it wasn't much at all." He did care about who, beyond the actual survivors themselves, would be receiving payments—"We didn't want everybody in the world just cashing in on this." But his major concern was the same as the Speaker's—that this was a highly volatile issue with moral, not just monetary implications for the entire state. Personally, he was ready to vote for the bill. But he knew his committee was not so inclined, at least not the majority. As soon as Barnett left, he put through a call to Bo Johnson.

The next morning, when the Appropriations Committee convened at eight A.M., Chairman Long made the unusual announcement that the Rosewood claims bill, scheduled to be heard that morning, would be postponed until that evening, after the full House finished its business. He and the Speaker were buying time for Barnett and her people to do what they could.

Meanwhile, Al Lawson decided the time had come to put pressure on the top. The black caucus was scheduled to have lunch that day at the Governor's Mansion, where Lawton Chiles was scrambling to salvage his health-care package, which was being shredded to ribbons by a hailstorm of amendments— nearly two hundred revisions had been attached to his proposals, which were up for a floor vote that evening.

Still, Chiles was upbeat as he took a seat that afternoon with eleven members of the caucus and about a dozen other guests. The meal was served—roast beef, asparagus, potatoes and cheesecake. A brief prayer was given, then Chiles turned to Lawson as the group began to eat.

"Well," said the governor, "what can I help you with?"

Lawson began slowly, politely, acknowledging the support the governor had given the Rosewood bill so far. Chiles had promised he would sign the bill if it passed the legislature, and Lawson told him the caucus appreciated that. But, he continued, at this point they needed more.

Heads turned. The eating stopped.

"It's getting to be mighty upsetting," said Lawson, his voice turning shrill, "that we've got Democratic members that are attempting to gut this bill in Appropriations. We've got a better shot at getting *Republican* help on Rosewood," he said, "than we do with Democrats."

Lawson had told no one he planned to lay down this gauntlet. The governor was stunned.

Lawson went on, telling Chiles they needed him to do more than simply follow the legislature's lead, that he needed to send his people out to help muscle this claim through that committee. If the governor *didn't* step in and do something, Lawson warned, he could not guarantee that the caucus would continue to support his health-care package. As a matter of fact, he said, they might just vote *against* it.

Chiles was dumbstruck.

"It was," said Lieutenant Governor Buddy MacKay, who was there at the table, "like watching a slow-motion accident."

Chiles finally gathered himself enough to speak.

"You're picking the wrong way to solicit my help," he said, scarcely bothering to conceal his rage. "I came out for Rosewood before anybody *asked* me, and now you're talking about shooting the one friend you've *got*. I don't like somebody coming and putting a gun in my ear and saying you're going to go vote with the *Republicans*."

"*I* don't like the tone of your *voice*, Governor," replied Lawson.

"I don't like hearing the tone of what *you've* said," shot back Chiles.

By then Lawson's black caucus colleagues were by his side. Cynthia Chestnut suggested the group walk out, which prompted MacKay to step in and play peacemaker. He half-jokingly asked that grace be said again and everyone start over. "You're all friends of ours," he said.

"I'm beginning to wonder," huffed Lawson.

Les Miller, a caucus member from Tampa known for a temper not unlike Arnett Doctor's, held court with reporters after the luncheon, reciting a list of black issues he claimed had been abandoned by his white colleagues in recent years, issues that ranged from creating a law school at Florida A&M to providing incentives for minority-owned businesses.

"When we want something, we can't get anyone to budge," said Miller. "We're not here to be ping-pong balls for the leadership of the House. We're tired of playing games, tired of being used, tired of being pawns."

No one knew what Chiles was going to do. On the one hand, he had nothing to lose by fighting for Rosewood. "He's not going to get those North Florida crackers' votes anyway," said one veteran Tallahassee lobbyist. But then there was the matter of the governor's pride. "You just can't push him," said that same lobbyist. "Lawton gets his *back* up if you threaten him, even if he agrees with you."

By late that afternoon, though, it was clear that Chiles had decided to help. MacKay, along with Chiles's chief of staff, Tom Herndon, were dispatched that afternoon to call on Appropriations Committee members. And once again Peter Wallace, the Speaker-designate, was on the scene, roaming the House floor, collaring each member of the committee in their seats. The press and the public watching from the glass-enclosed galleries above the chamber, looking down on the rows of cushioned seats, wooden desks, mounted microphones and computer monitors from which the 120 House members made their speeches and cast their votes, could see that Wallace was taking some sort of count, though most had no idea what it was about. Martha Barnett knew. It was about Rosewood. But she had no idea how it was going.

The House was scheduled to adjourn at five, which was when the Appropriations Committee would then meet on Rosewood. But the largest, most tangled issue on that year's legislative agenda, health care, was now on the floor, and the debate had just begun. It dragged on till six. Then seven. Barnett and Hanlon and Arnett went out to grab dinner, a cellular phone in hand in case the session adjourned while they were eating and they had to rush back.

At eight they returned, and the debate was nowhere near finished. Member after member rose to speak, amendment after amendment was read. Some were shouted down, others voted in. Nine o'clock. Then ten. Exhaustion was setting in. Impatience. Tempers were short. All Barnett and her crew could do was sit and watch. And wait.

Close to midnight there was a small commotion down in one corner of the chamber. It was the black caucus, huddled around Lawson. Another knot of members came together over by the Speaker's chair. Messages were relayed from one group to the other and back. At twelve-thirty, the fourteen black House members abruptly stalked out of the chamber, walked off the House floor and into a side room. Eventually they were coaxed back. Then, suddenly, the press corps came tumbling out of its upstairs gallery, rushing down toward Bo Johnson's office. Martha Barnett grabbed one reporter and asked what was up. He wasn't sure, he said. But the Speaker had called a recess to make a statement to the press. Something about Rosewood.

Johnson wasn't about to go into the details, but the fact was that the caucus was holding the health bill hostage again. So far that night, they had voted with the governor, stalemating the Republicans each time they tried to shoot down the bill. But the caucus's primary concern was Rosewood. The next day was Friday, when most of the legislature traditionally left early to get a head start on Easter weekend, before returning for the session's final five days. It was clear this health-care debate was far from over. The messages relayed down on the floor between the Speaker and the caucus had begun with the Speaker's suggestion that the Rosewood hearing be put off until Monday. The members were fried. They had no gas left for a late-night hearing on Rosewood. They wanted to go home.

But the caucus said no way. Beyond the Appropriations hearing, the bill still had to get through a House vote and then through the Senate and *its* committees. There was no time to do all that in a week. No, they said, the Speaker's suggestion was out of the question. They wanted their hearing *tonight*. And if they didn't get it, they said, they were ready to vote with the Republicans on health care.

So now Johnson was in his office, the reporters pressed wall to wall. He told them what was going to happen the rest of the night, that the health-care bill was going to take up the time they had left. Then he turned to John Long, who had an announcement to make "of great importance to many members of the House." The Rosewood bill, said Long, which was originally set to be heard tonight, had now been rescheduled for first thing the next morning.

The question of a quorum was raised by one of the reporters, who noted the imminence of Easter. Johnson nodded, then said he had informed every member of the Appropriations Committee that they were free to go home *after* the Rosewood claim was heard. Any absences, he said, had better have a good excuse, meaning any members who wanted to stay on that committee had better be there in the morning or be able to tell Bo Johnson why they were not. Even the most seasoned capitol-watchers were stunned.

"People were out in the halls going, *Whew, SHIT!,*" says Martha Barnett. "It was an extraordinary act of power for a Speaker to take."

And it was good enough for Barnett. As long as they had a quorum for that meeting, she was happy. De Grandy was not so pleased. His vote count of the committee came out almost dead even; they couldn't afford the absence of even one of their supporters, excused or not. Al Lawson was satisfied; he knew both the Speaker and the Governor were already leaning on those committee members to bring some swing votes Rosewood's way.

As for Arnett Doctor, he saw the entire situation as a plot, a deal among all sides—John Long, Bo Johnson, Peter Wallace, *all* of them—to sabotage this bill. Arnett had been walking these halls for the past sixteen hours. His legs were killing him. He'd heard promise after promise put off time and again.

Now it was being put off again. He didn't even wait to hear an explanation this time. He shoved his way out the door and stomped off into the night.

But he was back the next morning. They were all back. And when John Long called the Appropriations Committee to order at half past nine, thirty-seven of its thirty-eight members were in their seats—Daniel Webster of Orlando had been excused for religious reasons. There was little debate to speak of.

"If you search your heart and you search your conscience," proclaimed black caucus member Josephus Eggelletion, a schoolteacher and barber from Lauderdale Lakes, down near Miami, "I think you will agree this incident is like no other in the state of Florida."

Eighteen of Eggelletion's committee colleagues agreed, casting their votes with him in favor of the bill. Twelve disagreed, voting against it. And six—most of them North Florida legislators caught between constituencies furiously opposed to this claim and pressure from the House leadership to support it—simply abstained.

"God bless America," crowed Arnett, as a crowd of reporters again closed in around him.

And so the Rosewood claims bill had clawed its way out of committee. Monday it would face the full House. Passage there, wrote most reporters, would virtually assure endorsement from the Senate. Martha Barnett wasn't so sure, but she relished the opportunity to find out.

Meanwhile it was time for everyone to take the weekend off.

It was Good Friday.

THIRTY-ONE

Amen

Monday, the morning after Easter, the final week of the 1994 session of the Florida state legislature began. For the families and survivors of Rosewood, soaked in the spirit of resurrection and renewal, this was their day of reckoning.

Two dozen of them were seated up in the House of Representatives' glass-enclosed East gallery, gazing down on the floor below, along with the portraits of past Florida Speakers of the House hanging high on the wall that surrounds the elliptical chamber.

Lording over the gently curved rows of blue-cushioned legislators' seats was the Speaker at his rostrum, flanked by the flags of Florida and of the United States. Mounted behind and above him was a slab of black blank glass, an electronic toteboard that, when switched on, lit up with seven columns of names, each of the 120 members of the House. Every time they cast a vote, pushing a button at each of their seats, the board would light up like a Christmas tree, red dots beside the members who have voted no, green beside those voting yes. Voice votes, the traditional thunder of shouted *yeas* and *nays,* with exaggerated

---

gestures of thumbs up or down, were saved for the floor debates, the verbal tornado of procedures and amendments that preceded a verdict. But when it was time for that verdict, the voting was done silently, with the push of those buttons, the lights on the board flashing instantly and simultaneously, the totals tallied by a clerk at a computer, all in a matter of nanoseconds—lawmaking in the age of fiber optics.

At precisely ten A.M., Bo Johnson gaveled the session to order and the torrent began, the day's first bill announced by the clerk, amendments read aloud, then argued, struck down or adopted by the yells of the lawmakers, amendments to amendments dispensed the same way, a dizzying swirl of points of procedure and parliamentary convolutions, all somehow finally leading to a vote. And then on to the next bill.

There were dozens of bills scheduled ahead of Rosewood on that day's docket. Proposed laws on biomedical waste, bail bond agents, the moving and storage industry, motor vehicle registration, recreational boating, animal control regulations, insurance rates, public library funds, helmet laws for kids on bicycles—the lawmakers plowed through them all that morning, broke for lunch, then carried on into the afternoon, while the Rosewood families watched and waited.

Finally, near two, the agenda shifted to the day's list of claims bills. First up was the case of a motorcyclist permanently disabled after being hit by a bus in Broward County in the winter of 1987. A jury had awarded him $380,000— $280,000 over the state limit. He was here to ask that difference. The House voted to pay him $100,000 instead.

Next came a woman from Hernando County whose car had been pinioned by a government dump truck and a road grader in a three-way collision in 1988. She too now had lifelong injuries. A jury had awarded her $432,000. She was also asking $280,000 from the state, and she too received a positive but diminished verdict from the House—for $180,000.

Then, at two-thirty, the clerk announced the next item on the agenda, House Bill #591, "A bill," she read aloud, "to be entitled 'An act relating to Rosewood, Florida.'"

It was literally a defining moment, not just for the Rosewood families gathered up in the gallery and the lawmakers down on the floor, not just for the fourteen million people of Florida, but for an entire nation struggling perhaps more than ever with the uniquely American tendrils of shame, guilt, reparation and resentment that are rooted in race. W.E.B. Du Bois's words, spoken near the time of the Rosewood attack—that "the problem of the twentieth century is the problem of the color line"—had come to seem even more true now, at the end of the century, than they were at its beginning.

The civil rights laws and social programs of the 1950s and '60s were being retrenched in an atmosphere of white backlash; the principles of affirmative action and equal opportunity established and enacted in the '70s and '80s had become besieged both in the workplace and on college campuses, where cries of reverse discrimination were as loud from whites as complaints of racial exclusion had long been from blacks; the 1992 race riot in Los Angeles had shocked the nation into realizing the extent of rage and desperation simmering in its inner cities; and the warlike violence on those streets, graphically mirrored in wildly popular rap music and embraced by a new generation of young blacks and whites alike, seemed to overshadow any rays of hope and peace breaking through the gathering thunderclouds of anger and hate.

The time seemed anything but ripe for Rosewood.

And yet it had made it this far. No one had listened three years before, when Arnett Doctor had reached out for a lawyer. The legislature had hardly paid heed a year earlier, when the first Rosewood bill was filed. Even the second bill was not taken seriously until Richard Hixson delivered his verdict. But now, today, an entire nation was watching—squadrons of reporters from national publications and networks crammed into the press gallery—because the issues defined and decided in this debate would doubtless be echoed in courtrooms and legislative chambers across the country for years to come.

Down on the floor, however, there was no inordinate sense of drama. The room was not hushed. The lawmakers were not riveted to their seats. It was business as usual, small clusters of four and five House members huddled in various corners of the chamber, murmuring about one issue or another, others roaming from seat to seat, leaning over a colleague, mumbling earnestly even as someone rose to make a statement or a speech. The commotion, the din of ceaseless movement and chatter, like the background bustle in a busy restaurant, would continue throughout the debate, a noisy curtain of sound surrounding the statements being made for the record. To the casual observer, it would appear that few of the men and women on that floor were paying attention. But they were. This was how they always did business, and the business at hand was what finally to do about Rosewood.

After rushing through the reading of several minor amendments—a string of procedural items recited like a 78 r.p.m. chant—Bo Johnson called on David Thomas, a Republican from Venice, down the coast below Sarasota. Balding, roundish, bespectacled, the forty-eight-year-old ophthalmologist rose to strike the first blow against a bill he considered "dangerous."

"What do we *know* concerning the incident that occurred at Rosewood," asked Thomas, turning to his colleagues. "The report is fairly short," he said, tapping a copy of the study team's paper. "You can read it in an evening. And it will stay *with* you the rest of your life.

"The appendix," he continued, "is longer. Not as interesting. But every bit as crucial, as is the special master's report."

Then he zeroed in on his target, the assertion that the state had been derelict in its duty to protect Rosewood's residents. "Law enforcement has been painted ugly with a broad brush," he said, "and that's just not true."

He pointed to Margaret Cannon's testimony that her father, the deputy sheriff, had helped women and children out of the woods and onto a train. No one, added Thomas, should forget the white train conductors who carried the refugees to safety. He acknowledged the neglect of the county sheriff, Robert Walker, but noted that Walker resigned within a year after the Rosewood incident, perhaps, suggested Thomas, from shame. Thomas said he felt shame himself. Everyone in the state of Florida, he said, should feel shame. "We ought *never* be done with this issue," he said, "because it is an ugly part of our history. We ought to own up to it permanently."

But, he continued—and this would become the crux of the day's debate— money was not the way to make amends.

"I've heard people say we ought to pay these people and be done with it," said Thomas. "But I don't agree. I think that's an inappropriate way to handle this.

"Forgiveness," he continued, "is a two-way street, and we ought not *buy* our forgiveness with a series of compensatory pecuniary actions for this small, select group.

"It's enough," he said, "to have an admission of sorrow and a *recognition* of that admission."

And that, he said, was why he was now bringing the Thomas Amendment before the House. It would strike all cash payments from the Rosewood bill— payments he warned would set a dangerous precedent. Instead, his amendment would create a permanent exhibit at the state library in Tallahassee, as well as a monument at the site of the massacre.

The Speaker then opened the floor to debate on Thomas's proposal, and Cynthia Chestnut seized her microphone.

"Dr. Thomas talks about 'buying forgiveness,'" she proclaimed. "Every claims bill that comes before this *House* is about 'buying forgiveness.' There is no amount of money that can be paid to bring back the lives that were lost here. There is no amount of money that can restore the property that was lost.

"What we have before us today," she said, "is to only *begin* to try to make amends. And making amends does *not* mean simply establishing a marker or building an exhibit."

Al Lawson rose next, giving Thomas credit for helping move the bill out of the Judiciary Committee. That was an important step toward this day, said Lawson, but now that this day had come, it would be shameful to shrink the significance of this claim by hacking at its contents. The Rosewood bill, said Lawson, was about much more than money or monuments. It was about healing, he said, not just for the Rosewood families, not just for Florida's blacks, but for black people looking on from across the nation.

"This removes a dark side of Florida history," said Lawson. "And it gives the African-American hope that this legislature, this body, will try to erase some of the dark shadows that have been hanging over people's heads for so many, many, many years."

Ben Graber, a Democrat from Coral Springs, near Miami—like Thomas, a doctor—then rose and seized on the issue Lawson had raised, the idea of healing.

"We have something we call closure in our society," said Graber. "It's important to a society, but it's *more* important to individuals.

"If this had occurred five hundred years ago, and nobody could trace the relatives, I could understand a marker or a statue. But we *do* have relatives right here," he said, glancing up toward the gallery, "as well as some of the actual individuals who were directly harmed.

"When harm is done to somebody in our society," he continued, "and society stands by, for whatever reason, while that person suffers, some compensation is needed for closure. I think the amount of money appropriated here is really small, but it's not the amount that counts. It's the fact that these people need to know that society is saying, Yes, we do understand you are hurt, and, Yes, we are going to give you closure by saying we're sorry."

Graber concurred with Chestnut's assertion. "There's no way you can fully compensate for this type of tragedy," he said. "But we *can* try to compensate for people's feelings. We *can* try to allow people to close."

Josephus Eggelletion stood next, tapping his copy of the report the same way Thomas had tapped his, and disagreeing totally with Thomas's conclusions.

"I've read this report five times," said Eggelletion. "Eyewitness reports indicated that police officers stood back and allowed this to occur. That is *crucial*. That is *compelling*."

He stopped, drew a deep breath, gathered his thoughts. He spoke from no notes.

"I will tell you this," he continued. "There comes a time in everybody's life, and in the history of a state, when we have to stand tall as humans, to recognize our faults and our shortcomings and to do what we have to do in order to right a wrong.

"And this," he finished, "is a great wrong."

Tom Warner, a Republican from Stuart, east of Lake Okeechobee, chided Thomas, not for opposing the bill but for fiddling with it. "We should either vote this Rosewood bill up or vote it down in regard to the compensation," said Warner. "If the state of Florida has done something wrong, then we should do something right by these people. I *don't* think it's the right thing to do to gut the bill and replace it with a highway marker."

Stephen Wise, a community college administrator from Jacksonville, disagreed, and he raised a startling specter to make his point. "If you look at the Holocaust and what's happened with that," said Wise, invoking the slaughter of World War II, "we *have* that kind of memorial in Washington, D.C. I think we need to put together the same kind of permanent exhibit here, so people will not forget what took place in this dark hour of our history."

A memorial, argued Wise, like the Holocaust Museum in Washington, should be enough. Money, he maintained, was not necessary.

That brought Elaine Gordon bolting from her seat. Gordon had not planned on speaking that day. Her vote had been with the bill from the beginning, simply because she felt it was the right thing to do. Hardly any black people lived in her North Miami district—fewer than ten percent. But she understood and identified with the issue of displacement and dispossession. The people she represented were mostly like herself, transplanted northerners, mostly from New York, many of them Jewish.

When she learned about Rosewood—the details of the women and children hiding in the swamp, the train coming through at night, the evacuation to Gainesville—Gordon, who had grown up in the Bronx, moved to Florida with her husband in 1964, and in 1972, at age forty-one, was elected to the state legislature, couldn't help but think of her own cousins, who had escaped from Poland in 1944 by hiding in the forest, burying themselves beneath the soil so the dogs leading the German search parties could not pick up their scent, staying in those woods for three days and nights until they were able to finally escape, first to Belgium and then to New York, where Elaine Gordon's family took them in. Now, as she heard the Holocaust invoked as an argument against the Rosewood claim, she could not help but rise and respond.

"Members," she began, "there *were* reparations made to the German Jews whose property was taken without due process. There isn't *just* a memorial. The German government, recognizing what they owed to the survivors because they denied them the opportunity of being able to have their descendants inherit their property, their goods, their *mementos,* their *jewelry,* their *paintings,* acknowledged that recognition by paying compensation. There is not just a memorial. There is ongoing reparation that the German government is paying to those people for the taking of their property and goods without due process.

"And *that,*" said Gordon, "is what's going on here."

The final response to Thomas's amendment was made by Miguel De Grandy, who, in lawyerlike fashion, picked his adversary's argument apart, point by point.

The first point was the assertion that Margaret Cannon's father, by helping the refugees board the train, was proof that the state had provided protection.

"The testimony Representative Thomas refers to," De Grandy began, noting that it was not eyewitness testimony and not even necessarily true, "is that *after* the destruction, *after* everything that occurred, *one* deputy sheriff went to the woods and found some black people and helped them get on the train to go to Gainesville.

"Think about this," he said. "If it's true, what message was law enforcement sending here? The message was *Get out of town!* We will *help* you get out of *town!*

"To me," he continued, "that is far from compelling evidence that the authorities in charge did anything affirmative to protect these people's rights. On the contrary, this was evidence of a continuing *failure* on the part of the authorities to do their duty, which was to protect the lives and property of the citizens of Rosewood, to protect their right to remain in Rosewood, as *we* have a right to live and remain anywhere *we* want to live."

As for the issue of compensation, De Grandy was curt.

"I have yet," he said, noting the dozens of claims bills he had seen during his five years in the legislature and referring specifically to the landmark decapitation claim, "to see a case where a person has a DOT sign fall on their head and gets a memorial erected. They get *compensation*."

Finally, he addressed the question still bothering many of the members on the floor, the question of the floodgates of other claims this bill might open.

"We have talked a lot about precedent," he said. "Think about this. What type of dangerous precedent are we going to set if we were to pass Dr. Thomas's amendment and gut this bill? I would submit to you that it would set a very *dangerous* precedent if we were to violate the notion of equal protection under the law and treat these individuals any differently from the way we've treated everybody else who has ever come before this legislature with a claims bill.

"I agree with Representative Warner," he concluded. "If you feel for some reason that the claim is not proven, then vote against the bill. If you feel the evidence shows that the claim has been proven—which I think is clearly the case—then vote for it. But to do what Representative Thomas is asking, to gut the bill, *would* set a very dangerous precedent."

Thomas was then allowed a final comment.

"What we're saying with this bill," he warned, "is that we can take a horrible part of the history of Florida and buy off a handful of residents and forget it.

"I beg of you," he concluded, "that that is wrong."

Then came the vote, a loud chorus of *yeas* to adopt Thomas's amendment, followed by a louder chorus of *nays*. The volume decided the verdict. The amendment was defeated. The bill had withstood its first charge of the day, and now George Albright, an attorney from Ocala, rose to pick up the spear dropped by his Republican colleague.

Slim, blond, thirty-eight, Albright had served in the House for six years. He nodded toward his black caucus colleagues, told them what a pleasure it had been working with them over the previous years. Then he explained why he could not support this bill.

"I have a problem," said Albright, "with trying to interject our views of 1994 civil rights on acts of the past."

His amendment, hardly different from Thomas's, proposed to spend ten thousand dollars planning a "Rosewood Memorial Park" on state forest property not far from the site of the massacre.

"I think the issue here," he concluded, "is that we memorialize this, use it as a historical footnote, and go forward. But if you open this door, ladies and gentlemen, rather than closing anything, you'll be opening up something that will *never* be closed."

This time it was Les Miller who could not keep his seat. The slim, fiery, forty-two-year-old from Tampa was clearly furious as he rose to face Albright. As a member of the black caucus, he said, he was "appalled, hurt, and disgusted" by what he had just heard.

"But as I have sometimes lost my cool on this floor," he said, turning toward the Speaker, "I will try *not* to do that today."

He drew a deep breath.

"The whole crux of this bill," Miller began, "is that law enforcement, the governor, and other state officials knew what was being done in Rosewood and they turned their backs, closed their eyes and did absolutely *nothing.*

"These things happened many times in the state of Florida," he acknowledged, noting the dozens of lynchings that occurred before Rosewood. "But there were *none* like this. This lasted one week. One *entire week.*

"I've had people ask me," he continued, "I even had one member ask me *today,* 'Why didn't the people of Rosewood try to get law enforcement to help them?'

"Ladies and gentlemen, can you *imagine* what rights a black person in the South actually had in 1923? Can you imagine what rights they had to go to police officers in a situation like this and ask for help?

"The answer is absolutely zero. *None.* Null and *void. Nada.* Those rights weren't there. They just *weren't there.*

"So, Representative Albright," he said, turning again to his counterpart, "if you truly have respect for the judgment of the members of the black caucus, if you have respect for the judgment of Representative Miguel De Grandy, if you have respect for the judgment of the people who support this bill, you will withdraw this amendment."

De Grandy, a bit impatient now, took the floor again.

"Please," he implored his colleagues, "vote against this amendment and let's get on to the merits of the bill itself."

But Bill Posey, a realtor from Rockledge, just north of Cocoa Beach, was not about to miss the chance both to stick up for Albright's amendment and in the process, to share a bit of his own family's history.

"Everyone," he began, "has heard the cliché, *Your name is mud.*"

That quieted the room. Heads turned to hear where in the world *this* was going to lead. Posey paused, allowed his colleagues to wonder a moment longer, then launched into his parable.

"After Abraham Lincoln was assassinated," said Posey, "we had literally a lynch mob of elected, empowered officials that went out to convict somebody for the murder. You may know that a number of people were hung in connection with the Lincoln assassination. A lot of other people were punished.

"One of them that was *wrongly* punished," he continued, "was Dr. Samuel Mudd. He lost everything as he sat in a prison in Key West before he was finally released—sick, old, worn out, a waste of life."

Posey paused again, then delivered his kicker.

"Dr. Mudd," he said, "was a *relative* of mine."

Another brief pause.

"But I don't ever expect to be compensated for what the federal government did to *him.*"

It might not have been the day's most persuasive argument, but it was doubtless the most original.

Albright followed with his closing remarks, warning his colleagues of the "Pandora's Box" they were about to open. But the debate, for all intents and purposes, was over. Albright's amendment, like Thomas's, was shouted down, and the Speaker quickly moved the unamended bill onto the floor for discussion.

The only question came from Victor Crist, an ad executive whose Tampa district bumped up against Arnett Doctor's neighborhood. Crist wanted to know whether people who were hurt, killed, terrorized and even run off their property in urban high-crime areas might not qualify for compensation under this bill, loosing an avalanche of inner-city lawsuits against the state.

"No sir," answered De Grandy. "In a case where you have a high-crime area and the state does not have adequate notice that something is going to happen, the state cannot be held responsible. In other words, if someone in your city— and I live in Dade County, where there's high crime—gets mugged, and there's no police officer there because they were all on other calls protecting citizens, or writing their reports, or taking people to *jail,* the state cannot be held responsible. The state cannot be held responsible for not being everywhere at all times.

"But that's what makes Rosewood unique," he continued. "There was more than plenty of time for the authorities to respond.

"And there is no *question,*" he concluded, "that if this were a *white* town threatened by a *black* mob, there would have been adequate protection of those citizens."

Now it was time. No more questions. No more debate. No more witnesses or testimonies or studies or reports. Al Lawson and Miguel De Grandy had been working toward this moment for over a year now. Steve Hanlon had been at it for almost two. For Arnett Doctor it had been twelve years since the spring afternoon when Rosewood was first reawakened in his life. And for the survivors, for literally a lifetime, this had been a moment they dared not imagine, much less hope for.

Bo Johnson's voice shifted into a staccato, rapid-fire monotone as he announced that it was time to vote on House Bill 591.

"The clerk will unlock the machine," Johnson droned, "and all members will proceed to vote."

Two seconds passed.

"Have all members voted?"

Three seconds more.

"Have all members voted?"

One more time.

"Have all members voted?"

And again.

"Have all members voted?"

A final pause.

"The clerk will lock the machine and announce the vote."

Not a full second later, the clerk read the totals aloud, reciting the figures as rapidly as Johnson had requested them.

"Seventy-one yeas," she declared, "forty nays, Mister Speaker."

A smattering of applause swept across the floor. Nothing eruptive, but a polite acknowledgment among the lawmakers that this had been something historic. Several of them turned toward the gallery, saluting the survivors, who wept and hugged one another as cameras flashed all around them. Arnett Doctor thrust his arms in the air, like a heavyweight after a knockout. Wilson Hall stepped away from the celebration to answer some questions from reporters.

"They really don't have enough money to make up for my losses," he said. "How do I know what I really would have been? What could have happened? This was all stripped from me." Still, he added, this bill was a good thing, a healthy thing. "Sure it makes things better," he said. "If not for me, then for my grandkids."

The black caucus members too were elated. There was still rancor and rivalries among them, just as there were and always would be among the Rosewood families. But this was a day for coming together, and the caucus—for the first time, in the eyes of many—had done that. The *Tallahassee Democrat* called it "a great day for Florida politics," praising the caucus for its perseverance and boldness, for the fact that it had "stopped playing politics and started practicing it," that its members had been "steely-eyed and steady handed" at their luncheon showdown with the governor, and, all in all, for the fact that the black caucus had "finally grown up."

Even as the victors celebrated, however, one of the vanquished was holding court himself, reminding reporters that this fight was not over yet. Charlie Williams, the state senator from Live Oak, whose district included Levy County itself, cautioned that there were still four days left in this session, and this bill had yet to begin its trip toward Senate confirmation. Williams admitted it was going to be tough to block it, but he was going to do his damnedest to try.

"It's a sad part of Florida history," he had said back when the House fight began, "but I'm just opposed to paying that money when we have so many other pressing needs in education, prisons, transportation and other things."

Now, with the bill out of the House and on its way to his doorstep, he was more strident. "When will it ever *stop?*" he proclaimed. "If we can go back seventy-one years, why not a hundred? Why not a hundred and *fifty?*"

Charlie Williams had to take that stand. He had no choice. His constituents were the people in Cedar Key and Bronson, Chiefland and Sumner, the towns being dragged through the mud of this whole mess, places that would forever be linked with the evil done three generations ago. Most of the families in these places had never heard of the Rosewood massacre until the reporters started showing up. Their relatives had nothing to do with this assault that had occurred long before they were born. But now it was all they were hearing about, and they were sick of it.

Farmers and fishermen, outdoor folk, blue-collar Christians, simple people with simple values—those were Charlie Williams's constituents. Of course Charlie had made a bit more money over the years than most of them, selling insurance, but he had remained a farmer all along. Matter of fact, he still listed hay and tree farming as his primary occupations on the biography they passed out in his Senate office, still kept his hand on his land down in Suwannee County. He was a Baptist deacon, too, and that counted for a lot with the people who voted for him, his friends and neighbors, hand-clapping, back-slapping Baptists just like him.

Charlie had to fight this battle to the bloody end, and really, he had nothing to lose. The folks back home would thank him in the end, for at least sticking up for them, even if there was no way on God's green earth that this bill would be beaten now.

And there wasn't. Martha Barnett was still worried, but then that was her job. The first thing she did that Monday afternoon, once the House had passed the bill, was pay a visit to Robert Wexler, chairman of the Senate Finance and Taxation Committee, which, along with a special claims committee, would be hearing the Rosewood bill the next day. Wexler was charged with appointing the members of that claims committee, and when Barnett arrived at his door, he just smiled.

"You don't even need to talk to me," he said. "I'm *for* you one hundred percent."

Not only that, he said, but Barnett was welcome to help select the claims committee herself if she'd like. "Tell me who you want," said Wexler, "and we'll put those people on."

So it was not surprising when the Rosewood bill breezed through both those committees that Tuesday without a single dissenting vote. Wednesday was a bit more sticky, with Fred Dudley sitting on the Appropriations Committee. Dudley had been dead-set against the bill from the beginning, just like his constituents back home in Cape Coral. Though many of his Republican colleagues still disagreed with the bill, his was now the only voice besides Williams's still shouting out against it.

"It's money being paid out to people, that's all it is," spat Dudley on the eve of the Appropriations hearing.

But it was no use. Dudley tried the same ploy on Wednesday that Thomas and Albright had attempted in the House—striking the cash compensation and settling for a scholarship fund. But his amendment was voted down by the committee, eighteen to nine, and when the bill itself was put on the table to decide if it would go to the full Senate on Friday, it passed by that same two-to-one spread.

Coupled with the votes it had gotten in Tuesday's committees, the bill now had a majority of the Senate's forty members already on record in favor of it. Friday's final vote would be a formality—"As long as nobody bolts on us," cautioned Daryl Jones, who, along with Matt Meadows from Fort Lauderdale and Jacksonville's Betty Holzendorf, were the black caucus members guiding the bill through the Senate.

Jones needn't have worried. Friday morning the members of the Senate settled into their brown cushioned seats for the last time that spring. Two months of sixteen-hour days had finally come to this. Upstairs, the press and the public filed into the galleries, passing a floor-to-ceiling mural displaying various figures from Florida's march through history—a band of Spanish explorers, some Seminole Indians, a Confederate soldier with the flag of Dixie . . . and a black female laborer standing beside a crate of oranges.

Just as portraits of past Speakers were mounted on the wall ringing the House chamber, so did paintings of past Presidents of the Senate surround this room. At ten A.M., the sitting president, Pat Thomas, gaveled the session to order, and at 11:20 the Rosewood bill came up for debate. When Daryl Jones rose to speak, it was with a set of notes Martha Barnett had helped him prepare—"talking points," as she calls them, "a list of issues and ideas with bullets beside them," something she routinely puts together for each legislator making a speech on a bill for which she has lobbied.

With his notes and bullet points in front of him, Jones addressed the nearly silent room. The Senate is always more controlled, more mannerly, than the clamorous House, but as Jones spoke, the room was unusually hushed.

"This is your chance to rectify an atrocious wrong," he began, "to provide justice where there has been none.

"The simple truth," he continued, "is the whole world knew what happened in Rosewood, but we have buried it in our collective amnesia."

Martha Barnett especially liked that last phrase. She had used it herself in her speech before the House Judiciary Committee.

"It would be a sad day for Florida," Jones concluded, "to once again turn its back on the victims of Rosewood."

Charlie Williams weighed in one last time, pulling every point he had ever made about Rosewood into a single statement.

"How long do we have to pay for the sins of our forefathers?" he asked. "There are other pressing, pressing needs for our state, and this is 1994, not 1923. I can't go back to my eighteen counties and justify spending two million—plus or minus a hundred thousand—of their hard-earned tax dollars on something that happened seventy-one years ago!"

Fred Dudley tried one last time to amend the bill, but was beaten back by a vote of twenty-nine to eleven. "I'll just have to be the one to tell you 'I told you so' next year," he said, "when we've got some lawsuits to defend."

That was the last gasp. Jim Hargrett of Tampa wrapped things up. "Let's stop playing with this issue," he said. "This bill is sort of like a suture on an open wound. It brings it together so healing can begin."

At 12:28, in an atmosphere of anticlimax for all but the Rosewood families themselves, the Senate cast its vote.

Twenty-six in favor, fourteen opposed.

It was over. Only the governor's signature remained to turn the bill into law. That would come in a month.

Meanwhile, after an eruption of cheers, tears and shouts of "Praise the Lord," the family members, three dozen of them, gathered around Arnett Doctor in the foyer outside. Mama Dot. Willie Evans. The Halls—Wilson, Mary and Margie. They each clasped hands and bowed their heads as Arnett led them in prayer, his voice echoing off the rotunda above as he gave thanks for them all.

A crowd collected, including the press, looking on in silence from a distance as the relatives' heads remained bowed and Arnett recited the names of those who had passed on. Dozens of names. The ones who had died at Rosewood—Sarah and Sylvester, Lexie and Lord God, Sam Carter and James Carrier. And the ones who had passed on in the decades since. Beauty and Sweetie, Philomena and Lee Ruth. Family, all.

And then they said Amen.

And then they went home.

PART SIX

COMING HOME

THIRTY-TWO

Nothing But Scars

It had been ten months now since the sparkling May morning when Lawton Chiles took a seat in the Senate chamber of Tallahassee's Old Capitol building and signed the Rosewood bill into law. The members of the black caucus were there for that historic moment, beaming as they gathered behind the governor. Miguel De Grandy was there as well, standing by Chiles's right shoulder as Arnett Doctor, resplendent in a bone-white suit, leaned over his left. Looking on were fifty members of the Rosewood families, half of them dressed in the same white clothing as Arnett—symbolic, they explained, of the innocence of the Rosewood victims. The other half were clad in scarlet, for the blood that was spilled that week.

The governor proclaimed that "the long silence has been broken, the shadow has been lifted." He vowed that "this blind act of bigotry" would never be forgotten. Then he passed out souvenir pens to each of the seven survivors in attendance. Arnett accepted for the eighth, bedridden Lonnie Carroll.

Rosewood survivors at the Governor's signing of the Rosewood bill
(1-r, front row: Minnie Lee Langley, Wilson Hall, Margie Hall Johnson,
Willie Evans, Mary Hall Daniels and A. T. Goins)

"*Thank you,* Jesus," declared Minnie Lee Langley that morning, glad that this day had finally arrived. Glad, too, that the whole ordeal was now over.

But for Guy David Robinson—along with his colleague Frank Beisler, and their boss, Greg Durden—the ordeal had just begun. The day the Rosewood bill was signed into law, Durden, as chief of the state's Attorney General's Office of Civil Rights in Hollywood, near Fort Lauderdale, was charged with enforcing it, which meant finding, verifying and finally paying all qualified Rosewood claimants. Durden knew it was going to be a sticky, lengthy process—but he had no idea how tangled and inflamed it would actually become. Nor did Robinson, a thirty-four-year-old former running back at the University of Alabama who had just joined Durden's staff that month as an assistant attorney general when Rosewood was dumped in his lap.

Robinson had been aware of Rosewood long before he was assigned to it. He'd read about it in the papers, and he was struck by the shock of a group of people being so suddenly and completely severed from their past, having it just swept away. He couldn't imagine what that must feel like. He knew all there was to know about his own family. His father and mother were both from a little town called Wildwood, in the center of the state, just south of Ocala. He had dozens of aunts and uncles and cousins in Wildwood. He knew the place inside out, knew the neighbors, knew his kin, drove up from his office in Hollywood as often as he could, just to visit, just to keep in touch. Family.

Robinson had heard all his family's stories, every one, about every aunt and uncle and grandparent and great-grandparent, all the way back to slavery. But when his relatives heard he was working on Rosewood, they told him a story he had never heard before.

It happened to one of his aunt's families sometime during the Forties, they told him, though no one could say exactly when. The Strongs was their name, and they owned some property up around the middle of the state, though no one could recall just where. The story was that the Strongs were run off that land. Chased off by the Klan, so everyone said. Lost all that they owned and never came back. Just like Rosewood.

"I couldn't believe it," says Robinson. "We were just sitting around talking and this story came up. I looked over at my mom, and she just nodded her head. 'Yeah,' she said. 'that happened.' I was stunned, really shocked. I'd *never* heard this story."

It was easy to see why this assignment became more than just a job to Guy

Robinson. Not only was he black, but now he had learned there were skeletons in his own family's closet, bones that lay not far from Rosewood's. Frank Beisler, though—it would be hard to find a man whose background was further removed from Rosewood than his. A former Marine, a former cop, and a former undertaker, Beisler was from New England, German Catholic, the son of a professional hockey player. He'd come to Florida in the late '80s after banging up his fifty-year-old body training SWAT teams in Virginia. He'd hooked up with the Attorney General's office as a paralegal in 1991, and, in the summer of '94, at age fifty-five, he joined Greg Durden's staff as an "investigator." Like Robinson, he was given Rosewood as his first case. Unlike Robinson, he had never heard of the place. "I thought a Rosewood was a flower," he says.

But he learned. He spent his first week reading everything the state had on Rosewood. Depositions and affidavits. Transcripts of interviews. Transcripts of testimonies. The study team's report. The state's review of the study team's report. Correspondence between the state and the attorneys, correspondence between the study team and the state. Newspaper and magazine articles by the dozen. Ten hours a day he pored over the papers at the office, then he took them home at night, the same as Durden and Robinson had already been doing for three months, the three of them retracing the steps already made by the study team, taking nothing for granted, and, hopefully, taking those steps further. "We were starting over again from step one," says Robinson. "We *had* to, to make sure."

The law signed by the governor and handed to Durden and his staff was essentially as Richard Hixson had recommended. A $1.5 million fund had been established to pay $150,000 each to people who could prove they were Rosewood residents at the time of the attack—survivors. It also created a $500,000 fund to reimburse the families of Rosewood residents who lost property during the attack. A fund to provide twenty-five college scholarships a year was created for minority students, with preference given to Rosewood descendants. And the Florida Department of Law Enforcement was directed to begin a formal criminal investigation of the attack.

Claimants were given until the end of the 1994 calendar year to file an application with the Attorney General's office. Durden's staff, in an effort to toss the net as widely as possible, to contact anyone who might qualify for a claim, placed public notices in newspapers across the state, including black publications. Wire services picked up the notices and ran them in papers across the country. Responses came in from as far as California. Calls came from overseas, from Japan, France, Australia and England, the foreign press wanting information, interviews, maybe a live sound bite.

Durden's office wound up mailing out more than four hundred applications to possible property claimants. Follow-up correspondence with each of them began filling the drawers and shelves of Robinson's office, hundreds of letters and documents mailed back from dozens of families, any piece of paper anyone could find that might boost their connection to Rosewood.

Robinson and Beisler began drawing family trees. When the limbs outgrew their desks, they began taping them up on the wall. It wasn't long before the wall was covered, floor to ceiling, plastered with paper, more than thirteen hundred names, each one claiming a piece of what the government had to give.

As the number of branches grew, they began to tangle. Family lines began criss-crossing, zigging and zagging, looping and turning on themselves with unexplainable gaps. Some names appeared on several trees. Some children were listed with no biological parents. Aunts and uncles were claimed as parents. Grandparents were claimed as parents. Friends and neighbors were claimed as parents. Some children changed parents every few years. The word "family," so neatly stated in the legislation, became blurred in the convoluted reality of Rosewood's households and of those of the generations that followed.

"This legislation was lacking in how it defined 'family,'" says Robinson. "It didn't give us a lot to go on. As you get into a place like Rosewood, or into many African-American communities, especially back in that time, you see a lot of situations where children are not raised by their biological parents. I saw it in my own family. My father was raised by a married couple he called 'Mother' and 'Father,' and it wasn't until he was a teenager that he learned his 'Mother' was really his aunt, that he was born in North Carolina and was given away by his real mother when he was a toddler. He bounced around among several relatives during his early years, then wound up with this aunt down in Wildwood.

"That's similar to a lot of situations we found in Rosewood. Some of the families were structured traditional family units. But there were others where you had cousins living with uncles and aunts and calling them parents."

Tracing those twisted lines three and four generations forward to determine the legitimacy of each property claim became a dizzying nightmare. Almost every day Robinson got another call or letter from one of the families, and another couple of names went up on the wall.

The survivor claims were simpler to sort out. The four witnesses who testified at Hixson's hearing—Minnie Lee Langley, A.T. Goins, Willie Evans and Wilson Hall—qualified automatically by dint of the scrutiny they had already undergone. The remaining four survivors named in the bill—Lonnie Carroll, Dorothy Hosey, Mary Hall Daniels and Margie Hall Johnson—had to apply like everyone else. In all, Durden's office received twenty-two survivor applications, and Frank Beisler was dispatched to personally interview each one at their home.

Several were easily dismissed. Two came from white people. Others were blacks who told Beisler they had been infants at the time of the attack and had no proof other than family lore that they ever lived in Rosewood. "I got a lot of 'My mother told me we were there,'" says Beisler. "They were sincere, but they had nothing to support it."

Just as sincere was a man named George Davis, whom Beisler visited in Tampa. Davis was seventy-seven years old, living in a nursing home. He was five, he told Beisler, the night his house was set ablaze. A white man pulled him out of the burning building, he said. The man had a rifle in one hand as he lifted Davis with the other. Davis's pants were on fire, he said, as the man carried him to the front yard, where he put out the flames and bandaged the boy's leg. "He told me this man kept his gun lying on his lap while he took care of him," says Beisler.

When Davis was done with his story, he pulled back his bedsheet and showed Beisler his right leg. "Nothing but burn scars," says Beisler, "from the knee down to the ankle."

Beisler has no doubt Davis's story was true. "That's my gut hunch," he says. But his hunch was all he had. Davis had no documents, and none of the verified survivors knew who he was. There was nothing to support his claim but his scarred leg and Beisler's instinct. And that was not enough.

"It killed me having to turn him down," says Beisler. "There were several like that, people I just knew were telling the truth. But they had no proof, no support, so there was nothing we could do. Some who had proof weren't living within the line of the law. They were living *near* Rosewood and were run off their property, lost their homes, but they weren't living *in* Rosewood, so we had to turn them down, too.

"It was tough," says Beisler. "I'll tell you. It really hurt me, in my heart."

In the end, the survivor applications, along with Beisler's reports, were reviewed by a three-person committee that included Robinson, a vice-president of the state NAACP, and the director of the governor's Commission on African-American Affairs. They wound up approving the claims of the four outstanding survivors named in the bill—Carroll, Hosey, Daniels and Johnson. And they approved one more, a wild card, a name never mentioned in the dozens of depositions taken from Rosewood family members, a name not included in the study team's report, a name found nowhere on Guy Robinson's wall. Amidst all the clamor and chaos of the previous two years, this woman had sat quietly at her home near Palm Beach, watching the goings on from a distance and waiting to see how things would shake out. Then, when it was time, she surfaced.

Her name was Robie Mortin, and her house was less than an hour's drive north of Hollywood.

THIRTY-THREE

Wildflower

S he lives literally on the other side of the tracks. Start on the Atlantic sands of Palm Beach and go west, across the sparkling harbor of Lake Worth, with its multimillion-dollar yachts and condos. Pass the mere million-dollar estates on the harbor's west bank, through the neighborhoods of fenced lawns and swimming pools behind them, then cross over the Florida East Coast rail line and you're there, in Riviera Beach, which, despite its deceptive name, is home to the poorest people in Palm Beach County, many of whom work in those mansions by the sea, and almost all of whom, like Robie Mortin, are black.

Her place is right on Old Dixie Highway, U.S. Route 1, the traffic whooshing within a few feet of her front door. It's a small house, a cottage, really, with a chain link gate out front and a rainbow of tropical plants engulfing its tiny front yard. The inside, too, is green and lush with foliage, a jungle of limbs and leaves crawling up the living room's louvered windows, bending over the leopard print pillows and throws arranged on the sofa and chairs.

Robie takes a seat in one of the chairs, filling it from arm to arm. She's a stout woman, broad-shouldered, her biceps and forearms as thick as her son

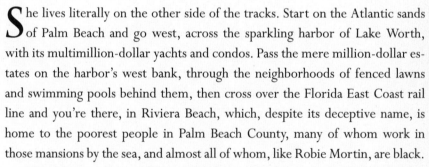

Robie Mortin

Geffery's, who is home on this Monday afternoon, taking a lunch break from his job at a nearby plumbing supply company. Geffery is thirty-seven, a big, beefy man. He's the youngest of Robie's five children. She's been married twice, is widowed now, living alone in this rented bungalow since her husband Johnnie died seven years ago.

Her physique says something about the work Robie did for most of her life, cleaning and loading laundry in some of those palaces across the tracks. She won't give too many details—she says she plans to write her own book some-day—but among her employers were the Pulitzers. "Worked for them eighteen years," she says. "Started out a laundress, and wound up doing *everything.* Cooking, cleaning. And parties, a *lot* of parties."

The Fords, the Kennedys, the Waterburys, they all dropped by, knew Robie by name, she says. Once a year, she says, the Duke and Duchess of Windsor would visit and stay for a week. "But I'm not going to tell you what they were like," says Robie. "That'll be in my book."

She's happy to talk about Rosewood, though, and when she does, Geffery comes out from the kitchen and takes a seat. It wasn't until eight years ago that he first heard of his mother's birthplace. "And that was just tidbits," he says, his voice deep but soft, a gentle baritone.

"I didn't know the whole story," he says, "until this stuff all came up with the legislature. When we were growing up, my mother never told us a *thing* about this."

"Of *course* I didn't," says Robie. "I didn't want my children to grow up hating people. Hate destroyed Rosewood. Why should I let it destroy *me?* Or *them?*"

Geffery nods.

"My parents never taught us to hate," he says. "I've never had that feeling in me. And I'm glad now that she never *did* let me know, because it would have set something off in me that I don't even want to *think* about.

"It hurt me so much when I learned about this," he continues. "To realize that my mother could have been so much more, that *I* could have been more than what I am today."

He squeezes his hands together and shakes his head.

"I watched my mother and father struggle their whole lives . . ."

Robie cuts him off. She'll have none of this. No regrets. No pity. No whining.

"You've got to *live* in this world," she says. "You've got to go *on.* It's like my grandmother said. 'Don't look back. Pick up what you got and *go* with it.'"

Robie was startled when she saw the "60 Minutes" broadcast in 1983. "It was like a bolt out of the blue," she says. But even then she didn't tell her children that that was *her* story on that TV screen.

"I was trying to figure out who and what everybody was going to *do* about this thing," she says. "Personally, I couldn't see any sense in revisiting it. I had put this all back in my mind, and that's where I kept it."

Minnie Lee and Lee Ruth were Robie's cousins. They'd come up together as children in Rosewood, and they'd kept in contact for a while afterward. But they had lost touch over the years, so Robie knew nothing about the reunions or the family friction, or even the claim itself—not until she read about it in the newspaper. And even then, when she saw that Minnie Lee and Lee Ruth were filing their bill, Robie kept her silence.

"Frankly," she says, "I didn't believe anything would come of it."

But she began clipping every story she saw, everything that was printed about Rosewood. She dropped each clipping in a bag, and by the winter of '93, the bag was stuffed.

"It was clear to me about then that they were fixin' to do something about this thing, so I said it's time to make a move."

She went to a local attorney, a black lawyer named Richard Ryles, dropped the bag of clippings on his desk and told him she was from Rosewood. "I didn't have a birth certificate, nothing like that," says Robie. "But I had my memory."

That was enough to convince Ryles. He took her case and, heeding his client's wishes, they both sat back and watched that spring's legislative fireworks from afar. Robie had no desire to get involved, not yet.

"Really, I didn't care if the thing passed or not," she says. "I couldn't care less about the money. I could *use* it, but I certainly didn't *need* it. I've never wanted for anything in my life, and I've never needed *anybody's* help. I am not, and I never have been, a welfare, state-assisted person. I never wanted to take one dime from the state. I did for *myself*.

"Whether I got anything out of this or not didn't matter to me," she says. "All that mattered to me was letting them know who I *was,* that I was *there*. And there was no rush for that."

Even when the bill became law, Robie felt no rush. She didn't write Durden's office for an application form until August. But when she received it, she sat with it for days before filling it out, letting the pages stay blank while she called up memories she had suppressed for a lifetime.

She thought about the mother she never met, who died when she was eighteen months old. She thought about her father, Nathan Robinson, who worked at the sawmill in Sumner. When her mother died, he gave Robie to her grandmother to raise. Polly Carter was the woman's name, Sam Carter's mother.

"Uncle Sammy," that's what Robie called Sam Carter. She remembered the wagon rides he gave her, their trips to the beach, the times they'd go wildflower picking in the woods. Robie's father lived just two miles away, on the other side of town, but Robie remained with Polly and Sam Carter and Sam's wife Katie. They were the people who raised her, brought her up as if she were their own.

Robie was at her father's house the day it began, visiting him along with her older sisters Sebie and Esther, who had come down from Chiefland for the holidays. None of them knew anything was wrong until their father rushed in the door Tuesday afternoon and told them to dress warm and dress fast. He was taking them to the Sumner station and putting them on the train to Chiefland. He didn't take time to explain. There was no time. It wasn't until they got off the train that the girls learned Sam Carter had been lynched the night before. It wasn't until late that week that they learned the whole town of Rosewood was under attack. And it wasn't until two years later that Robie saw her father again.

He had escaped the same way as Robie's grandmother Polly—on foot. Polly showed up in Chiefland a day after the girls got there. She was wet, shivering, half dead after hiking through the woods. She had walked all night to reach Otter Creek, where a mailman hid her in the back of his car and drove her to safety. Robie's father had gone east, too, but apparently he had kept going. No one knew where. Not until two years later, when Robie moved to the Riviera Beach area with her sister Esther, was she reunited with their father. They ran into each other in church. Five years later he died, and according to Robie, her father isn't the only Rosewood native buried in Riviera Beach.

"Omigod," she says nodding her head toward the north end of town, "the cemetery up there is *full* of them."

Once she was ready, Robie sat down that August with a granddaughter and filled out the Attorney General's affidavit in a single five-hour session. She got it notarized and mailed it back that same day. A month later, the last day of September, a skeptical Frank Beisler arrived to interview her.

"I had doubts about her at first," says Beisler. "*Extreme* doubts."

He came prepared, peppering Mortin with questions only someone who knew Rosewood inside out could answer. How far was Junior Hudson's barn from the rail depot? What buildings were between the depot and the Rosewood jook? Who shot Elias Carrier the night of the Christmas pageant? Beisler even tried a trick question, mentioning in passing how hard the chairs must have been in the Rosewood school's classroom.

"No," Robie corrected him. "They didn't *have* chairs. They had *benches*."

Beisler knew that.

"She was amazing," he says. "Every question, no hesitation, no thought. *Bang,* she had the answer. I couldn't trip her up."

Beisler came away a believer. With confirmation from Minnie Lee and some of the others that Robie Allenetta Robinson had indeed been among them at Rosewood, a ninth, and final, survivor, was added to the Attorney General's list. That fall, along with the eight others, Robie received a check from the state for fifty thousand dollars. The following January, again like the others, she was given a second check, this one for a hundred thousand.

Robie hasn't really done much with the money. She's looking at buying her own home, a place not more than a mile from where she now rents. It needs a little work, but at $38,000, "it's a steal," she says. "Hardwood floors. A nice place, something I can really make my own."

She bought herself a new car, too, a '95 Cutlass Supreme, to take the place of the old '79 Chevy that used to sit out in her carport. And she's thinking about taking her granddaughter on a trip to Greece. She points at a pair of paintings of the Parthenon hanging on the wall above her sofa.

"Greece is the beginnings of civilization," she says. "That's the beginnings of who we *are*."

She chuckles.

"Or at least who we'd like to *think* we are."

Other than those three things—the house, the car and the trip—Robie doesn't plan to spend a dime more on herself. Whatever's left, she says, will go into a trust fund for her children.

"Why should I change?" she asks. "I was doing fine before all this happened, and I'm doing fine now."

Geffery pats her knee as he heads back to the kitchen.

"You can't teach an old dog new tricks," says Robie, "and I'm one *happy* old dog."

THIRTY-FOUR

Family

~~~

It would seem they would all be happy, the dozens of Rosewood families that had endured so much and come so far, who had kept their feet through decades of fragmentation and fear, hard times and hurt, who had finally reached out and reunited, joining hands and gathering strength, then turning to face the most powerful of foes—the state of Florida itself—and against all odds, had emerged victorious, standing on those steps of the Capitol building that golden morning in May, the warm glow of glory, justice and redemption washing over them all.

But the glow faded fast, replaced by rancor. And rivalry. And resentment. All because of the very thing the government had tried to keep out of the Rosewood bill.

Money.

There were signs as early as July, when the 1995 Rosewood Family Reunion was staged down in Micanopy, just outside Gainesville. The press flocked to the scene, reporters from across the state and beyond, descending on that quiet hamlet, recording the hugging, the hand-shaking, the Saturday picnic and the

Willie Evans

big Sunday dinner, the talk of a Rosewood museum, of a family quilt, and a monthly newsletter. It was a feel-good story, great footage to cap off the eleven o'clock news, a nice piece for the feature front of the morning papers.

No one paid much attention to the fact that there were almost as many journalists there as family. Sixty—that's how many survivors and descendants showed up that weekend. Thirteen hundred names were on that wall down in Guy Robinson's office, and sixty came to Micanopy.

They all knew why. Those who had come and the ones who had stayed away, they all knew that a battle was already brewing, a backlash among factions within some of the families themselves, kin turning on kin. Finger-pointing. Name calling. And worse. Now that the law was spelled out, now that the hard figures were set in stone, now that there was nothing left to imagine, no lottery-like prize to dream of, now that it was clear who would get how much and who would have to fight for what was left, the hand-holding and praying subsided, replaced by outstretched fingers and raised fists.

The first targets, incredibly, were the survivors.

Dorothy Hosey was so overrun with relatives—some she hadn't seen in years, some she didn't even recognize—calling her on the phone, knocking on her door, asking for cash, *demanding* it, cursing her if she refused—that she went into hiding. She bought a new house, which she had planned to do from the beginning, leaving behind the bullet-riddled, roach-infested east Tampa housing project she had lived in for so many years. But she told no one where she had moved, and she discarded her phone number as well. Not even Arnett Doctor knows Mama Dot's number now. No one does. She has, in essence, carefully and with forethought, disappeared, like a political exile.

Mary Hall Daniels has moved as well, from her small Jacksonville apartment into a house whose address she too has kept a secret. Her number, like Dorothy's, is unlisted, but her daughter Alzada has permission to share it with people Mary knows.

"I *had* to do it this way," explains Mary, speaking by phone from her new home, north of the city. "It seemed like everybody in the world started calling me after I got this money. People I don't even *know* called me up, telling me they were my relatives. And it's funny, you know? Because everybody *knew* where I was living before. They all knew my telephone number. But none of them ever came to visit me, none of them stopped by. None of them called. People walked right *by* me, which was all right. It never bothered me, because I *had* my friends. I knew who they were, and I know who they are now. But the rest of them, the ones who been trying to get to me now? Forget it. *None* of them knows where I live."

Even if they did, there's nothing any of them could get from Mary. She's put every cent she received from the state into her new home and a car, and she's happy.

"All the money that God blessed me to have, it's all gone," she says. "The house, my new furniture, and a new car, I paid it all off with cash. I don't want to be owing anybody *anything.* I'm right back where I started from, living off my same social security. The only thing different is I'm in my own home now, and that is *so* pleasant.

"It's true," says Mary. "If you wait on the Lord, He'll make a way for you."

Mary's brother Wilson hasn't had to hide. No one would be foolish enough to face off against Wilson Hall, though he's heard more than a few unkind words over the past year.

"It's the younger ones that are talking," says Wilson. "The nieces and nephews. They're looking at me now like I cheated them *out* of something, like I got something *they* should've had.

"But I don't worry about them, 'cause I've never been close to them anyway. They live different lifestyles, those younger ones. They're in a different *world* from mine."

Wilson's world has been, and still is, centered on his wife, his sister up the street—Margie—and his club, which, he says, has been completely remodeled with the money he got from the state.

"You wouldn't *recognize* the joint," says Wilson, speaking by telephone from the bar of the *new* 705 Club. "That old, smoky, rundown place that was here, man, this place is like *sunshine* compared to that."

The club is half again larger, says Wilson, with a brand-new kitchen. "Shiny stuff," he says. "Even a new cooler box." The booths are gone, replaced by tables and chairs and a bar that runs the length of one wall. "Fifteen tables," says Wilson, "and thirty-five stools at the bar. With mirrors all the way around."

The dirt lot out front is paved now, lined off for parking, with signs posted on all sides: NO DRUGS, NO LOITERING, NO LITTERING.

"Those signs are *inside,* too," says Wilson. "Ain't gonna be none of that kind of trouble around here no more."

He now has the cash to pay the security guards required by the city, and he's bought a new mini-van for his wife Stephanie, who teaches special education at a school across the state line in Georgia. "She needs something with some room in it," says Wilson, "to carry those kids around."

As for Wilson's sister Margie, nothing in her life has changed. She is still fighting leukemia, still making regular trips to the hospital for radiation treatment. "She had a bad spell of the sickness not too long ago," says Wilson, "and it's taking effect on her."

Wilson's the one who drives Margie to the clinic for her treatments. He's the one who pays the home nurse who sits with Margie each day. He helps her sign any papers she needs to keep her affairs in order—"For social security and such," he says. And he's the one making sure the money Margie was paid by the state is safe.

"Right now she's just sitting on it," says Wilson. "She says she's saving that money to take care of her sick days. What she don't realize is her sick days are *here*."

While folks around Hilliard have left Wilson alone, there have been a few pecking at Margie's windows. "Not relatives so much as some of her neighbors and friends," says Wilson. "People think she's got a house full of money, and they try to get in there any way they can."

Willie Evans doesn't have to worry about his windows. He's got a new security system installed in his house in Sanford, the same house he bought back in 1968, the year he had to quit work because his eyesight was gone. Twenty-two years of sawing cement and bricks, the dust and chips flying in his face eight hours a day, had done him in. It had been tough work at the start, when they paid him fifty cents an hour, and it was just as hard when he retired, at sixteen dollars a day. But he still wishes he could have hung on a couple more years. "To when the money started gettin' *really* good," he says.

It was the fall after the Rosewood bill had been signed—a September evening—when Willie sat out front of his home, with its tin roof, its pink trim around the windows and the pink pillars holding up the porch, and talked about the difference in the generations he was seeing these days. He made his point by talking about mullet. Fresh mullet. "That's *west* coast mullet I'm talking about," he cautioned, "not that east coast stuff." He said he often picks some up when he pays a visit to one of his friends.

"The older people," said Willie, "they *love* you to bring them something when you go to see 'em. They just appreciate it so *much*.

"But the younger ones," he said, "they see me bringing that fish, and they ask me where's *theirs* and why didn't I buy *them* some. They're *expecting* it, see? I tell 'em, 'Go catch your *own* damn fish.'"

It was raining that September night, a light drizzle dripping off the sagging roof of Willie's porch. It was dark out, but he still had his sunglasses on. He always puts his sunglasses on when he steps outside. That's been his habit ever since he went blind. He keeps the TV going almost all the time—"More for company than anything else," he said—though there are two shows he never misses. "'Wheel of Fortune,'" he smiled, "and 'The Price is Right.' I just *love* that 'Price is Right.'"

Word had come that afternoon from the Attorney General's office that Rosewood survivors would soon be receiving early payments of $50,000 apiece, rather than waiting until January for the full $150,000 each. Arnett had pushed Greg Durden's office for that, saying these people were getting old, and some might not still be around in January. Willie would be turning eighty-seven on Christmas Day, but he waved away any notion that *he* might be checking out anytime soon.

"Got a little arthritis in my left knee," he said, "but then that's been worrying me about forty-five years now, so I don't pay it much mind."

He's got one child, his son Donnell, who lives up in New York, where he works in warehousing at the World Trade Center. A framed high school graduation photo of Donnell's daughter Libra sits on Willie's bureau, though he can't see it. It's inscribed, *Your one and only granddaughter.*

Willie's wife Edna passed away in 1992, and he's lived alone since. His neighbor Edlina James does some cooking for him, and Meals on Wheels takes care of the rest. Three days a week—Sundays, Tuesdays and Wednesdays—he spends at church. Willie's always been a churchgoing man. His grandmother Julia raised him that way back in Rosewood. They went to the AME church there, and Willie goes to the AME church now—the St. James AME there in Sanford, just across the street from his house.

When he mused that September evening about how he might spend the money he had coming to him from the state, Willie talked about fixing up his porch—"The termites been eatin' it up real bad," he said, poking at the rotting wood with his cane. He talked about maybe giving the house a new paint job as well. And he said he was definitely going to give something to the church.

When he answers his telephone eight months later, he still has the TV going. "Yes," he says. "Matter of fact, 'The Price is Right' is just comin' on."

His front porch is fixed now, says Willie, and the house has been painted. "Outside *and* in," he says. It was Arnett who insisted Willie put in the security system, though Willie says he really doesn't see the need.

"I ain't had nobody come here bothering me at all," he says. "Nobody's bothered me about my money. 'Course hardly anybody knows where I *am*."

His only splurge, he says, was the new living room chair that now sits in front of his television. "It's one of them—whatcha call it—one of them *Lazyboy* chairs," he says. "You know, that lift you up, stretch your feet out, lay you back. It's real nice."

And he certainly did give some money to his church. "Fifteen thousand dollars," he says, proudly. Ten percent. The standard tithe. "I *believe* in tithing," says Willie.

As for his health, the arthritis is still the only thing bothering him. "It causes me some misery," he says. "But I can live with it. You *learn* to live with things like that."

Up in Jacksonville, Minnie Lee Langley's health problems have been a bit more serious than Willie's. There was another bout with pneumonia and she's had some recent surgery for a blocked artery in her left leg. But she says she's getting better, and she's lost none of the defiance that has carried her through all these years. Ask her what she's done with the payment she received from the state, and she almost spits into the telephone.

"You got your womens mixed *up* when you go and ask me about my *money*," she says.

Her daughter Dorothy is more forthcoming. Minnie never gave a thought to leaving her home, says Dorothy, but she has fixed it up with a new living room suite, a new refrigerator, new cabinets for the kitchen, and, most notably, says Dorothy, a new washer *and* dryer.

"She washes all the *time*," says Dorothy. "She always has. She's got a lifestyle that doesn't change too much. But she was getting too feeble to keep going outside and hanging things up, so she went and got herself a dryer."

Minnie won't talk about how she does or doesn't spend her money, but she knows what money has been doing to some of the Rosewood families, and she's happy to explain why it's done nothing to her.

"I ain't never been crazy about money," she explains. "I worked all my life, I worked *hard*, and I made what I needed. I made money, but money ain't *never* made *me*. It would never *change* me. Not money, not *nothin'* gonna' get between me and the Lord.

"Them people that's having trouble with all this," she says, "they don't know nothin' about family, about *being* family. I don't even *know* none of those people."

Minnie knows A. T. Goins, but it would be hard for her to get in touch with him, even if she wanted. His daughter Annette has moved into a place near his home in St. Petersburg, and when the phone rings at A. T.'s house, it's either Annette or her mother, Anna Maude, who answers.

"He can't come to the phone right now," says Anna Maude, answering a recent call. "He's feeling depressed today."

The next day Anna Maude answers again.

"He can't talk right now," she says. "He's out in the yard."

Could she call him in?

"No, I can't. The person you need to talk to is my daughter, Annette."

When Annette answers her phone, she says she needs to talk to her own attorney before she speaks to anyone about her family. Furthermore, she says, she has power of attorney for her father. "And I would appreciate it," she says, "if you don't try to call my father anymore."

Frank Beisler, who visited each of the survivors' homes during the Attorney General's investigative process, is amazed at the disputes that have arisen among some of the Rosewood families. But none bewilders him more than what has happened to A. T. Goins.

"When I went to interview him, what I saw was a gentle man, just a nice guy," says Beisler. "He told me all he wanted out of this money was to pay off his newspaper bill. His *newspaper bill,* that's it. And he can't even read, because his eyes are so bad. He said he likes to keep the paper around for friends when they come to visit.

"And now here are these people trying to beat the shit out of this man for his money," says Beisler. "Unbelievable."

You have to go through a lawyer, too, if you want to speak to Lonnie Carroll, but that's because Lonnie is unable to speak for himself, as he has been for the past ten years, ever since he had a stroke and was put in a nursing home there by the ocean in New Smyrna Beach.

That same week last September that Willie Evans sat on his porch and talked about his life, Lugenia Carroll and a dozen or so of her family and friends gathered in the living room of her little house on Hickory Street there in New Smyrna and talked about Lonnie. They set out a nice spread of food—barbecued chicken, collard greens, cornbread, rice, potato salad and iced tea— pulled up every chair they could find, and spent a couple of hours sharing stories.

Lugenia and Lonnie have had that same place—a white cinderblock bungalow with plants hanging on the porch—ever since Lonnie's brother Aaron died there in 1966. "A. C.," they called Aaron. This little tree-shaded neighborhood, just off the main drag in New Smyrna, was where both Aaron and Lonnie wound up after leaving Rosewood. Lonnie and Lugenia married here in 1944. Lugenia said Lonnie told her all about Rosewood when he first met her, told her about his father James, who was shot dead that week, and about his mother Emma, who left Rosewood with bullet wounds in her hand and wrist and died a year later. Aaron never did like to talk about Rosewood, said Lugenia, not the way Lonnie would.

Lonnie was a logger, said Lugenia, "following that wood," she said, wherever it took him. Mostly he worked in the forests around Palatka, halfway between Gainesville and the Atlantic. He was a big man—six foot, two hundred pounds—strong enough to earn some extra money boxing on the side. "Four dollars a fight," said Lugenia, "that's what they paid him."

Toward twilight the talk turned to the claims bill, to the money that was starting to come to the survivors and to the property settlement that had yet to be worked out.

"Lord," said Lonnie's cousin, Rose Edwards, whose father Hubert was a deceased Rosewood survivor, "I just hope this money doesn't destroy our people."

Then it was time to take a drive over to visit Lonnie. The trip was short, just a couple of miles, out of the crowded little neighborhood of Hickory Street, onto the main drag, up over the Intracoastal Waterway and down to the oceanfront, the resort section of New Smyrna Beach, where condos and small seedy motels are painted various shades of pink and aqua. The place where Lonnie lives, the Ocean View Nursing Home, looks like just another motel, painted coral and turquoise, with sand sweeping across its parking lot.

Inside, the halls were crowded with elderly men and women, black and white, parked in wheelchairs, some speaking with one another, a few speaking to themselves, most just sitting in silence.

Lonnie was in his room, in darkness, the shades drawn. A transistor radio sat on the bureau, tuned to a soul station, the voice of a singer named Babyface crackling from the little box:

> *"I'm gonna keep on searchin' till I find you, baby...*
> *Please tell me where, where, where is my love."*

Lonnie was on his back in bed, his mouth open, his eyes closed, his chest rising and falling as he breathed.

Lugenia leaned over him, put her hands on his face and began rubbing it—his cheeks, his forehead—pressing the skin till he knew she was there.

His mouth closed, the lips pressed tight, and his eyes opened. They were white, his eyes, as white as milk. Lonnie is completely blind.

He groaned, moved his head slightly from side to side. The rest of his body remained inert. Then he shut his eyes again, and his mouth fell open, and he lay back as he was when Lugenia arrived, as he has lain every day for the past decade.

For the first seven years Lugenia came to see Lonnie every day. But then she got sick herself, began bleeding out of her left ear and found out she had a brain tumor. Now one side of her face is paralyzed, and though she can hear fine, she has trouble speaking, because half her mouth is paralyzed too.

But she still visits Lonnie at least once a week. That's the way it was that September evening, as she kissed his face and left him in his room. And that's the way it is today. Lonnie's money has paid for a new sofa, a new bed, a new Frigidaire for the house, a chain link fence out front and some air-conditioning that's getting put in any day now, says Lugenia. She's also getting $300 a month from Lonnie's claims payment, to help pay the bills. Other than that, the money is paying for Lonnie's care.

"Nothing's changed too much," says Lugenia. "We're just goin' on living."

It was understandable in a way, say Frank Beisler and Guy Robinson, to see the conflicts that arose around some of the survivors and their families. The money, after all, was a significant sum. But the property payments—Beisler and Robinson were initially amazed at the infighting that grew among some of the families over those. Still, it didn't take long to understand.

The half-million-dollar pie created by the state to pay Rosewood's property claims could be sliced only so many ways. The more slices there were, the smaller each slice. Thirteen hundred names added up to some very thin slices—a fact that did not escape some of the claimants, which Beisler and Robinson discovered as they went about the business of verifying those claims.

"People were purposely leaving other people out," says Beisler. "Their own relatives, their own family. We found that out after digging and digging into this thing. There were a couple of *ministers* who filed papers conveniently leaving family members off their trees. I'm talking about their own sisters and brothers. Now I'm *sure* they knew their own sisters and brothers were alive."

Then again, adds Beisler, there were those on the flip side, qualified descendants who turned down payments to which they were fully entitled.

"We've got a whole drawer full of people who are eligible for property payments who just don't *want* them, for whatever reason," says Beisler. "I've had several people tell me, 'Look, I wasn't *at* Rosewood. Those are my *ancestors*. I'm not entitled to that money and I don't want it, period.'

"And there are some who told me they didn't want anything to do with this money because they were afraid it would start a battle in their family."

There was a small eruption in March of 1995, when Greg Durden arranged a meeting at a church in Orlando with all families whose property claims appeared at that point to have merit. The intent was to have the families themselves help comb and complete the trees that had been drawn by Beisler and Robinson. Seventy people showed up, representing sixteen families. At one point Durden said he'd had complaints from some family members that they were not being kept updated on what was happening with these property claims.

Arnett, sitting in the front row, took the comment as an affront to him and the Committee. He was irate. He told Durden he wasn't about to sit still and listen to accusations from unnamed sources. Durden told him he could leave if he'd like. Arnett shot back that he wasn't about to leave. "This is *my* family that you're talking about," he said. An echo of *Amens* came from around the room.

But that was about the last sign of solidity the families would show. The complaints Durden had heard continued, and soon the situation had deteriorated into a case of every family for itself.

"It hasn't been pretty," says Beisler.

And it shouldn't be surprising, says Arnett's sister, Yvonne. Through all of this, Philomena Doctor's first child had kept her silence. From that weekend in 1982 when her brother came back from his trip to Rosewood and told their mother he wanted to know more about this thing, through the ensuing decade of shouting and tears, from her mother's death in 1991 through the twisting journey that finally led to the passing of this law, Yvonne Doctor had kept her silence.

And this—the acrimony that was now tearing some of these families apart—was why. This—more than fear, pain, trauma, anger or hate—was why Yvonne's mother had so fiercely forced her family to keep this matter to themselves. Yes, the damage done that winter week in 1923 was immeasurable. But Philomena Doctor knew just as well the further damage that would surely be done by using the ghosts of Rosewood to unleash the evil of greed.

"My mother understood people," says Yvonne, speaking from her home in St. Petersburg, the same home in which her mother died. "She knew human nature. And she *knew* what was going to happen if people went and tried to do something about this."

Like Robie Mortin—only for much longer—Yvonne Doctor watched from the sidelines as the Rosewood forces, led by Arnett, fought their way toward Tallahassee. Yvonne respected what her brother was doing, even though she disagreed with it.

"Whatever my mother said to Arnett, I don't know," says Yvonne. "But till her dying day, her wishes to *me* were to keep this quiet."

Yvonne respected those wishes, long after her mother was dead. Not until the day the Florida Senate voted on the bill did she show her face, sitting with the families in the gallery. It was important to her to be there that day, because that day was not about money. It was about justice, acknowledgment, a tribute her mother would have appreciated, a tribute her mother and those who died before her deserved.

But after that day, Yvonne watched it all dissolve. It even washed up on her own doorstep, there in St. Petersburg.

"When it hit the papers that this law had passed," she says, "they all started showing up here, faces I'd never seen, coming to my door, asking questions, wanting to find out how they were connected so they could make a claim.

"I'd open the door and see this *stranger* standing there, and I'd say, 'God, I can't believe this. What wind blew *you* here?'

"There's one cousin I haven't seen in over twenty years, and she lives right here in this city—*she* showed up."

It's not everyone, cautions Yvonne, who has been stained by this catfighting.

It's not everyone who's guilty of greed. The older generations, she says, and some of the younger ones, too, those who have been showing up at funerals and baptisms for years, who have come together at holidays, who have sent cards on birthdays and presents at Christmas to nieces and nephews and grandsons and granddaughters, who have been family—actively *been* family—long before any of this talk about a claims bill began, those people's concern all along has been that this be a good thing, a healing thing for the family, that the beauty of this bill was what it represented, not what it repaid.

They are hurt, many of them say—some say they are embarrassed—by what they have seen. Yvonne has no doubt her mother is watching, and that Philomena feels the same.

"I don't think she's happy about this, not at all," says Yvonne. "The fact is," she says, "it's turning out just the way she was afraid it would."

THIRTY-FIVE

Sylvester's Shadow

When the dust had finally settled on the Rosewood property payments, when the names were drawn up, the figures computed and the checks finally mailed in June of 1995, the money hardly seemed worth the bloodletting it had caused.

Out of four hundred property claim applications, fewer than seventy claimants actually wound up with a check from the state. And those checks were not life-changing. The largest were for five thousand dollars, to each of the four children of Fred Edwards, who had owned two acres of land in Rosewood at the time of the attack. The smallest were those received by the eight surviving sons and daughters of Galvester Nada Bradley, who was one of Rosewood resident John Bradley's twelve children. By the time the math was done, John Bradley's eight surviving grandchildren each got a check from the state for $104.17.

It was worse than anticlimactic. Even after a year's effort, the Attorney General's office, like everyone else who had waded into the subject of Rosewood, was left with a sense of incompletion. Tens of thousands of state dollars sat unclaimed. Hundreds of acres of Rosewood property were unaccounted for.

Rosewood family reunion, Washington, D.C., 1993

"Add it up," said Guy Robinson, scanning the 1922 Levy County tax rolls and reading aloud. " '250 acres unknown . . . 400 acres unknown . . . ' There's a *lot* that hasn't been accounted for."

Just as bewildering were the number of property shares that wound up unclaimed. Among John Bradley's family, for example, almost $12,000 of the $20,000 award went uncollected, with no heirs surfacing among the families of ten of Bradley's twelve children. It was the same story, more or less, among each family that applied. By law, every one of those unclaimed dollars were returned to the state's general fund, from which they were originally drawn.

"As of right now," said Frank Beisler in June of 1995, "there's about a hundred and seventy grand going back to the state."

By then, the buzz among the Rosewood families had shifted from property claims to Hollywood. Not Hollywood, Florida; Hollywood, *California*.

Ever since the Rosewood story had broken nationally, calls had begun coming in to Arnett from producers and motion picture companies, people sniffing around about a possible Rosewood project. Maybe a full-length film, maybe a TV miniseries. Rumors began flying. Louis Gossett, Jr. was supposedly interested. Maybe John Singleton. Quincy Jones. Spike Lee. The families—Arnett and the Advisory Committee—hired an entertainment attorney in Orlando, a man named Greg Galloway, to represent them, to sort rumor from fact and to get them a deal.

As for Michael O'McCarthy, he was out of the picture. That 1993 "Maury Povich" broadcast had been his parting shot. When Arnett and the other family members surfaced, O'McCarthy, who had his contracts with Minnie Lee Langley and Lee Ruth Davis, found himself dealing with people who had little interest in dealing with him. The families' rift with Minnie Lee and Lee Ruth apparently extended to O'McCarthy as well. After a single phone conversation that spring with Arnett Doctor, Michael O'McCarthy heard no more from the Rosewood families. He tried selling what he had with just Minnie Lee and Lee Ruth, but no one was interested. This was no longer just two women's story. And so, as the legal gears he had helped set in motion began to turn, O'McCarthy found himself on the outside looking in. "I guess," he said in a *Los Angeles Times Magazine* story published the autumn after the bill was passed, "I was the wrong color."

Six months later O'McCarthy denied at least the spirit of that quote, saying it was taken out of context. He is living in South Carolina now, still modeling, still making movie deals, still selling stories to "Hard Copy" and "A Current Affair." "I do think I deserve credit for what I had to do with Rosewood," he says, "and I haven't gotten it. But that's all right. I remain very proud that I had the opportunity to help even the scales of justice in my home state of Florida. That's my reward, period. If I die today, I'll know I've done some small thing to make my nation better, period. And that's enough, man. That's it."

Far more than O'McCarthy, a man who feels he has not gotten proper credit for his role in the Rosewood story is the reporter who first wrote about it and has continued researching the subject ever since—Gary Moore. Moore's path has wound far from St. Petersburg since he left the newspaper there not long after his first Rosewood story was published in 1982. Over the ensuing decade, he roved from Central America to Seattle, finally settling in Tupelo, Mississippi, where he lives today, not far from where he was born and raised. He teaches a course in computers, but Rosewood remains the focal point of his life. An eight-hundred-page manuscript sits on his desk, the sum of fourteen years spent digging like an archaeologist into every detail of that 1923 town, from the bricks that formed the chimneys of those houses to the names and ancestry of every man, woman and child who inhabited them. He has tried getting his book published, tried getting it made into a movie, all so far to no avail. Like O'McCarthy, Moore has found himself pushed aside by the course of events, standing offstage while the spotlight falls on others. "This story is an endless locus of bitterness," he says. "Reality itself becomes a labyrinth, and you find yourself falling into it. . . . I just couldn't begin to express to you the subterranean aspects of this thing."

Steve Hanlon wouldn't bother trying. Side streets and alleys, layers beneath layers, they don't interest him. Keep it simple. Stay on track. That's his mantra. Always has been, always will. His current cause is a case against the public housing authority in St. Petersburg, on behalf of a three-year-old boy suffering from lead poisoning. But he's still involved with the Rosewood families, helping them sort out the financial and legal affairs that continue to linger. He looks back on what was an ordeal for so many with the fondness of a mother sorting through baby photos. He keeps a postcard from Jim Peters in his desk. It arrived from England not long after the Hixson hearing was finished. "London By Night," the card is titled, completely black on its front, with an inscription on the back:

Have come to the Queens' Asylum and infirmary to have the track marks re-
moved from my carcass. Doc says the scars should heal. You do good work. Let's try
it again in another lifetime.

                                                                    P.

Martha Barnett, too, has moved on, lobbying her way through Florida's
1995 legislature, a group quite different both in content and in spirit from the
'94 body that passed the Rosewood bill. The right-wing wave that swept America in the fall elections of 1994 washed over Florida as surely as it did through
every state in the nation. Lawton Chiles barely beat back a brutal challenge
from George Bush's son Jeb for the governor's seat. In the Senate, for the first
time since Reconstruction, Florida's Republicans became the majority party. In
the House, the Democrats held on, but by the barest of margins, and a core of
them—including most of the strongest opponents to the Rosewood bill—were
more conservative than their Republican colleagues.

Miguel De Grandy bowed out of the whole scene, choosing not to run for
re-election, returning instead to his private law practice in Miami. Bo Johnson
chose not to run again as well; he's back in Milton, selling real estate. Charlie
Williams was re-elected, despite embarrassing many of his colleagues by de-
claring at a public rally that the school prayer bill he had pushed in the '94 legislature was defeated by "South Florida Jewish members who don't believe in
Jesus." And Al Lawson was back again, too, though he and his black caucus colleagues were barely heard from in an environment whose terms were largely
dictated by the Republicans' national Contract With America—a contract that
would have no room at all for an item like Rosewood.

"There is no doubt in my mind," says Martha Barnett, "that the Rosewood
bill would not have stood a *chance* of passing this year's legislature. If it hadn't
made it last year, it would never have made it."

Arnett Doctor agrees. He's back in his home in Tampa now, still working
the phone day and night, but he's not calling legislators anymore. He's calling
movie producers, though he can't give any details. "Big things are brewing," is
all he'll say about that. "Big, big things."

He's calling for money, too, trying to raise $600,000, he says, to build a
memorial park—the same sort of project Arnett's legislative opponents tried
to put in the bill instead of money. The memorial he has in mind would be built

near Rosewood, on land to be donated by a Levy County resident—a *white* resident. Arnett has a blueprint of the place, drawn by a team of students and professors in the school of architecture at Florida A&M. He unscrolls it on the floor of his office, pointing at the outdoor gardens, the benches and fountains, the museum itself, as if the blue-inked structures are real. "It's going to happen," he says. "Make no mistake about it. It's *going* to happen."

He still keeps his shades drawn, even in the middle of the day, as he has for the past two years. He still freezes each time he hears a car engine slow in front of his house. He hasn't gotten one of those odd late-night calls in months, but he feels no safer now than he did that Saturday in 1982 when he first drove up to Rosewood, with a pistol in his slacks. "They're out there," he says, stroking his goatee. "I *know* they're out there."

He still keeps a gun in every room, as he has for the past two years. There's a Winchester .22 rifle propped in the corner of his office, a shotgun back in the bedroom, a Colt .32 revolver and the old .357 Magnum tucked away in various drawers, along with a new Beretta .25 automatic pistol he bought for his girlfriend Loretta. "I'm not paranoid," says Arnett. "Let's just say I'm *protected*."

But despite the wariness and the weaponry—steel-edged shadows of his great-uncle Sylvester—Arnett has softened. His fuse is longer, and he's more philosophical about those who stand against him. A year ago, when the government seemed to him to be dragging its feet in paying the survivors, he was furious. "What they don't have the backbone to say," he had declared one afternoon, driving to the coast to visit Lonnie Carroll, "is 'We don't *mind* if we're giving money to the Japanese, or if we give it to the Hispanics, or to the whites, but we don't want to *give* it to the goddamn *niggers*.'"

Today, though, he is a different man. Ask him how he feels about the amounts of money everyone has received, especially the property claimants, and he sounds like one of those senators up in Tallahassee. "I think," he says, "that the fact that the state of Florida has seen fit to pay at *all,* that they would reach into their pockets at *all,* speaks volumes about the state of mind of our elected legislators and how far we've come in the past seventy-three years."

Unlike his sister, Arnett is convinced his mother is looking down on all this with a smile. "Yvonne's entitled to her opinion," he says, "but I think my mother is *ecstatic* about what has happened."

He won't say how much he personally received from the state for his share of his mother's property claim, but it couldn't have put a dent in the twenty thousand dollars he figures he has spent over the past decade pursuing this dream of his. And that, he says, doesn't bother him. "At this juncture, quite honestly," he says, "I'm not in the complaining mode."

As for his dream, it's hard to say exactly what it is, because Arnett's dreams seem to shift with time and circumstance. At first he just wanted to find out what happened at Rosewood. Then he wanted to bring his family together, to make it whole again. Then rose the idea of justice, of making somebody pay for the damage his relatives had suffered.

Now he dreams of that memorial park.

And the movie.

And he has begun dreaming as well about his Seminole Indian roots, something he stumbled across during his research on Rosewood.

"That's right," he says. "My great-grandfather on my *father's* side of the family was a *war* chief in the Seminole Nation."

Arnett pulls a copy of Florida's statewide Seminole tribal membership voting list from a cabinet, and there indeed, among the columns of names, more than a hundred names to a column, among the Gophers and Tigers and Cypresses and Youngbloods, are the Doctors. Nathan Dean Doctor and Minnie Billie Doctor. Toka Carrie Doctor and Susie Osceola Doctor. Two dozen Seminole Doctors, and Arnett intends to track down every one, to trace his connections to them all, and theirs to one another.

"These are my *people*," he says, the late afternoon light slanting through his windowshades. "These are my *relatives*. This is where I came from, *too*."

He folds the list and puts it back in the cabinet.

"That's going to make me feel more complete than I used to feel," he says, closing the drawer. "It's going to make me even more aware of who I am," he says, as his telephone rings.

He lets the answering machine take the call, his recorded voice filling the room.

Hello! . . .

Better it is to be of humble spirit with the lowly, than to divide the spoils with the proud. . . .

After the beep, please leave your telephone number. . . .

Thank you, and God bless.

They still say there are bodies buried back in this swamp. Blacks and whites alike, they still believe there are piles of bones sleeping deep beneath the sand and mud, covered by the thick canopies of oaks and palms and palmettos that have risen like a green cathedral since the day the dead were dropped into the ground.

How many dead is hard to say. The Florida Department of Law Enforcement began combing this forest the same summer the Attorney General's office began counting survivors. A team of state agents pushed through the shrubs and briers, swatting at clouds of mosquitoes and sand flies, stepping over sluggish creeks and black bogs, picking through the eighty acres of dense woodland that was once called Goins Quarters, searching for the mass grave so many told them was here.

They talked to old Fred Kirkland, and he said there were thirty-five women and children dropped into a well a couple of days after the attack on the Carrier house. They listened to Jason McElveen's account of a mule-pulled fire plow dragging dirt over the bodies of twenty-six more. And there was the testimony of a man named James Turner, who was just a fourteen-year-old boy at the time but would later become Levy County sheriff. Turner said he was led to an open grave a few days after the attack and was shown a pile of bodies too tangled to count. He guessed there were at least seventeen, all of them black.

Turner and McElveen are long dead. Fred Kirkland is too old to tromp through those thickets. And even if he weren't, he told the agents, there was no way he could find that well after all this time. Eighty acres, and it's been almost eighty years.

The agents did get Kirkland's help in identifying suspects. Ernest Parham helped as well. As did Gary Moore, the newspaper reporter whose notes and tapes included interviews done in the early 1980s with many white and black witnesses who have died since then.

Moore shared his notes, and the Levy County sheriff's office lent a hand. Court records were pulled, death certificates were gathered, and state agents fanned out across the county, from Chiefland to Cedar Key, interrogating witnesses as well as possible suspects, old men and women not many steps from the grave, each of them struggling to recall details of neighbors who had long ago gone to theirs.

The result—discounting the crowds of the curious who came to Rosewood that week to simply watch as the town burned down, the throngs who arrived in their Model Ts to witness the torching as if it were a carnival, the two to three thousand onlookers Fred Kirkland says filled the village's streets by week's end to witness the smoking ruins—setting all those people aside, the state arrived at a final list of sixteen suspects, men who were witnesses to and possibly involved in the killings that took place in Rosewood that week.

Only one was listed as an actual murderer—a man named Bryant Hudson. He was twenty-five at the time. Four witnesses named Hudson as the man who shot Sam Carter that night by the edge of the woods. "Hudson," states the FDLE report, "is the only suspect identified as having committed a homicide." Records show Bryant Hudson died at a Veterans Hospital in Lake City in 1931, from injuries, friends say, he received in a fight.

Three other names were on the list as witnesses to Sam Carter's murder. One was Garrett Kirkland, Fred Kirkland's uncle. He died in 1952, according to the report, at age seventy-eight. Another was Jason McElveen, who was also present at the Carrier House shootout three nights later. McElveen died in 1983, at age eighty-eight. The third was Orrie Kirkland, Fred Kirkland's father. He was fifty-two the night Sam Carter was killed, but no one, not even his son, can recall the year he died. The FDLE could find no official record of Orrie

Kirkland's death. The best they got was the word of one Levy County old-timer who said old man Kirkland died "many years ago."

Four more names on the suspect list are men who were wounded the night of the shootout at the Carrier House, according to newspaper accounts from the time of the attack and according to witnesses interviewed by the FDLE. Two of those men—Cephus Studstill and Henry Odom—were seen in Sumner late that Thursday night, bloody and bandaged, by Ernest Parham. Studstill, who was twenty-three at the time, died fourteen years later, on the last day of December. Odom is more of a mystery. The FDLE found a 1971 death certificate for a Henry A. Odom in Jacksonville, but they are not sure it's the same man. It is possible, the report concluded, that Odom is alive today. If so, he would be at least ninety-seven years old.

The other two men listed as wounded that Thursday night were Fred Kirkland's brothers, Bryan and Warner. Again, the FDLE could find no record of either man's death, so it is assumed they could possibly still be alive. If so, Bryan Kirkland would be ninety-nine. His brother Warner would be at least ninety-seven.

The last name that appears on the Rosewood suspect list is Red Raulerson. He was a witness to the Carrier house shootout, according to Fred Kirkland. Kirkland says Raulerson is dead now, but he can't recall when he passed away.

The remaining six people on the list are identified by numbers, not names, "due to the weakness of the allegations against them," according to the FDLE. Two were "possibly involved" in the shooting death of Mingo ("Lord God") Williams, and one was "possibly involved" in the killing of Lexie Gordon. Five of these suspects are now dead. The sixth, were he still alive today, according to the report, would be at least ninety-seven.

That was the gist of it. "The Rosewood investigation has now been completed," wrote FDLE Commissioner James Moore in a cover letter to the report, delivered to the state's Attorney General in January of 1995. "All investigative efforts," the report stated, "have been pursued to their logical conclusion."

That included the hunt for bodies possibly buried out in those woods. The FDLE team spent two days pushing through the swampland behind Doyal Scoggins's house and came away with nothing but scratches and insect bites. The last paragraph of the thirteen-page report sums up that search: "The mass grave issue may never be resolved."

And strangers may never stop knocking on the door of Wesley Thompson's trailer to ask about it. No one has heard more about this mass grave than Thompson. It's his property on which the grave supposedly sits. It's his land Arnett Doctor walked around that spring afternoon in 1982, when he stumbled on the headstones of his ancestors. It was Wesley Thompson who offered Arnett a beer that afternoon.

The headstones are still there, still covered with tangles of vines and poison ivy, deep in these woods back behind Doyal Scoggins's house. There are still gators back there, too. And snakes. And green turtle and black catfish, hogs and wild turkeys, possum and rabbits and otter and deer—all the meat a man would need if meat were what he was after. And that is what a group of men huddled here on a recent, wet autumn afternoon were after—meat.

Their bows were strung taut, their steel-tipped arrows glinting in the glow cast from the porch light of the hut behind them. Around the hut perched a half dozen trailers, bent, rusted, empty. A battered pickup truck leaned by a split-rail fence, its windshield shattered, its wheels swallowed by weeds. Beside it, beached like a lost fish, sat an airboat, its caged propeller looming above its stern, the steel wires sharp and shining in the midday mist.

The men were clad in camo fatigues, four of them, each clutching a cold can of beer. They laughed and cursed, paying no mind to the soft sheets of rain sweeping down from the gray sky above, to the sound of their hounds baying in a distant pen, to the chickens and children rooting in the mud by the porch.

There were women inside the hut, tending a pot of beans picked fresh that morning, lima beans. A television was tuned to the Florida–Ole Miss football game, which was just about finished, the Gators ahead by three scores, and so the men had moved outside, where the smallest of them, a wiry fifty-year-old, his chin speckled with stubble, his damp gray hair dangling from beneath a sweat-stained ball cap, was holding court.

Wesley Thompson.

The shack, the trailers, this land, it's all his, his and his family's, he said. "Unless," he added, draining a last swallow from his can and flinging it toward the fence, "the niggers take it away from us."

His companions grinned. One had a compass pinned to the crown of his cap. The small clear bulb bobbed like a Christmas ornament, its tiny arrow quivering as the man laughed.

Thompson pointed toward a stand of cabbage palms, their gnarled trunks smeared with splashes of orange paint. "It was the state government people did that," he said. "They come in poking around, measuring this and that, checking their maps, trying to figure out where such and such was, where the *town* used to be."

A woman—big, brunette, clad in shorts and a T-shirt, with flip-flops on her feet—stepped out from the hut, waving a spoon. Her name is Christy Thompson, Wesley's wife.

"What the shit were they measuring for *anyway?*" she said. "What's to *measure?*"

Her husband nodded, then continued.

"It's been aggravatin'," he said. "People drivin' up in my yard night and day. White people. Black people. Tellin' me they want me to take 'em down to where the train trestle used to be, or over to the cemetery, or what have you. All these news people, all these reporters. I'm *sick* of it. That that happened was in 1932 or 1923 or whenever it was. That is *history.*"

He popped open another can.

"Shit, what has happened is this thing has gotten blowed way out of proportion. Every person in the state of *Florida* is paying for this, and that just don't get it. That's our *tax* money."

His wife took a seat on a wet plank of pine.

"What are *we* getting out of this?" she asked. "We're right in the middle of it, and we ain't got a damn *thing* out of this except people comin' in here and nosing around.

"What I want to know," she said, "is with all this talk about the coloreds and what they're owed, there hasn't been nothin' said about the *white* people. I mean, from what I've heard, the first persons *shot* in this thing were white people."

Her husband nodded.

"Nigger shot a white man," he said. "That's what started it all. Naturally they all come down and started killin' after that."

The dogs had stopped howling. The TV was turned off. The only sounds were the children splashing in the mud and the rain swishing through the trees. A puppy crawled out from under the porch and curled by the woman's feet, beneath her makeshift bench.

"I don't think it was right what they done," she offered, "I mean, these coloreds were human just like we are. But I don't think these ones out there *now* ought to be reapin' all this profit off it either, not when there's other families that suffered from this, too, *white* families, and nobody's said *diddley*squat about them, and they're not speaking for themselves because they just want to let the past *die*."

Her husband stood and stretched his thin, ropy arms.

"That's the way it's always been, up till now," he said. "Nobody ever said much about this, 'specially those that were actually there. You never heard a word from them, not a *word*.

"I bought this place in 'seventy-two," he said. "From the timber company, *that's* where my deed came from. These niggers talking all about how this land was theirs and they're owed something for it? Are you *kiddin'* me? Those people didn't own this land. Shit, *they* were owned, basically. That's what they were, owned by the lumber company."

The others chuckled again. The rain was falling harder now, beads of water hanging from the brims of their caps.

"Those '60 Minutes' people," he said, "I never will forget that. I come home from work over at the power plant, and here's a TV crew set up out there by the gate, and there's two old niggers sitting there in chairs, and here's this other nigger I recognized from the television, that Bradley man, and he's leaning on the fence, talking to the camera and interviewing these other two niggers, and all I could think was what the *hell* is goin' on here?"

He took another draw from his beer.

"I mean, most of the time a black man comes up in this yard, I turn the *dogs* loose on him. We got to feed our dogs every now and then."

His companions snickered. His wife waved them quiet.

"Blacks have *never* been welcomed around here," she said.

"You got *that* right," said her husband. "When I was growing up over in Cedar Key, we didn't know what a nigger *was*. There used to be a few livin' up on what they called Nigger Hill, but there ain't none there now, not 'less they import 'em in and they leave before dark."

More snickers.

"You see them come in once in a while to visit the island," said the woman. "Just like the other tourists. I saw a couple of 'em not long ago, a black man and woman riding bicycles down by the pier, but I guarantee they didn't spend the night. They've *all* been told there's only one way in and one way out and you better be out before dark."

"That's just the way it is," said the man. "This is not just history. I was working with a company out of Gainesville, buildin' a water plant over at Suwannee, down at the mouth of the river, and a bunch of them old-timers was sittin' around there. We had some black men working with us, and one of these colored guys walks over to these old crackers and says, 'Where do the *black* people hang out around here?'

"And this one old fella, he looked at him a little while, not sayin' a word, then he pointed up at a branch on this big oak tree and said, 'Well, the last black that hung out around here hung right up there.'

"Needless to say, them blacks went back up to Cross City for the night, where there's some of their kind, and that's where they stayed."

The others were picking up their weapons now, moving toward the woods. The woman was back in the hut, tending the stove. Wesley Thompson collected some crushed beer cans and dropped them in a pail.

"I don't like any of this," he said, shaking his head and grabbing his bow. "I don't like it worth a *shit*.

"And I'll tell you where it started," he said, lifting his cap and wiping his brow. "It started that Saturday, I think it was, when that colored man come up here poking around."

He pulled his cap back on and shook his head.

"Yep," he said, spitting on the ground by his feet, "that's what it was."

He rubbed the spit into the mud with the toe of his boot.

"Colored man with a cane."

ACKNOWLEDGMENTS

First, I must thank the survivors, who had the courage, kindness and grace to open their lives and share their stories with a stranger: Minnie Lee Langley; A. T. Goins; Wilson Hall; Willie Evans; Dorothy Goins Hosey; Mary Hall Daniels; Margie Hall Johnson; Robie Mortin; and, through his wife Lugenia, Lonnie Carroll.

My gratitude also to the relatives of Rosewood's survivors and deceased alike, who took me into their trust to help me understand: Arnett Doctor; Yvonne Doctor; Eva Jenkins; Vera Goins Hamilton; Mae McDonald; Annie Bell Lee; Altamese Wrispus; Janie Bradley Black; Anna Maude Goins; Dorothy Smith; Gregery Mortin; Albert Edwards; Sylvia Juanita Richardson; Gwendolyn Johnson; and Katherine Hall.

Special thanks go to Ernest Parham, Doyal and Fuji Scoggins, Martha Pillsbury Thompson, and Walter and Carolyn Pillsbury for sharing their own stories and those of their forebears. Also thanks to George Sandora, Leonard Reynolds, Wesley and Christy Thompson, Herb Wilkerson, Eleanor Travers, Kellie Meyhoff, Don Hatcher, Kenny Collins, Lloyd Collins, Liza Collins, Randolph J. Hodges, and scores of others who asked not to be mentioned by name, for helping me see and understand Levy County, both present and past.

In terms of general historical direction, I must first thank the professionals themselves, the members of the state's Rosewood investigative research team: Maxine Jones, Tom Dye, Bill Rogers, David Colburn and Larry Rivers. The staff at Florida State University's Robert Manning Strozier Library, particularly Gay Dixon and Grace Brock, helped steer me into some of the more arcane corners of the state's history. I am also indebted to the staff of Florida A&M University's Black Archives Research Center and Museum. Others who helped with various local history were Midge Laughlin, archivist with the St. Petersburg Museum of History; Liz Ehrbar, director of the Cedar Key Historical Society Museum; the staff at the Cedar Key State Museum; the staff at Dade City's Hugh Embry Public Library; and Jan H. Johannes, Sr., whose history of Nassau County included useful background on the town of Hilliard.

For their guidance through the legal and legislative layers of this story, I thank Steve Hanlon, Martha Barnett, Jim Peters, Richard Hixson, Greg Galloway, Al Lawson, and Miguel De Grandy. I would also like to thank Bo Johnson, Elaine Gordon, Richard Trammell, Pete Antonacci, Manny Dobrinsky, John Long, Bill Posey, Robert Wexler, Daryl Jones and Charlie Williams for sharing their own roles in the Rosewood bill's legislative journey. I am deeply indebted as well to the staff of the Florida Legislative Library Services Division in Tallahassee, especially archivist Delbra McGriff, and to the Florida State Archives, where David Coles and James Helms shared their expert advice.

I offer my gratitude to Greg Durden, Guy David Robinson and Frank Beisler of the Florida Attorney General's Office of Civil Rights for their assistance above and beyond the call of duty.

The library staffs of several Florida newspapers were immensely generous in opening their files to me. Those newspapers, and the particular people who helped me, include: the *Tampa Tribune* (Alyce Diamandis and Buddy Jaudon); the *Tallahassee Democrat* (Deborah Galloway); the *St. Petersburg Times* (Caroline Ziadie); the *Orlando Sentinel* (Cate Nolan); the *Palm Beach Post* (Sammy Alzofon); and the *Nassau County News-Leader* (Mary Hurst).

Journalist Gary Moore, whose 1982 investigation of Rosewood was a catalyst for many of the events that followed, was very generous in sharing his insights and overviews. Also helpful were reporters Peter Gallagher and Charles Flowers of the *Seminole Tribune* and Eric Harrison of the *Los Angeles Times,* producer Joel Bernstein of CBS News, Brad Wasson of the University of Florida's office of news and public affairs, and Judy Sedgeman, former editor of *The Floridian,* the *St. Petersburg Times*'s Sunday magazine. I would like to thank as well Joe Capozzi of the *Palm Beach Post.*

For the photographs that so enrich these pages, I must first thank the families who trusted me with truly priceless personal snapshots and portraits, particularly Arnett and Yvonne Doctor, Martha Pillsbury Thompson, and Walter and Carolyn Pillsbury. I would also like to thank Joan Morris with the Florida State Archives, Kelly Cooley with Florida State University, Lissette Nabut with the *Miami Herald,* Ron Kolwak and Michelle Dwaskin with the *Tampa Tribune,* Hugh Scoggins, Wendy Ledis with the *Palm Beach Post,* and Terry Witt. Beth Bergman of the *Virginian-Pilot* deserves a special nod for her sensitive eye and magical touch.

On the home front, for their support, encouragement, advice, and—in several cases— sheer sweat, I want to thank Millie Johnson, Joan Ange Shepard, Fred Kirsch, Erika Reif, Cole Campbell, Marvin Lake, Wil Haygood, Randy Jessee, Dave Potvin, Carol Taylor, Cass Fullerton, Susan Raihofer, and Kate Murphy.

Finally, for her wisdom, patience and unending enthusiasm, I will always be grateful to my editor Jane Isay. And, yet again, for his faith and guidance I thank my agent David Black.

NOTES AND SOURCES

PROLOGUE

This account of the January, 1923, attack on Rosewood is based on a synthesis of sources. As Florida State University history professor Maxine Jones told me after she and her colleagues on the state's academic study team had finished investigating this event, "It would be impossible to recreate exactly what happened."

My primary sources were the nine living survivors, each of whom I visited at their homes in Florida during the summer and fall of 1994 and the spring of 1995. Two other primary sources—Ernest Parham, whom I interviewed at his home in Orlando in the fall of 1994, and his sister-in-law Martha Pillsbury Thompson, whom I interviewed several times by telephone at her home in Jacksonville—were witnesses to that week's events and helped provide the perspective of the white community in Sumner. All of these men and women—except for survivor Lonnie Carroll, who is too ill to speak—shared with me the experience as seen through their own young eyes. Several spouses and direct descendants of Rosewood survivors shared with me as well the stories their parents had told them about the town and the attack.

Besides my own interviews, I was able to refer to transcripts of sworn statements made by each of the survivors to attorneys from the law firm of Holland and Knight in 1992 and '93. The state's academic study team members interviewed each of the survivors as well in the fall of 1993. The transcripts of those interviews were helpful, as were the transcripts of all testimonies given at the Florida House of Representatives Special Master Hearing conducted in Tallahassee during February and March of 1994.

I was also able to review all affidavits filed with the Florida Attorney General's Office of Civil Rights by Rosewood survivor claimants; many of those affidavits contained useful details about the town and the attack. Also helpful were transcripts of interviews with survivor claimants conducted in the fall of 1994 by Investigator Frank Beisler of the Attorney General's Office of Civil Rights.

The dozens of state and national newspaper accounts published the week of the attack in January, 1923—though conflicting in many cases—were helpful in providing some details of events. Also helpful were several modern-day newspaper and magazine articles written about Rosewood, most notably two lengthy pieces written by journalist Gary Moore—the first published in the *St. Petersburg Times* in July, 1982, and the second published in *The Miami Herald* in March, 1993. An unpublished paper on the Rosewood attack titled "Rosewood, Florida: The Destruction of an African-American Community," written by historian Tom Dye, who was a member of the study team commissioned by the state to investigate Rosewood, provided useful information as well. The state's study team's report, *A Documented History of the Incident Which Occurred at Rosewood, Florida, in January 1923,* along with a detailed review of that report, included a multitude of facts which were crucial in piecing together what transpired that week.

Finally, of course, it was necessary to personally visit the site itself, which I did numerous times during the spring, summer and fall of 1994, walking the acreage behind the old John Wright house, as well as exploring the ground around Sumner where the old sawmill town had once stood.

CHAPTER ONE: OLD NEWS

I first met Arnett Doctor in the law offices of Holland and Knight in downtown Tampa in April of 1994. It had been only twelve days since the Florida Senate had voted in favor of the Rosewood claims bill. Governor Lawton Chiles had yet to sign the bill into law.

Doctor was wearing an Orlando Magic sweatsuit, a ball cap, a pair of high-topped Reebok tennis shoes—and a witheringly skeptical expression. We sat in a conference room with a commanding view of the city's skyline. His leather briefcase, spilling over with papers, file folders and lists of addresses and phone numbers, sat open on the table. During the course of this first conversation, Doctor was coy, careful, suspicious. We were interrupted several times by telephone calls buzzed in by the firm's receptionist. One, Doctor whispered, was from a movie producer. Another, he told me, conspiratorially, was from an *Esquire* magazine reporter. This was apparently a busy man, and he wanted me to know it.

During the ensuing fall, as we spent days together in Doctor's home in east Tampa, he was constantly interrupted by a ringing telephone. The process of verifying and paying Rosewood bill claimants was ongoing by then, and Doctor considered it his duty to hound the Attorney General's office. If he wasn't dialing attorneys or newspaper reporters, prodding the state, he was answering calls from family members anxious to know about the status of the government payments, as well as about any information Doctor could give them concerning the movies and books and magazine articles all rumored to be in the works. So much was in the works in the wake of the families' legislative victory that spring.

As we spent more time together, Arnett began to relax, to open up, to share personal details he had been reluctant to divulge in the beginning, details about both himself and his relatives. Much of the first half of this book revolves around those details, around the shadow Rosewood threw over scores of these families through the better part of this century, and around the struggles and squabbling they faced among themselves during the decade it took for them to finally come together and take action against the state.

This first chapter is based primarily on Arnett's recollections of his boyhood in St. Petersburg. I visited the places Arnett described: Jordan Park, 22nd Street, the Manhattan Casino, South Mole Beach, the Million-Dollar Pier. I also interviewed Arnett's uncle, Arnett Turner ("A. T.") Goins, in August, 1994, at his home in St. Petersburg, where he corroborated, corrected and fleshed out many of Arnett's memories. Arnett's sister, Yvonne, was also helpful during numerous telephone conversations we had in the spring and summer of 1995. Midge Laughlin, archivist of the St. Petersburg Museum of History, shared her personal knowledge and recollections of the city—including her own memories of the Manhattan Casino—as well as providing other details about St. Petersburg's history. An excellent source on the history of St. Petersburg is Raymond Arsenault's *St. Petersburg and the Florida Dream* (Norfolk: The Donning Company, 1988).

I interviewed John Taylor, owner of Lundy's Liquor Store, by telephone in the spring of 1995. Taylor confirmed Arnett's account of the Friday afternoon in 1982 when Arnett first met Gary Moore, although Taylor did not know about Arnett's pistol. "I didn't know he carried a gun on the job," Taylor told me. "I kept a pistol in the store myself, but I didn't *carry* it."

Gary Moore verified the account of his first encounter with Arnett Doctor during a June, 1995, telephone interview from his home in Tupelo, Mississippi.

Arnett could not provide a specific date, or even year, for the death of Wallace Jordan in Lacoochee, nor could any of his Lacoochee relatives, although they all recalled it. In May of 1995, I obtained a copy of Wallace Jordan's death certificate from the Florida Office of Vital Statistics in Jacksonville. The date on the certificate, which did not include the cause of death, was March 7, 1957. That would mean Arnett was fourteen when Jordan died, not ten, as Arnett remembers. But Arnett insisted he was ten, even after I told him about the certificate. "There is no way that happened in 1957," he said. "I was still living in the quarters in Lacoochee when Wallace Jordan was killed. We lived three doors down from the Jordans there. By 1957 we had moved over to Mosstown. There's no *way* that happened in '57."

I then called the Pasco County Sheriff's Department, where Denise Mills, the records clerk, spent two days searching for the record of Wallace Jordan's death. She found nothing. "It's odd," she told me. "There *was* a death, so we should be able to show something. Of course," she added, "way back then there's no telling how they handled things."

As for the account of Arnett's prison experience, it is based on interviews with him and on a copy of his prison record, which I obtained in January, 1995, from the Florida Department of Corrections in Tallahassee. The file described Arnett as "an above average inmate," who "spends his spare time reading."

CHAPTER TWO: A WALL OF DARKNESS

This chapter is based primarily on interviews with Arnett and Yvonne Doctor. A. T. Goins also shared his memories of his sister Philomena's emotional pain about Rosewood. When I visited Vera Goins Hamilton in August, 1994, at her home in Lacoochee, she talked about her older sister, Philomena, and what life in Lacoochee had been like for them all in the 1940s and '50s.

Historical information on the Cummer and Sons Company was found in many newspaper stories and columns on file in the library of the *Tampa Tribune* newspaper. Most notable was a September 15, 1979, article by Dale Wilson titled "Lacoochee Just Couldn't Keep Lumbering Along." Biographical background on the Cummer family and their business interests both in Michigan and in Florida is included in *Florida: Historic—Dramatic—Contemporary: Family and Personal History* (New York: Lewis Historical Publishing Company, 1952).

CHAPTER THREE: "IF THAT AIN'T COUNTRY"

The description of the drive down Route 19 from Tallahassee to Levy County came from my notes taken while making that trip several times during the spring, summer and fall of 1994. The descriptions of modern-day Cedar Key came from several visits made during that same time period.

I interviewed approximately two dozen Cedar Key residents during this time, many of whom asked not to be identified. Among those who did not mind giving their names and who were most hospitable as well as helpful were Eleanor Travers ("Miss El"), owner of the Cedar

Inn motel; Kellie Meyhoff, who tends bar at the L&M; Don Hatcher, a local clam farmer; and the Collins family—Kenny, who runs a small machine shop on the island, his brother Lloyd, who guides tourists on fishing excursions into the Gulf, and their mother Liza, who has spent all seventy-seven years of her life on Cedar Key.

George Sandora, executive director of the Levy County Development Authority in Bronson, spent an October, 1994, afternoon gathering and helping me understand the current demographic and economic statistics of Cedar Key and its surrounding inland area, including Rosewood.

The Cedar Key Historical Society Museum was a source for some of the history of this region. Another source was the Cedar Key State Museum, located at the north end of the island. It was there that I found a copy of *A Thousand-Mile Walk to the Gulf,* by John Muir, edited by William Frederic Bade (Boston: Houghton-Mifflin, 1944), which includes Muir's account of his visit to Florida and Cedar Key, from which the quotations in this chapter were taken.

Search for Yesterday: A History of Levy County, Florida (Bronson, Fla.: Levy County Archives Committee), a series of interviews, oral histories, records and photographs collected by Levy County historians during the late 1970s and early 1980s, contains a wealth of detailed information about day-to-day life in early twentieth-century Levy County. A short, but fascinating section on that same period of time in this region is included in *Florida: A Guide to the Southernmost State,* compiled and written by the Federal Writer's Project of the Work Projects Administration for the State of Florida (New York: Oxford University Press, 1939). An invaluable source as well for the area's history is Tom Dye's master's thesis, titled "Race, Ethnicity and the Politics of Economic Development: A Case Study of Cedar Key, Florida," submitted to the Florida State History Department in the fall of 1992.

Cedar Key's violent heritage is vividly recounted in a July 25, 1959, *Tampa Sunday Tribune* story titled "Cedar Key Old Timers Recall Wild Gun Fights," by Sam Mase. The story, with photographs of barefooted fishermen and graphic accounts of gun battles and knife fights, called turn-of-the-century Cedar Key "probably the toughest town in the South."

Gary Moore described his discovery of the Rosewood story during our June, 1995, telephone interview. The account he shared with me was the same as the author's note that appeared with his March 7, 1993, *Miami Herald Tropic* magazine story titled "The Rosewood Massacre." "I would take weekend trips, looking for color stories," he wrote. "The more obscure, the better." He described coming to Cedar Key seeking a "travel story," but once he was there, he "felt something much deeper." That feeling led him to the discovery of Rosewood. In a synopsis of his research, included among the documents stored at the Florida State Archives, Moore wrote, "Like the public at large, I personally had never heard of Rosewood."

The tales of Rosewood victims' body parts in Levy County abound. Gary Moore described several in his 1982 newspaper account. Twelve years later, an October 16, 1994, *Los Angeles Times Magazine* story on Rosewood by the *Times*'s Atlanta bureau chief, Eric Harrison, quoted former *Cedar Key Beacon* editor Robin Raftis as saying she had seen "penises, testicles, fingers, even toes. You name it," she said, "they jarred it." I had tried calling Robin Raftis myself six months earlier, at the *Beacon* office in Cedar Key. Her husband, Mike "Salty" Raftis, answered the phone and told me Robin had left the newspaper and was no longer in town. When I asked how to contact her, he told me they were both working on their own book about Rosewood and neither she nor he would be able to talk to me. This was something I discovered early in my reporting on this story—that a lot of people seemed to be working on a lot of books and movies about Rosewood.

I heard several Rosewood body parts stories myself during my visits to Levy County. The most vivid came from a man I interviewed at his home in Chiefland on the last Friday night of September, 1994. The man—a former administrator with the Levy County Public School system—had written an unpublished, fictionalized account of the Rosewood attack, which was referred to in a December 28, 1992, *Miami Herald* story by a reporter named Lori Rosza. The man told me Rosza had promised she would not use his name in the story, but then did. I left several phone messages on Rosza's answering machine at her *Herald* office over the course of several months, to ask about this and other matters concerning Rosewood, but I did not hear back from her.

The Chiefland educator was reluctant at first to meet with me. Ultimately he invited me to his home, where he and his wife prepared a meal of fried catfish and grouper, caught fresh that day, he pointed out. He exacted the same promise of anonymity from me that he had from Rosza, then he proceeded to talk for several hours about the tales he had heard over the years from old-timers about Rosewood. He too had heard about body parts, but he never believed the stories, he said, until he stopped for gas several years ago at a Pure Oil filling station in Bronson. He was inside chatting with the owner when "a man" walked into the office: "He had something in a bottle and was showing it off. I didn't say a word, not till he left. Then I asked Len what was that in that jar? He said that was that black man's thumb that they cut off in Rosewood. They cut off the man's ears too, he told me. He said some say they cut off his *dick*. That was the first time I ever saw anything like that."

The only threatening encounter I had during my time in Levy County was with a man named Jesse Taylor. People around Cedar Key call him "'Ol Cuz," and I was told he was the brother of James Taylor, Fannie Taylor's husband.

It was a rainy Sunday morning when I knocked on the screen door of Taylor's tin-roofed home at the end of a dead-end lane in the center of the island. A large, bald man in stocking feet, slacks and a light sportshirt answered the door. He wore eyeglasses. A slight pot belly sagged over the belt of his trousers. Behind him, a formica table was covered with neat rows of playing cards. I had interrupted a game of solitaire.

I told him I was a writer working on a book, that I was interested in some of the history of Cedar Key, and that I'd heard he was a man who knew more about this town than just about anyone on the island—all of which was true. I did not mention Rosewood.

He remained behind the locked screen door, his eyes squinting as I spoke. "You're not a *reporter* now, are you?" he asked. "Now don't you *lie* to me."

I said again that I was writing a book, not a newspaper article. Again, I did not mention Rosewood—not yet. He stared hard, then let me in, told me to take a seat and settled himself in a large lounge chair. I began to ask a few questions, just chatting—Did he live here alone? Was he retired? What did he used to do for a living?—and he immediately cut me off.

"I thought you wanted to know about Cedar *Key*," he said, narrowing his eyes again and leaning forward. "You *sure* you're not a goddamn reporter?"

So we talked about Cedar Key. In the course of the conversation, he shared a few things about himself. He was about to turn eighty-five, he said. He was a bachelor, never married. He'd done some time as a merchant seaman during his middle years, but most of his working life had been spent right here, on the decks of those fishing boats down by the Cedar Key waterfront.

"Now if you want *bullshit,*" he said, "go on down to those docks. I've heard so many goddamn stories about this and that that was supposed to have happened around here from people who weren't even *born* then. None of 'em knows what the hell they're talking about. Those bastards *love* gossip, and that's what they do. Gossip. Pure bullshit."

The house we sat in was at the island's highest point. I asked him if we were anywhere near the place they called "Nigger Hill."

"This *is* Nigger Hill," he said. "There was niggers lived in this house right here. Almost three hundred of them lived up around here at one time. But ain't none of 'em here any more. Not one. They just left. Left and died out."

We went on chatting for another half hour, talking about hurricanes, about the big cocaine bust they had in town a few years back—"Operation Fishhook," the DEA agents called it—and we talked about the island's art festival, how large it had grown. Then I mentioned this story I'd been reading so much about during the past year, the story of this place they called Rosewood.

He bolted from his chair, sprang to his feet and thrust a thick, quivering finger toward my face.

"*Goddamnit!*" he yelled. "I *knew* it! *Rosewood! That's* why you came to my house. *Shit! I knew* it."

That was the end of the interview. Later that afternoon, with rain still falling in sheets, I drove past the end of that lane. As I went by, I could see four pickup trucks parked in front of Taylor's house. A group of five men, younger than Taylor, a couple cuffing cigarettes, were standing on his front porch, out of the rain. I didn't know if the gathering had anything to do with me, but I wasn't about to stop and find out.

CHAPTER FOUR: GROUND ZERO

The details of Philomena Doctor's life came from interviews with Arnett Doctor in Tampa and with Yvonne Doctor in St. Petersburg, as well as with Philomena's sister Vera Hamilton in Lacoochee. I also spoke by telephone in March, 1995, with Janie Bradley Black in Miami. Black was Lee Ruth Bradley's niece and was very involved in the Lacoochee branches of the various Rosewood families. Her memories of Philomena Goins's matriarchal power within those families concurred with the accounts of virtually all the survivors and descendants whom I interviewed.

Arnett's mother may indeed have shared a stage with Ella Fitzgerald, but Fitzgerald's spokespeople say she did not. When I called Salle Productions, Fitzgerald's production company in Beverly Hills, in October, 1994, Margaret Nutt, who said she has worked with Fitzgerald for thirty years, told me it was "highly unlikely" that Philomena Goins ever sang with Ella Fitzgerald during the 1930s. "As far as we know," said Nutt, "Ella never sang with anyone. They didn't have any 'backup' singers, no chorus. Ella sat with the band back then, as a member of the band. There were no 'warmup' acts either. There was never any other woman but Ella, no woman, period."

The account of Arnett's Saturday visit to Rosewood with Gary Moore comes from interviews with Arnett, with Wesley and Christy Thompson, who own the property on which the small Rosewood cemetery is located, and with Moore. When I visited the Thompsons at their home in Rosewood in October, 1994, Thompson and his wife took me through the woods behind their trailer to the cemetery, where the gravestones still lay, including Martine Goins's, which had been knocked over since Arnett first discovered it. "See," said Christy Thompson, pointing at the stone, "what's the big deal?"

CHAPTER FIVE: THE DEATH OF A DOG

The January, 1923, Florida and national newspaper reports of the events in Rosewood were found in both the microfilm periodicals collection and the special collections department at Florida State University's Robert Manning Strozier Library.

A proliferation of books and articles exists on the "lynching era" in America. Those which provided source material for this chapter, both general and specific, include: *A Festival of Violence: An Analysis of Southern Lynchings, 1882–1930,* by Stewart E. Tolnay and E.M. Beck (Urbana: University of Illinois Press, 1995); *Lynching in the New South,* by W. Fitzhugh Brundage (Urbana: University of Illinois Press, 1993); *The NAACP Crusade Against Lynching, 1909–1950,* by Robert L. Zangrando (Philadelphia: Temple University Press, 1980); *The Anti-Lynching Movement: 1883–1932,* by Donald L. Grant (San Francisco: R and E Research Associates, 1975); *Race Riot: Chicago in the Red Summer of 1919,* by William M. Tuttle, Jr. (New York: Atheneum, 1970); *Racial Violence in the United States,* edited by Allen D. Grimshaw (Chicago: Aldine Publishing Co., 1969); *Urban Racial Violence in the Twentieth Century,* by Joseph Boskin (Beverly Hills: Glencoe Press, 1969); *A History of the South, Volume X: "The Emergence of the New South, 1913–1945,"* by George Brown Tindall (Baton Rouge: Louisiana State University Press, 1967); *Race Riot at East St. Louis, July 2, 1917,* by Elliott M. Rudwick (Carbondale: Southern Illinois University Press, 1964); *Mark Twain on the Damned Human Race,* edited by Janet Smith (New York: Hill and Wang, 1962); *Mark Twain: Social Critic,* by Philip S. Foner (New York: International Publishers, 1958); and *Rope and Faggot,* by Walter White (New York: Alfred A. Knopf, 1929). Of all these books, and dozens more written on the subject of lynching in the South, the only one that mentions Rosewood is Tindall's—and the single sentence it gives the subject short-counts the damage and the deaths: ". . . the race riots petered out in 1923," wrote Tindall, on page 154 of his text. "The last serious affair was at Rosewood, Florida, where a white mob in search of an alleged Negro rapist ran amuck through the Negro community, burned six houses and a church, and left five Negroes and two whites dead."

Details of several of the specific lynchings described in this chapter come from the NAACP lynching records stored at the Tuskegee Institute and included in the appendix to *A Documented History of the Incident which Occurred at Rosewood, Florida, in January 1923,* by Maxine D. Jones, Larry E. Rivers, David R. Colburn, R. Tom Dye and William R. Rogers. This report was the result of the 1993 study commissioned by the Florida legislature to investigate the attack on Rosewood.

An excellent source for the etymology of the term "cracker" is an article titled "Cracker: The History of a Southeastern Ethnic, Economic, and Racial Epithet," by John Solomon Otto in the March, 1987, issue of *NAMES, the Journal of the American Name Society.*

CHAPTER SIX: SWEET POTATOES

This chapter is based primarily on my interview in September, 1994, with Minnie Lee Langley at her home in Jacksonville and several subsequent telephone interviews with her. Supplemental information came from a copy of Minnie Lee's sworn statement recorded by attorneys from Holland and Knight in June, 1992; from a transcript of her September, 1993, interview with Tom Dye of the academic investigative team; from a transcript of her testimony before the Florida House of Representatives Special Master in February, 1994; and from a copy of Florida Attorney General's Office of Civil Rights Investigator Frank Beisler's notes from his interview with Langley in September, 1994.

CHAPTER SEVEN: HARD DIRT

This chapter is based primarily on an interview I had with Arnett T. ("A. T.") Goins at his home in St. Petersburg in August, 1994. Additional information came from Goins's sworn statement given to Holland and Knight attorneys in February, 1993; from a transcript of Goins's September, 1993, interview with Dr. Larry E. Rivers of the state's academic investigative team; from a transcript of Goins's testimony before Florida's House Special Master in February, 1994; and from Investigator Frank Beisler's notes from his interview with Goins in September, 1994.

Information on Goins's life also came from interviews with his wife Anna Maude and with his nephew and niece, Arnett and Yvonne Doctor. When I tried to interview Goins's daughter, Annette Goins Shakir, by telephone in May, 1995, she refused, saying she would call me back after she spoke to her attorney. I did not hear from her again.

The CBS News "60 Minutes" segment on "The Rosewood Massacre" aired December 11, 1983. A videotape of that broadcast provided some of the visual details A. T. Goins referred to during our interview.

The description of "harvesting" logs in the early part of this century came from viewing a videotape I discovered while visiting Lacoochee in August, 1994. I had stopped at the town's only medical facility—a rural health clinic housed in a trailer near the old "quarters" section of town where Arnett Doctor had once lived—to gather what information I might find there about modern-day Lacoochee. As I chatted with Paula Knight, the clinic manager, she mentioned a tape they had in the back room on the history of the old Cummer and Sons Company logging operation. She fetched it for me to watch on the waiting room's television. The tape, narrated by an unidentified former manager of the Cummer operation, included film footage of loggers in the 1940s wading into the swamp to cut timber. "The same way," noted the narrator, "they been doing it since the 1920s." As the huge cypresses fell on film, the narrator lamented, "Almost makes you want to cry when you see them great big old trees taking their final dive." He lamented, too, in his own way, the harsh working conditions endured by the loggers. "It was a hard way to make a living," he said, "but regular work was hard to find in those days, and this was regular work."

The old days of logging in Lacoochee were also detailed in a May 19, 1985, *Tampa Tribune* story by Sara Nichols titled "Loggers Remember When Timber Business Was King."

Several of the Rosewood survivors I interviewed, as well as Ernest Parham, recalled how central the weekend baseball games were to the social culture of Rosewood. The same was true, said many of the old-timers I talked to, of most rural communities—white or black—in this section of the state. Even Martha Pillsbury Thompson, Ernest Parham's sister-in-law, who was fourteen at the time of the attack on Rosewood, recalled how popular the game of baseball was with the men and boys in both Sumner and Rosewood. Her explanation was simple. "There wasn't much to do back then for entertainment," she said. "You found your fun where you could. The men and boys found it in baseball."

The game of "fireball" was described in great detail by Wilson Hall during my interview with him at his home in Hilliard in September, 1994. A. T. Goins concurred with Hall's description of this game.

A definitive source for the history of black professional baseball leagues, teams and players, many of whom were recalled by A. T. Goins, is *The Biographical Encyclopedia of the Negro Baseball Leagues,* by James A. Riley (New York: Carroll & Graf, 1994).

CHAPTER EIGHT: NO EAR ON EARTH

This chapter is based on interviews with Arnett Doctor and his sister, Yvonne, as well as on interviews with various survivors and descendants who shared many of the same rumors about Rosewood, ranging from Sylvester Carrier's escape to the suggestion that Fannie Taylor is still alive. Some—perhaps all—of these stories may be true, but I was unable to verify any of them.

Ed Bradley of "60 Minutes" responded by letter in early March of 1995 to my inquiry if he was indeed related to the Bradleys of Rosewood. "I am satisfied," he wrote, "that there are no family connections."

Joel Bernstein, producer of that "60 Minutes" piece, was the man who, accompanied by Gary Moore, visited Philomena Doctor's home in the fall of 1993 to ask her to appear on the program. He recalled the meeting when I asked him about it during a telephone interview in June, 1995. "She was very persistent, very stubborn," said Bernstein, "and she made it clear in no uncertain terms that she was not interested. But there was nothing confrontational about it. She didn't throw us off her property. It wasn't like that at all. We just said, Okay, and left."

The notion of interracial Masonic brotherhood as an explanation of why a white fugitive would have fled to the black community of Rosewood is embraced by many of the Rosewood families today. But the history of Freemasonry in the South indicates otherwise. In his book *Middle-Class Blacks in a White Society* (Berkeley: University of California Press, 1975), William Muraskin traces the history of black Masonry in the United States from its beginning in Boston in 1775. A "primary attraction of the Order," writes Muraskin, was the vision of this secret society as a future bridge between blacks and whites in America. "The original hope that Masonry offered black men," writes Muraskin, "was the integration of the races in a common brotherhood."

The reality, however, was that black Masons were rejected by their white counterparts from the beginning, especially in the South, especially after the Civil War. "The South did not like the idea of blacks meeting together without supervision," writes Muraskin, "and an organization such as Masonry appeared especially dangerous to them."

By the turn of the century, the climate among white and black Masons in the South reflected the climate among white and black southerners in general. "Scorpio Africanus is simply a brute, with no revenge or resentments, and no regard for the truth or the purity of women," wrote the Grand Secretary of Mississippi's white Masons in 1909. "Whiskey and co-caine and miscegenation are his bane and until some remedy is found for these great evils, the poor fellow will continue to go down lower and lower in the social scale."

According to Loretta J. Williams, author of *Black Freemasonry and Middle-Class Realities* (Columbia: University of Missouri Press, 1980), even Albert Pike, a nineteenth-century Mason regarded as the leading scholar of his time on the history of the sect, stated more than once that he would leave the Order before he would recognize a black Mason as a brother and risk being "contaminated by the leprosy of Negro association."

While history seems to refute the notion that Rosewood burned because of interracial Masonic loyalty, the fact that there was a Masonic lodge in Rosewood and that many of the men among that community were high-ranking members of that Order bolsters the claim that this was more than a mere collection of shanties in the swamp, that Rosewood was a viable middle-class community. Masonry, writes Muraskin, has always been "one of the bulwarks of the black middle class. It has worked to separate its members, both socially and psychologically, from the black masses." It has done so, writes Muraskin, by emphasizing, "the values of work, thrift, charity, property ownership, and business efficiency"—precisely the qualities so many Rosewood descendants point to with pride when they recall the black community their parents and grandparents built.

CHAPTER NINE: SMOKE AND FOG

The account of Arnett Doctor's visit to the Levy County Courthouse comes from my interviews with him. Physical descriptions of the drive to Bronson and of the town itself come from those interviews and from my own visit to Bronson in October, 1994.

Much of the census and property records information cited in this chapter comes from Arnett's personal files. Some comes from records included in the appendix to the state's investigative study team's report. And some comes from microfilm copies of the 1900, 1910 and 1920 federal census reports for Levy County, which I examined at the Florida State Archives in Tallahassee during my visits there in the fall of 1994.

Details of Ed Goins's business and property holdings in Rosewood can be found in the state's study team report. Statistics indicating the area's economic decline by the early 1920s are also included in that report, as well as in Tom Dye's study of the history of Cedar Key, cited earlier.

CHAPTER TEN: SOUL FOOD

The account of the beginnings of the Rosewood Family Reunions and the conflicts and confrontations that occurred during the ensuing years are based on interviews with Arnett Doctor, Yvonne Doctor, Vera Goins Hamilton, Annie Bell Lee, Altamese Wrispus, Eva Jenkins, Janie Bradley Black, A. T. Goins, Willie Evans and Dorothy Hosey.

I found several accounts of the history of the Mosstown section of Lacoochee—including various references to the Depression-era gathering and selling of moss—in the files of the *Tampa Tribune*. The most detailed account of moss gathering was a *Tribune* column by Carol Jeffares published in December, 1984.

Vera Goins Hamilton shared her recollections of Rosewood and of her life after the attack when I visited her home in Lacoochee in August, 1994.

Dade City's Hugh Embry Public Library was a source of several newspaper stories and locally produced pamphlets describing the history of the city's citrus packing industry—particularly that of the Pasco Packing Association, which is known today as the Lykes Pasco Packing Company. A May, 1986, *Tampa Tribune* story written by Leland Hawes, marking the fiftieth anniversary of the Lykes Pasco operation, provided several details included in this chapter.

The Rosewood family members' 1987 visit to the old Wright house was recalled in interviews with Vera Hamilton, Eva Jenkins and Willie Evans, as well as with Doyal and Fuji Scoggins, whom I visited at their home in October, 1994.

The accounts of the interfamily disputes in Rosewood are based on interviews with Arnett Doctor and other family members. The record of Sylvester and Hayward Carrier's 1918 arrest is included in the *State of Florida Prison Record Book, 1900–1920,* which I examined in the Florida State Archives in Tallahassee in October, 1994.

The account of Philomena Doctor's death is based on interviews with Arnett and Yvonne Doctor.

CHAPTER ELEVEN: THE FIRE THIS TIME

I interviewed Michael O'McCarthy several times over the telephone at his home in South Carolina, beginning with two extensive conversations in January, 1995. By then I had already spoken with scores of Rosewood survivors, descendants and attorneys. Whenever Michael O'McCarthy's name was mentioned by any of them, it was with a raised eyebrow and a tone of skepticism, if not outright disdain.

The man I spoke with on the telephone seemed straightforward, if a bit aggressive. He was candid about the details of his past struggles with alcohol and drugs, of his incarceration both in reform school and in prison, and of the variety of motivations that drove him as a political activist, as a radical journalist, and finally as the film producer he is today. As he detailed the twisting arc of the lifelong journey that led him to Rosewood, I found the story both improbable and preposterous, too incredible to believe. Then I checked out what facts I could, and they were all true. His account of the Florida reform school was there, on page 122 of *Growing up Southern* (New York: Pantheon Books, 1981). His behind-bars relationship with George Jackson was there, on page 31 of *Soledad Brother* (New York: Coward-McCann, 1970). He and the counterculture co-authors he claimed were out to expose the entire police state in America were there, lined up in a photograph on the title page of *The Glass House Tapes* (New York: Avon Books, 1973). And there was his photo again, eight years later, in the July 23, 1981, issue of *Rolling Stone* magazine, this time posed alongside some of his Vietnam veteran buddies.

Gary Moore recounted his initial contact with O'McCarthy during our June, 1995, telephone interview. Again, Moore's memory concurred with an account he had already written, this one in a letter dated August 10, 1993, sent to the state's academic investigating team as they were launching their study. "In the summer of 1991," wrote Moore, "McCarthy called me because of my research and expressed eagerness to make a movie about Rosewood, which he said would be built around a presentday [sic] hook: testimony in a courtroom-style setting by aged survivors decades after the destruction. I demured [sic], saying no such public testimony had ever occurred in real life. McCarthy then stopped calling me. I heard no more from him for more than a year."

O'McCarthy's account of his first meeting with Lee Ruth Davis was corroborated by Davis's niece, Janie Bradley Black. The racial strife and rioting during the 1980s in both the Liberty City and Overtown sections of Miami are well documented in national newspapers and magazines. I drove to Liberty City in March, 1995, retracing O'McCarthy's route through the neighborhood where Lee Ruth Davis lived in 1992. This chapter's physical description of that community comes both from O'McCarthy's memories and from my own notes.

The quotation from the NAACP letter to O'McCarthy comes from a copy of that letter, dated October 29, 1991, mailed from the organization's national headquarters in Baltimore and signed by then-NAACP Deputy Executive Director George E. Carter.

An account of O'McCarthy's pursuit and discovery of Lee Ruth Davis and Minnie Lee Langley is included in the October 16, 1994, *Los Angeles Times Magazine* story by Eric Harrison, titled "A Massacre, The Movies, and the Obligations of Memory."

CHAPTER TWELVE: EAT WHAT YOU KILL

I first met Steve Hanlon at his law office in Tallahassee in April, 1994. In September of that year, I returned for two days of interviews there, followed by numerous telephone interviews during the ensuing months. This chapter is based on those interviews, as well as on interviews with Michael O'McCarthy which confirmed the details of O'McCarthy's initial contact with Hanlon concerning Rosewood.

The descriptions of previous cases handled by Hanlon's Community Services Team came from Holland and Knight records shared by Hanlon and from newspaper accounts. Hanlon's legal services work in Tampa was the focus of a March 13, 1991, *Tampa Tribune* story by Suzie Siegel titled "In Defense of the Poor."

The pro bono division of Holland and Knight was the subject of a *Wall Street Journal* article by Eric Morgenthaler titled "For the Public Good," published April 8, 1994.

Profiles of Chesterfield Smith—each highlighting his housecleaning attitude as president of the American Bar Association and his controversial condemnation of Richard Nixon—appeared in the February 18, 1974, issue of *Time* magazine and in the April 15, 1974, issue of *Newsweek*.

CHAPTER THIRTEEN: TINY ISLAND

This chapter is based on interviews with Arnett Doctor at his home in Tampa, where he shared his files of correspondence from 1991 and '92, when he was trying without success to find legal representation for the families' case.

"Grunting gators" was a common practice among some of Lacoochee's white population as well as its blacks, according to one of the town's white old-timers, a man named Horace Morgan, who described the practice in an August 23, 1987, *Tampa Tribune* story titled "He Recalls Days of Fish and Gators," by Carol Jeffares.

Arnett's account of the monkey on the island was confirmed by Steve Shepard, manager of the John B. Sargent Sr. County Park, where the fishing spot Arnett described is located. "A lot of people have seen this 'monkey,' including some of our staff," Shepard told me when I called him in May, 1995. But the animal, said Shepard, is actually not a monkey at all. "We suspect it's probably a *coatimundi,*" he said, "a member of the raccoon family. It's not an animal usually found in this area, but some people like to keep them as pets, and this may be one that got away, or that someone wanted to get rid of. It's got a long tail, it likes to climb trees and forage along the riverbank, and it's bigger than a raccoon. If you're at a distance, it can sure *look* like a monkey."

Albert Edwards confirmed the account of the claims bill discussion he had with Arnett in a June, 1995, telephone interview from Edwards's home in Deland.

CHAPTER FOURTEEN: ORIGINAL SIN

This chapter is based on interviews with Steve Hanlon, Michael O'McCarthy, Minnie Lee Langley and Janie Bradley Black.

CHAPTER FIFTEEN: A DELICATE DANCE

I interviewed Al Lawson at his insurance office in Tallahassee in October, 1994. A month after that, I interviewed Miguel De Grandy by telephone at his law office in Miami. Subsequent telephone interviews with both men, as well as with Steve Hanlon, confirmed and fleshed out the facts contained in this chapter.

Also helpful were several newspaper profiles of both men. Two *Tallahassee Democrat* accounts of Al Lawson's 1982 and 1986 campaigns were especially useful in understanding his approach to politics. The first, written by Ann M. Doyle and titled "House 9 a Race of Quiet Dignity, Rags-to-Riches," detailed Lawson's 1982 campaign against Bette Wimbish. The second, by Jan Goodwin, described Lawson's 1986 re-election campaign, focusing on his "curious" constituency, including the "Rednecks for Lawson."

In De Grandy's case, the *Miami Herald*'s annual rankings of state legislators were revealing. Each year's ranking provides thumbnail sketches of the leading lawmakers, and De Grandy was ranked among the leaders during his entire time in office, primarily because of his efforts on behalf of his largely Hispanic constituency. After the crucial redistricting process that occurred during the 1992 legislative session, the *Herald* called De Grandy that year's "unquestioned star" and predicted that "when a slew of new minority legislators are swept into office this fall, he can rightly claim a leading role." That prediction would prove prescient when it came time to decide who would sponsor the Rosewood bill.

CHAPTER SIXTEEN: ROAD KILL

Arnett's account of the family uproar that Tuesday in December of 1992, after the news of Minnie Lee Langley's and Lee Ruth Davis's lawsuit was published in the *Miami Herald* and went out on the Associated Press wires to newspapers across the country, was corroborated by several family members, including those named in this chapter. Steve Hanlon verified this chain of events, as did Manny Dobrinsky. Hanlon also verified details of his first phone conversation with Arnett Doctor.

The January 1, 1993, kidnapping and torching of Christopher Wilson was national news, documented in newspapers and magazines across the country, as well as throughout Florida.

Details of Steve Hanlon's drive to Lacoochee came from his memory and from my own trip taken along that same route in August, 1994.

The Lacoochee murder story, titled "Presumed Guilty," written by David Finkel, was published in the March, 1989, issue of *Esquire* magazine.

Some details of Lacoochee's history were found in the Dade City Public Library's file of locally written pamphlets and brochures—collections of local remembrances such as *East Pasco's Heritage,* edited by Eleanor Dunson (First Baptist Church of Dade City, 1976). Much of the Cummer and Sons information came from the sources cited in the notes for Chapter Two.

The descriptions of modern-day Lacoochee were based on my visit there in August, 1994. Background information on the town's economic and racial problems came primarily from newspaper pieces in the *Tampa Tribune,* which routinely covers this west-central section of the state. The recent beatings, shootings and cross-burning were all reported in *Tribune* stories. The community's current poverty and decay were extensively reported in a 1989 series of *Tribune* stories titled "Lacoochee: Forgotten Town," written by Lisa Demer.

The newspaper series on the Ku Klux Klan in Florida, by Fred Smith of the *Tampa Tribune,* was published in April, 1965.

The account of the church meeting in Lacoochee came from interviews with Hanlon and Doctor, as well as with various family members.

CHAPTER SEVENTEEN: THREE MORE NAMES

Michael O'McCarthy shared both his memories and his January, 1993, correspondence with the producers of the "Maury Povich" show to help recount the sequence of events that led to that broadcast. Minnie Lee Langley also shared her memories of that experience during my interview with her. The description of the broadcast itself came from a videotape of that January 18 program.

I interviewed Wilson Hall at his home in Hilliard in September, 1994. We spent half a day at his club, then walked up the road to his sister Margie's home, where I talked with her on her front porch for about an hour. Margie was not doing well; she had just been released from the hospital the day before. A yellow plastic identification bracelet was still on her left wrist.

The 1993 arrest and conviction of former Nassau County Sheriff Laurie Ellis on charges of selling cocaine and marijuana were reported in the *Nassau County News-Leader* in a series of stories written by reporter Sarah Bottoms.

The account of the Hall family's life in Rosewood is based on interviews with Wilson and Margie, as well as an interview I had with their sister, Mary Hall Daniels, in September, 1994, at her apartment in Jacksonville. More information came from subsequent telephone interviews with both Wilson and Mary.

The murder of Emmett Till is probably the most well-documented lynching in American history. A detailed account of his killing is included in Stephen J. Whitfield's *A Death in the Delta: The Story of Emmett Till* (Baltimore: The Johns Hopkins University Press, 1991).

Wilson Hall's account of his brother Sam's whereabouts during the attack on Rosewood differs from that of Sam Hall's granddaughter, Katherine Hall, whom I interviewed by telephone in June, 1995, at her home in Jacksonville. "What I was told by my grandfather," she said, "is he was *there* in Rosewood at the time of the attack. He was working in Sumner, but he was still living in Rosewood. He said he went out in the woods with the rest of them, hiding in the swamp so they wouldn't get killed. I don't know what anyone else says, but that's what he told *me*."

CHAPTER EIGHTEEN: "ATTENTION WHITE PEOPLE"

The account of the September, 1993, gathering at Florida A&M University is based on interviews with Al Lawson, Steve Hanlon and Arnett Doctor, as well as with the survivors who attended the conference that week and the members of the state's study team who interviewed them there.

I visited the campus of Florida A&M several times during September and October of 1994, primarily to visit the university's Black Archives Research Center and Museum.

Dozens of newspaper stories have been written about Bo Johnson and his political family. Probably the most definitive was a February 14, 1993, *Tallahassee Democrat* examination of Johnson's controversial career titled "Johnson Built His Career on Determination," by Judy Doyle and Dana Peck. A companion piece to that story, titled "Connections With Bond Company Were Secret," examined questions about ties between Johnson's political position and his personal finances. The description of Johnson's personal background is based primarily on those stories and on a June, 1995, telephone interview with Johnson.

The testy relationship between Al Lawson and Bo Johnson was confirmed in interviews with both men.

The problems with the 1993 Rosewood bill and the subsequent funding of an academic investigative team were detailed in newspaper stories and recounted in interviews I had with Steve Hanlon, Martha Barnett, Al Lawson, Miguel De Grandy and Bo Johnson.

The families' anger in the wake of Minnie Lee Langley's and Lee Ruth Davis's original claims bill was typified by a letter written by Yvonne Doctor to Davis following that January's "Maury Povich" broadcast:

"Everyone is upset about the lies that were told," wrote Doctor. "We would appreciate it very much if you would stop now. Because this thing could become very, very ugly in the long run. . . . You know, Lee Ruth, we all have to be careful, because you never know to whom you're speaking and in fact, to whom they are acquainted. There is still alot [sic] of hate crimes being committed today . . . We are not going to stand by and let this continue to open old, old wounds. . . ."

Arnett's hyperbole with reporters during the summer of 1993 was typified by a set of articles published that May in the *Tampa Tribune*. Titled "Razed by Racism," written by *Tribune* reporter Suzie Siegel, the stories contained Arnett's references to Rosewood as a "Black Mecca," etc. Arnett says today that his reference to Atlanta was taken out of context. "I consistently compared Rosewood to Atlanta from the perspective of black unity, black business, and strong civic pride," he says. "The comparison was not intended to suggest that Rosewood was on the same scale, or of the same size, as Atlanta. That would have been ludicrous."

Doyal Scoggins recounted the visit to his home by the Ku Klux Klan during our interview there in October, 1994.

A copy of the "ATTENTION WHITE PEOPLE" flier was included among boxes of records, tapes, transcripts and other material related to the Rosewood bill stored at the Florida Legislative Library in Tallahassee, which I visited in April, 1994. That material has since been transferred to the Florida State Archives.

I called John Baumgardner at his home in McIntosh, Florida, March 27, 1995. We had an extensive telephone interview that evening, and he subsequently mailed me his Ku Klux Klan business card and several recent copies of his monthly *Florida Interklan Report,* featuring articles with titles such as "Who Is White?," a column ridiculing a photograph of Bill Clinton in a yarmulke and calling the President "a closet Christ-hater, a little Jewish want-to-be," and several columns on the subject of Rosewood, which was referred to as "Lawton's Folly."

CHAPTER NINETEEN: DOC WILLIE'S LITTLE GIRL

I interviewed Martha Barnett at her law office in Tallahassee in September and October, 1994, followed by several telephone interviews during the subsequent months. This chapter is based on those conversations, as well as interviews with Steve Hanlon and Arnett Doctor.

CHAPTER TWENTY: SATISFACTION

I visited Maxine Jones at her office on the campus of Florida State University in September, 1994. We had several telephone conversations following that meeting, to confirm, correct, and add to information from that interview.

A week after I met with Jones, I interviewed Tom Dye on the FSU campus as well. I also interviewed William Rogers, David Colburn and Larry Rivers by telephone in June, 1995.

The study team's report and appendix, as well as transcripts of the team members' testimony before the Florida House Special Master in March, 1994, were helpful in reconstructing their experience.

In the course of my own research, I came across many of the same documents the investigative team had studied and so was able to describe some in detail. An example was the Florida State Prison Record ledger book, which a staff member at the Florida State Archives pulled from a back storage room when I asked if they had anything beyond the typed, Xeroxed, second-hand compilations of prison records available in the front room.

The *Washington Post* story which included quotations from Tom Dye appeared May 30, 1993. Titled "Rosewood: The Town That Burned in Shame," it was written by William Booth.

Jason McElveen's account of the attack on Rosewood came from pages 69–72 of Tom Dye's master's thesis on Cedar Key, cited earlier in these notes.

CHAPTER TWENTY-ONE: BACKWOODS FOLKS

I visited Ernest Parham at his home in Orlando in September, 1994. I had come across a photograph of him earlier that fall in the Cedar Key Historical Society Museum, a gangly big-eared boy lined up with his Cedar Key High School classmates on the last day of November, 1922—less than two months before the attack on Rosewood. I could still see some of that boy in the elderly man who answered his door that September afternoon. This chapter is based on that interview with Ernest Parham, as well as on several follow-up telephone conversations we had in the ensuing months.

The account of John Wright's later years came from conversations with several Levy County residents, most notably former Florida state senator Randolph J. Hodges, who recalled his father telling him of the pistols placed throughout John Wright's home, and Doyal Scoggins, who took me to John Wright's grave in the Shiloh Cemetery.

I interviewed Ernest Parham's sister-in-law Martha Pillsbury Thompson by telephone at her home in Jacksonville in May, 1995. Martha is the only living child of Walter Harlan Pillsbury, who was superintendent of the Sumner sawmill at the time of the attack on Rosewood. Her father was indeed part Indian, she said, but like Parham, Martha, who was born in 1908, has no idea of her father's exact ancestry. She did say, however, that her daughter-in-law Carolyn had recently been researching the family's history and might know. So I called Carolyn Pillsbury at her home not far from Martha's.

"We've been trying to track it down for years," said Carolyn, the forty-two-year-old wife of Walter Pillsbury, W. H. Pillsbury's grandson. "What we *do* know," she told me, "is that the Pillsbury family were highbrow people up in Michigan. Very wealthy, very uppity. When one of their sons, Edward, married an Indian woman, they completely ostracized him, paid him his share of the family's business and told him to leave. 'See ya. Take *off.*' Just like that."

By the turn of the century, she continued, "nobody in the family wanted to recognize their background at all. The attitude was, 'No, no, no. No Indians in *this* family.' So now here we are. My children are fifth generation Pillsburys, and they want to know where they came from. *I* want to know."

What Martha Thompson knows is that her father was Edward Pillsbury's oldest son, that he was born in 1875 and that he grew up playing with the sons of a man named Jacob Cummer in the Clam Lake (now Cadillac) area of Michigan. Jacob Cummer was a logging magnate up in Michigan, and by the turn of the century he had moved his business and his family to Jacksonville. According to Martha, her father was a young man playing on a traveling semi-professional baseball team when he bumped into the Cummer boys while passing through Jacksonville, and they convinced him to stay and join the family's business.

"Papa was a sawyer at first," said Martha, "pulling logs out of the St. Johns River right here, where the Cummers had a sawmill. Later they sent him down to the Bahama Islands to build a mill for the company there. It was when he came back from the Bahamas that they asked him to go on over to Sumner."

That was in 1913, just after the Cummers had opened a new sawmill on the Gulf Coast and begun harvesting the abundant cypress there. Ten years later, those woods were almost completely logged out, the company was already opening another mill further south, in Lacoochee, and the Sumner operation was slowing down. That was in 1923, the year the attack on Rosewood occurred.

Martha was fourteen at the time of the attack. She didn't go near Rosewood that week— "I never did go closer to Rosewood than Mr. Wright's house, where we'd go to pick grapes." But she remembers how busy her father was that week, beginning with the first day, the day Aaron Carrier was tortured and Sam Carter was lynched. It was Martha's older brother, Edward, she said, who drove Aaron Carrier to safety that day.

"Edward was four years older than me," she said, "and his friend Burt Phillips had come down to visit from Jacksonville, to go hunting over Christmas season. When this trouble started, my father put this black man in the back of a car, covered him with a quilt, and told Edward to drive him to Bronson, to put him in the jail there for safety. Burt went with him, and I remember, as soon as they got back, *that day,* my father put Burt Phillips on the train home to Jacksonville."

The next two days were frightening, recalled Martha. "There were people just driving up and down the streets with shotguns sticking out of their cars."

The day after the shootout at the Carrier house, Martha said Sumner was filled with refugees from Rosewood. Several of her families' neighbors took in black women and children and hid them from the mobs, she said. Her own family hid "between ten and twenty" women and children in a small building behind their home, said Martha, where they stayed for two nights. "My mother would wait till dark," she said, "and then she'd cook a big old pot of grits and greens, you know, *cracker* food, and she'd carry it out to them."

The blacks weren't the only people terrified of those mobs, said Martha. "Some of the *white* people in Sumner came and stayed in our house," she said, "'cause they were scared to stay in their own. We were *all* afraid. All these cars riding up and down the road with all those guns. We didn't know when somebody was gonna try to shoot *us*. . . . It was just an exciting time," said Martha, "a scary week."

Finally, she said, it ended when the Bryce brothers' train arrived that weekend to pick up the blacks hiding in Sumner and carry them to safety in Gainesville. "I thought it was mighty nice of them to make arrangements to do that," said Martha.

Martha's father left for Lacoochee the next year, but unlike Ernest Parham, Martha does not remember W. H. Pillsbury having any particular problems with the workers there. "In fact," she said, "the Cummers sent Papa a letter commending him for saving all those lives. They said anything they could ever do for him, they would."

And they did, said Martha. Her father left Lacoochee and the company in 1925, retired from the logging business and moved his family back to Jacksonville. A year after that, on a hot June evening, he was driving home from Fernandina Beach when his car developed engine trouble. He pulled off the road, climbed under the gas tank, found a leak, plugged it, stood back up and—"Like an idiot," his grandson Walter told me—lit his pipe.

"He burst into flames," said Martha. "They couldn't do anything for him. He died that night."

CHAPTER TWENTY-TWO: SPECIAL MASTER

I interviewed Richard Hixson at his office at the state capitol building in Tallahassee in October, 1994. This chapter is based on that interview, along with two subsequent telephone conversations.

CHAPTER TWENTY-THREE: THE ELEVENTH HOUR

Interviews with Steve Hanlon, Arnett Doctor, Martha Barnett, Al Lawson and Miguel De Grandy formed the basis of this chapter.

Biographical information on former Florida Governor and U.S. Senator Spessard Holland is abundant. The titles alone of the many newspaper and magazine articles about Holland indicate the man's political complexity: "Sen. Spessard Holland 'Brings Home the Bacon'" (*Tallahassee Democrat,* Oct. 3, 1965); "Holland: 'They Call Me Hopelessly Reactionary'" (*St. Petersburg Times,* Oct. 10, 1965); "Spessard Holland Was a Man of Many Labels" (*Polk Country Democrat,* Nov. 8, 1971). The two instances in which Holland personally confronted lynch mobs were detailed in a *Polk County Democrat* story written on the occasion of his death in 1971.

CHAPTER TWENTY-FOUR: ONE LAST MATTER

Steve Hanlon, Martha Barnett, Richard Hixson, Bo Johnson, Pete Antonacci and Robert Trammell shared with me details of the discussion and decision to have the state defend itself at the House Special Master's Hearing.

I interviewed Jim Peters at his office in Tallahassee in October, 1994, and interviewed him again by telephone in April, 1995, to confirm and add to the information he had already shared with me.

Earnest Lee Miller and William Riley Jent were the subjects of the *Esquire* magazine article cited in the notes to Chapter Eighteen.

Steve Hanlon's comments about Peters came from our interviews at Hanlon's office in Tallahassee.

CHAPTER TWENTY-FIVE: LIKE AN ANT

I visited both the old and the new Florida State Capitol buildings many times during the spring and fall of 1994. The staffs at both buildings—particularly Pete Cowdrey at the Old Capitol—were very helpful in providing historical background on the structures.

Florida State University Professor William Rogers, who was a member of the investigative team that wrote the report on Rosewood, has also written extensively on the history of Tallahassee. The center of the city's slave business, said Rogers, was not far from the capitol, at the city's largest outdoor market. But he has never been able to confirm the popular rumor that slaves were actually sold off the steps of the Old Capitol. "If they did buy and sell slaves there," he said, "it was clearly an exception. Although," he added, " I wouldn't rule anything out, the South being what it was."

Although the Florida Department of Law Enforcement offices in Tallahassee and Tampa could find no official record of patrols provided in response to threats received by Arnett Doctor when I called them in June, 1995, the FDLE office in Tampa acknowledged that they may have provided "unofficial drive-bys" of Doctor's house at the time he received the threats.

The account of the House Special Master's Hearing's opening day—as well as the twenty-four hours preceding it—came from interviews with Richard Hixson, Steve Hanlon, Martha Barnett, Arnett Doctor, Jim Peters, the four Rosewood survivors who testified that day—Minnie Lee Langley, A. T. Goins, Willie Evans and Wilson Hall—Miguel De Grandy, and Al Lawson.

The physical description of the hearing room came from notes made during my visits to the Capitol building.

The dialogue in this chapter was taken directly from transcripts provided by the state Legislative Library in Tallahassee.

That first day's testimony had a particularly strong impact on Bo Johnson, who told me he watched a videotape of the day's proceedings that evening in his office. While he was watching the testimony, said Johnson, two of the Capitol's cleaning staff—both African-American women—peeked in to take a look. Johnson turned and asked them what they thought. "It looks," said one of the women, "like the hometown folks are whippin' up on the big boys."

CHAPTER TWENTY-SIX: AMBUSH

This chapter is based on interviews with Jim Peters, Steve Hanlon, Richard Hixson, Maxine Jones, Tom Dye, William Rogers and Arnett Doctor.

Stan Smith's economic calculations came from a copy of his report submitted to the Special Master, now part of the Rosewood file stored at the Florida State Archives.

Again, the Hearing dialogue came from taped transcripts provided by the Legislative Library.

CHAPTER TWENTY-SEVEN: "HE DIDN'T HAVE A HOLSTER"

Jim Peters shared with me the details of his excursion to Levy County during our interview at his office. I spoke with Herb Wilkerson several times by telephone in April, 1995, to confirm and add to Peters's account of his interview with Wilkerson and Wilkerson's father, James. The description of that videotaped testimony came from viewing a copy of the tape at the state's Legislative Library.

CHAPTER TWENTY-EIGHT: HANDS UNKNOWN

Next to the opening day testimony of the Rosewood survivors, the testimony of Ernest Parham was the most climactic of the hearing's three weeks.

The heart of this chapter comes from transcripts of Parham's testimony that day. Interviews with Parham himself, as well as with Richard Hixson, Steve Hanlon, Martha Barnett, Bo Johnson, Arnett Doctor, Al Lawson, Maxine Jones, David Colburn and Martha Pillsbury Thompson provided context for that testimony as well as for the Rosewood team's behind-the-scenes strategy that preceded it.

Numerous newspaper accounts provided the public statements quoted in this chapter.

A copy of the March 17, 1994, letter from Florida NAACP President T. H. Poole to state Attorney General Robert Butterworth regarding Jim Peters's tactics was sent to me by Guy Robinson of the Attorney General's Office of Civil Rights.

Ernest Parham's interview with David Colburn of the academic investigative team is found in the appendix to the team's report, as cited in this chapter.

The Florida Department of Law Enforcement interviews to which Ernest Parham referred in his testimony were ordered by the Attorney General's office just prior to the start of the House hearing in late February, 1994, according to FDLE agent Arthur Erickson, whom I interviewed by telephone in June, 1995. Erickson said Parham was first interviewed by agents from the FDLE's Orlando office at his home on February 25, the same day the House hearing began in Tallahassee. Erickson himself interviewed Parham at his home in May, after the bill had become law and the FDLE's official investigation had begun.

A thorough account of the Byron De La Beckwith case is Maryanne Vollers's book, *Ghosts of Mississippi* (New York: Little, Brown and Company, 1995).

CHAPTER TWENTY-NINE: A MORAL OBLIGATION

Richard Hixson was very open in sharing and clarifying the reasoning and research that went into the decision he wrote after the Rosewood hearing concluded. That reasoning forms the heart of this chapter.

The copy of the coroner's verdict on Sam Carter's death was provided by Tom Dye.

Robert Trammell and Bo Johnson both confirmed the discussion of Hixson's decision on the amount of compensation to be included in the recommendation.

A copy of Hixson's report is included in the records on Rosewood now filed at the Florida State Archives. I obtained my copy from the state's Legislative Library, where the records were stored at the time I was in Tallahassee.

The account of Arnett Doctor's volatile reaction to the report came from interviews with Doctor, Steve Hanlon and Martha Barnett.

Again, public statements about Hixson's decision came from numerous newspapers' accounts of his report's release.

CHAPTER THIRTY: GOOD FRIDAY

This chapter is based on interviews with Richard Hixson, Martha Barnett, Arnett Doctor, Al Lawson, Miguel De Grandy, Bo Johnson, Robert Trammell, and John Long.

Legislators' public statements included throughout the chapter came from numerous newspaper accounts of the Rosewood bill's journey through the House committees, as did the excerpts from various editorials and letters-to-the-editor.

Official House Committee records were provided by the state Legislative Library Services Division.

The luncheon showdown between Governor Chiles and the black caucus was gleefully covered by the press, which provided many of the details—such as the meal served that afternoon—which are included here.

CHAPTER THIRTY-ONE: AMEN

The heart of this chapter—the House floor debate on the Rosewood bill—came from a tape recording of that debate provided by the state Legislative Library. The physical descriptions of the House and Senate chambers came from notes made during my visits to the Capitol.

The Journals of the Florida House of Representatives provided a detailed account of all bills voted on by the House the day it debated the Rosewood bill.

Interviews with Miguel De Grandy, Al Lawson and Elaine Gordon, as well as observations from Steve Hanlon, Martha Barnett and Arnett Doctor, helped provide background details to what was on the official record.

When I called Bill Posey in May, 1995, to ask how exactly he was related to Samuel Mudd, he couldn't tell me. "I don't really know directly," he said. "My dad told me we were related by marriage somewhere back through there."

Posey's reference during the Rosewood debate to Samuel Mudd's imprisonment in Key West was actually incorrect. Mudd was jailed at Fort Jefferson, a federal prison located sixty-eight miles west of the Keys, among the cluster of islands known as the Dry Tortugas. Several accounts of Mudd's life have been written, the most thorough being *The Riddle of Dr. Mudd* (New York: G. P. Putnam's Sons, 1974), by a historian whose name echoes the dead of Rosewood: Samuel Carter III.

The Senate section of this chapter is based on the Journals of the Florida Senate, as well as on interviews with Barnett, Robert Wexler, Daryl Jones, and Charlie Williams.

CHAPTER THIRTY-TWO: NOTHING BUT SCARS

I visited the Attorney General's Office of Civil Rights in Hollywood in March, 1995, where I spent the day with Guy Robinson and Frank Beisler, who, along with Greg Durden, had spent the previous ten months enforcing the law prescribed by the Rosewood claims bill. During that day's interview and in numerous subsequent telephone interviews, they shared both their personal experiences as well as the official records of their research.

The description of the governor's bill-signing came from newspaper accounts and from interviews with various Rosewood family members.

CHAPTER THIRTY-THREE: WILDFLOWER

I visited Robie Mortin at her home in Riviera Beach the day after I met with the Attorney General's staff. This chapter is based on our interview that day and on several subsequent telephone conversations. I also was able to refer to Mortin's survivor affidavit filed in August, 1994, with the Attorney General's office, and to Frank Beisler's notes made a month after that during his interview with Mortin at her home.

Several newspaper stories were written about Mortin in the *Palm Beach Post* after she surfaced as a Rosewood survivor, and she was featured in the January 16, 1995, issue of *People* magazine. These articles provided additional background for this chapter.

CHAPTER THIRTY-FOUR: FAMILY

In May of 1995, as I neared the conclusion of writing this book, I set out to call all of the Rosewood survivors for final interviews, to catch up with each of their lives at that point. The first section of this chapter is based on those interviews—the ones I was able to obtain as well as the ones I was not.

The chapter's second section focuses on the Rosewood property claimants and is based on interviews with Guy Robinson, Frank Beisler and Greg Durden of the Attorney General's office, as well as on interviews with various Rosewood family members, including Arnett and Yvonne Doctor.

CHAPTER THIRTY-FIVE: SYLVESTER'S SHADOW

This chapter is based on interviews and records shared by Robinson, Beisler and Durden as well as interviews with Arnett Doctor, Michael O'McCarthy, Gary Moore, Steve Hanlon, Martha Barnett, Bo Johnson, Miguel De Grandy, Al Lawson, and Charlie Williams.

Epilogue

A copy of the Florida Department of Law Enforcement's final report on its Rosewood investigation, dated January 18, 1995, was provided by Greg Durden's staff at the Attorney General's office in Hollywood, Florida.

My visit with Wesley and Christy Thompson at their home in Rosewood took place in October, 1994.

The Survivors

Minnie Lee Langley: Nine at the time of the attack, she lived in Rosewood with her grandparents, James and Emma Carrier. She now lives in Jacksonville, Florida.

Arnett T. (A. T.) Goins: He was eight, staying with his grandmother, Sarah Carrier, when the attack occurred. His parents, George and Willie Retha Goins, were away at a logging camp that week. He now lives in St. Petersburg, Florida.

Willie Evans: Born in Sanford, near Orlando, his mother died when he was four and he moved to Rosewood to live with his grandparents, Ransome and Julie Edwards. He turned sixteen a week before the attack. He now lives in Sanford, Florida.

Lonnie Carroll: The son of James and Emma Carrier, he was twelve when Rosewood was attacked. He later changed his name to Carroll. He now lives in New Smyrna Beach, Florida.

Wilson Hall: One of Charles Bacchus Hall's nine children, he was seven the week of the attack. He now lives in Hilliard, Florida.

Margie Hall Johnson: Wilson Hall's sister, she had just turned fourteen at the time of the attack. She now lives in Hilliard, Florida.

Mary Hall Daniels: The youngest of the Hall children, she was three when Rosewood was attacked. She now lives in Jacksonville, Florida.

Dorothy Goins Hosey: The daughter of Perry and Hattie Goins, she turned four the first day of the attack. She now lives in Tampa, Florida.

Robie Allenetta Robinson Mortin: Born in 1915, she was living with her uncle, Sam Carter, and her grandmother, Polly Carter, at the time of the attack. She now lives in Riviera Beach, Florida.

Lee Ruth ("Mossy") Bradley Davis: One of the original two Rosewood bill claimants, along with Minnie Lee Langley, she was seven at the time of the attack. She died in 1993, as the second claims bill was taking shape.

Vera Massadeas Goins Hamilton: A. T. Goins's baby sister, she was with her parents at a logging camp the week Rosewood was attacked and so did not qualify for state compensation as a survivor. She now lives in Lacoochee, Florida.

Eva Jenkins: Born and raised in Rosewood, she was thirteen and staying in Gainesville with an aunt at the time of the attack. She too was disqualified as a survivor. She now lives in Orlando, Florida.

Berthina Edwards Fagin: Born and raised in Rosewood, she was nine when she and her parents moved to the town of Steinhatchee three weeks before Rosewood was attacked.

Her parents owned a home and land in Rosewood, which they lost. She too was disqualified as a survivor. She now lives in Deland, Florida.

Thelma Hawkins: Nineteen at the time of the attack, she had been raised in Rosewood by her uncle and aunt, Ed and Eliza Bradley, who lost their home and five acres of land during the attack. She had moved to Jacksonville before the attack occurred and so was not considered a survivor. She now lives in Dade City, Florida.

Lillie Washington: Born in Rosewood in 1910, she and her family were living in a small village called Lenin, six miles from Rosewood, at the time of the attack. They left soon after, because of the attack, but she was not considered a survivor. She now lives in Gainesville, Florida.

THE ANCESTORS

Sam Carter: A forty-seven-year-old blacksmith, he became the first victim of the attack on Rosewood when he was lynched Monday night, January 1, 1923.

Sarah Carrier: She was the week's second victim, shot to death in her home Thursday night, January 4.

Sylvester Carrier: The thirty-year-old son of Sarah Carrier, he died during the January 4 gun battle at his mother's house.

Lexie Gordon: A fifty-five-year-old widow, she was shot to death fleeing from her burning house on Friday morning, January 5.

Mingo ("Lord God") Williams: A fifty-year-old turpentine worker, he was shot to death Friday afternoon, January 5, while working in the woods outside Rosewood.

James Carrier: Sarah Carrier's brother-in-law, he emerged Saturday morning, January 6, from hiding in the swamps around Rosewood and was murdered execution-style beside the grave of his sister-in-law Sarah and his nephew Sylvester.

Hayward Carrier: Sarah Carrier's husband and James Carrier's brother, he was away on a hunting trip the week of the attack.

Annie ("Sweetie") Carrier: Sylvester Carrier's sister.

Lelland ("Beauty") Carrier: Sylvester Carrier's sister.

Bernadina ("Honey") Carrier: Sylvester Carrier's sister.

Willie Retha Carrier: Sylvester Carrier's sister.

Emma Carrier: James Carrier's wife.

Aaron Carrier: The son of James and Emma Carrier, he was tortured, then escaped the first day of the attack.

Beulah ("Scrappie") Carrier: Emma Carrier's daughter, she helped care for some of the smaller Carrier children in the woods after the attack on Sarah Carrier's house.

Elias Carrier: A Carrier cousin, he was gunned down by Charlie Goins during a church Christmas pageant in Rosewood several years before the town was destroyed.

Lee Carrier: A Carrier cousin, he survived into the 1980s and was a strong voice at family reunions.

Martine Goins: Born a slave in North Carolina, he established the M. Goins & Brothers' turpentine distilling company in Rosewood in the mid-1880s. He died in 1905.

Ed Goins: Martine's younger brother, also born a slave, he ran the family's turpentine business until 1916, when he moved to Gainesville.

Charlie Goins: One of Ed Goins's ten children, he was the man who murdered Elias Carrier.

George Goins: Another of Ed Goins's sons, he married Willie Retha Carrier and had five children, including Philomena, A. T. and Vera.

Philomena ("Sissy") Goins Doctor: A daughter of George and Willie Retha Goins, she was eleven at the time of the attack and was in her grandmother Sarah Carrier's house the night of the January 4 shootout. The mother of Arnett and Yvonne Doctor, she died in St. Petersburg in 1991.

Daisy Mitchell: A daughter of James and Emma Carrier, she was Minnie Lee Langley's mother. She died giving birth to Minnie Lee in 1915.

Theodore Mitchell: Daisy's husband, he left his children with his wife's parents after her death and went to work along the Gulf Coast as a sponge diver.

Ruben Mitchell: Minnie Lee's brother, he lost an eye the night of the shootout at the Carrier house.

Charles Bacchus Hall: He owned a small store, farmed and ran a sugar-cane grinding business, all on his property in Rosewood.

Mary Davis Hall: Charles Hall's wife.

Sam Hall: One of Charles and Mary Hall's nine children, he was fifteen at the time of the attack. He died in Brunswick, Georgia, in 1984.

Dosha Hall: Second-oldest of the Hall children, she was married and moved from Rosewood by the time of the attack. She later settled in Hilliard, Florida, with her sister Margie, where they both eventually reunited with their brother Wilson.

Polly Carter: Sam Carter's mother, she raised survivor Robie Allenetta Robinson Mortin in Rosewood, after Robie's parents divorced when Robie was a baby.

THE WHITES

Fannie Taylor: The twenty-three-year-old wife of a Sumner sawmill worker, she was assaulted in her home New Year's morning, 1923. That assault precipitated the attack on Rosewood.

James Taylor: Fannie Taylor's husband, he was an employee at the Cummer and Sons sawmill in Sumner.

Robert Walker: He was Levy County's sheriff at the time of the Rosewood attack.

Clarence Williams: He was the Levy County deputy sheriff in Sumner at the time of the attack.

Walter Harlan (W. H.) Pillsbury: General superintendent of the sawmill in Sumner at the time of the attack, he is credited with saving the lives of blacks both in Rosewood and in Sumner.

Bryant Hudson: Twenty-five at the time, he was the man who shot and killed Sam Carter the night of January 1, 1923.

Fred Kirkland: A witness to the lynching of Sam Carter, he is still alive today.

Garrett Kirkland: Fred Kirkland's uncle, he was among the mob that witnessed Sam Carter's lynching.

Orrie Kirkland: Fred Kirkland's father, he was also present at the lynching of Sam Carter.

Jason McElveen: A logger and fisherman from Cedar Key, he was present at both the Monday night lynching of Sam Carter and the Thursday night attack on the Carrier house.

C. P. "Poly" Wilkerson: A storekeeper and former quarters boss from Sumner, he was shot and killed by Sylvester Carrier the night of the attack on the Carrier house.

Henry Andrews: A logging foreman from Otter Creek, he was also shot and killed by Carrier the night of the attack.

Bryan Kirkland: He was wounded during the attack on the Carrier house.

Warner Kirkland: He was wounded during the attack on the Carrier house.

Cephus Studstill: He was wounded during the attack on the Carrier house.

Henry Odom: He was wounded during the attack on the Carrier house.

Manny Hudson: He was wounded during the attack on the Carrier house.

Red Raulerson: He was among the group that attacked the Carrier house, but did not take part in the attack.

John Wright: A storekeeper in Rosewood and the town's only white resident, he hid a number of black women and children in his home during the week of the attack.

John and William Bryce: Two railroad conductors from Cedar Key, they brought a train through Rosewood at the end of that week and carried carloads of women and children to safety in Gainesville.

THE DESCENDANTS

Arnett Doctor: The son of Philomena Doctor, he spearheaded the families' pursuit of a legal claim against the state of Florida.

Yvonne Doctor: The daughter of Philomena Doctor.

Annie Bell Lee: The daughter of Rosewood resident Josephine Evans, she, along with her sister, Altamese Wrispus, organized the first Rosewood Family Reunion in 1985.

Annette Goins Shakir: The daughter of Rosewood survivor A. T. Goins.

Janie Bradley Black: The niece of Rosewood survivor Lee Ruth Davis.

Geffery Mortin: The son of Rosewood survivor Robie Mortin.

Dorothy Smith: The daughter of Rosewood survivor Minnie Lee Langley.

Albert Edwards: The son of deceased Rosewood resident Earl Edwards and a cousin of Arnett Doctor, he was with Doctor when the idea of filing a claim against the state was first discussed.

SPOUSES

Lugenia Carroll: Lonnie Carroll's wife

Anna Maude Goins: A. T. Goins's wife.

Walter Doctor: Philomena Doctor's husband.

PHOTO CREDITS

INDEX

Page entries in **boldface** indicate illustrations in the text.

E

F

G